By Order of the Kaiser

By Order of the Kaiser

Otto von Diederichs
and the Rise of the
Imperial German Navy,
1865–1902

BY
TERRELL D. GOTTSCHALL

Naval Institute Press
Annapolis, Maryland

Naval Institute Press
291 Wood Road
Annapolis, MD 21402

© 2003 by Terrell D. Gottschall

All rights reserved. No part of this book may be reproduced or utilized in any form or by any means, electronic or mechanical, including photocopying and recording, or by any information storage and retrieval system, without permission in writing from the publisher.

Library of Congress Cataloging-in-Publication Data
Gottschall, Terrell D., 1951–
   By order of the Kaiser : Otto von Diederichs and the rise of the Imperial German Navy, 1865–1902 / Terrell D. Gottschall.
      p.   cm.
   Includes bibliographical references and index.
   ISBN 1-55750-309-5 (alk. paper)
   1. Diederichs, Otto von, 1843–1918. 2. Admirals—Germany—Biography. 3. Germany—History, Naval—19th century. 4. Germany—History, Naval—20th century. 5. Germany. Kriegsmarine—History—19th century. 6. Germany. Kriegsmarine—History—20th century. I. Title.
V64.G32D544 2003
359'.00943—dc21

                                          2003001565

Printed in the United States of America on acid-free paper ∞
10 09 08 07 06 05 04 03   9 8 7 6 5 4 3 2
First printing

Contents

	Preface and Acknowledgments	vii
1	With Duty and Honor: Diederichs and the Prussian Navy, 1843–1867	1
2	Training for Preparedness: Diederichs and the Evolving German Navy, 1867–1878	29
3	To East Asia: Diederichs and SMS *Luise,* 1878–1880	57
4	Defending the Coasts: Diederichs and Strategic Planning, 1880–1890	85
5	The Kaiser's Navy: Diederichs and the New Course, 1890–1897	109
6	A Mailed Fist: Diederichs Takes Kiao-Chou, 1897–1898	131
7	The Philippines: Diederichs and Dewey at Manila, Summer 1898	181
8	Constant Strife: Diederichs and the Admiralty Staff, 1899–1902	223
9	Watching from Afar: Diederichs in Retirement, 1902–1918	257
	Notes	267
	Bibliography	305
	Index	319

Preface and Acknowledgments

To scholars of German naval history before World War I, the Tirpitz era is quite well known. Yet Alfred von Tirpitz dominated German naval development only after 1897. In the less familiar and less dramatic period before 1897 were laid the foundations for the future overall development of the Imperial German Navy, the *Kaiserliche Marine*. That period, after all, saw the navy grow from a small Prussian coastal defense force (*Küstenflotille*) with limited power and mission to the imperial German High Seas Fleet (*Hochseeflotte*) with aspirations of world power. The naval career of Otto von Diederichs (1843–1918), who entered the Prussian Navy in 1865 and left the Kaiserliche Marine in 1902, provides an excellent model for tracing German naval development during the period.

Two major themes dominated Diederichs's career. The primary theme draws from the statement, "I am here, Sir, by the order of the Kaiser," a formulaic phrase used by German naval officers on overseas station to announce their arrival in foreign ports. For Diederichs, the son, grandson, and great-grandson of Prussian civil servants, the phrase also exemplified a family tradition of service to the German crown. The second theme marks Diederichs's "presence at the creation" as he participated in almost every major step in German naval development from 1865 to 1902. He took part in the strategic and operational development of the Kaiserliche Marine; served in the Franco-German War of 1870–71; was involved in political and diplomatic controversy arising from military intervention in Asia; headed a naval confrontation with one superpower and a naval arms race with another; and, finally, engaged in a bitter intraservice debate with Tirpitz over the future strategic development of the navy. An examination of Diederichs's career thus offers a new and more complete perspective on German naval history before World War I.

Many friends and colleagues contributed to this project. I would particularly like to express my sincere gratitude to my colleagues at Walla Walla College for their advice and support. From the Department of History, Professors Roland Blaich, Monty Buell, Robert Henderson, Terrie Aamodt, and Greg Dodds survived the development of this manuscript and patiently read and commented on various early fragments. Likewise thanks to Professors Carolyn Shultz, Gary Wiss, and Dan Lamberton from the Department of English, and Professor Nancy Semotiuk, from the Department of Communications, who provided similar assistance. I owe particular appreciation to Herr Doktor Professor Blaich for his assistance with difficult translations. Beyond the borders of the Walla Walla Valley, Dr. Patrick Kelly, Adelphi University; Dr. Lawrence Sondhaus, University of Indianapolis; Dr. Rolf Hobson, Norwegian Defence Studies Institute, Oslo, Norway; Dr. Karl-Heinz Wionzek, Düsseldorf, Germany; and Dr. Milton Nathanson, Emeritus Professor of Microbiology, Queens College of the City University of New York, contributed guidance and inspiration. Stuart Haller, Bernhard Sage, and Tim Hughes provided answers to always difficult and occasionally trivial questions. Jennifer Boyden dispensed many hours of editorial advice. The staff of the Bundesarchiv-Militärarchiv, Freiburg, Federal Republic of Germany, toiled at length in response to my many requests for documents and photographs. I would also like to extend my thanks to Herr Hartmann Wedding, Munich, Bavaria, for permission to use the Hintze *Nachlass*. Likewise, I am forever grateful to *gnädige* Frau Gisela von Diederichs, Diederichs's granddaughter-in-law, who graciously provided me with additional information and insight as she guided me on a tour of the family's former estate in Lichtenthal, Germany. Finally, I reserve my greatest thanks and love for Merry, my first and best editor, and our children Meghan, Jordan, and Nicholas, and to my parents, Marvin and Donna Gottschall, whose patient and loving support saw me through the end of this project.

By Order of the Kaiser

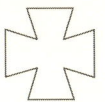

1

With Duty and Honor: Diederichs and the Prussian Navy, 1843–1867

Flags snapped overhead in the cool morning sun and breeze of Danzig's northern latitude as Cdr. Carl Batsch mustered the crew of SMS *Niobe* in the ship's waist at 0900 on 7 September 1865. With the crew at attention, Batsch directed Seaman Second Class Otto von Diederichs to place his left hand on the Prussian flag and raise his right hand. The oath began solemnly: "I, Ernst Otto von Diederichs, swear this oath before the Almighty and All-Knowing God, that I will serve His Majesty Wilhelm I, the King of Prussia, with duty and honor." Diederichs stepped back to join twenty-two other young men as Commander Batsch read out the royal decree appointing them as officer-cadets in the Royal Prussian Navy.[1] For Diederichs, this ceremony began thirty-seven years of active duty in the service of successive German states. Continuing a tradition of family service to the crown, Diederichs would truly serve with "duty and honor."

OTTO VON DIEDERICHS

Ernst Otto von Diederichs was born in Minden, Westphalia, on 7 September 1843. His father, Friedrich von Diederichs, was a provincial Prussian official; his mother, Henriette Molinari Diederichs, was the daughter of an expatriate Italian merchant family that had settled in Cologne. Seven weeks later, on 27 October 1843, Diederichs was christened in Minden's Lutheran cathedral. Geheime-Oberrechnungsrat Bormann, a family friend and official of the Prussian Ministry of the Treasury, traveled from Berlin to serve as godfather.[2]

Otto, as he was known, was born into a family with a tradition of service to the Prussian state. His great-grandfather, Leopold Diederichs (1721–1809) was a member of the professional middle class in Bad Pyrmont, Westphalia. He later became *Brünnencommissar* (commissioner of water works), an important and influential position in the resort town. Diederichs's grandfather, Christoph (1772–1839), was a provincial judicial official, later appointed to the Royal Prussian Council in Berlin. The Hohenzollern kings of Prussia often elevated worthy members of the middle class, particularly municipal or judicial officials, to the nobility to award service and offset the power of the landowning Junker aristocracy. Accordingly, King Friedrich Wilhelm III awarded Christoph Diederichs a patent of nobility in 1816. Christoph's new status allowed him to use the aristocratic *von* and a coat of arms centered on a skeleton key (a *Dietrich*).[3]

Friedrich von Diederichs (1805–88), Christoph's son and Otto's father, followed this emerging family tradition. In order to prepare himself for service, he studied economics and law at the University of Halle (Saxony) to earn the doctorate that had become mandatory for employment with the Prussian state. Following his marriage to Henriette Molinari (1812–80) in 1832, he published his dissertation—*Concepts of Political Economy*—as a preliminary step to joining the civil service in 1833.[4] He was an official financial administrator in Minden when Otto was born there in 1843. After revolution brought down the existing Prussian regime in March 1848, Friedrich transferred to Berlin, where he joined a new government headed by Otto von Bismarck. He moved his family to the royal suburb of Potsdam, where a daughter, Elizabeth, was born in 1850. Friedrich retired some twenty-five years later with the subcabinet rank of *Oberregierungsrat* (senior privy councillor).[5]

Thus Otto von Diederichs was marked for public service from birth. The first step toward filling that role was for him to obtain the appropriate education, culminating in a university doctorate. Education, however, soon became an obstacle, rather than a path. Diederichs spent his elementary years

(1849–55) at a Potsdam *Vorschule*, but chronic ill-health, a foreshadowing of lifelong pulmonary problems, stretched the three-year curriculum to six years. One 1854 grade report noted that his attendance was "irregular due to illness," while another recorded that his attention in class was somewhat "indifferent." His early accomplishments ranged from poor (French, Latin) through satisfactory (drawing, arithmetic) to the occasionally excellent (history, geography). One teacher even noted that he had "great enthusiasm, if little talent" for music.[6]

Diederichs and his parents hoped that a successful *Vorschule* experience would allow him to move on to a *Gymnasium*, one of the elite secondary schools that prepared students for a university education. The Gymnasium's rigorous nine-year program emphasized the classical Greek concept of *arete* (excellence or virtue) and character development. The curriculum included courses in history (classical, Prussian, German), *Germanistik* (German grammar and literature), literature (classical, German), foreign languages, geography (physical, political, cultural), mathematics (algebra, geometry, trigonometry), and natural sciences (biology, chemistry, physics). Students who completed these courses then sat for the state-sponsored *Abitur*, a comprehensive final examination that had become mandatory for admission to university and a prerequisite for a career in government.[7] In short, Diederichs needed a Gymnasium diploma if he were to follow family tradition into Prussian service. The Gymnasium curriculum in history and literature by then included an element of nationalism that further intensified his and his family's expectations of him. His favorite poet, Friedrich Schiller, illustrated this concept in a single stanza of "Ode to Joy" ("An die Freude," 1785):

> *Stalwart courage in the face of suffering,*
>   *Kindness to those who weep,*
> *Eternal commitment to obligation,*
>   *Honesty to friend and foe,*
> *Humility before the thrones of kings.*
>   *Comrades, serve the crown with blood and courage.*[8]

Despite his nationalist fervor, Diederichs's secondary education developed a disappointing pattern. When admitted to the Gymnasium in 1855, he was twelve years old, three years older than his classmates. Thus, since royal statute made it mandatory to report for military duty at age eighteen, he would not be allowed to complete the Gymnasium's nine-year program. Meanwhile, however, his health remained good, at least temporarily, as he made steady, if slow, progress, earning "good" to "very good" grades in the core curriculum for the next three years. He performed well in history, geography, and mathematics, but his penmanship was abysmal at best—a circumstance that would later hamper scholars attempting to read his personal and service correspondence. He now studied piano with "little enthusiasm" (but later developed into a pianist good enough to play his favorite piece, Beethoven's Waldstein Sonata, for his family). A brief brush with smallpox in 1858 revived his health problems and hampered his academic progress. He missed forty-one days of classes in spring term, 1859, and a grade report for fall term, 1860, noted, "No week passed during which Diederichs did not report sick. This circumstance will keep him back."[9]

Although his subsequent career abundantly confirmed that he had absorbed the character training of the Gymnasium to an exceptional degree, his professional future looked bleak when he completed his formal education in December 1861. His final transcript placed him far short of the requirements that would allow him to take the *Abitur*. Without this credential, he had no chance of admission to university and therefore little opportunity to follow his father and grandfather into the Prussian civil service. Moreover, he had turned eighteen in September and now faced the *allgemeine Wehrpflicht*, obligatory military service. Enlisted conscripts were required to serve for three years; officer aspirants served from one to three years, depending on academic qualifications. Diederichs's aristocratic roots made him eligible for admission to the army officer corps, the most honored profession in Prussian society, but again his academic record proved to be a problem. Officer candidates who had completed Gymnasium and passed the *Abitur* qualified for a normal tour of three years, with the hope of a full career in the regular army. Because Diederichs had completed only six years of secondary school, he could serve only a single year as a temporary reserve officer. Thus, he had little hope of an army career.[10] He nonetheless sat for the *Portepee-Fähnrich Prüfung*, the officers' entrance examination, which resembled the comprehensive *Abitur*, and passed with a satisfactory score.[11]

Diederichs reported for duty at the Cologne *Kaserne* (barracks) of the Thirty-third Infantry (East Prussian Fusiliers) Regiment on New Year's Day, 1862. The Fusiliers, a line regiment, was not an elite unit like the *Garde* or cavalry regiments, but it did have a long and famous tradition of service. The regimental adjutant entered Diederichs's name in the muster book as an *Offizieraspirant* with the substantive rank of ensign (*Fähnrich*) and assigned him to Seventh Company, First Battalion.[12]

Diederichs's army service came to an abrupt halt after only six months. Cologne's damp winter climate and Diederichs's cold quarters in an aging stone barracks exacerbated his pulmonary condition. After a physical examination by the regimental surgeon in early June, Diederichs resigned his temporary commission. As one possible solution to his chronic physical problems, the surgeon recommended that Diederichs take a sea cruise.[13]

These circumstances left Diederichs with two problems. Prussian law still required him to fulfill his military obligations; family expectations continued to demand public service. As it happened, his poor health provided a potential solution to both problems. When it became clear that he had to leave the army, Diederichs wrote to the Ministry of the Interior for an explanation of his legal liability if he were unable to complete his military obligation. The response informed him that military regulations allowed him to satisfy his *Wehrpflicht* with a two-year stint in the merchant marine. A second letter, this one to the *Seekadetten-Institut* in Berlin, elicited the response that service with the merchant marine could in turn provide him with an alternative route to a new career, this time with the Prussian Navy.[14] Although Diederichs was older than the preferred age—seventeen—at entry, he learned that older applicants or those with deficient academic or medical records could qualify for admission with official proof of three years' service at sea.[15] Because Diederichs, already overage and subject to recurring health problems, fit this bill of exceptions, a sea cruise would both fulfill his military obligation and pave the way to a naval career. And as a young man poised to take on his life's work, he might just have thought, with Herman Melville's Ishmael: "I thought I would sail about a little and see the watery part of the world."[16]

Yet, a sea cruise was not without danger, and Diederichs's plan not surprisingly provoked opposition from his parents. Fearing that his poor health would inhibit the pursuit of such a physically active profession, they initially resisted his interest in naval service, advocating a more traditional career instead. They pointed to the recent sinking of SMS *Amazone,* the navy's primary training ship, in which an entire class of naval cadets had died.[17] (Ironically, it was the sinking of *Amazone* that undermined the navy's effort to recruit qualified applicants and thus aided Diederichs's admission to the navy.) Diederichs eventually overrode his parents' opposition and reaffirmed his decision to go to sea. After all, he later noted, "Poor health and medical advice ended my army experience but gave me the opportunity to fulfill a youthful aspiration to go to sea."[18]

Diederichs began his service with the merchant marine immediately. Only twelve days after his formal separation from the army, Diederichs arrived in Hamburg from Cologne. He immediately signed on aboard the bark *Amaranth* as an apprentice seaman on 24 June 1862. The ship departed a day or two later with a full cargo of trade goods for China.

His new employment tested both health and character as Diederichs faced hard work, dangerous conditions, and nasty weather. He bunked in a crowded forecastle, breathing fetid air and sleeping in a damp, swaying hammock. He toiled aloft on swaying masts and pitching yards where a single slip could cause a fatal fall to the deck below. He ate hardtack biscuits inhabited by weevils (which often provided the diet's sole protein) and drank foul water from the scuttlebutt. He endured hot and humid weather that could sear the mind or rot the soul. Nonexistent hygiene and the constant presence of disease could kill as quickly as sharks or pirates. He thus discovered that life aboard a sailing ship was unrelated to his sense of romantic adventure. Yet, he survived this and more for three years. For some, a strong character is forged in the hot fire of experience, and Diederichs emerged from his odyssey stronger for its adversities and ready to take on the world.

One of his first tasks aboard ship was to learn the strange vocabulary of topgallants and bowsprits. Working at the command of the ship's mates and bosun, he learned the complex commands needed to handle a ship under sail (Heiss Bramsegel! "Hoist the topgallant sail!"), row small boats (Streich überall! "All back together!"), weigh anchor (Klar bei Steuerbord-Anker! "Stand by the starboard anchor!"), and serve a watch as helmsman (Komm auf! "Ease your helm!").

Amaranth followed a course south through the North Sea and English Channel into the Atlantic, past the Iberian peninsula and down the coast of Africa, around the Cape of Good Hope and into the Indian Ocean. The ship sailed through the pirate-ridden Strait of Malacca, past Singapore and Hong Kong, which were rapidly developing as British trading centers and naval bases, and proceeded through the South China Sea to Chinese waters in December 1862. Before *Amaranth* reached East Asia six months later, Diederichs had earned promotion to seaman.[19]

Diederichs arrived in China at a time of great ferment. Western imperialism threatened *Ch'ung-kou,* the "Middle Kingdom," from every corner of the compass, undermining China's political sovereignty and territorial integrity. Similar problems threatened China from within; an ineffective ruling dynasty proved unequal to the country's problems, natural disasters produced floods and famines, opium addiction crippled the civil service, the Taiping Rebellion (1856–64) devastated central China, and pirates menaced coastal waters and foreign trade. Only the hovering presence of foreign warships allowed Western trade to continue.[20]

Chaos and anarchy notwithstanding, German merchants found East Asia to be a profitable site for trade. German traders first visited Canton in 1828 and Shanghai in 1853. Trade flourished quickly thereafter, as evidenced by the more than 175 German ships that visited Hong Kong in 1861 and German tonnage in Chinese waters that exceeded 580,000 tons by 1864.

Amaranth's first port of call was Amoy, a major port north of Hong Kong, which had become the unofficial center of German trade in East Asia. Diederichs and his fellow crewmen worked hard, exchanging the ship's cargo, German industrial goods, for Chinese silk and Amoy's famous tea. Once their work was done, they had a brief opportunity for shore leave before moving on to the next port of call. Amoy offered sights to intrigue any European traveler, including a famous Buddhist shrine and a large but decaying fortress with stone fortifications and obsolete cannon. Although Diederichs was no stranger to the royal monuments of Berlin and Potsdam, the mysterious and novel Chinese architecture and culture impressed him greatly.[21]

Diederichs served aboard *Amaranth* for another six months before the ship set course for Germany in June 1863. With two years remaining before he would be eligible to apply to the Prussian Navy, he stayed in Chinese waters, transferring aboard a second trading ship, *Marie Wilhelmina*. This new ship was a coaster carrying general cargoes between Hong Kong in the south and Shanghai in the north. Six months later, in December 1863, he joined the crew of the bark *Friendship* for service in Southeast Asia. His new ports of call now included Singapore, another center of British colonial and commercial activity, and Bangkok, the capital of the kingdom of Siam—whose reigning monarch, King Rama IV, had recently hired a British governess, Anna Leonowens, to tutor his children. When *Friendship* departed for Germany in May 1864, Diederichs remained ashore in Bangkok for the better part of two months while awaiting another ship. As an experienced seaman, he eventually found service aboard merchant ship *August,* which made several round trips between Bangkok and Hong Kong during late 1864.

Diederichs finally transferred aboard *Suchow* for the return voyage to Germany, arriving in Hamburg in April 1865. *Suchow*'s master formally discharged him from service on 8 May with a strong recommendation: "He fulfilled his duties aboard ship to my complete satisfaction. His conduct toward me and his fellow crewmen was always good. His skills and knowledge testify to his abilities as an efficient seaman." Diederichs forwarded this recommendation and a copy of his service record to the Prussian Navy on 13 May 1865 as the first formal step toward seeking admission to the naval officer corps.[22]

THE PRUSSIAN NAVY BEFORE 1865

The Prussian Navy that Diederichs entered in 1865 had existed for little more than fifty years. During that period, the navy had endured as the military stepchild of the Prussian state, subject to insufficient funds, subordinate status, and chronic disorganization. Because the "soldier kings" of the Hohenzollern dynasty had fought mostly continental foes, Prussia had always depended on its famous army and therefore had seen little need for a navy. Not until the revolutionary and Napoleonic Wars (1792–1815) did it appear that Prussia might need a permanent naval force. Accordingly, Lt. Col. Gustav von Rauch produced Prussia's first fleet development plan in 1811. He justified the need for naval forces on the grounds that Prussia confronted three potential maritime foes—Denmark, Sweden, and Russia—in the Baltic region. As a soldier unacquainted with the needs of sea power, he identified coastal defense as the fleet's only strategic mission. He therefore proposed the establishment of a flotilla consisting of three large and twelve small warships with a combined complement of four hundred men. Although fiscal problems prevented the full implementation of these proposals, Prussia converted several small ships to operate as warships in the War of National Liberation in 1813–14.[23]

After Napoleon's final defeat at Waterloo in 1815, the Congress of Vienna worked to restore peace. As a means of maintaining stability in central Europe, the Congress created the *Deutsches Bund,* the German Confederation, which consisted of thirty-eight German states, including Austria and Prussia. The Congress also provided additional impetus for the development of a Prussian fleet when it compelled Sweden to cede Pomerania, with a port at Stralsund, and six small gun sloops to Prussia. This settlement assuredly justified the existence of a Prussian fleet: "A major power, whose northern borders consists of a coastline extending 140 miles along the North and Baltic Seas, cannot reject the power of the sea but, rather, needs a fleet to fulfill its responsibilities as a European state."[24]

Lt. Dietrich Longe (1779–1863), a Finnish naval officer in Swedish service, led the gun sloops into Stralsund in October 1815. He remained to become commander of this newly constituted *Küstenflotille* under the aegis of the Ministry of Trade. Longe directed the development of sites at Danzig and Stralsund as the coastal flotilla's first naval bases, the construction of SM Schooner *Stralsund* (ten guns) as the flotilla's first capital ship, and the establishment of the Navigation School as the flotilla's initial training facility. In fact, Longe and a fellow Finn, Lt. Heinrich Murck, remained the coastal flotilla's only professional naval officers until 1843.[25] A related lack of funding forced Longe to deactivate the gun sloops by 1819 and the *Stralsund* in 1829, restricted active duty to only a few months per year, and severely limited any sort of operational role. The flotilla's limited mission—coastal defense—also made it difficult to develop an independent identity. In fact, the flotilla operated as little more than an adjunct to the army, particularly when transferred to the jurisdiction of the Ministry of War in 1847 as "Department 4: Naval Affairs (provisional)" with only four commissioned naval officers.[26] According to an early history of the force, these circumstances nonetheless "established the foundation of gunnery training for our seamen and the tactical development of our officers."[27]

The German revolutions of 1848 briefly produced new impetus for naval development when a rebellion against autocratic rule, which began in Berlin in March, quickly spread to other German states. Stimulated by nationalism and liberalism, voters elected representatives to the Frankfurt Diet with the intent of establishing a united Germany under a constitutional monarchy. (Coincidentally, the political upheaval in Berlin led to the transfer of Friedrich von Diederichs from Minden to Potsdam.) The possibility of a united Germany, however, also provoked war with Denmark, which had territorial interests in the German duchies of Schleswig and Holstein. Indeed, the small Prussian force, plus a few converted warships belonging to Hamburg and Bremen, proved incapable of protecting the combined German merchant marine, which totaled sixty-eight hundred ships and forty-five thousand seaman.[28]

The Frankfurt Diet therefore moved quickly to repair this lack of naval power. Delegates appropriated six million talers for the construction of a united German fleet and appointed Prince Adalbert of Prussia (1811–73) to a position equivalent to minister of the navy. Although trained as an army officer, Adalbert had studied the naval activities of other powers, particularly Britain, at length. He hoped to establish a fleet consisting of twenty frigates and twenty sloops but succeeded, given limited time and funds, only in creating a jury-rigged force of river gunboats and converted passenger liners.[29]

Prussia also responded to the war with Denmark. A royal decree in September 1848 elevated the Prussian naval force from Küstenflotille to the navy proper. A second decree in March 1849 appointed Prince Adalbert, who would now direct two fleets, as chief of the *Oberkommando der Marine* (OKM), the Naval High Command, with administrative responsibility, and Dutch-born Commo. Jan Schröder as commander in chief of the fleet, with operational authority. The naval officer corps expanded to include eight commissioned naval officers and three officers seconded from the army to command a battalion of naval infantry.[30] As the new fleet slowly expanded, Adalbert faced difficulty in finding crews for his new ships. He therefore drew gunnery officers and marines from the army and recruited able seaman from the merchant marine. Adalbert even arranged to place midshipmen aboard American warships for training.[31]

Given Prince Adalbert's dual roles, there was remarkably little cooperation between the Prussian and Frankfurt fleets. Conservative Prussia refused to allow its ships to fly the flag of the liberal Frankfurt Diet, contending instead that it would wait until a unified and sovereign German state actually existed. The Prussians argued further that international convention did not yet recognize the black-red-gold Frankfurt flag and that other countries, particularly Britain, would therefore treat any ship flying it as a pirate.[32]

Such problems dimmed briefly when united Germany achieved a signal, if minor, victory in the war against Denmark. A Danish squadron of five warships, including ship-of-the-line *Christian VIII* (84 guns) and frigate *Gefion* (48 guns), had escorted an amphibious force into Eckernförde northwest of Kiel. German shore batteries drove off the Danes on 5 April 1849, destroying *Christian VIII* and forcing *Gefion* to run aground and surrender. The Frankfurt fleet added a repaired *Gefion* to its small force of ships. The battle had more propaganda value than strategic success but did briefly increase popular interest in German naval development.[33]

In any event, the collapse of the Frankfurt Diet in 1849 and peace with Denmark in 1850 ended the experiment with a united fleet, suspended plans for German unification, and curtailed Prussian naval development. The Prussian Navy ended the war with three small warships, forty gunboats, and eighteen hundred officers and men. The Frankfurt fleet's officer corps quickly dwindled to fifteen officers (five Germans, five Belgians, three English, one Dutch, and one American) before the sale of its few ships to Prussia in 1852.[34] The Prussian Ministry of War opposed every increase in naval construction thereafter and even proposed the allocation of the remaining gunboats to the various coastal fortresses and the assignment of naval officers to the Army Corps of Engineers.[35]

Despite the odds, Prince Adalbert persuaded the king to remove the navy from administration by the Ministry of War and place it under a separate, if not always independent, *Königliche Preussische Admiralität* in November 1853. Otto Freiherr von Manteuffel served as the Royal Prussian Admiralty's first chief, while Prince Adalbert, promoted in 1854 to the pretentious rank of "Admiral of the Prussian Coasts," continued as chief of the Oberkommando der Marine. Rear Admiral Schröder remained as operational commander.[36]

Over the opposition of the army, which believed that the navy should uphold coastal defense as its primary purpose, Prince Adalbert sought to give the navy a broader mission beyond Prussian coasts. Although Prussia's continental preoccupation limited extensive naval developments, the acknowledgment that Prussia possessed growing interests overseas—a far-flung merchant marine and German immigration to North and South America—led to strategic changes in the 1850s. An 1855 tactical memorandum, which reflected lessons learned from the Crimean War, concluded, "A naval power which cannot undertake offensive operations has no value in European waters."[37] To prove this dictum, Prince Adalbert personally led a small squadron into the Mediterranean in 1856, in the navy's first operation outside of home waters, a punitive expedition against North African pirates. He also organized and dispatched a naval force, with diplomatic and scientific intentions, to East Asia in 1859.[38]

Adalbert encouraged the king, his cousin, Wilhelm I (r. 1861–88), to take an active role in naval development. At Adalbert's behest, the king now transformed the Royal Prussian Admiralty into the Ministry of the Navy (*Marineministerium*) in April 1861 and gave its portfolio back to the minister of war, now Lt. Gen. Albrecht von Roon. Roon, who served in that capacity from 1859 to 1873, was an able and creative administrator. He proposed the navy's first unified construction program to the Prussian *Landtag* (the provincial diet) in 1863 with a formal statement of the fleet's purpose: "Prussia must create a fleet that will protect overseas trade and support naval war which in turn will provide the capability to defend our coasts and attack the enemy." Although Roon intended to maintain the navy's traditional emphasis on coastal defense, he nonetheless planned to develop a battle fleet constructed around a core of six armored frigates. Roon also convinced the Landtag to appropriate 2.3 million talers to support these proposals. Although this figure significantly exceeded the navy's 1837 budget, it still did not compare well to the army's 38.5 million talers out of a total royal budget of 140 million talers.[39]

The Prussian Navy played a somewhat greater role in the Danish War of 1864, one of Otto von Bismarck's "wars of unification." When the conflict broke out in January 1864, the Danes immediately blockaded Prussia's Baltic coast. Capt. Eduard Jachmann won Prussia's only, and minor, naval victory on 17 March when he led a handful of Prussian warships to drive off Danish blockaders at Jasmund. Prussian ships also operated in the North Sea and supported the army's amphibious attacks against Danish fortresses at Düppel (March–April) and Alsen (June).[40] The navy's limited role in the war produced only minor benefits. For example, Alfred von Tirpitz later noted, "When I was a boy there was scarcely any trace left of the enthusiasm for the navy which the revolution of '48 aroused in Germany, although it flickered up once more in the year 1864 after the Battle of Jasmund."[41]

Having learned lessons from the recent conflict, Roon replaced his earlier proposals with a major new plan in April 1865. Although he acknowledged that current Prussian maritime interests remained limited, he nonetheless told the Landtag that the "Prussian Navy must assume a position in the second rank of sea powers" on par with Denmark, Sweden, and Holland. He believed that such advancement would allow the fleet to undertake three specific missions with matching ship types. The navy's primary mission, the defense of Prussia's North Sea and Baltic coasts, required gunboats and floating batteries. A second role, the protection of Prussian and German merchant shipping overseas, required cruisers (i.e., sloops or corvettes). The fleet's final role, the projection of Prussian naval power on the high seas, required armored frigates. Roon anticipated that his plan needed twelve years and fifty-seven million talers for fulfillment. This would provide for the construction of ten armored frigates, fourteen overseas cruisers, and ten coastal defense ships.[42]

Roon's plans also provided funds for the development of new bases at Kiel and Wilhelmshaven. Based on lessons learned from the First Danish War (1848–50) and the Crimean War (1854–56), Prussia had already begun to convert its fleet from sail to steam. This new technology, however, increased the need for regular access to logistical and technical support and the stockpiling of materials and equipment. Likewise, strategic issues now required that the Prussian fleet operate in both the North and Baltic Seas. The navy's existing naval base at Danzig proved too small and isolated to provide the necessary facilities for these new developments. Prussia secured a land grant on the Jadebusen from the Grand Duchy of Oldenburg in 1853 for a new naval base. This site, named Wilhelmshaven at its formal opening in 1869, had a strategic location that allowed it to command the Ems (Emden), Weser (Bremen), and Elbe (Hamburg) estuaries. A sortie by a Wilhelmshaven-based squadron would easily prevent an enemy blockade of Germany's North Sea coast. Prussia acquired Kiel from the settlement of the Second Danish War (1864). Kiel, which already had a link to the North Sea via the shallow Eider Canal, would allow the fleet to dominate Baltic sea lanes. The further development of a canal would also allow Prussia to concentrate its fleet in order to project sea power into either the Baltic or North Seas. Meanwhile, Danzig reverted to the status of a naval depot while Stralsund continued as the site of the navy's reserve, and deactivated, gunboats.[43]

Because the growing fleet also needed more personnel, Roon proposed the expansion of the navy to approximately two hundred naval officers (*Seeoffizier*), two hundred warrant officers (*Deckoffizier*), and fifty-four hundred enlisted men. This would require a significant increase in the existing *Seeoffizierkorps*, which currently numbered approximately 120 officers. Prince Adalbert, who wore two hats as commander in chief and chief of the OKM, and Rear Adm. Eduard von Jachmann, who was operational commander as *Geschwaderchef* (squadron chief), served as the fleet's only flag officers. Line officers included four captains, eight commanders, twenty-seven lieutenant commanders, thirty senior lieutenants, and thirty-nine junior lieutenants. Approximately one-third of the officers, thirty-five, had aristocratic status. The navy's officer training establishment numbered more than one hundred midshipmen and cadets, of whom forty-four bore the aristocratic *von*.[44]

OFFICER TRAINING IN THE PRUSSIAN NAVY

Like every institution and procedure in the incipient Prussian Navy, officer training had evolved as the fleet developed. Longe established the Navigation School in Danzig in 1817 to train naval and merchant marine officers. Thirty years later, Prince Adalbert created a more structured system based on a combination of training cruises that provided practical experiences and theoretical work at the *Seekadetten-Institut* (Midshipmen Institute), which replaced the Navigation School in 1851. Modeled after the United States Naval Academy, the school had a two-year curriculum of navigation, gunnery, seamanship, ship design, naval science, English, and French. Training did not forgo education of the body; cadets studied gymnastics, fencing, and dancing. In two years, the midshipmen received commissions as lieutenants, junior grade, if they passed the final exam.[45]

Adalbert also sought to develop the naval officer corps along more professional lines. His first step was to seek candidates who had a "good origin and upbringing, a healthy body, and an unspoiled character open to all noble impressions." He would then use officer training to enhance character and professional development. Since the naval officer corps had only recently come into existence, he also sought to develop maritime traditions and customs, using the British Royal Navy and the Prussian Army as models.[46] Given the increasingly technical nature of the navy, Adalbert saw the need to refine training procedures by establishing a four-year program. Beginning in 1864, he sought candidates between the ages of fourteen and seventeen who would take an entrance exam testing their academic proficiency. Successful cadets would then board one of the navy's training ships for a year-long cruise to the South Atlantic. These voyages would provide practical nautical experience and weed out cadets who were physically or intellectually deficient. Cadets then took a midshipmen's exam (*Seekadetten-Prüfung*), which evaluated proficiency in gunnery, navigation, and seamanship. Newly rated midshipmen would next embark on a two-year training cruise, initially to the South Atlantic but later to East Asia, for additional practical experience. The midshipmen would complete their training with a year of academic studies at a new institution, the Naval School (*Marineschule*), which Adalbert intended to establish in Kiel for the 1866 academic year. Midshipmen who passed their final exams would receive commissions as lieutenants, junior grade, and swear an oath of duty and honor ("Auf Ehre und Pflicht") to the Prussian king and flag.[47]

At the time of Diederichs's application in May 1865, the Prussian Navy was desperate for cadets. Following the tragic loss of SMS *Amazone* in 1861, only three candidates applied for admission to the naval officer corps in 1862. The Navy Ministry sought applicants from the Prussian Army and called up reserve officers from the merchant marine, but these candidates did not always meet Adalbert's expectations; the quality of reserve officers was particularly deficient. Although these expedients temporarily filled vacancies, the navy still lacked qualified applicants for active naval careers, particularly when Adalbert moved to weed out the unqualified.[48]

These personnel problems undoubtedly worked to Diederichs's advantage. He learned upon his return to Germany in May 1865 that he had already missed the regular date for the naval entrance examination. Twenty-six candidates had taken the exam in April, but only eleven had passed. Because Adalbert wanted at least twenty-five cadets to fill out the year's draft, he decided to solicit more applications to allow for additional entrants.[49] Upon receipt of Diederichs's application a few days later, the Seekadetten-Institut invited him to sit for the exam, which tested his knowledge of mathematics, physics, geography, drafting, French, and English. Because he had a substandard academic record from secondary school, he took an additional exam in history, German, and Latin.[50]

SMS *NIOBE*

The Navy Ministry notified him in August that he had passed the exams with a score of "excellent" and directed him to report to the Danzig naval station for duty in September aboard SM Training Ship *Niobe*.[51] The Prussians had purchased *Niobe,* a sixth-rate sail frigate, from the Royal Navy to replace *Amazone* in 1862. Workmen at the Danzig naval yard converted her to a training ship, reducing her armament from twenty-six to fourteen guns and converting gun-deck space to cadet and midshipmen quarters. *Niobe* joined the navy's British-built training sloops *Rover* and *Musquito* to form a training squadron in 1863. The three ships operated in the western Baltic in the war against Denmark in 1864 before resuming training cruises in early 1865.[52]

Niobe carried an experienced crew. Under Cdr. Carl Batsch, the ship had a complement of twelve watch and warrant officers, two hundred enlisted men, a training contingent of four officer-instructors, and space for forty cadets and midshipmen. The Seekadetten-Institut assigned Lt. Cdr. Paul von Reibnitz as director of cadet training, and Lt. Cdr. Louis von Blanc, Lt. (jg) Viktor Valois, and civilian *Navigationslehrer* Eduard Albrecht as training officers.[53]

Accompanied by his father, Diederichs took the train to Danzig and reported aboard *Niobe* on 6 September 1865. As Diederichs unpacked his sea chest in the crowded cadet quarters, he met his fellow officer candidates. *Niobe*'s contingent included four future admirals: Diederichs; Alfred Tirpitz, the eventual father of the "risk fleet" and Diederichs's rival in the later development of the navy; Wilhelm Büchsel, who would become a devoted member of Tirpitz's "torpedo gang" and another rival; and Iwan Oldekop, a

Hanoverian subject who had also joined the navy from the merchant marine and who became Diederichs's lifelong friend. The cadets were immediately fitted for uniforms and then granted liberty to say good-bye to their families. Diederichs, who began a practice of maintaining a personal logbook during *Niobe*'s cruise, concluded the day's entry with a succinct and melancholy, "Took leave from my father."[54]

Batsch officially mustered Diederichs and twenty-two other cadets into the Prussian Navy on 7 September 1865, Diederichs's twenty-second birthday. The navy rated Cadets Diederichs and Oldekop as seamen second class because of their previous experience in the merchant marine. The other cadets, who lacked prior service at sea, received a lower rate—seaman fourth class—and less pay. The navy paid Diederichs the handsome sum of twenty marks per month but required him and the other cadets to pay for their own uniforms, effectively weeding out applicants from less affluent families.[55]

Niobe weighed anchor on 9 September for a brief orientation cruise around Danzig harbor. Batsch timed his departure poorly, however, as *Niobe* promptly ran aground in the low tide. Towed off by a steam tug, the ship proceeded on her way before returning to Danzig in the afternoon. Diederichs's prior experience at sea served him in good stead during this early period; while the other cadets were still—literally—learning the ropes and other basic ship routines, he and Oldekop stood anchor watches as signalmen.[56]

The ship departed on the sixteenth for a shake-down cruise to Kiel. As *Niobe* proceeded on a westerly course, Diederichs used his spare time to record the minutiae of naval life. He made repeated references in his personal log to sail drill aloft and gunnery drill on deck, as the cadets learned the complicated art of operating sailing ships in often difficult conditions. Diederichs did not limit his log to memories of training alone. When *Niobe* passed through the Fehmarn Belt, which separated Prussia from Denmark, he noted a tense exchange of formal salutes with Danish ships and fortifications in an area where the Prussian and Danish ships had exchanged gunfire only months earlier. He also noted that danger existed even in peacetime. When heavy fog obscured navigational buoys marking the narrow entrance into the Kiel fiord, Batsch had to send a seaman into the chains with a sounding lead to find the channel and prevent the ship from running aground.[57]

This was Diederichs's first visit to Kiel, recently replacing Danzig as the navy's primary naval station in the Baltic. After the navy acquired property on the Kiel fiord as part of the peace settlement arising out of the Danish War of 1864, the new *Marinestation der Ostsee* slowly had begun to develop along both sides of the long (twelve kilometers) and narrow (one to two kilometers) fiord. Kiel offered several advantages over other sites: It already had a link to the North Sea via the shallow Eider Canal; its location would allow the fleet to dominate Baltic sea lanes; and it was ice free most years and certainly navigable each winter four to six weeks before ships could leave Russian ports.

Diederichs saw a vibrant and flourishing base at Kiel. The navy's initial establishment lay between Friedrichsort and Holtenau on the west side, at the point where the Eider River, the later site of the Kaiser Wilhelm Canal, drained into the fiord. The navy had already begun to construct barracks and training facilities for the enlisted personnel attached to the *Matrosendivision* (Seamen Division) at Holtenau and research and development facilities at Friedrichsort. A new *Königliche Werft* (Royal Shipyard), for the construction and repair of warships, was simultaneously developing on the eastern side of the fiord at Ellerbek. Four companies of the First *Seebatallion,* the navy's equivalent of Royal Marine Light Infantry, and two companies of naval artillery provided security from their fortified positions at Friedrichsort.[58]

This was an active period for Diederichs, as *Niobe*'s cadets commenced final preparations for the training cruise. His logbook notes a series of events, including formal naval ceremonies, regular work details, and the occasional liberty ashore. Often accompanied by Oldekop, he went ashore to taste the delights of Kiel or made informal visits to other warships anchored in the roadstead. Diederichs became an avid sailor, at one point joining other cadets to sail a pinnace across to Holtenau. (In later years Diederichs would participate regularly in Germany's annual *Kielwoche* regatta at the naval station.)

After a busy week, the ship was finally ready for sea. Rear Adm. Eduard von Jachmann, commander of the Baltic squadron, came aboard on 27 September to inspect the ship and observe the cadets at their drills. At the end of the day, in a formal speech to the crew, he declared *Niobe* "ready in all respects for sea" and granted permission to Batsch to commence the training cruise.[59]

Niobe weighed anchor and proceeded to sea on 29 September 1865. Although a temporary lack of winds forced Batsch to heave to off Skagen, passage out of the Baltic and down the North Sea coast to the English Channel was largely uneventful. Diederichs noted regular course changes to avoid English fishing boats off Dogger Bank and the flogging of a sailor for unspecified misdemeanors. A brief call at Plymouth (5–7 October) provided a momentary respite from ship's routine as the cadets attended a performance of *Macbeth*.[60] At sea again, *Niobe* weathered rough autumnal conditions in the Atlantic. Heavy squalls struck the ship repeatedly, causing extensive damage to sails and spars. Batsch suspended drills as the cadets joined the crew to complete the required repairs in hazardous conditions.

No sooner had the weather moderated and the ship returned to normal routine when disaster struck yet again. Diederichs noted in his entry for 20 October that the day's training had included both gunnery and boarding drill. Perhaps the youthful cadets, boisterous after several days of stress and tension, had grown careless. A missed step, an inadvertent stumble on a crowded deck, a momentary distraction to observe the sights and sounds of an active ship and, suddenly, fire, the most fearful threat possible to a wooden ship, flared up near the forward magazine. The crew responded quickly to put out the flames before the fire could spread to the gunpowder stored below, but not before the mainmast sustained damage. New squalls further damaged the ship's masts and rigging on 21 October, when the foremast topyards fell and became entangled in the jib and bowsprit. Cadets and crew worked hard for two days to make the needed repairs.[61] By then the drama of *Macbeth*, which Diederich had seen only a few days before, must have appeared mild in comparison with life-and-death shipboard urgencies.

To the relief of all aboard, lookouts sighted Madeira Island, a Portuguese possession off northwest Africa, on the morning of 23 October. The sight of land brought relief—both emotional and meteorological—to the tired crew. As light winds and warm temperatures replaced bitter autumnal storms, the crew hoisted out all boats to tow *Niobe* into Funchal harbor. Early the next morning, in clear weather and with the temperature approaching ninety degrees, the crew spread awnings for shade. They welcomed the German consul aboard with a formal seven-gun salute and his cargo of fresh fruit and water with enthusiastic cheers.[62]

Niobe, joined by *Rover* and *Musquito*, remained anchored in Funchal Roads for two weeks while Batsch implemented a more regular training schedule. The ship's bosun piped the cadets out of their hammocks for reveille at 0600. Inspection and breakfast followed at 0640 with a formal cadet parade at 0800. The daily training schedule commenced promptly at 0930. The cadets paused for lunch at 1200 before resuming training at 1400. The training officers again paraded the cadets for inspection by Captain Batsch at 1630. The cadets then had an hour of boat or sail drill at 1700. Supper followed at 1800. The cadets returned to their quarters at 2000 for studies—reviewing navigational and gunnery manuals—or free time before the bosun piped lights out at 2200.[63]

Diederichs used his limited free time to keep up his personal log. His entries are succinct and informative as he records the minutiae of shipboard life: wind and sea states, temperature, and a brief reference to the day's activities, all in a quick, spidery script. A few diversions interrupted the tedium he recorded. On one day, training officers led the cadets on a mad scramble up *Niobe*'s towering masts to study the ship's rigging. On another day, the cadets disassembled and cleaned small arms—the needle gun made famous only a few months later at the Battle of Königgrätz—and practiced sword drill with cutlass and rapier. On a third day, Diederichs commanded a gun crew of cadets as they manned one of *Niobe*'s gundeck 68-lb guns in competition with the regular crew at the quarterdeck 32-pounders. On the next, the cadets learned that etiquette and protocol were an indispensable part of an officer's education when they hosted a dinner party to celebrate the birthday of His Royal Highness Admiral Prince Adalbert of Prussia. And, occasionally, the cadets rested on a seventh day. Momentarily relieved from training for a few hours of recreation ashore, Diederichs notes joyously that "beautiful weather (clear, 36 C) and a fresh sea breeze favored the day."[64]

Niobe weighed anchor and proceeded south to the Cape Verde islands, another Portuguese possession, in November. With the ship sometimes at anchor and sometimes under way, the training continued. The cadets would alternate sail drill and gunnery practice, relieved only by the occasional trip ashore to practice with small arms. The monotonous routine of training filled Diederichs's log for November, December, and January with little variation. For example, the entry for 21 November notes laconically, "Removed and repaired bowsprit spars and rigging. Cadet small-boat drill." Diederichs notes a few incidents, some near tragic, some merely social, to break the monotony. Seaman Eberhardt fell overboard while the ship was under way but Bosun's Mate Selpin dove into the water to save him; a court-martial punished Marine Lemke for sleeping on duty.[65]

The cadets received substantial training in amphibious operations. Although *Niobe* carried a small contingent of twenty-five naval infantrymen from the First *Seebatallion* for training purposes, Prussian warships did not usually embark such units. Instead, the navy gave its officers and seamen extensive training with small arms and infantry tactics. Diederichs, who had brief military experience, unlike his younger peers, noted with some pride that he had qualified on the rifle range ashore, shooting at fixed targets over difficult terrain. He admitted to less success with revolvers—shooting only 32 percent—but cited long range and active winds as mitigating factors.[66]

An occasional opportunity for recreation ashore broke the monotony of training. On one occasion, Diederichs and his peers challenged *Rover*'s cadets "to meet ashore to play ball." Although he did not record the ensuing score (perhaps *Niobe* lost), the soccer game nonetheless allowed Diederichs to become more acquainted with *Rover*'s training detachment, which included Lt. (sg) Eduard von Knorr as well as Mdn. Gustav von Senden-Bibran and Paul Hoffmann.[67] All three would rise to flag rank and serve with Diederichs in later posts.

The Christmas holidays brought new diversions. The cadets visited the 60-gun Russian steam frigate *Dimitri Danskov,* which had stopped briefly to load fresh food supplies while in transit to East Asia. Diederichs and several other cadets returned to the Russian ship the next day. His log entry for Christmas Day contains no melancholy reference to his absence from distant family celebrations but notes rather succinctly, "Good Russian brandy."[68]

Following the brief holiday season, the cadets took mid-cruise exams. Batsch and the training officers proctored oral and written exams on navigation and seamanship on 28 December, followed by gunnery exams on the twenty-ninth. The cadets first constructed a wood-and-sailcloth target, eight feet by ten, and then cleared the portside guns for action in two minutes and thirty seconds. The exercise became less successful at that point, however, as the cadets hit the target only twice out of thirty-six rounds. Diederichs's relevant log entry made no mention of the captain's scathing evaluation of the cadets' performance.[69]

During this time, Batsch himself complained in a report to the OKM in early December that the number—forty—of cadets and midshipmen aboard *Niobe* had proven excessive. The four training officers were unable to provide adequate opportunity for individual or small-group direction. This was particularly true, he noted, in ship-handling, navigation, and sail drill. He therefore recommended that the OKM either reduce the number of trainees or increase the number of training officers.[70]

New Year's Day, 1866, began with a formal address by Captain Batsch and ended with liberty at Porto Grande on St. Vincente Island. Gunnery results notwithstanding, the cadets had passed at least the navigation and seamanship portions of the exams and now had an opportunity to celebrate. Wearing their dress uniforms and with the ship decorated for the holidays, the officers and cadets hosted a ball to mark Twelfth Night, inviting civilian guests from several visiting steamers.[71]

Batsch suspended training to prepare the ship for the next leg of his training itinerary. Work details filled water casks (Diederichs recorded a total of fifteen thousand gallons of drinking water), slaughtered and salted oxen, and loaded fresh provisions. *Niobe* set sail on 26 January, proceeding northwest toward Funchal, Madeira, for a final visit. The ship's brief return brought some excitement to island life and filled the pockets of island businessmen. In return, one local merchant hosted a masked ball for the cadets.[72]

Niobe's departure from Madeira on 16 February 1866 marked the end of the first and most significant phase of the training cruise. This segment had focused on fundamental naval skills—seamanship, navigation, and gunnery—intended to educate the cadets as sailors. The next stage, based on visits to various European cities, would educate the cadets more thoroughly as "officers and gentlemen." Because German naval officers in the nineteenth century often represented their country as diplomats, their training needed a cultural and political element.

Niobe arrived in Cadiz, once the center of Spanish naval and colonial power, on 22 February 1866 and remained for more than a month. Accompanied by their training officers, the cadets toured the port, inspected the existing naval base at Rota, rode inland to Seville, and watched a bullfight. *Niobe*'s crew hoisted flags overall and raised the Prussian flag at the fore to celebrate the birthday of Wilhelm I, His Majesty King of Prussia, on 22

March. Batsch marked the occasion by awarding prizes to the leading cadets, presenting Diederichs with a special edition of Feodor von Klön's *Struggle for Schleswig.*[73]

Diederichs's stay in Cadiz was not all fun and games. When high winds caused a passenger ferry to capsize and a schooner to go aground, Diederichs joined the crew to rescue the passengers, saving all but two, and tow the grounded schooner into deeper water. Diederichs also recorded events reflecting political unrest in the city. In fact, Spain was then embroiled in political upheaval that would lead eighteen months later to the overthrow of Queen Isabella and result in events that would cause the Franco-German War in 1870.[74]

Niobe continued northwest around the Iberian peninsula to Lisbon, where Prince Henry the Navigator had once dispatched Portuguese explorers to span the globe, in early April. *Niobe* exchanged salutes with USS *Kearsarge,* which arrived in port following antislavery patrols on the African coast. The ship, which had gained fame during the American Civil War for a famous ship-to-ship duel with CSS *Alabama,* reported the presence of the dreaded "yellow jack," or cholera, aboard. Two officers, the surgeon, and four stokers had already died. Under normal conditions, Diederichs and the cadets would have visited *Kearsarge,* but the ship remained in quarantine, maintaining only limited contact with the shore to replenish supplies.[75] Batsch used the incident to report to the OKM that the health of the cadets and crew aboard *Niobe* was good.[76]

Before *Niobe*'s departure on 13 April 1866, Batsch briefed the crew on growing tensions with Austria. Although the two states had fought against Denmark as allies only two years earlier, renewed tensions over the fate of Schleswig and Holstein caused both states to break off negotiations and mobilize for war. The Prussian consul in Lisbon warned Batsch that several Austrian warships, including the modern steam sloop *Erzherzog Friedrich,* were operating in Atlantic and English Channel waters. *Niobe* therefore assumed a war footing upon departure from Lisbon, alert for the imminent outbreak of hostilities.

Niobe's initial passage out of Iberian waters and into the Atlantic was quiet. That all changed on 25 April, however, as *Niobe* entered the English Channel with Falmouth over the horizon to the northwest. Batsch had mustered crew and cadets in the waist to celebrate *Buss- und Bettag,* a day of prayer and thanksgiving, when a lookout sighted an unidentified steam warship trailing astern. As the warship, provisionally identified as Austrian, secured sails and raised steam, a sure indication of hostile intent, Batsch ordered all hands to clear for action. This was at best a symbolic gesture. Outfitted as a training ship with armament reduced to fourteen obsolete cannons, sailing ship *Niobe* was no match for a modern steam warship. *Niobe* lacked the guns and crew to fight even a sail frigate, much less *Erzherzog Friedrich,* which carried twenty-two modern rifled guns and could easily outmaneuver *Niobe* under steam. Although the mystery ship soon disappeared in the fog, *Niobe*'s crew remained on alert for the next twenty-four hours. The ship did not secure from general quarters until 1100 on 26 April, when a lookout again sighted the mysterious warship, this time flying Swedish colors. A few hours later, *Niobe* put into Plymouth, where Batsch learned that the threat of war had briefly waned. She put to sea on 2 May, sailing without incident through the English Channel and North Sea before reaching the sanctuary of the Baltic five days later.[77]

The ship's arrival in home waters signaled both the end of the training cruise and the onset of final examinations. Diederichs and the other cadets sat for the Seekadetten-Prüfung as *Niobe* lay anchored off Friederichsort at the mouth of the Kiel fiord. These midshipmen's tests, which began on 11 May and continued for several days, contained oral and written sections evaluating the cadets' knowledge of gunnery, navigation, and seamanship. The gunnery exam required the cadets to demonstrate proficiency in both ship's artillery and small arms and the mathematical skills necessary to lay individual cannons. The navigation section tested knowledge of astronomy, the use of navigational instruments and charts, meteorology, and hydrology. The seamanship section examined cadets in their knowledge of sail, signal, and small-boat drill.[78]

Batsch informally notified the cadets of their individual examination results on 20 May. Diederichs had performed well, receiving scores of "excellent" in all three categories. Based on a favorable recommendation by the captain and confirmation by the Seekadetten-Institut, he would now advance to the rate of midshipman. Before he packed his logbook away in his sea chest on 21 May, Diederichs paused to make a final entry: "Cadets left the ship to begin four weeks' leave."[79]

The navy formally notified Diederichs on 17 June that he had passed the midshipman exams and promoted him to midshipman a week later. A total of twenty-three cadets had passed the exams, but only Diederichs and four others, including Tirpitz and Oldekop, received "royal commendation" (*Allerhöchster Belobigung*) for their high scores.[80]

WAR AND PEACE

Mr. Midshipman Diederichs had no opportunity to enjoy his achievement. When the long-awaited war between Prussia and Austria broke out on 14 June, the navy ordered him to report for duty aboard SMS *Gefion*. The Frankfurt fleet had captured *Gefion*, a sailing frigate armed with forty-eight guns, in the First Danish War in 1849 and then had sold her to the Prussians in 1852. The Prussian Navy then converted her to an artillery training ship and assigned her to the Kiel station. Anticipating an attack on Kiel by Austrian forces stationed in Holstein, the OKM decided to restore *Gefion* to regular duty. Diederichs's first task, therefore, was to assist *Gefion*'s first officer, Lt. Cdr. Adolf Butterlin, in restoring the training ship to combat status. The frigate could serve as a floating fortress and provide artillery support for the defense of the naval station. *Gefion*'s 24-, 36-, and 60-lb cannons were more than a match for Austrian field artillery, and the ship could serve as a floating battery and provide artillery support in defense of the naval station.[81]

The Austro-Prussian War produced little opportunity for the Prussian Navy to prove itself. Gen. Helmut von Moltke, chief of the Prussian General Staff, quickly ended the war with an early form of blitzkrieg in which the more mobile Prussian forces forced Hanoverian forces to surrender on 29 June and decisively defeated the Austrians at Königgrätz, Bohemia, on 3 July. Although a Prussian naval squadron operated briefly in the North Sea, the Peace of Prague formally ended the war on 23 August before Diederichs could see any action. Instead, his log entries focus primarily on work details and patriotic celebrations of army victories.[82]

War's end returned Diederichs to a training regimen. The 1864 protocol required new midshipmen to embark aboard another training ship for an additional two years at sea. Diederichs's prior experience in the merchant marine, however, exempted him from this requirement and allowed him instead to proceed directly to the next, and final, step of officer training.

While other midshipmen, including Tirpitz, soon left Kiel aboard *Niobe*, *Rover*, and *Musquito* for the second training cruise, Diederichs and Oldekop prepared to report instead to the Marineschule.[83]

Prince Adalbert intended to make the Marineschule, which by now had replaced the Seekadetten-Institut, the Prussian Navy's premier undergraduate program for officer training. As outlined in his formal proposal, the school would offer "a systematic education whereby the officer-candidate may develop the necessary professional skills for service as a regular officer." Directed by Lt. C. A. Liebe, the school drew its regular faculty from the navy's "best and brightest" officers and adjunct faculty from the University of Kiel. Appointment to the school faculty became a professional honor as active-duty officers rotated through the post in four-year tours.

Adalbert's plan called for the academic year to begin on 1 August and conclude on 30 June. Each year would have two terms—fall (August to December) and spring (January to June)—and mid-term and final examinations, both written and oral, in every subject. Locating a new site, revising the curriculum, and transferring faculty and staff to Kiel took well into autumn and required a temporary postponement of the new academic year. The navy leased the Dürstenbrook Hotel for a temporary site and then purchased property at the intersection of Mühlinstrasse and Waisenhof for a permanent site. Because of the delays, Adalbert abbreviated the first term to three months (November, December, January) and the second term to five (February through June).[84]

Diederichs, Oldekop, and fourteen other midshipmen formally reported to the Marineschule on 30 October 1866. Diederichs's final log entry aboard *Gefion* noted in his typically succinct manner: "2nd pinnace carried coal from base. Cleaned hand weapons. Reported to Marineschule."[85] Six of the sixteen midshipmen eventually achieved flag rank: Diederichs, Oldekop, August Thomson, Gustav von Senden-Bibran, Paul Hoffmann, and Max Plüddemann.

When classes began on 1 November, the midshipmen faced a rigorous curriculum. For example, the fall term blended professional courses with the liberal arts. From Monday through Saturday, Diederichs attended a total of twenty-four ninety-minute lectures on mathematics (five class periods), natural science (five), French (two), and English (two), with additional lectures on navigation (three), gunnery (four), and military tactics (four). He spent Tuesday and Thursday afternoons in labs. The spring term consisted of seventeen weekly lectures on professional subjects, including navigation (three), naval tactics (two), gunnery (four), ship design (four), steam engineering (three), and naval protocol (one). Diederichs studied navigation with reserve Lieutenant Albrecht, who had held a similar post aboard *Niobe*. His former executive officer aboard *Gefion*, Lieutenant Commander Butterlin, taught gunnery. Lieutenant Neber, from the First Seebattalion taught military tactics.

The curriculum did not neglect physical education. Adalbert had originally intended that the midshipmen practice gymnastics and fencing in winter months and take swimming lessons during the spring. Since the new school still lacked adequate athletic facilities at its Mühlinstrasse location and Kiel's cool climate prevented swimming lessons until June, Diederichs and the other midshipmen fenced and danced their way through Kiel's cold and damp winter months.[86]

Director Liebe filed mixed reports on his students toward the end of the first term. He praised the students, singling out Diederichs, Oldekop, Hoffmann, and Senden, for their academic achievements but also reported that more than one quarter of the students, whom he did not identify, had contracted syphilis. To deal with the problem, he invited Rear Admiral Jachmann to speak to the midshipmen about their reckless behavior. Liebe also reduced the two-week Christmas break to nine days to make up for the late start and perhaps to reduce the amount of free time available to the high-spirited midshipmen.[87]

Diederichs sat for the lieutenant's exams in Kiel at the end of the spring term in June 1867. He received formal notification in July that he and only four other midshipmen— Oldekop, Senden, Plüddemann, and Thomson— had passed the exams. The other eleven had failed.[88] Diederichs's highest score was in drafting, for which he received a mark of excellent. He did well in navigation, seamanship, general service knowledge, naval design, and English, received a fair score in gunnery, steam engineering, and French, and performed satisfactorily in military tactics.[89]

New orders assigned Passed Midshipman Diederichs to temporary duty with the Seaman Division in Kiel on 26 June 1867. The Matrosendivision provided training for enlisted personnel and acted as cadre for the mobilization of reserve forces. Junior officers such as Diederichs often served briefly with one of the division's four detachments while awaiting permanent assignment. In fact, he barely had time to unpack his gear before receiving new orders on 14 August 1867 transferring him to SMS *Musquito* as a training officer in preparation for a new training cruise in Atlantic waters.[90] After a brief furlough, Diederichs reported for duty aboard *Musquito* on 26 August.

A newly minted tradition in the young Prussian Navy was for new officers to receive their commissions aboard ship. Diederichs therefore stood before the officers and crew of *Musquito* at noon on 27 August 1867 while Cdr. Adolf Berger administered the same flag oath that Diederichs had taken two years earlier as a cadet aboard *Niobe*. After a lifetime of familial expectations, after years of academic struggle and physical illness, after nearly four arduous years at sea, Diederichs now stood proudly at attention as he received his commission as *Unterleutnant zur See* (lieutenant, jg) and committed himself to the service of the crown with "honor and duty."[91]

In retrospect, it is clear that, health problems notwithstanding, Diederichs's irregular education fulfilled its role in character development. As his older son Fritz noted, the Gymnasium had indeed inculcated in him a strong sense of virtue: "His essential character traits included moral courage, equanimity, clear and quick decisiveness, iron diligence, absolute reliability in every task, goodwill toward every man." Others would comment on his modesty and directness, and his strong sense of civil obligation. Frau Elisabeth von Heyking, wife of the German ambassador to China, much later confirmed this trait, referring to Diederichs in a positive way as a "simple man" in sharp contrast to the many ambitious intriguers of her acquaintance.[92] Already evident in his steady ascent through the hurdles of training, such traits would serve him well throughout his career. They also would make him intolerant of the dishonest and deceptive politicians whose actions would impinge on his career. In his later years, responding to political problems in Germany's governmental and naval leadership, he again invoked Schiller: "Against stupidity, the gods themselves battle in vain."[93]

2

Training for Preparedness: Diederichs and the Evolving German Navy, 1867–1878

As Lt. (jg) Otto von Diederichs assumed his duties aboard SMS *Musquito*, he could look back on the previous two years with a sense of pride. Motivated by strong family expectations, he had succeeded in overcoming significant obstacles on his course toward a naval commission. He could now look forward to a career in the service of the Prussian state. That service now assumed specific responsibilities, well summarized by the observation of the naval strategist Capt. Alfred Stenzel: "Crews are recruited, clothed, trained, and fed, while ships are constructed, equipped, and armed—solely to fight at the right time and place."[1] That dictum effectively described Diederichs's duties for the next decade.

SMS *MUSQUITO*

Prussia purchased *Musquito*, along with her sister ship *Rover*, from the British Royal Navy in 1862. The Danzig shipyard promptly refitted both ships, originally designed as brigs armed with ten 24-lb guns, as training ships with quarters for forty midshipmen and cadets. *Musquito* departed Kiel on 18 September 1867 in concert with *Niobe* and *Rover*. The training squadron touched briefly at Plymouth, England, where Commander Berger transferred over to *Niobe* to replace her former captain, Cdr. Erwin Schelle, who had died en route. Cdr. Archibald MacLean, an expatriate Scot and most recently first officer aboard SMS *Kronprinz,* came aboard as *Musquito's* new commanding officer. The squadron then proceeded south, reaching new training grounds in the vicinity of Lisbon two weeks later.[2]

Musquito arrived in Portuguese waters under new colors. Bismarck had abolished the German Confederation following the Prussian defeat of Austria in 1866. He replaced it with the *Norddeutschen Bund* (North German Confederation), which included most German states north of the Main River, in August 1867. Thereupon the Prussian Navy became the core of a new *Bundesmarine,* the Federal Navy, under the direction of the Prussian Ministry of the Navy. Lt. Gen. Albrecht von Roon (minister of the navy), Admiral Prince Adalbert (Naval High Command), and now Vice Admiral Jachmann (operational commander) assumed comparable posts in the new navy. To the sound of twittering pipes and salutes, *Musquito's* crew hoisted the Confederation's new black-white-red colors in place of Prussia's black eagle on a white field on 1 October 1867.[3]

Training continued, however, no matter what flag flew from the mast. In fact, Diederichs quickly learned that service as a commissioned officer differed greatly from his earlier experience as a cadet and midshipman. *Musquito* was much smaller than frigates *Niobe* or *Gefion,* and overcrowded cadet quarters caused disciplinary and health problems. For example, Diederichs and his fellow training officers placed two cadets in irons for insubordination and punished others for minor infractions (returning late from liberty, negligent treatment of seamen) by arrest in quarters. When two cadets contracted typhus, a deadly disease spread by lice, during shore leave in Lisbon in January 1868, MacLean sailed to Vigo to avoid the further spread of the disease. The crew washed down the ship with chlorine, ventilated below decks, and found a new source of fresh water. Citing crowded conditions as the cause of these problems, MacLean recommended that the *Oberkommando der Marine* reduce the number of cadets and midshipmen aboard from forty to twenty on future training cruises.[4]

Musquito returned to Kiel after an otherwise uneventful cruise in May 1868. Almost immediately, Diederichs escorted a parliamentary delegation on a tour of *Musquito* on 25 May. The Bundestag deputies visited Kiel as they prepared to consider an increase in the navy's budget for the next fiscal year. Navy Minister Roon, who had introduced a new fleet development plan in October 1867, had asked for additional funding in order to construct a fleet of sixteen armored ships for offensive operations, twenty-two corvettes for overseas service, and twenty gunboats for coastal defense.[5]

Before *Musquito* departed for her fall cruise, new orders detached Diederichs in August 1868 and transferred him to temporary duty with the Matrosendivision in Kiel. The Seaman's Division trained new recruits and provided billets for seamen transferred ashore from ships deactivated at the end of summer operations. Because the navy lacked adequate funding for year-round operations, most ships were placed out of service in the fall. Their captains assumed temporary billets on the staff of the Kiel naval station while their crews came ashore to temporary quarters billets with the Matrosendivision for additional training. Junior officers such as Diederichs served as detachment or company commanders with the Matrosendivision and participated in training exercises. A small maintenance contingent under a junior officer or senior petty officer remained aboard each deactivated ship during the winter. The navy simply reversed this sequence in the spring, placing ships in service and embarking crews.[6]

Following brief service with the Matrosendivision, Diederichs received orders in November 1868 that transferred him to SMS *Gefion*. Although officially placed out of service in September, *Gefion* had received a recent refit that replaced her original smooth-bore muzzle loaders with more modern guns. Diederichs worked hard through the winter months with a small crew of petty officers and seamen as they mounted guns on new carriages, rearranged powder magazines, and rewove tackle to prepare the ship for the next season's gunnery practice.[7]

Diederichs's work aboard *Gefion* and his growing reputation as a gunnery expert led to his transfer to SMS *Arcona* in February 1869. Commissioned a decade earlier following construction at the Royal Dockyards at Danzig, *Arcona* was the lead ship in a new class of screw frigates designed for overseas service as *Auslandskreuzer*. Diederichs served aboard *Arcona* for five months, supervising her refit, which replaced her original 68-lb carronades with modern 150-mm guns. His new post seemed not without relief; a cryptic penciled reference in his personal copy of his service file says simply, "Lilli Lehmann an Bord!"[8]

Arcona put to sea in May 1869 for a trial cruise in the Baltic before proceeding into the North Sea to inaugurate the navy's new *Marinestation der Nordsee* at Wilhelmshaven. *Arcona* served as fleet commander Jachmann's flagship as Wilhelm I formally opened that naval base on 17 June 1869. Located on the Jadebusen, it gave the navy an outlet to the North Sea and provided protection for the strategic Elbe (Hamburg) and Weser (Bremen) estuaries. The nearby Eider River combined with inland canals to provide transit between the Baltic and North Seas for shallow-draft warships. Wilhelmshaven, which housed the Second Matrosendivision, provided logistical and technical support for approximately half of the Bundesmarine's ships hereafter. During Diederichs's career, however, Wilhelmshaven never developed the military significance of its Kiel counterpart.[9]

Following the end of the festivities, Diederichs received another set of orders. These detached him from *Arcona* and assigned him to SMS *Grille*, the royal yacht, for a three-week cruise through the Frisian islands. Diederichs's brief tour aboard *Grille* probably had more to do with his aristocratic background and paternal connections to the royal family than to his gunnery skills, and it taught him, as well, that naval service was not always about military considerations. Originally commissioned in 1858 as the royal yacht of the Hohenzollern family, *Grille* carried two 12-lb guns, more for formal salutes than naval combat, and a crew of seventy officers and men. A recent refit that included the installation of more modern engines had produced a more comfortable and seaworthy ship.[10]

Diederichs reported aboard *Grille* at Geestemünde, a small naval depot in the Weser estuary, on 3 July 1869. Commanded by Lt. Cdr. Julius Ratzeburg, the yacht raised anchor and proceeded by way of the Eider Canal to Kiel. Following two weeks of preparation, *Grille* reversed course and returned through the canal to the Elbe River to rendezvous with the royal family at Hamburg-Altona. To twittering pipes and a twenty-one-gun salute, Crown Prince Friedrich (son of Wilhelm I), Princess Victoria (daughter of England's Queen Victoria), and their five children embarked aboard *Grille* on 20 July. Two days later, *Grille* put to sea on a southerly course, reaching Emden on the twenty-third. For the next three weeks, with Emden as her base, *Grille* cruised back and forth between Borkum and the other Frisian islands. On one day, the royal family enjoyed a picnic lunch on the island of Norderney, after which Diederichs and the other officers demonstrated a rocket-powered rescue apparatus for the amusement of the royal children. Ten-year-old Willy, who later became Kaiser Wilhelm II, and seven-year-old Heinrich, who entered the navy in 1872 and rose to the rank of grand admiral, particularly enjoyed the *Raketenrettungsaparat* demonstration. *Grille* visited Borkum on 27 July to allow the children to enjoy sand dunes and beaches. Good weather allowed the yacht to cruise leisurely through the rest of the picturesque islands, whose infamous mud flats made sailing both challenging and exciting. The idyllic voyage ended on 16 August when the crown prince's party disembarked with appropriate ceremonies at Altona.[11]

Although *Grille* proceeded back through the Eider Canal to Kiel to prepare for another mission, Diederichs left the ship on 26 August with new orders. He now returned to *Musquito* for another training cruise to Spain and Portugal. Only days later, on 31 August 1869, he received formal notice of his promotion to *Leutnant zur See,* or lieutenant, senior grade. The standard time-in-grade for promotion from junior to senior grade was three years. Diederichs had received the promotion after only two, a rapid pace even for a navy under expansion. He had proven himself to be a dependable and versatile officer, willing to undertake a variety of assignments. His early promotion also allowed him to pass more senior officers, including Gustav von Senden-Bibran and Paul Hoffmann, on the seniority list.[12]

Diederichs's second tour aboard *Musquito* resembled his previous commissioned training cruises. He worked hard to train the cadets and midshipmen, earning praise from MacLean, who cited excellent results in the trainees' seamanship and gunnery. Weather conditions and shipboard hygiene had improved since Diederichs's earlier tour, with no repeat of the typhus epidemic suffered the previous year. Perhaps the moral health of the cadets and crew produced some problems, however, since MacLean complained about the absence of a chaplain. Superstitious seamen preferred to serve without a chaplain, but the Calvinist MacLean had other views. MacLean's only other complaint was that the cadets were not able to complete swimming instruction before *Musquito*'s return to Kiel in late April 1870.[13]

THE FRANCO-GERMAN WAR

For the second time in four years, Diederichs returned to Kiel to find Prussia on the brink of war. Tensions between Prussia and France had developed since 1868 over the issue of the "Spanish candidature." The political unrest in Spain that Diederichs had witnessed while aboard *Niobe* in 1866 had led to the overthrow of Queen Isabella in September 1868. The Spanish sought a new ruler from among various European princes, finally offering the throne to Leopold von Hohenzollern-Sigmaringen, a south German and Catholic cousin of the Prussian king, Wilhelm I, in early 1870. (The Prussian Navy had a coincidental tie to the diplomatic crisis; Leopold's father, Karl Anton, had briefly served as chief of the Prussian Admiralty from 1858 to 1861.) The French, however, opposed the placement of a German prince on the Spanish throne because it would have encircled France and upset the existing diplomatic balance of power.

The crisis climaxed with the famous Ems Telegram, which Bismarck released for publication on 14 July 1870, Bastille Day, the French national holiday. The telegram, edited by Bismarck, suggested that the French ambassador and the Prussian king had treated each other rudely. Angered by this perceived insult, the French declared war on Prussia on 19 July. This Franco-Prussian conflict became the Franco-German War when Bismarck raised the specter of another Napoleon—Emperor Louis Napoleon III—invading German soil, enabling him to recruit the south German states (Bavaria, Baden, and Württemberg) to his cause.[14]

Vice Adm. Eduard von Jachmann assumed primary responsibility for the naval war when Wilhelm I recalled his cousin Admiral Prince Adalbert to serve with the First Army in the land campaign against France. Jachmann therefore served as commander in chief of allied naval forces and assumed command of naval forces in the North Sea. Rear Adm. Edward Heldt, chief of the Kiel naval station, commanded naval units in the Baltic. Jachmann and his staff possessed few options as they developed strategic plans for the war, since France had clear quantitative superiority. When the war broke out, Prussia had only sixteen warships (three armored frigates, two coastal defense vessels, four screw frigates, and seven gunboats) in service, with eighteen warships (frigate *Renown,* one screw frigate, and sixteen gunboats) laid up in ordinary. Prussia's allies could add only a handful of coastal defense ships, auxiliaries, and armed merchant cruisers. On the other hand, the French fleet contained two armored battleships, fifteen armored frigates, twenty-nine ships-of-the-line, seventeen screw frigates, and numerous small warships. Jachmann immediately concluded that to commit German (i.e., Prussian) naval forces to battle on the open sea would only invite a quick and decisive defeat that would leave Germany's coasts vulnerable to attack.[15]

Jachmann therefore decided to wage a defensive war, giving first priority to the defense of Germany's strategic ports and river estuaries, and distributed his forces accordingly. He concentrated the North Sea forces at Wilhelmshaven, with defensive responsibility for the Elbe, Weser, and Ems estuaries. He created a special flying squadron of Prussia's only capital ships to serve as a sortie force. This *Ausfallflotte* included armored frigates *König Wilhelm* (10,500 tons, eighteen 240-mm guns), *Friedrich Carl* (sixty-eight hundred tons, sixteen 210-mm guns), and *Kronprinz* (sixty-two hundred tons, sixteen 210-mm guns). He assigned his two other major warships—armored monitor *Arminius* (eighteen hundred tons, four 210-mm guns) and armored ram *Prinz Adalbert* (sixteen hundred tons, one 210-mm and two 170-mm guns)—to the Elbe. He allocated several gunboats to defend each of the river estuaries with orders operate no more than twenty nautical miles from the coast and hinder any French approach with hit-and-run attacks. Likewise, the armored squadron, with Jachmann flying his flag aboard *König Wilhelm,* would advance out of the Jade to strike at any French movements. Thus, any French attempt to transit the North Sea and enter the Baltic would face a constant threat of flank attack. Jachmann allocated fewer units to the Baltic, centered at Kiel and Stralsund, where he could depend more on coastal fortifications and mobile army units for defense.[16]

At the outbreak of the war, Diederichs received orders to proceed to the Stralsund naval depot on the Baltic coast and assume command of SM gunboat *Natter.* Constructed in 1860 but only intermittently in service thereafter, *Natter* was a *Jäger*-class steam-sail gunboat designed expressly for littoral defense. Classified as a second-class gunboat, *Natter* displaced three hundred tons and carried one 24-lb gun forward and two 12-lb rifled guns aft. She had a limited operational radius, which confined her to the coast, and a top speed of nine knots under steam. The *Dampfkanonenboot II. Klasse* gunboats had earned the nickname *Seeferkel* (sea piglet) for poor handling characteristics even in moderate seas. Moreover, the gunboat's design hindered combat, since the crew had to unstep the mizzenmast before firing the after guns.

When Diederichs arrived at the Stralsund depot, he found *Natter* laid up on land. Work crews had removed her boilers and guns and constructed a protective roof over the hull in 1864. Diederichs, his executive officer, and thirty-eight enlisted men worked hard to prepare her for activation, mounting guns, stepping masts and funnel, and loading supplies and munitions. Diederichs hoisted his commissioning pennant on 24 July, formally placing *Natter* in service only days after the declaration of war.[17]

Diederichs's orders directed him to proceed to Wilhelmshaven to serve with the Jade squadron in the North Sea. In company with gunboats *Jäger* and *Salamander, Natter* first proceeded to Kiel to load additional supplies and then entered the Eider Canal, where her two-meter draft and seven-meter beam allowed her to transit to the North Sea for passage on to Wilhelmshaven. As soon as Diederichs arrived in the Jade, he received new orders, directing him to continue south to the Ems estuary. Gunboat *Drache,* originally assigned to the Ems, had developed engine problems en route from Stralsund. Jachmann therefore decided to send Diederichs, who had navigated the area aboard *Grille* in 1869. Diederichs arrived at Emden in company with gunboat *Wespe,* under the command of Lt. (sg) Johannes Meller, on 31 July. Their mission was to defend the Ems estuary—an important shipping and commercial region—against French attacks. Meller, who was senior officer by six months, remained at Emden with *Wespe*. Diederichs and *Natter* steamed upriver to Leer, a small but active port at the confluence of the Ems and Leda rivers, on 2 August.[18]

Jachmann planned a joint defense of the Ems estuary. *Natter* and *Wespe* would patrol out to twenty nautical miles to detect any signs of a possible French threat, while the local army commander coordinated infantry and artillery units for coastal defense. The army had already supplemented the existing coastal defense batteries stationed on Borkum with two heavy field artillery batteries mounting 240-mm guns. The Emden garrison itself numbered approximately two thousand troops from the Seventy-eighth Infantry and Thirteenth Landwehr Regiments plus attached coastal defense and field artillery batteries. A chain of semaphore stations, stretching from the Ems to the island of Sylt near the Danish border, provided both an early warning system and a means of communication along the North Sea coast.[19]

Natter and *Wespe* arrived none too soon. As the gunboats proceeded south through the shallow waters of the Frisian islands, lookouts sighted the vanguard of advancing French forces to starboard. Vice Adm. Louis Bouet-Willaumez had assumed overall command of French naval forces on 22 July. He identified three primary missions for the French fleet: (1) to blockade the German coast and disrupt coastal trade; (2) to bombard strategic coastal targets, to force the Germans to retain more army units for coastal defense and therefore weaken the land attack against France, and (3) to support amphibious operations against various targets in both the North and Baltic Seas. He likewise selected likely targets for amphibious assault: Borkum island, which protected the Ems estuary; Cuxhaven, which would allow French troops to move against Hamburg, Bremen, or Wilhelmshaven; and Wismar, near Lübeck, on the Baltic, which would place French forces within striking distance of Kiel to the northwest and Berlin to the southeast.[20]

As it happened, the French battle plan had little impact on Diederichs's wartime service, which proved somewhat anticlimactic. The French all but ignored the Ems estuary because of Dutch neutrality—Netherlands shared the Ems with Germany—and the region's comparative lack of strategic value. Instead, the French concentrated their North Sea operations around Helgoland, which would allow them to move against more strategic targets. Adm. Martin Fourichon, commanding eight armored ships as well as smaller warships, blockaded Germany's North Sea coast from positions near Helgoland. Fourichon kept his capital ships under steam on the leeward side of the island while smaller warships patrolled closer inshore. If French ships approached too close, however, the *Ausfallflotte* sortied to drive them off.

The French were more active in the Baltic. The French squadron, under Bouet's command, entered the Baltic on 29 July, paused briefly in the Copenhagen roads, and then proceeded into German waters on 5 August. The French steamed into the sight of the Friedrichsort batteries at the mouth of the Kiel fiord on 6 August but never approached within range of the large German guns. Although Bouet cruised offshore as far east as Neustadt, the strong German coastal defenses dissuaded him from launching an amphibious assault. At one point, when French ships lay anchored off Neufahrwasser in West Prussia, Cdr. Johannes Weichkhmann's small sloop *Nymphe* raided the French anchorage on the moonlit night of 21–22 August, raking the enemy line with two broadsides before withdrawing. The French squadron retired to a semipermanent anchorage in Danish waters thereafter. According to the official Prussian account, "The French Baltic fleet remained as a rule inactive after the foregoing collision, and was therefore frequently harassed by German ships even in Kjöge Bay." It noted further that the French blockade of the North Sea coast "assumed the same character as in the Baltic."[21]

As the naval war declined into stalemate, German victories on land quickly turned the tide of war. Gen. Helmut von Moltke repeated the tactics he had used so effectively in the Austrian war of 1866, dividing his forces to launch a two-pronged advance into northern Alsace and Lorraine. One column decisively defeated French forces at Sedan, personally commanded by Emperor Napoleon III, on 2 September 1870. The other column surrounded and besieged remaining French forces at Metz, forcing them to surrender a month later on 3 October. Moltke then combined his forces to besiege Paris.

The French defeats on land affected the French actions at sea. Catastrophic losses sustained at Sedan and Metz forced the French to recall their naval forces from German waters to bring seamen ashore to fight as naval infantry in the defense of French soil. *Natter* and *Wespe* steamed out into the Ems estuary to Borkum on 10 September when semaphore signals advised Diederichs and Meller of the approach of French warships. They watched as Admiral Fourichon's North Sea squadron withdrew from German waters and returned to Cherbourg. Admiral Bouet's Baltic squadron attempted a final sortie against Germany's coast in response to the defeat at Sedan but turned back in the face of adverse weather. When the French steamed out of the Baltic on 26 September, Heldt followed them at a distance. After their withdrawal from German waters, the French maintained limited operations along a line from Cherbourg to Dunkirk to prevent a sortie by Jachmann's *Ausfallflotte*, now reinforced by Heldt's Baltic squadron, into French waters.

Prussian naval operations were not limited to home waters. Jachmann sent a commerce raider, SM sloop *Augusta* (14), into the Atlantic to interdict arms shipments to France from the United States and Britain. The sloop captured two prizes and sank a third before a squadron of French armored frigates blockaded her in neutral Vigo. SM Gunboat *Meteor*, commanded by Lt. Cdr. Eduard von Knorr, achieved the most memorable success in a minor single-ship action against the French packet *Bouvet* on 9 November 1870 in the Caribbean. *Meteor* had a slight disadvantage, armed with one 150-mm and two 120-mm guns with a crew of sixty-four, against *Bouvet*'s one 160-mm and four 120-mm guns and a crew of eighty-five. The two ships exchanged gunfire for two hours before *Bouvet* rammed *Meteor*, which promptly lost both masts. *Bouvet*, which had lost her engines due to gunfire, set sail and proceeded into neutral Havana, ending the battle.[22]

Although the retreat of the French naval forces from the North Sea left Diederichs without a mission, *Natter* remained on patrol in the Ems estuary for several more months. The war's essential inactivity allowed Diederichs occasional free time to explore Leer and meet its residents. A photograph in the Diederichs *Nachlass* shows Diederichs and his executive officer, Lieutenant von Debschietz, playing skat with several municipal officials. On another occasion Diederichs met Herman Klopp, a local merchant and ironmonger who also served as Austrian consul. More importantly, Klopp and his wife Amalie were the parents of several daughters, including seventeen-year-old Clara Elisabeth Henriette (Henni). Diederichs began to court Henni in late 1870; the couple became engaged in early 1871 even though their courtship proved somewhat difficult in wartime.[23]

When an armistice finally ended the fighting on 28 January 1871, Jachmann recalled *Natter* and *Wespe* to Wilhelmshaven in February. Diederichs steamed out of the Ems estuary for the last time on 18 February, steering a northerly course through the islands and along the mud flats that had provided such excellent natural defenses for the region. On 12 April, Diederichs mustered *Natter*'s small crew and formally lowered his commissioning pennant, declaring the gunboat out of service. His war service had lasted for eight months and eighteen days. The Treaty of Frankfurt formally concluded the war in May 1871, requiring France to cede Alsace and Lorraine to Germany and pay a hefty indemnity of five billion francs.[24]

KAISERLICHE MARINE

Prussia's victory finally permitted Bismarck to fulfill his long ambition of creating a unified German state. Even before the French capitulated, Bismarck had declared the creation of the Imperial German Empire, the *Kaiserlich Deutsche Reich,* on 18 January 1871, the 170th anniversary of the establishment of Prussia and the Hohenzollern dynasty. Territorially, the new German state simply added the three south German states to the existing map of the North German Confederation. Bismarck's actions also created the *Kaiserliche Marine,* the Imperial Navy, meaning that Diederichs would now sail under another flag, the third in four years, as the German fleet hoisted a black-white-red ensign. The newly reborn navy did not get a warm reception. Compared to the victorious army, the navy had achieved little success in the recent war, earning more criticism than praise. Thus, the naval contingent that marched in a victory parade in Berlin in summer 1871 included only twenty-two officers and men. Moreover, Bismarck refused to demand French ships as war booty in the Treaty of Frankfurt, noting that "the acquisition of a portion of the French fleet does not fit my intentions." Instead, his continental policies, which sought to avoid colonial or navalist entanglements, meant that he would oppose significant plans to aid the further development of the fleet.[25]

The new navy also needed a new administration. Accordingly Kaiser Wilhelm I transformed the Naval Ministry into the Imperial Admiralty (*Kaiserliche Admiralität*) on 1 January 1872 and appointed Lt. Gen. Albrecht von Stosch as its new chief. Stosch's appointment, on the heels of General Roon's tenure as minister of the navy, meant that army generals, the so-called *Marinegenerale,* continued to administer the navy. The ailing Admiral Prince Adalbert returned to naval service from the war against France in the new office of general inspector of the navy, which he held until his death in 1873. Jachmann, who had expected to succeed Adalbert as head of the navy, felt slighted by Stosch's appointment and retired.[26] General Stosch, who had entered the army in 1835 and had no prior experience in naval matters, nevertheless brought significant administrative talent to his new post. He characteristically told a friend, "You know that the navy itself does not particularly excite me but the uniqueness and difficulty of the task do."[27]

Stosch, who was to gain admiral's rank in 1875, largely maintained strategic continuity in his fleet development plan in 1873. His *Flottengründungsplan* continued the emphasis on coastal defense as the navy's primary mission and likewise echoed Roon's analysis of Germany as a second-rate naval power.

The army would thus remain Germany's premier armed force. As Mantey notes, "[Stosch] perceived the power of the German Empire only in terms of the tip of an army bayonet, which was wholly natural because the army had accomplished the successful unification of the Reich."[28] Stosch therefore linked ship construction to that mission, calling for monitors and floating batteries for coastal defense, cruisers to protect Germany's overseas interests, and armored frigates and corvettes for squadron operations. He eventually envisioned a force that would include eight armored frigates for the North Sea, six armored corvettes for the Baltic, and twenty cruisers for service overseas. This program would cost 218 million marks and require an expansion of naval personnel to more than four hundred officers and five thousand enlisted men by the plan's anticipated completion date in 1883.[29]

A RETURN TO PEACETIME ROUTINE

After *Natter*'s deactivation in April 1871, Diederichs received new orders assigning him to temporary duty at Geestemünde, a small naval depot at the confluence of the Geeste and Weser rivers. The navy had opened the depot in January 1867 to provide temporary repair and support facilities pending the completion of the Wilhelmshaven naval station. Army engineers constructed ammunition and coal stores, a small repair station, and defensive positions. A small detachment from the Second Seebattalion garrisoned Fort Wilhelm and provided gunners for a coastal defense battery. Since the opening of Wilhelmshaven had made Geestemünde's facilities redundant, the navy had decided to close down the depot. The navy briefly considered using the depot as a site for torpedo research and development, but Wilhelmshaven's superior facilities provided a more functional site.[30]

Diederichs traveled by train from Wilhelmshaven to Geestemünde and reported to Engineer-Major von Hirsch, Fort Wilhelm's commander, for duty on 20 April 1871. His task was to supervise the closure of the navy's facilities there and lead naval personnel back to Wilhelmshaven. Diederichs and his detachment worked to divide up Geestemünde's facilities between the Railroad Ministry for use as a steam engine repair depot and the Ministry of Public Works to support the local fishing industry. Diederichs left only a small repair facility under naval administration, to provide emergency support for warships transiting the nearby Eider Canal. Diederichs finished the work in early August, returning with the other naval personnel to the Second Matrosendivision at Wilhelmshaven on the sixth.[31]

Diederichs's service with the Second Matrosendivision coincided with Stosch's campaign to apply army standards and methods to naval training. Stosch had decided to end the practice, which had begun in 1852, of placing small contingents of marines from the *Seebattalion* aboard warships. He instead adopted a new regimen, known as *Infanterieismus,* which would train seamen as naval infantry in the use of small arms, infantry tactics, and amphibious operations. Warships would now carry appropriate stores of infantry weapons, ammunition, and equipment necessary for operations ashore. Stosch further directed that crew members serving aboard ships on foreign station qualify annually with small arms, using the standard infantry rifle, Mauser *Jägerbüsche* M/71, for seamen and revolvers for officers.[32] These army methods did not particularly please the naval establishment. Tirpitz, for example, noted, "Many of the older officers grumbled; there used to be one spot left in Prussia where one could live, they said, and that was the navy."[33]

One momentous event broke Diederichs's routine with the Matrosendivision. He had petitioned the Admiralty for permission to marry Henni Klopp, now eighteen. Granted a week's furlough, he hurried by train to Leer, where Pastor Harms officiated at a small, quiet ceremony in the Lutheran church on 14 November 1871. The couple had time for only a brief honeymoon, as Diederichs returned to duty three days later to assume the post of executive officer for the Matrosendivision's First Battalion. Henni followed him to Wilhelmshaven, where the couple rented a small apartment near the naval station and lived simply and frugally on a lieutenant's pay.[34]

On the basis of his work with seamen-recruits in the Matrosendivision, the navy assigned Diederichs to SMS *Friedrich Carl* for summer 1872. Because the navy lacked the funds to keep all ships in service during peacetime, the Admiralty would decide in January to activate certain ships for brief training exercises in the summer. This practice had minimal value, since the limited operational time allowed only for practical shipboard training with little opportunity for tactical exercises or squadron maneuvers. In fact, any attempt to carry out complex maneuvers generally led to a circumstance that, according to one admiral, resembled "'an attempt to mould something solid out of loose sand.'"[35] In any event, Diederichs received orders in July to report aboard the armored frigate as a watch officer. Commissioned in 1867, *Friedrich Carl* was the largest ship that Diederichs had yet served aboard, displacing sixty-nine hundred tons and carrying sixteen 210-mm guns. His service was quite brief, however, since *Friedrich Carl* was only operational from 20 July to 24 August 1872, ultimately allowing for only two weeks of training and exercises in the Baltic Sea. Henni happily welcomed Diederichs's return to Wilhelmshaven and the Second Matrosendivision, but he would need to leave again soon. He had just received new orders to report to the newly created *Marineakademie,* the Naval War College, on 1 October 1872.[36]

MARINEAKADEMIE

With the recent introduction of armored warships, steam engines, and large-caliber weapons, Stosch believed that seamanship alone was no longer sufficient for a naval officer "who is to command the large and expensive armored ships now used for naval warfare." In March 1872, he therefore proposed the creation of the Marineakademie, which he hoped would improve the professionalism of the naval officer corps. Stosch had a familiar model to draw from, given his own experiences with the famous and effective Army War College (*Kriegsakademie*) in Berlin. He envisioned a two-year program, combining professional and liberal arts courses, with graduates assuming staff positions after graduation. He intended to draw faculty from those active officers who had proven themselves best able "to uphold the academic and professional standards of the navy." The Marineakademie was the world's first naval war college, anticipating the foundation of the United States Naval War College at Newport, Rhode Island, by twelve years.[37]

When the emperor agreed to his proposals in May, Stosch immediately published an invitation in the *Marineverordnungsblatt* for applicants. He directed interested officers—commanders, lieutenant commanders, and lieutenants, s.g.—to submit a résumé plus three essays from a list of topics including naval history, seamanship, navigation, gunnery, steam engineering, and naval architecture. Sample questions included such diverse topics as "Evaluate the respective roles played by the English and French fleets in the Black Sea during the Crimean War," "Describe handling procedures of a screw steamer under steam at minimum and maximum speeds in harbor, in the roadstead, at sea, in a current and in still water," and "Describe navigational requirements in the North

Sea and the entrances to German river estuaries during inclement seasons." A committee evaluated the dossiers and essays before forwarding recommendations to the Admiralty by the 15 August deadline.[38]

Col. C. A. Liebe, who would now serve jointly as director of both the Marineschule and the Marineakademie, welcomed twelve officers to the school's inaugural term on 2 October 1872. This first class included four future admirals: Lt. Cdr. Viktor Valois and Lieutenants (sg) Otto von Diederichs, Felix Bendemann, and Gustav von Senden-Bibran.[39] The students faced a rigorous program, attending five hour-long lectures per day during the six-day academic week. Over the course of the first academic year, they studied ten different subjects, divided into three areas: military science (naval tactics, amphibious tactics, fortifications, military law), science (mathematics, physics, chemistry, public health), and humanities (logic and ethics, French).[40]

When classes began on 3 October, Diederichs faced a time filled with distractions. Henni had returned to Leer for the birth of their first child, while Diederichs attempted to give adequate attention to his new classes. Fortunately, he did not need to juggle his worries for long. He received a telegram a week later on the tenth that Henni had given birth to a boy. They named him Friedrich (Fritz) after Otto's father. As soon as he could, Diederichs arranged a brief furlough to speed to Leer to visit Henni and their newborn son. Mother and son remained in the care of her family once Diederichs returned to Kiel to continue his studies. He and Henni had a second reason to celebrate six months later, when he received notification of his promotion to lieutenant commander in May 1873.[41]

Diederichs proved to be an exceptional student. Following final examinations in late May, he learned that he had earned a score of excellent in five courses (land tactics, physics, chemistry, civil and military law, and public health), good grades in four courses (logic, naval tactics, fortifications, and mathematics) and a satisfactory mark in French. He and his colleagues had presumably maintained a higher level of student conduct than his cadet peers years earlier at the Marineschule. Liebe's reports contain no accounts of ungentlemanly behavior.[42]

As usual, Diederichs had little time to enjoy his latest accomplishment. At the end of his first school year, he received orders to report aboard SMS *Vineta* as gunnery officer for summer exercises. He and Valois, appointed as *Vineta*'s executive officer, promptly boarded a train for the four-hour journey from Kiel to Wilhelmshaven, embarking aboard their new ship on the late afternoon of 1 June. Commissioned in 1864 as a frigate but now re-classified as a corvette, *Vineta* carried a main battery of seventeen 150-mm and two 125-mm guns. Diederichs joined a crowded wardroom that included fifteen commissioned and warrant officers and, because this was a training exercise, seven cadets. Officers and crew worked hard for the next three days, allowing Cdr. Wilhelm von Wickede to declare *Vineta* in service at 0800 on 4 June 1873.[43]

SMS *Vineta* joined corvettes *Hertha, Arcona,* and *Ariadne* to form a new unit, the Training Squadron (*Übungsgeschwader*), for squadron maneuvers. Before summer 1873, German warships tended to train individually, with only occasional exercises involving multiple-ship maneuvers. Rear Adm. Wilhelm Henk, director of the Admiralty's Central Directorate, had proposed in 1872 that the navy undertake more formal maneuvers at the squadron level in order to improve personnel training and enhance fleet readiness. With Stosch's concurrence, Henk assumed command of the operation and commenced preparations in May 1873. His orders called for a training cruise in home waters where the purpose was to "develop the military and maritime knowledge of officers and crews." Exercises would include conventional (ramming) and novel (torpedo) tactics, squadron maneuvers, and squadron communications.[44]

Henk activated the Übungsgeschwader at Wilhelmshaven on 13 June. Since most of the crew and many of the officers had spent the previous months quartered ashore with the Second Matrosendivision, personnel spent the first few days relearning basic seamanship and ship handling. The training squadron departed for the Baltic on 20 June, proceeding slowly under steam to practice basic squadron evolutions, and arrived at Kiel on the twenty-fourth. The squadron then spent the next ten days in Baltic waters, exercising more complex tactical maneuvers.[45]

The squadron's secondary mission was showing the flag in foreign waters. Henk therefore set course for Stockholm in July to participate in a naval review celebrating the coronation of King Oscar I of Sweden. As gunnery officer, Diederichs directed *Vineta*'s twenty-one-gun salute to King Oscar on 13 July. The new monarch observed a formal parade of foreign warships from the quarterdeck of screw frigate *St. Olaf* the following day. The squadron spent two weeks in Swedish waters, allowing *Vineta*'s officers and crew the opportunity for shore leave in Sweden's beautiful capital city, Stockholm. At one point, Diederichs met with Swedish, Danish, and English officers as King Oscar hosted a formal reception aboard *St. Olaf.* The usual problems occasionally also intruded, including an incident in which a seaman from *Vineta* deserted; Swedish authorities arrested him and returned him to the ship.[46]

Henk next led the squadron east across the Gulf of Finland to Helsinki in late July for joint exercises and ceremonial visits with Russian warships. This reflected a diplomatic role for the squadron, since Bismarck, who had once served as Prussia's ambassador to St. Petersburg, had long promoted close ties to czarist Russia. In fact, the squadron's visit coincided with secret negotiations between German, Russian, and Austrian diplomats that resulted in the signing of the *Dreikaiserbund* (the Three Emperors' League) in October 1873.

The squadron reversed course in early August to visit Norway, still a part of Sweden. The ships rendezvoused with imperial yacht *Grille,* which carried Crown Prince Friedrich, and escorted her to Christiansand (Oslo), where the prince joined King Oscar in a formal inspection of the squadron. Christiansand must have presented too many temptations, however, as six seamen from *Vineta* overstayed their liberty. Three returned in time to depart with the ship, but three others remained behind in the custody of the German consul for later transport to Kiel. With international protocol satisfied, Henk returned briefly to Kiel on 14 August to coal and then continued squadron maneuvers. Tactical exercises and drills continued until early September. Henk formally reported the squadron out of service on 11 September 1873. *Vineta* briefly put into Kiel to offload guns and ammunition before departing for Danzig for repairs and deactivation on the twenty-fourth.[47]

Diederichs himself had not completed the maneuvers. During gunnery exercises in late August, he had become ill. He transferred ashore, spending time at the station hospital at Kiel before a brief assignment with the Second Matrosendivision in Wilhelmshaven. Diederichs had never fully recovered from his childhood illnesses. He continued to suffer from pulmonary problems and, according to his son Fritz, was chronically ill for the first decade of his married life.[48]

In any event, he recovered in time to return to Kiel in October for his second term at the Marineakademie. The second-year curriculum focused more heavily on professional courses. His gunnery course, for example, reunited him with Captain Wickede, recently promoted from commander and just detached from *Vineta*. Over the academic year, Diederichs continued to maintain a strong performance, earning excellent scores in gunnery, naval design, electrical engineering, and physical geography, good scores in steam engineering, nautical astronomy, and military leadership, and, his lowest score, fair, in cultural history. His instructors praised him for his excellent technical demonstrations and outstanding leadership skills.[49]

Following his graduation from the Marineakademie in May 1874, Diederichs received orders assigning him as a gunnery instructor aboard SMS *Renown,* the artillery training ship at Wilhelmshaven. The navy had purchased *Renown,* a 74-gun ship-of-the-line, from the Royal Navy in 1870. The Wilhelmshaven shipyard reconfigured her as a training ship, removing her original smooth-bore cannons and replacing them with more modern guns. When Diederichs reported aboard on 15 May 1874, he observed a diverse armament aboard his *Artillerieschiff,* ranging from 37-mm boat guns to 240-mm main batteries. His students included thirty-four midshipmen in a basic gunnery course and fifteen lieutenants, junior grade, in an advanced course. They studied the mathematics and physics of gunnery, handled various calibers of guns, and then participated in extensive live firings of single guns and massed broadsides. At home, Henni worried that gunnery training was dangerous. In fact, the explosion in 1876 of a 240-mm gun killed two men and wounded a dozen more.[50]

TORPEDOS, LOS!

Diederichs received a new assignment in October 1874. Based on his academic work at the Marineakademie and his professional experience in gunnery, the navy now assigned him to the Torpedo Research and Development Commission (*Torpedo-Versuchs-und-Prüfung Kommission,* or TVK) in Berlin. Although the term "torpedo" had long applied to static mines, developing technology soon provided an alternative version, the self-propelled "fish" torpedo (*Fischtorpedo*). This new weapon owed its origins in part to Robert

Whitehead, an English engineer, who had immigrated to Austria in 1849 to work for a marine engineering firm designing steam engines. He tested his first self-propelled torpedo, which used an air-compression engine, in 1866, selling the first production model to the Austrian Navy in 1867.[51]

The Bundesmarine sent Cdr. Alexander Graf von Monts to Fiume, Austria, to visit the Whitehead firm in 1869 for a firsthand look at the new weapon. Two years later, Monts proposed the establishment of the Torpedo Service (*Torpedowesen*), which would consist of Torpedo Detachments for static mines and the TVK for torpedoes. The plan further intended to establish research and testing sites at Kiel (Friedrichsort), Wilhelmshaven, and Geestemünde.[52] Stosch formally implemented the program in 1873, appointing Monts as director and authorizing the purchase of one hundred torpedoes from Whitehead's firm. Stosch also proposed the construction of ten torpedo boats and the purchase of a tender, SMS *Zieten,* in his Flottengründungsplan for 1873. Monts set to work immediately, hiring a physicist, Dr. Theodor Hertz, to begin preliminary tests with the new torpedoes on Lake Remmelsburger in Berlin. Meanwhile, work crews mounted a single torpedo tube on SM Gunboat *Basilisk,* which began trials at Kiel, with Stosch aboard, in June 1873.[53]

With this background, Diederichs reported for duty at TVK headquarters in Berlin on 4 October 1874. Although this was his first tour of duty in the capital, he knew the city well since he had grown up in nearby Potsdam. Henni and Fritz, approaching his second birthday, soon followed, staying with Diederichs's parents until they could rent an apartment. The TVK staff in Berlin included two other naval officers, two army engineers, and Professor Dr. Hertz. Diederichs split his time between Berlin and the new Torpedo Depot, Friedrichsort, where he reported to Cdr. Eduard von Heusner. Diederichs's first task was to study the current Whitehead torpedo, which had a 33-cm diameter and a 12-kg warhead. A three-cylinder air compression engine could propel the torpedo at seventeen knots with a range of 750 meters.[54]

Initial tests of the Whitehead torpedo at Friedrichsort proved unsatisfactory, as it failed to meet the Torpedo Service's contractual standards for speed and accuracy. When technicians concluded that the problem lay with the torpedo's air-compression engine, Heusner dispatched Diederichs to Fiume in April 1875 to resolve the problem. He remained there for the next fifteen weeks, working with Whitehead on a new design. Whitehead retooled the torpedo's configuration and replaced the existing engine with a new English model. The result was the Fiume Mark 1, which became Whitehead's standard production torpedo in 1876. Diederichs briefly returned to Berlin in early August 1875 to report his activities to the TVK and spend a few days with Henni and Fritz. He then continued on to Friedrichsort to resume his involvement in the testing program.[55]

Soon after Diederichs returned to Berlin in the late fall, his professional status again changed. Following on the heels of the establishment of the Marineakademie, Stosch had decided in April 1875 to create an elite cadre of staff officers (*Admiralstabsoffizier*) who would direct the future technical and tactical development of the navy. He particularly sought officers for the Admiralty Staff who possessed "a zeal for service and a desire for knowledge," a label that certainly described Diederichs. Stosch believed that such service would provide aspiring young officers with the opportunity to enhance their professional skills, while inspiring a much-needed *Korpsgeist* to mitigate the decline in morale that followed the navy's poor performance in the Franco-German War. Staff officers would serve a three-year tour and wear a golden imperial crown on their uniform sleeves in lieu of the standard watch officer's star.[56]

Kaiser Wilhelm formally announced the new appointments on 14 December 1875. The inaugural list included Diederichs and twelve other officers. In fact, Diederichs was one of the most junior officers to achieve the honor. The thirteen initial appointees included one captain, nine commanders, and three lieutenant commanders. Six would serve in the Admiralty and a seventh as senior adjutant at the Kiel naval station, where they would focus on readiness, naval strategy and tactics, and intelligence. Three, including Diederichs, continued their service on the TVK, and three also served on the Artillery Research and Development Commission, where they would specialize in technical fields.[57]

Diederichs himself became a roving troubleshooter for the Torpedo Service. He initially alternated between Friedrichsort and Berlin but then, in April 1876, added Wilhelmshaven to his regular itinerary. When the first production models of the new Whitehead torpedo arrived in Germany in 1876, the navy distributed them between the TVK's facilities in Berlin, the Torpedo Depot in Kiel, and a new facility in Wilhelmshaven. Diederichs transferred to Wilhelmshaven in April 1876 to make preparations for testing of the new torpedoes. Because construction workers had not yet completed the Wilhelmshaven Depot, Diederichs worked out of temporary facilities at the Naval Artillery Depot. His first task was to convert SMS *Elbe,* formerly a barracks ship for the Second Matrosendivision, which the navy now intended to use as a test bed for torpedo research. He directed a crew seconded from the imperial *Werft* (dockyard) in mounting a single 380-mm torpedo tube in the bow.[58]

As soon as he had completed the work aboard *Elbe,* Diederichs transferred to the navy's newest torpedo tender, SMS *Zieten,* for a similar task. Stosch had commissioned the ship, constructed by the Thames Iron Works, in 1875. Diederichs's TVK colleague, Cdr. Franz Mensing, proceeded to London to accept delivery and assume command of *Zieten* in August 1876. After a brief trial run in the North Sea, *Zieten* arrived in Wilhelmshaven on 11 August 1876. Fresh from his experience with *Elbe,* Diederichs directed work crews in mounting two underwater 380-mm torpedo tubes, bow and stern, and preparing a magazine for ten Whitehead torpedoes. Once Diederichs had finished his work, *Zieten* departed for Kiel. Because it was too late in the season to commence testing, Mensing placed *Zieten* out of service on 17 September 1876. Diederichs himself returned to Berlin to resume his staff work with the TVK. Even though most of the actual torpedo tests now occurred at either Kiel or Wilhelmshaven, the TVK still retained testing facilities, in addition to design and development offices, in Berlin.[59]

After six months in Berlin, Diederichs received new orders in March 1877 to proceed to Kiel and prepare SMS *Zieten* for service for the 1877 testing season. Furthermore, he would assume the post of acting head of the Torpedo Service in May when Commander Heusner, accompanied by Lt. Cdr. Alfred Tirpitz, departed for Fiume to study the latest technical developments at the Whitehead factory. (Tirpitz, recently named to the Torpedo Service as an *Admiralstab* officer, was in charge of detonators and warheads.)[60]

Following Heusner and Tirpitz's departure, Diederichs faced several problems related both to the activation of *Zieten* and torpedo testing as the Torpedo Service faced its full season at the Torpedo Depot at Kiel. Although the depot had recently received a supply of copper pipes, belt pulleys, and material to fuel and repair the torpedoes, he complained that the main air-compression pump continued to break down. Without the pump, he noted, he could not undertake a full course of testing. He asked Station Chief Reinhold Werner to expedite repairs through the Artillery Depot.

The burden of simultaneously activating *Zieten* and testing torpedoes had become even more demanding when he discovered that a design flaw in the torpedoes' horizontal steering vanes caused torpedoes to porpoise and then dive into the muddy bottom of the Kiel fiord. This had come to light in part because existing shore-based test facilities had proved inadequate. Because *Zieten* was not yet in service, Diederichs had originally test-fired torpedoes from a dock, using an above-water torpedo tube but shallow—three meters—water, and the flawed steering vanes had caused problems. An earlier attempt to jury-rig a torpedo tube on a barge had also proven ineffective. He proposed developing an underwater torpedo tube to be mounted approximately one meter under water with a rear breech mechanism for easy loading, but this would not solve the problem of steering vanes. Diederichs hoped that Heusner's visit to Fiume, which was intended to work on the technical problems, and the activation of *Zieten,* which would allow testing in deeper waters, would solve some or all of the problems.

Diederichs also worried that the Torpedo Depot lacked sufficient technical personnel both to crew *Zieten* and operate the special equipment at the depot. He currently depended on temporary transfers or personnel borrowed from the Artillery Depot. He did have *Zieten*'s Engineering Chief Petty Officer Groth and Machinists Wismede and Minks, but they were overwhelmed with the work necessary to commission *Zieten* and were therefore not always available to the depot. Furthermore, Diederichs had concluded that *Zieten* herself needed an auxiliary tender. This second craft could assist in the recovery of torpedoes and provide additional transportation from Friederichsort to the firing range. He recommended the assignment of Minelayer No. 6, which the Torpedo Service had used during the previous year and which still contained appropriate equipment. He also requested the immediate assignment of one bosun's mate and one seaman from the First Matrosendivision, and one machinist mate and two stokers from the First Dockyard Division as crew for the new tender.[61] Stosch approved Diederichs's recommendations and directed the chief of the naval station to comply in regard to seamen and supplies. Based on these improvements, Diederichs notified his superiors on 11 June that he had activated *Zieten* and hoped to commence sea trials and test the torpedo equipment within a few days.[62]

When Heusner and Tirpitz returned from Fiume in late June, Diederichs again became *Zieten*'s executive officer. He turned responsibility for testing over to Tirpitz and began to focus solely on the ship, which had, among other troubles, problems with her engines. Diederichs also spent time on fitting out a second tender for *Zieten*. The navy had struck *Scorpion*, a *Jäger*-class gunboat, from the Navy List in January 1877. Diederichs arranged to have the craft, familiar to him from his days aboard sister-ship *Natter*, reactivated as an auxiliary torpedo test bed. As with Minelayer No. 6, his work crews mounted a single torpedo tube forward of the mainmast.[63]

The summer's climax came with a final demonstration of the Torpedo Service's abilities on 18 September 1877. Heusner welcomed Admiralty Chief Stosch, Station Chief Werner, and other high-ranking officials aboard *Zieten*. Over the course of the next several hours, with a single break for a formal brunch in late morning, the personnel and vessels of the *Torpedowesen* demonstrated their technical facility with torpedo firings at moving and stationary targets. First, with Heusner at the helm and Tirpitz serving as torpedo officer, *Zieten* scored three hits on a stationary target. Next, *Minenlager 6* demonstrated the basic physics of firing a torpedo from a moving platform. Finally, gunboat *Scorpion*, under Diederichs's personal command, fired several torpedoes during a "high-speed" run to again confirm the versatility of the new weapon. Heusner deemed the day's tests a great success.[64]

The September tests concluded the summer trials. As executive officer, Diederichs directed the fall ritual of placing *Zieten* out of service. Torpedo technicians began to transfer torpedoes and equipment ashore to the new testing and storage facilities at the Torpedo Depot in Friedrichsort, while the regular crew greased the moving parts of *Zieten*'s steam plant and stored sails and rigging below. Diederichs had barely begun his work when he received a telegram from Berlin that Henni had again gone into labor. Their second son, Herman, was born on 26 September 1877. Diederichs, however, was unable to return to Berlin for several days. When Heusner formally declared *Zieten* out of service on 2 October, Diederichs left the ship and hurried to Berlin to meet his new son, joining Henni and five-year-old Fritz.[65]

Following a brief furlough, he returned to work at the Torpedo Service.

Although the testing season had ended, Diederichs and his fellow officers now had to evaluate test results, analyze performance of torpedoes and torpedo tubes, make preparations for the next year's experiments, and begin to develop ideas for the tactical use of the new weapon. Since the Whitehead torpedoes had not always operated effectively, Heusner also decided to send Tirpitz back to Fiume in the spring.[66] Diederichs then had a momentary respite from these tasks. He requested and received a six-day furlough that allowed him to spend the holidays with Henni and the boys in Berlin. His parents also came down from their retirement home in Marienwerder, north of Berlin, to celebrate the new year.[67]

AUTUMN WILL BRING ALL TO AN END

When he returned to duty in January 1878, Diederichs found a series of new tasks awaiting him. His recent work had impressed Stosch, who now assigned him to direct a major refit for *Zieten* to make the ship more functional. The season's tests had shown that the current arrangement of *Zieten*'s torpedo tubes, one fore and one aft, was not adequate. Stosch therefore appointed Diederichs to chair a joint design commission, which included the director of the Friedrichsort Artillery Depot and a senior naval engineer from the Imperial Dockyard, to develop new plans. Diederichs's committee produced a plan that would not only relocate the forward tube but also add two new 120-mm guns as well. This would make the ship more versatile in the defense of Kiel and provide protection against attack by small craft. At the same time, Stosch asked Diederichs to design a new arrangement for torpedo tubes aboard the new armored corvette SMS *Prinz Adalbert* (forty-six hundred tons, twelve 170-mm guns). Additionally, Stosch requested that Diederichs study the possibility of mounting shore-based torpedo tubes to guard the Kiel shipping channel at Friederichsort.[68]

Under Diederichs's direction, *Zieten*'s refit began in March 1878 at the Kiel *Werft*. Shipfitters moved the forward torpedo tube from its original position in the bow to a swivel mount near the foremast, improving *Zieten*'s forward draft. The work crews then mounted the two 120-mm guns in the after part of the ship and constructed a shell and powder magazine below decks. Diederichs signed off on the work on 16 April. Tirpitz, who had returned from his Fiume trip, assumed command of *Zieten* on 6 May 1878. Diederichs himself replaced Heusner, appointed to command SMS *Hansa*, as the new director of the Torpedo Service.[69]

Although his new position possessed some prestige, Diederichs had grown restive after nearly four years as a staff officer with the Torpedowesen. He certainly enjoyed the challenge of working with the new torpedo technology but preferred to return to sea with the *Seeoffizierskorps.* Diederichs likewise doubted that staff duty would earn him the credentials needed for command. Thus, he began a campaign in spring 1878 to secure appointment to a warship on overseas duty. His rank—lieutenant commander—made him eligible to command a gunboat or serve as first officer aboard an overseas cruiser. He knew that such service would bring both hardships—taking him away from his family for at least two years—and challenges, more professionally demanding than his command of SMS *Natter* during the Franco-German War and as physically exacting as his earlier service in East Asia.

Diederichs also knew that the fiscal realities of the German fleet limited his opportunity to return to sea. Funding allowed the Kaiserliche Marine to activate only a few ships every year: perhaps four to six to participate in brief maneuvers in home waters and another dozen or so for two-year tours on foreign station. The *Rangliste* for 1877–78 noted, for example, that the Imperial Navy had six regular corvettes and four gunboats patrolling the various stations and two training corvettes on extended cruises. Competition for service aboard such ships was also problematic since the navy had sixty lieutenant commanders. Two of them commanded gunboats on overseas duty and another four served as executive officers aboard *Auslandskreuzer.* Another handful served briefly on the few ships activated for maneuvers, with the remainder holding staff or technical posts. Diederichs, who stood fifteenth on the seniority list for lieutenant commanders, would thus need something approaching divine intervention if he were to secure a transfer to sea duty.[70]

Diederichs had already confided his desire to return to sea to his friends. He had complained to his good friend Iwan Oldekop at New Year's 1878 that he wanted to escape staff duties and return to sea. His complaint fell on sympathetic ears, since Oldekop, an Admiralstab officer with the Artillery Testing Commission, had similar frustrations. (Oldekop, like Diederichs, had not served at sea since his own days as a gunboat commander in the Franco-German War.)[71] Diederichs confided the same feelings in a letter to another friend, Lt. Cdr. Heinrich Jeschke, a staff officer attached to the Admiralty in Berlin. Jeschke responded with a compliment, calling Diederichs a "fine fellow" (*ganz guter Mensch*) and offering a "heart-felt hope that you will gain a first officer's post." Jeschke concluded his letter on an optimistic note, "I firmly believe that autumn will bring you salt water and flowing seas."[72]

Diederichs, in fact, had now discovered a possible solution to his problem. In January 1878, when the navy published its annual list of ships to be placed in service for the new year and assigned officers to command them, he noticed a familiar name. The Admiralty had decided to appoint Cdr. Rudolf Schering to command SMS *Luise* for a two-year tour on the East Asian station beginning in October 1878. Diederichs and Schering had become friends when both attended the Marineakademie in 1872–74 and then both again served together in the initial group of Admiralstab officers. Based on his current post as director of the Admiralty's *Zentralabteilung*, where he was Stosch's executive assistant, Schering was in a good position to make his own selection for *Luise*'s first officer.[73]

Believing that he had the necessary credentials, Diederichs wrote Schering to request consideration for appointment as *Luise*'s first officer. He cited his experience at sea, which included tours as training officer (*Musquito*), watch officer (*Grille, Musquito, Vineta*), and gunnery instructor (*Gefion, Renown*). He had served as first officer of a naval auxiliary (*Zieten*) and even commanded one of His Majesty's ships, albeit a gunboat. Schering was quite responsive to Diederichs's entreaty. He spoke to the director of the Admiralty's personnel department and succeeded in arranging Diederichs's appointment. In his response to Diederichs, Schering wrote of his pleasure in once again serving with his long-time colleague. He believed that Diederichs's seniority and experience were appropriate to the post, particularly citing Diederichs's professional record as an asset in dealing with a young and inexperienced crew. He also noted that Diederichs's tenure with the Torpedo Service would prove useful, since *Luise* would carry four Whitehead torpedoes for testing under actual sea conditions.[74]

The news brought Diederichs plaudits from several sources. Oldekop, who heard the news directly from Schering, congratulated Diederichs on his new assignment. Acknowledging his own professional frustrations, Oldekop wrote with a tinge of envy that "Autumn will bring all to an end." Oldekop noted, too, that Diederichs's service aboard *Luise* was an excellent step to becoming "master and commandant" with a command of his own.[75] Another friend was equally envious. Lt. Cdr. Carl Barandon, an instructor at the Marineakademie, congratulated Diederichs on his appointment while acknowledging his own disappointment over his failure to secure a similar assignment aboard SMS *Ariadne*.[76]

Before he could prepare for his new assignment, Diederichs carried out one final mission for the Torpedowesen. He boarded armored frigate *Friedrich der Grosse* on 14 May and remained aboard for three weeks with instructions to train the crew in use of her five 350-mm torpedo tubes.[77] In the course of his work, he discovered that many of his fellow officers had serious misgivings about the value of torpedoes. One, in fact, described the idea as "humbug."[78]

Diederichs briefly returned to Berlin in June to finish up paperwork and clean out his desk at the Torpedowesen. He then obtained a six-week furlough to spend time with his family before his departure for East Asia. He and Henni vacated their apartment in Berlin and moved their possessions to a flat in Leer, where Henni and the boys would live during his overseas tour. He also took his family north to Marienwerder to visit his parents before he reported back to duty in Wilhelmshaven. Although he was anxious to return to sea, he would leave with some remorse, particularly since Henni also suffered from chronic ill health. His overseas tour would be their first extended separation since their marriage almost seven years earlier.[79]

As expected, new orders soon arrived, formally assigning him to temporary duty with the Second Matrosendivision, Wilhelmshaven, where he began to assemble an enlisted crew for SMS *Luise*. At the same time, the Admiralty formally transferred him from duty as an Admiralstab officer to the *Seeoffizierkorps,* pending his assignment as first officer aboard SMS *Luise*.[80]

Diederichs's departure from the Torpedo Service in June 1878 marked the end of the second phase of his naval career. For more than a decade, since he first boarded *Musquito* in August 1867, he had faithfully attempted to fulfill Stenzel's dictum, training crews and preparing ships to "fight at the right time and place." Now, he could look forward to a new phase in his professional career—at sea.

3

To East Asia: Diederichs
and SMS *Luise,* 1878–1880

Upon returning from furlough in late August, Diederich reported to Wilhelmshaven to begin preparation for his new appointment as executive officer aboard SMS *Luise* by studying available information on the navy's overseas operations. Although its primary mission was coastal defense, the navy had long considered the projection of sea power, particularly to protect German interests and nationals overseas, as an important, if secondary, role. SMS *Amazone* had made the first voyages out of Prussian waters, visiting Constantinople in 1844 and 1846 and sailing across the Atlantic to New York in 1847. Commo. Jan Schroeder led a small squadron into the South Atlantic to show the flag in 1852, following a great circle route that took the squadron to Liberia on the west coast of Africa and then across the Atlantic to Rio de Janeiro and Buenos Aires before returning to European waters via Norfolk, Virginia, and Portsmouth, England, in 1853. SMS *Gefion* sailed into the Black Sea in 1854 to observe the Crimean War in 1854. Two years later, Prince Adalbert himself hoisted his admiral's flag in SMS *Danzig* to lead a punitive expedition against Moroccan pirates. The prince personally led an expeditionary force ashore at Cape Tres Forcas in August 1856 to attack the pirate stronghold. Although the ensuing engagement was largely indecisive, Adalbert succeeded in deterring future attacks against German shipping.[1]

THE GERMAN NAVY IN EAST ASIA

As Diederichs quickly recalled from his own service in the merchant marine, the opening of German markets in East Asia provided an additional incentive for overseas operations. The first Prussian trading ship, *Prinzessin Louise*, had reached Canton in 1828 to trade for tea, silk, and spices. Another ship, *Danzig*, had carried cargo to Shanghai in 1853. On the eve of Diederichs's initial arrival in East Asia aboard *Amaranth* in 1862, more than two hundred German merchant ships plied East Asian waters. A decade later, forty German firms had offices in China employing nearly five hundred German nationals. But the increased economic presence subjected German merchants to attacks by Chinese pirates, and that, in turn, mandated a German naval presence.[2]

Likewise, political and strategic conditions further justified a German naval presence. China, once, the dominant state in East Asia, had declined to a point of imperialistic vulnerability. A series of domestic crises (opium addiction, natural disasters, peasant rebellions, incompetent government) combined with external threats (successive wars with Britain and France, conflict with Russia) to seal China's fate. Beginning with the cession of Hong Kong to Britain in 1842, a series of bilateral treaties forced China to surrender political sovereignty and territorial integrity as European states established spheres of influence on Chinese soil. Thereafter, Britain quickly came to dominate the lower Yangtze River basin from a strong position in Shanghai. At the same time, France moved to assert control in southern China from its position in Indochina and Russia began to encroach on China's western territory.

Japan experienced a more peaceful, if equally distasteful, experience with Western intrusion. Commodore Matthew Perry led an American naval squadron across the Pacific to "open" Japan in 1853. Ensuing treaties with the United States and several European countries established diplomatic relations and opened Japanese ports to foreign trade for the first time in more than two hundred years.

In light of these circumstances, the Prussian government had decided to send a naval expedition to East Asia. A squadron, commanded by Commo.

Henrik Sundewall and consisting of steam frigate *Arcona* (27), sail frigate *Thetis* (38), schooner *Frauenlob* (1), and armed transport *Elbe* (6), departed Prussian waters in October 1859. Sundewall's orders directed him to project Prussian naval power in East Asian waters and to investigate the potential for further trade in the region. The squadron also carried Ambassador Friedrich Graf von Eulenburg, who succeeded in signing treaties with China and Japan in 1861. While still in school, Diederichs had followed news of the expedition with great interest.[3] The treaty with China granted Prussia the same rights already accorded other states under the "unequal treaty system." For example, Article 6 granted German trading ships access to treaty ports such as Canton, Swatow, Amoy, and Shanghai. Article 30 specifically allowed Prussian warships to operate in Chinese waters for the protection of trade or the suppression of piracy. Additional articles required the Chinese government to pay compensation for financial losses caused by pirates and promised swift punishment of crimes committed by Chinese against German nationals.[4]

The navy also began to factor East Asia into strategic planning. Roon formally established the need for overseas operations in his fleet development plan of 1865, directing the construction of an appropriate class of ships—steam-sail corvettes of the *Ariadne* class—to carry out the mission. He also designated East Asia as a formal area of operations in 1868, usually assigning two corvettes and a pair of small gunboats to the station thereafter. Because the navy had no permanent naval facilities in East Asia, Prussian warships depended on British (Hong Kong), Chinese (Shanghai), or Japanese (Nagasaki) facilities for logistical and technical support. Prussian warships on the East Asian station quickly learned that the lack of a base hindered operations. A survey undertaken in 1869 and 1870 identified potential base sites, but the outbreak of the Franco-Prussian War postponed any decision. Chancellor Bismarck's continental preoccupation following German unification in 1871, in addition to strategic decisions by the navy, deferred final resolution of the base issue for a generation (see chapter 6).[5]

Yet, as Diederichs learned, naval operations had since become even more critical. Ambassador Maximilian von Brandt, the German ambassador to China from 1874 until 1893, reported in July 1877 that xenophobic groups had begun to threaten the lives and property of German merchants in

Tientsin. The businessmen attributed the local unrest in part to a "poor harvest and famine" and asked the navy to station a warship at Tientsin through the coming winter and conduct more regular patrols in Chinese waters thereafter.[6] It therefore became immediately clear to Diederichs that *Luise*'s mission had taken on some urgency.

In fact, Commander Schering's orders reflected these issues: "When in all respects ready for sea, SMS *Luise* will proceed to Hong Kong and take up station in Chinese waters for the protection of German interests." Additional instructions further directed Schering to "show the flag on all parts of the station" and center his operations on Amoy, China, and Yokohama, Japan. Pursuant to existing instructions, which included "Imperial Directions for the Operation of Ships on Station in East Asia" and "Standing Instructions in regards to the Suppression of Pirates in Chinese Waters," Schering would provide all necessary assistance to Ambassador Brandt as diplomatic needs dictated. Schering's mission was nonetheless peaceful, with his orders directing him, insofar as possible, "to undertake no military action without first notifying imperial representatives." With memories of the Franco-German War still fresh, the Admiralty also cautioned Schering to avoid confrontations with French ships at sea and French sailors ashore. His concluding instruction was clear and concise: "Take all necessary precautions to ensure that the ship under your command is prepared for combat and to carry out projected military and maritime duties."[7]

That latter task was largely the responsibility of Diederichs. As executive officer, he stood between the commanding officer on the navigating bridge and the crew in the crowded forecastle. His primary duty was the day-to-day supervision of the ship as he executed the commanding officer's orders, directed the other officers, and applied discipline to the crew. He was responsible to see that the rigging and sails were kept in good repair and that the ship's new steam engines operated properly. These were not simple or easy duties, particularly since *Luise* would soon depart for a two-year cruise to a part of the world that lacked a German naval base and would therefore need to depend on foreign facilities for technical and logistical support. The navy also assigned him a series of technical duties, including the testing of a full load of Whitehead torpedoes, which he had just worked on at the

Torpedowesen, and a series of oceanographic experiments in conjunction with the Hydrographic Bureau.[8]

Diederichs brought several strengths to his new assignment as executive officer. First, he was familiar with East Asia, having spent three years there as an able seaman in the 1860s. Although that voyage was fifteen years in the past, Diederichs could nonetheless advise Captain Schering on issues and situations in Chinese and Japanese waters. Secondly, his service with the Torpedowesen would enable him to properly direct experiments with *Luise*'s new Whitehead torpedoes. Finally, he had already begun to train her crew, a mixed draft of seasoned seamen and recent recruits, at the Second Marinedivision. Now he must also begin to integrate them into a collective crew—first, to place *Luise* in service, and then to man her during a long sea cruise.

SMS *LUISE*

Designed specifically for overseas service, *Luise* was an *Ariadne*-class corvette. Launched at the Danzig *Werft* in 1874, *Luise* displaced approximately two thousand tons and carried a main battery of six 150-mm guns. She had a rated flank speed of fourteen knots, with a range of over thirteen hundred nautical miles at a more economical cruising speed of ten knots. To provide auxiliary power, her three masts carried sixteen hundred square meters of sail. Her complement included more than 230 officers and men, who lived in a hull that measured sixty-six meters long by eleven meters broad with a draft of six meters.[9]

Diederichs's initial responsibility as executive officer was to prepare *Luise* for sea. Because the navy's limited budget and mission meant that few ships could remain operational at any one time, *Luise* had been placed out of service in September 1877 at the end of her inaugural overseas tour. A work crew had converted her to bark rigging but had done no other maintenance for more than a year. Therefore, when Diederichs and his crew boarded *Luise* early on the morning of 20 November 1878, they found her in poor shape. Diederichs's initial log entry notes, "In dock at Wilhelmshaven. Commenced pumping ship at 0915. Dry after 5 ¾ hours."[10] Once the ship's pumps had completed this necessary task, Diederichs began the arduous job of preparing the ship for her two-year mission on foreign station. He worked at a hard pace throughout, leaving himself only enough time to record the same phrase—"Continuing to place ship in service"—for seven consecutive days in his log.[11]

Diederichs himself went from one task to another. He and Lt. Cdr. Alfred Herz, the ship's navigator, pored over charts, making corrections and identifying potential dangers for the voyage ahead. His experiences as a gunnery instructor served him in good stead as he directed the gunnery officer, Lt.(sg) Richard Hildebrandt, to mount *Luise*'s 150- and 120-mm guns on new carriages and cut new gun ports in her hull. Diederichs also drew on his work with the Torpedowesen as his gunner's mates mounted two torpedo tubes in the ship's bow and hoisted six new Whitehead torpedoes aboard. He tried to calm the frustrations of Chief Engineer Thomas Fontane, who complained repeatedly that a lack of spare parts prevented him from getting the engines in operating condition. Finally, Diederichs supervised Purser Hugo Butterwegge and another work crew in loading provisions and fresh water.[12]

After ten days of hard labor, Diederichs completed the arduous task of preparing *Luise* for sea. To the trilling of bosun's pipes and the salutes of Schering and his officers, Rear Adm. Carl Batsch, commander of the Wilhelmshaven station, came aboard on 30 November to celebrate the ship's activation. As the station band played martial tunes, Schering hoisted his commissioning pennant and formally placed SMS *Luise* in service at 1000 hours. Schering then hosted a small reception for station representatives and the wives and families of *Luise*'s officers. This allowed Diederichs one more opportunity to say his sad good-byes to Henni and their boys before he ushered them over the side and returned to work.

As soon as the guests had left the ship, *Luise* steamed over to the ammunition dock in the outer harbor and anchored for the night. At dawn the next day, the crew loaded six hundred rounds of ammunition into her magazines. Forty-eight hours later, with the barometer rising and the temperature hovering at freezing, the crew again manned the side as the bosun piped Admiral Batsch and the station's chief engineer aboard for sea trials and a final inspection. Diederichs had done his job well. Batsch declared the ship in all respects ready for sea and granted Schering permission to proceed on his mission.[13]

GING MIT DER MASCHINE AN!

Schering gave the long-awaited order at 1700 hours on 3 December 1878—

"Ging mit der Maschine an!" "Proceed under steam!"—as he directed the helmsman to set a course through the Jade and into the stormy North Sea. The North Sea is unfriendly to mariners in any season but at its worst in winter. As *Luise* steamed slowly south through the North Sea and into the English Channel, Diederich's log noted freezing temperatures, chilling winds, and turbulent seas. Heavy fog punctuated by sleet made navigation difficult, requiring Schering to stop engines and anchor until visibility returned. Even under these conditions, Diederichs established a shipboard routine, mustering the crew for inspection at 0800 and make nightly rounds at 2100 hours. In between he set watches, trained the crew, supervised gunnery drill, and presided over the officers' wardroom.

Engine problems further impeded progress, causing what would become a too familiar pattern. *Luise*'s quirky engines would break down every few hours, forcing Schering to heave to or proceed under sail. These problems, which continued throughout the voyage, required Schering to put into Plymouth on 7 December for minor repairs.[14]

Under normal circumstances, this would have caused no extraordinary degree of frustration for First Officer Diederichs and Chief Engineer Fontane. Now, however, the delays threatened to upset *Luise*'s new itinerary. Schering's original orders had directed him to proceed down the west coast of Africa, around the Cape of Good Hope, and on to East Asia. New orders now diverted him through the Mediterranean and Suez Canal on a direct course for India, where *Luise* would be the first German warship to show the flag in Indian waters.

The Admiralty had originally assigned that task to SMS *Prinz Adalbert*, whose torpedo mounts Diederichs had recently designed, until mechanical problems with that ship's engines delayed her departure for several weeks. Bound for a training cruise to the Pacific, *Prinz Adalbert* would have been the ideal ship for a ceremonial visit to India, because His Royal Highness Lieutenant (jg) Prince Heinrich of Prussia (1862–1929), grandson of Kaiser Wilhelm I and the younger brother of the future Kaiser Wilhelm II, was aboard. Now, however, *Luise* would have that honor if she could overcome her own mechanical problems. Schering also worried that the combination of engine problems and the diversion to India would delay *Luise*'s arrival on the East Asian station, scheduled for mid-April 1879. Frankly, he wrote the

Admiralty, antipiracy patrols in Chinese waters were more important to him than flowery protocol at Indian banquets.[15]

If that wasn't enough, poor weather conditions persisted, hampering Diederichs in his duties as first officer. During *Luise*'s passage through the Bay of Biscay, lookouts sighted an English bark making slow progress against headwinds. The ship heaved to and signaled *Luise* with a desperate request for food and water. In high winds and freezing temperatures, Diederichs launched *Luise*'s cutter to carry supplies over to the beleaguered ship, which then proceeded north. When *Luise* put in to the British naval base at Gibraltar to replenish her bunkers, high winds forced Diederichs to temporarily suspend coaling. Although weather and wind conditions improved as soon as *Luise* entered the Mediterranean, mechanical difficulties persisted, requiring Schering to proceed largely under sail. The heavy easterly winds that had impaired coaling at Gibraltar made amends by driving *Luise* through the Mediterranean at a satisfactory pace. Moderating weather—a balmy 65 degrees Fahrenheit—at least allowed Diederichs to exercise the crew in gunnery and sail drill.[16]

Luise's brief visit to Gibraltar, which the English had seized from Spain in 1704, also provided the first demonstration of Britain's imperial and naval might. In fact, it quickly seemed to Diederichs as though each stop *Luise* made on the trip out to East Asia was at one British outpost or another. Schering's decision to make a brief visit for coal and repairs at Valletta, Malta, which the British had acquired in 1798, only confirmed this suspicion. *Luise* arrived on 23 December and remained for several days to allow Fontane to again overhaul her engines. Because he anticipated a difficult passage through the hotter climate of the Suez Canal and Indian Ocean, Schering wanted the ship's engines in better shape. Fontane's "snipes" scoured port-side boiler tubes, repaired the starboard boiler, and replaced an engine piston. Another work detail cleaned the bilges, which had been emitting an offensive odor into the crew spaces. Diederichs's torpedo technicians dismantled and repaired several torpedoes which, stored on deck, had sustained damaged during inclement weather. The tired crew observed a brief Christmas respite—though "O Tannenbaum" seemed rather incongruous in sunny, 70-degree weather—before Diederichs directed the grueling and filthy task of coaling. With work completed, *Luise* raised anchor and put to sea on 28 December, several days behind schedule.[17]

New Year's Day found *Luise* at sea in the eastern Mediterranean. As Diederichs mustered the crew in the waist, Schering used the holiday to offer his hopes for a successful mission in the new year. Diederichs responded by leading the crew in a "dreimal Hurrah" for His Majesty the Emperor and King. Holidays passed quickly as sea, however, as Diederichs immediately returned the crew to more drills.[18]

Before entering the Suez Canal, Schering halted briefly at Port Said, the canal's northern terminus, to coal and provision. Constructed by a joint Franco-Egyptian company, the canal had opened in 1869. Using the canal, rather than steaming around the Cape of Good Hope, reduced *Luise*'s voyage to East Asia by more than forty-five hundred nautical miles. *Luise* embarked a pilot and cautiously entered the canal on 5 January. Almost immediately, the canal's narrowness (fifty-eight meters) forced *Luise* to tie up to allow the passage of two merchant ships and an English transport. Heavy currents also forced Schering to use steam from two boilers to propel *Luise* through the northern canal. Because of the perilous nature of the canal passage, Schering dropped anchor for the night at Ismaili, the midpoint of the canal's hundred-nautical-mile length and the entrance to the southern canal at the Great Bitter Lakes. *Luise* reached the port of Suez, the canal's southern terminus, on the evening of 6 January. The crew loaded twenty-six tons of coal the next morning before proceeding into the Gulf of Suez and beyond to the Red Sea in the afternoon.

As the barometer fell and temperatures climbed, the heavy seas and high winds of a tropical storm struck *Luise* as she steamed south through the Red Sea on the evening of 14 January. Diederichs's log dramatically recorded the crew's strenuous labors as the mounting storm caused damage to *Luise*'s spars and rigging. Schering ordered Diederichs to strike down the maintop yards and lower the topyards to avoid further damage. Dawn on 15 January saw the crew cleaning the ship during a temporary lull in the storm. A heavy current compelled Schering to light all boilers, but fear of wearing out the machinery, along with a broken piston ring, soon required him to reduce speed to three knots.

Disaster struck the next day—16 January—at the second bell of the noon watch. In heavy seas, the bowsprit suddenly splintered as a forward section broke away and trailed down the starboard side. The crew leapt into action, quickly cutting away the broken spar and reweaving tackle to reduce pressure on the jib, but the damage was done, crippling *Luise*'s sailing ability. Schering's report of the incident cited an additional problem that only compounded the crew's miseries: Inadequate ventilation in engine spaces produced temperatures exceeding 120 degrees Fahrenheit, forcing Fontane to rotate his stokers to avoid heat prostration. Schering planned to put into Aden for repairs to his rigging and also hoped to hire native stokers once *Luise* reached East Asia.[19]

Luise limped into Aden, which commanded the southern entrance of the Red Sea and further illustrated British imperial power, on 19 January. Schering had originally intended to remain only briefly, but repairs forced him to extend his stay to nine days. Diederichs and a work crew mounted a block-and-tackle on the foremast, unstepped both the jib and the broken bowsprit, and then lowered the spar into a waiting barge for transport to the repair facilities of the Aden Coal Company.

Diederichs at least found some advantage to the longer stay, using the time to provide additional training for *Luise*'s crew. He particularly wanted to exercise the landing force—regular seamen trained as naval infantry—to test the *Infanterieismus* (small-arms practice and infantry tactics) policy recently implemented by Admiralty Chief Stosch. While in Aden, Diederichs focused on small-boat practice with sail and oars, amphibious operations, and infantry maneuvers ashore. He had also wanted time to test *Luise*'s Whitehead torpedoes and torpedo tubes. The Torpedowesen had specifically requested tests that included firing the torpedoes at static and moving targets while the ship herself was at rest and in motion. Diederichs also wanted to test the tubes' experimental air-compression firing mechanism. The bowsprit problems, however, forced a postponement of the tests because Diederichs had to dismantle the tubes to replace the damaged bowsprit.

Diederichs had the crew restep the bowsprit on 25 January. He worried, however, that its seventeen-meter length was too great to withstand the stress of its rigging. He believed that a more practical length, given *Luise*'s rigging, was fourteen meters. He doubted that it would long survive continued use and therefore recommended to Schering that he replace it with a new spar in Bombay. Until then, he feared that ship-handling would be difficult and that he would have to restrict full use of sails. There was, however, some good news. Because of local competition between chandlery and coal suppliers, the price of machine oil had declined by 25 percent, and Schering could purchase high-quality coal at forty schillings per ton, ten schillings less than usual.[20]

The passage to Bombay (28 January to 14 February) across the Arabian sea was largely uneventful. Good weather and sea conditions allowed *Luise* to transit the 1,650 nautical miles in eighteen days, an average of four knots per hour. At one point, with the engines admittedly operating better than usual, *Luise* traveled two hundred nautical miles in a single day, using two boilers and auxiliary sails. Schering noted only one mishap: A seaman had fallen to the deck from the mainmast; he was expected to resume his duties after a day's recovery in sickbay.[21]

High temperatures, however, again forced Diederichs to revise his training regimen. He hoped that a more moderate climate beyond Singapore would allow him to complete training before *Luise* arrived on station in East Asia. He nonetheless used the time for a series of oceanographic experiments, requested by the Admiralty's Hydrographic Bureau, with water temperature at various depths. He also had his torpedo artificer disassemble and clean several of the torpedo firing and steering mechanisms. On 9 February, Diederichs noted an unusual weather phenomenon. Towards dusk the sea suddenly turned a warm yellow color, and then changed to milky-white. As the swells dropped and a light fog settled over the water's surface, sea and air took on a ghostly white appearance until the rising moon dissipated the fog, restoring the water to its original color.[22]

Bombay was the first major stop on *Luise*'s itinerary. The Honorable East India Company, the joint-stock company that had ruled India for a century before 1858, had once headquartered its naval force—the famous "Bombay Marine"—there. Although the opening of the Suez Canal had reduced Bombay's maritime importance, it was still the major port on the west coast of India and thus an opportunity for *Luise* to show the flag and illustrate the power, albeit limited, of the German fleet. Accompanied by Diederichs and the German consul, Schering made a series of official calls on the local political and military officials. *Luise*'s officers attended a formal reception ashore honoring the former American president U. S. Grant, who was on a transglobal cruise, and hosted a series of functions aboard *Luise* to honor local dignitaries and members of the German community. German expatriates, mostly employees of various business firms, hosted a ball and fireworks display for *Luise*'s crew in turn.[23]

Diederichs, as always, remained busy with his responsibilities as executive officer. Following negotiations ashore, he advised Schering to replace *Luise*'s bowsprit in Singapore or Hong Kong, since the local dockyard's bid of two hundred pounds sterling was exorbitant. He also tested the new Whitehead torpedoes. During his work with the Torpedowesen, Diederichs had identified two persistent problems: The torpedo's gyro system regularly failed, and the Whitehead-designed launching tube often functioned improperly. As noted in chapter two, the first test was a failure. As in the earlier test, although the torpedo tube operated effectively this time, the guidance system failed, causing the torpedo to arc and then plunge to the bottom of the bay. When an extensive search failed to locate the torpedo, Diederichs postponed further tests until *Luise*'s technicians could test the gyros on the other torpedoes.[24]

Luise departed Bombay on 23 February. Favorable winds allowed Schering to set sail, using only auxiliary power when necessary as *Luise* proceeded around the southern tip of India and then east to Ceylon. Because the temperature often reached 100 degrees in the shade with a correspondingly high humidity, Diederichs adopted a tropical routine, limiting work details and training exercises to morning and evening hours. The ship touched briefly at Colombo, on the west coast of Ceylon, allowing the crew a brief respite from weather and routine and enabling Diederichs to meet the small German community—approximately eighty nationals—who lived there.[25]

Departing on 5 March, *Luise* steered northeast through the Bay of Bengal for Calcutta. For the first time on the long voyage out from Wilhelmshaven, neither Schering's reports nor Diederichs's log notes any problems. The ship proceeded primarily by sail unless light winds forced Schering to light off the boilers and proceed under steam. Diederichs maintained his limited training regimen, stopping only briefly to carry out the oceanographic studies. When the ship reached the mouth of the Hooghly River on 17 March, Schering anchored overnight. Because the Hooghly estuary suffered from high tides and the river itself wound through a dangerous and narrow channel, all ships proceeding to Calcutta—fifty miles upriver—required daytime passage and a qualified pilot. *Luise* had barely begun to move when busy traffic heading downstream forced Schering to drop anchor and again wait overnight.

Luise finally reached the Calcutta anchorage early in the postnoon watch on 19 March. Founded in 1690 by the Honorable East India Company, Calcutta had become the capital of British India in 1773. Although eventually supplanted by Singapore, Calcutta was still a flourishing port, serving northeastern India and Bengal. Schering went ashore to begin the ritual round of formal calls on viceregal and military officials. The local German community, which numbered about two hundred, welcomed *Luise* enthusiastically, sponsoring a ball for the crew and a formal dinner at the German Club for the officers. Schering in turn hosted a birthday celebration in *Luise*'s wardroom on the twenty-second to honor the emperor. The British welcome was equally effusive. Viceregal officials hosted a dinner for *Luise*'s officers and sponsored a visit by the crew to Calcutta's world-famous botanical gardens. In his ensuing report, Schering commented favorably on Anglo-German relations and noted, as he had in Bombay and Colombo, that an occasional visit by a German warship would suffice to protect German nationals and interests.

Luise's visit had other benefits. The Hooghly River's swift current and fresh water scoured her hull of algae and other marine growth. Schering did complain, however, that the bill for the pilot and anchorage fees had totaled almost nine hundred rupees (about seventy-five pounds). He hoped to have the amount refunded to his purser by the German consul in Singapore, *Luise*'s next destination. During the ship's nine-day stay, Diederichs used the time to make minor repairs on engines and rigging and to load coal, provisions, and fresh water.[26]

Luise steamed down the Hooghly to open water on 27 March. As she proceeded southeast through the Bay of Bengal and into the Malacca Strait, Diederichs accelerated training. Poor weather—the temperature rarely dropped below 90 degrees and humidity remained high—nonetheless continued to impede exercises. Other problems also developed. When Diederichs led gunnery drills with the ship's 150- and 120-mm batteries, the explosive noise broke the ship's mercury barometer.[27]

With the Dutch East Indies to starboard and the Malaysian peninsula to port, *Luise* arrived in Singapore on 11 April for a week-long stay. Britain had acquired Singapore Island as a crown colony in 1824 and had developed its harbor as a major naval base. While Schering made the usual round of ceremonial and social visits, Diederichs used the time to clean, coal, and provision the ship. Circumstances also allowed him to test the torpedoes on 15 April. Placing a floating target two hundred meters from the anchored ship, he fired several torpedoes. None hit the target. Torpedo no. 633, trailing a visible line of air bubbles, dove deeply and hit the muddy sea bottom 150 meters from the ship. A boat crew immediately marked the site with two buoys, allowing *Luise*'s diver, Machinist's Mate Kaufmann, to dive on the site. When Kaufmann was unable to locate the torpedo after a six-hour search, Diederichs the next day hired two native divers who found the torpedo and aided Kaufmann in raising it. Diederichs decided to suspend further testing until his torpedomen could tear down the torpedoes and check the air bladders.[28]

Luise departed on the final leg of her voyage out from Germany on 17 April, steering a northeasterly course through the South China Sea. With French Indochina to port, the Spanish Philippines to starboard, Singapore astern, and Hong Kong ahead, Diederichs saw only imperial outposts belonging to other countries. *Luise* arrived in Hong Kong, the western terminus of the East Asian station, on 30 April 1879, 149 days after leaving Wilhelmshaven. Diederichs's log notes the minutiae and protocol of arrival:

> 0620: Chinese pilot on board. 1057: Moored by starboard and port anchors with 75 fathoms of chain. 1110: Saluted the English flag with 21-gun salute and the English commanding officer with 11-gun salute. Both salutes were returned. 1130: Embarked German consul with a 5-gun salute. 1140: Visit from the commanding officer of SMS *Freya*.

Freya (twenty-four hundred tons, eight 150-mm guns) was the warship that *Luise* would replace on the East Asian station. Schering therefore met with her captain to take possession of station records and formally assume the position of senior officer present on station. Schering also spoke with the commanding officers of gunboats *Wolf* (six hundred tons and two 125-mm guns) and *Cyclop* (five hundred tons and two 120-mm guns), which, with *Luise*, now comprised the active German naval presence on the East Asian station.[29]

Diederichs used the stay in Hong Kong, which lasted for a month, to undertake repairs and continue training. Proximity to a shipyard allowed him to replace the bowsprit and give the engines a long-needed overhaul. Although the crew had time for liberty, Diederichs increased the tempo of training. He used a total of eight days for Infanterieismus—in case *Luise* needed to send ashore a landing force that could handle small arms and deploy infantry tactics.[30]

Meanwhile, Schering, as senior officer on station, dealt with the vagaries of command. German ships on the East Asian station did not operate as an integrated squadron but rather as independent units under the direct orders of the Admiralty. Schering's limited control of the two gunboats tended to reduce the effectiveness of German sea power in the region. The need to respond to specific diplomatic requests also limited Schering's freedom of action. In fact, his first problem on station was an immediate conflict with Ambassador Brandt.

The Admiralty had recently instructed Schering to proceed from Hong Kong to Japan, rather than to Chinese ports as originally planned. Schering welcomed these new instructions for several reasons. The mechanical problems arising from the outbound voyage, along with the heat and humidity of equatorial travel, had prevented the completion of the crew's training. There were also two cases of cholera aboard. Schering believed that a summer spent in Japanese waters, where the climate was much more moderate and refreshing than in China, would allow him to complete training and resolve the crew's health problems.[31] This plan did not please Ambassador Brandt, who argued that various threats to German interests in China required *Luise*'s continued presence in Chinese waters.

Brandt cited the ubiquitous pirates, xenophobic riots in treaty ports, and Sino-Japanese and Sino-Russian tensions that threatened to erupt into war any moment. He opposed *Luise*'s mission to Japan, citing an Admiralty promise to keep half of the station's ships in Chinese waters at all times.[32]

Schering nonetheless intended to give each of his three ships (*Luise*, *Wolf*, and *Cyclop*) a brief respite in Japanese waters to escape the miserable and unhealthy Chinese summer weather. *Luise* would depart for Japan in June, returning to Chinese waters in September. *Wolf* would tour Chinese treaty ports before steaming to Japan in July. *Cyclop* would remain temporarily in

Chinese waters before visiting Japan in August. Thereafter, Schering intended to base *Cyclop* in northern Chinese waters during the winter, supported, weather permitting, by regular visits from *Luise*. Schering thus emphasized to Brandt, "Your Excellency will thus note that the flag will remain permanently on the [Chinese] coast."[33]

Before proceeding to Japan, Schering visited the island port of Amoy in mid-June. Lying approximately equidistant between Hong Kong and Shanghai, Amoy possessed a good harbor with a spacious anchorage. The port had become the unofficial center of German naval and mercantile operations in Chinese waters in the past twenty years. Twenty years after *Luise*'s visit, when Diedrichs returned to East Asia as commander of the Cruiser Squadron, Amoy topped the navy's list as a prospective site for an official German naval base in China.[34] Diedrichs used *Luise*'s brief stay to test torpedo no. 634. Test-fired four separate times, the torpedo ran accurately over distances up to five hundred meters. Amoy's rapid tidal race prevented further tests, however, particularly of torpedo no. 78, which had evinced constant technical problems since its purchase from the Whitehead firm.[35]

Diedrichs faced a potential second problem, this time involving the crew, before *Luise* departed for Japanese waters. One of the other warships present at Amoy was U.S. sloop *Ranger* (4), whose under-strength crew numbered only 114 out of a regular complement of 165. Because American ships had been known to recruit German seamen, Diedrichs took extra precautions to see that none of his own crew deserted.

A more dangerous problem presented itself midway to Japan. A fire broke out in the after port engine space near midnight on 5 June. Although the well-drilled crew responded quickly to put out the flames and the engines were not damaged, the fire burned a large hole in the bulkhead. On 6 June, *Luise* proceeded under sail rather than losing the six hours it took to clear the poorly ventilated engine room of smoke.

Nagasaki was *Luise*'s first port of call in Japan. Located on the west coast of Kyushu Island, Nagasaki was the center of German naval operations in Japanese waters. Nagasaki had a natural harbor and well-developed maritime facilities. Its location provided ready access both to Chinese waters and Japan's east coast. The port's weather was cool and comfortable, allowing Diedrichs an excellent opportunity to complete *Luise*'s formal training regimen. In fact, he notified Schering that the crew had completed all training requirements as set by Admiralty regulation. *Luise* had now achieved operational readiness for all required duties, including combat. Fulfilling his responsibilities as executive officer, however, had come at some personal cost. The rigors of his duties as first officer, in addition to the strain of the long voyage out from Wilhelmshaven, had left him exhausted and revived his persistent pulmonary problems.[36]

Joined by *Wolf* (Cdr. Willibert Becks), *Luise* steamed through the Inland Sea to Kobe, a major port on the southern coast of Honshu. The passage, via narrow and difficult inland waters, required a pilot. Because Japanese pilots were inexperienced in navigating steam ships, Schering hired an American pilot named Smith who charged a bargain six dollars for the run.

Kobe had excellent weather and a healthy climate. However, it lacked Nagasaki's facilities, and Diederichs complained to Schering that Kobe's lack of competitive ship chandlers meant that he had to pay a high price for coal and provisions. Diederichs also used *Luise*'s brief stay to exercise his boat crews. While practicing amphibious operations, one boat lost its machine gun overboard. Machinist's Mate Kaufmann used the launch to locate and recover the weapon. *Luise* again launched her boats when a fire broke out in the local moorage and Diederichs dispatched the ship's firemen to assist.[37]

When cholera, an illness endemic to East Asia, suddenly struck ashore, *Luise* weighed anchor and proceeded to Yokohama with *Wolf*. Passage, for which Pilot Smith charged eighteen dollars, was again slowed by unpredictable inland waters and inadequate charts. The two warships arrived at Yokohama, the port serving Tokyo, on 1 July.

Luise dropped anchor next to SMS *Prinz Adalbert,* one of the navy's new training ships. The steam-powered *Prinz Adalbert,* which had replaced the old sailing ships like *Niobe* and *Musquito,* was on the first leg of a two-year training cruise and not actually attached to the East Asia station. Diederichs knew her commanding officer well. He had served with Capt. Archibald MacLean, years earlier aboard SMS *Musquito*. As the senior officer present, MacLean assumed temporary command of the three ships to practice squadron maneuvers and amphibious operations. He came aboard *Luise* to inspect ship and crew and observe various drills and exercises. Diederichs came away from the experience somewhat disappointed when *Prinz Adalbert*'s boats defeated *Luise*'s in an intra-squadron regatta. Diederichs also renewed his acquaintance with seventeen-year-old His Royal Highness Lieutenant (jg) Prince Henry of Prussia, who came aboard *Luise* for a formal reception and dinner. Diederichs had first met the prince aboard SMS *Grille* in 1869.[38]

Yokohama's spacious anchorage offered Diederichs prime opportunity to test torpedoes. From a stationary position, Diederichs fired torpedoes 634, 833, and 835 at fixed targets. Only 634 operated effectively, hitting targets at two hundred and four hundred meters. Torpedoes number 833 and 835 had problems with their guidance systems that caused the torpedoes to swerve away as much as 30 degrees at the end of their runs. Diederichs was unable even to fire 633 when its propulsion system again broke down. Diederichs also noted problems with *Luise*'s Whitehead-designed launching tubes.

Further work on the torpedoes' guidance system and launching tubes gave Diederichs greater success. His technicians fired three times from the starboard tube and three from the port tube with the ship under way, scoring four hits at a stationary target two hundred meters away. Two torpedoes, though, still ran ten and twenty meters left of the target even with constant corrections to the guidance system.[39]

Since the Meiji Restoration a decade earlier, Tokyo had become the capital of a resurgent imperial dynasty open to Western ideas while retaining a strong foundation of traditional Japanese culture. Yokohama, as its port, attracted distinguished visitors from abroad, giving *Luise*'s officers and crew several opportunities, planned and unplanned, to break the monotony of shipboard life. They participated in a harbor-wide celebration of American Independence Day with fireworks and twenty-one-gun salutes in the presence of former President Grant on 4 July. The Japanese Minister of the Navy and the German ambassador paid formal visits to *Luise*. *Prinz Adalbert*'s chaplain came aboard on Sunday, 13 July, to celebrate divine services on *Luise*'s deck. (*Luise* was too small to rate her own chaplain, a fact that pleased the crew since the superstition still reigned that chaplains brought their ships bad luck.)

There were other, less formal events. When the German consul requested the assistance of *Luise*'s firemen because of fire danger ashore, Diederichs detailed Lieutenant (jg) Hugo Pohl to set off with two boatloads of men and equipment. Also, Diederichs used some of the time in Yokohama to provide swimming lessons for the crew, since only seven of *Luise*'s 220 crewmen could swim! Sudden high winds created a less benign diversion when USS *Monongahela* dragged her anchor and fowled *Luise*'s rigging, causing a yard to splinter and some backstays to part. And at one point during gunnery exercises, a seaman stumbled and fell against a machine-gun director, knocking it overboard. Diver Kaufmann dove for two hours to recover it.

Luise also suffered her first fatality at Yokohama. Although most ailing seamen had recovered in the healthy climate, Able Seaman Schubert died of cholera. His messmates buried him in a small cemetery on the grounds of the German Naval Hospital, Yokohama. (The navy had established the facility in 1878.) Diederichs himself had spent some time ashore at the hospital, convalescing from his pulmonary problems. Under the excellent care of the resident German naval physician, Dr. Gutschow, he had fully recovered.[40]

The departure of *Prinz Adalbert* on 22 July on a transpacific voyage to South American waters once again left Schering as senior officer present.[41] *Luise* next turned north for Hakodate, a port on the southern tip of Hokkaido Island, on 5 August. Due east of the Russian naval base at Vladivostok, Hakodate was strategically located to command the northern Sea of Japan. It was also a haven for international whaling crews operating in the northern Pacific. As always, *Luise*'s visit was intended to make Schering and his officers familiar with various parts of the station, including this port so regularly visited by foreign warships.

Diederichs kept busy during the voyage north. He detected mechanical problems with *Luise*'s propeller shaft and coupler. Although the shaft was raised when *Luise* proceeded under sail, water pressure rotated both propeller and shaft. This movement had damaged the shaft and worn out the coupling. He noted that *Luise* would eventually need major repair facilities, which Hakodate lacked, to repair the damage. Diederichs also used the voyage to test *Luise*'s sailing capabilities. She made good movement in light winds with no water flowing over the deck but suffered from significant rolling—often as much as 10 degrees—in high seas and before the wind. The helmsman also reported some problems with rudder response in moderate to high winds. *Luise* was most maneuverable with approximately 130 tons of coal as ballast. Diederichs reported to Schering that, despite her shortcomings, he was satisfied with *Luise*'s seaworthiness and performance.[42]

Luise remained at Hakodate for a week, during which Diederichs maintained a steady tempo of gunnery and small-arms training. By the time *Luise* departed for the Chinese waters, Diederichs could report that fifty-two of her crew had qualified as first-class marksmen with small arms. This was important because the sailors would need to serve as naval infantry in case of any amphibious operations. While exercising the main battery, Diederichs also concluded that the ship's rigging and some design flaws impeded the crew's efforts to work the guns. He therefore requested permission from Schering to rerig the forward mast and cut new gunports.

Luise suffered a second tragedy on the passage to China. Sometime around midnight on 30 August, Seaman Schroeder, who suffered from diarrhea, left his hammock in the crew's quarters to seek fresh air on deck and use the ship's "head." No one saw him again. An investigation by Diederichs turned up no evidence of suicide or unusual weather or sea conditions, but the combination of a rolling ship and a sick crewman was a prescription for tragedy.[43]

Luise steamed into Chinese waters on 1 September, touching first at Chefoo, a small treaty port on the northern tip of the Shantung peninsula. Although notorious as a poor anchorage for warships, Chefoo dominated the entrance to the Gulf of Chihli and the approaches to Peking. The region itself had long been a center of xenophobic sentiments, producing numerous acts of anti-Western violence. Recent crop failures and famines had further increased tensions between Chinese and Western residents to the extent that Ambassador Brandt had requested that the navy base a warship in Chefoo to protect German interests. Although the German community in Chefoo numbered only twenty, 150 German-flagged ships visited there annually.[44]

The return to Chinese waters provoked Schering to comment on the status of German naval operations in East Asian waters. He noted first that there were simply too few ships on station. A single corvette and two gunboats could not possibly patrol both Chinese and Japanese waters adequately. The rapid growth of German trade and diplomatic crises cried out for naval reinforcements. Secondly, he complained about the command ambiguity on the station. Although Schering was senior officer, he had only limited authority to direct the actions of *Wolf* and *Cyclop,* nominally under direct orders from the Admiralty in Berlin. Because of this circumstance, he feared, German warships would not be able to react quickly in a major crisis. Finally, he criticized the amount of paperwork that he and his executive officer needed to complete in order to fulfill Admiralty directives. For example, although he acknowledged the value of annual small-arms qualifications—157 more crewmen qualified as either first- or second-class marksmen at Chefoo—he resented the bureaucratic requirements of the activity. Regulations required him to submit one report to his superiors in Wilhelmshaven by 1 September and then a copy of the same report to the Admiralty in Berlin by 1 December. He and his clerk had better things to do, he contended, so let the paper-shufflers at Wilhelmshaven pass on the report to Berlin.[45]

Diederichs had his own difficulties when he lost a torpedo. When the guidance system for torpedo 634 caused it to dive into the sea bottom, boat crews spent four fruitless days dragging for the missing torpedo. His gunner's mates had better success repairing the launching mechanisms for the two torpedo tubes, and he could report effective exercises with torpedoes 633 and 635. Diederichs nonetheless wasted more time filling out the necessary paperwork for the lost equipment.[46]

Diederichs also reported to Schering that *Luise*—after eleven months in service and several thousand miles under way—needed extensive repairs. Since Chefoo lacked the necessary facilities, *Luise* weighed anchor on 20 October and proceeded down the coast to Shanghai. Diederichs's noon sight for 21 October placed *Luise* slightly southeast of Kiao-chou Bay, a site that he would come to know well eighteen years later.[47]

Shanghai was the primary treaty port in northern China. Located near the mouth of the thousand-mile-long Yangtze, the city dominated the profitable riverine trade with the interior. Shanghai supported a large and thriving European community with all the comforts of home. Kept aware of local and world events by the English-language *North China Daily News*, Shanghai offered *Luise*'s tired crew everything from opera and symphony concerts to baseball and cricket, as well as other pleasures usually available in liberty ports.[48]

Diederichs had little time to enjoy such pleasures, involved as he was with *Luise*'s overhaul. Crewman and Chinese workers from the Royal Navy dockyard caulked the hull and painted the maindeck, gundeck, forecastle, and quarterdeck. Engineer Fontane supervised repairs to *Luise*'s engines and propeller shaft and replaced boiler tubes that had become clogged by salt water. Dockyard workers also replaced the bowsprit, damaged six months earlier in the Red Sea, at a cost of eight hundred marks (two hundred dollars). Diederichs was able to recover part of the bowsprit's replacement, cutting the original spar into board lumber to replenish *Luise*'s carpentry stores.[49]

Although *Luise*'s busy two-month stay was pleasant, Shanghai's frigid weather in late December convinced Schering of the need to turn south. Most warship commanders chose to winter in southern ports like Hong Kong or Manila. Schering decided instead to proceed south to Amoy, toward which the Germans had an almost proprietary attitude. *Luise*, in fact, remained there from 30 December 1879 until 17 March 1880, providing time for work, drills, and the occasional liberty ashore. The local *Amoy Gazette* welcomed *Luise*'s lengthy stay and cultural contribution. When *Luise*'s band backed up an amateur theatrical group, a reporter noted, "[The band's] efforts, in no small degree, added to the success of the evening's entertainment."[50]

Luise and her crew were called upon for other services at Amoy, notably at attempt to clear the harbor of a shipwreck. At the request of the Amoy authorities, Diederichs assigned a work crew to remove the navigational hazard with explosives. Diver Kaufmann spent two hours in freezing cold weather planting three explosive charges underwater. The triple blast, however, did little more than muddy the water and blow away parts of the wreck's superstructure. The surgeon forbade Kaufmann to dive again because of the cold, and other efforts had equally little effect. Diederichs detailed small boats and crews on eight separate occasions to work on the hulk but attributed their poor results in part to *Luise*'s lack of appropriate equipment for underwater demolition, such as electric batteries and firing caps. The project was abandoned.[51]

As always, Diederichs worked to maintain a high level of readiness in both officers and men. The officers themselves were quite involved, required by regulation to qualify as marksmen and participate in all aspects of infantry training. Diederichs noted in his log at one point that the officers—probably to the amusement of the enlisted witnesses—acted as a boat crew to launch and arm one of *Luise*'s small boats and then fire its 80-mm boat gun.[52]

When winter storms began to affect training and torpedo experiments,

Schering decided in late March to leave Amoy. He had selected Mirs Bay, near Hong Kong, as *Luise*'s next destination, but a series of frantic messages from Ambassador Brandt in March turned *Luise* north toward Shanghai. Brandt feared the possibility of a war between China and Russia in Central Asia when Russia seized control of Ili, a part of western Sinkiang province. As Schering and Diederichs knew, such imperialistic crises generally produced xenophobic violence, which in turn endangered German nationals and interests. Brandt had therefore requested that *Luise* return to Shanghai and that gunboat *Wolf* proceed to Tientsin.[53]

Schering's response to Brandt's entreaties was not enthusiastic, as he understood all too well Germany's relative inability to project naval power in East Asia. *Wolf* was scheduled to depart on a tour of Southeast Asian ports as soon as the winter weather broke. *Cyclop* had reported a major mechanical problem with her main 120-mm battery, rendering her temporarily incapable of combat. *Luise* herself was due to rotate back to Germany. Schering had standing orders to return to Hong Kong no later than 20 April to prepare for departure for Germany on or about 1 May. This deadline was firmly fixed, since the crew's commission ended in September. Because any change in operational plans required Berlin's consent, Schering agreed to proceed to Shanghai but for a limited stay.[54]

Luise reached Shanghai on 23 March as the Ili crisis heated up. Only forty-eight hours later, the *North China Daily News* reported, "Grave rumors were circulated in the Settlement yesterday to the effect that affairs in the North had assumed a most serious aspect—an unknown number of foreigners or natives had been massacred and the German Minister at Peking had hauled down his flag and left the capital. . . ." The article refuted the rumors but nonetheless noted the diplomatic and imperialistic problems associated with Ili.[55]

Brandt had not left Peking, but his regular messages to Schering spoke of his anxiety. He reported outbreaks of xenophobic violence in the capital and feared that Chinese preparations for war might lead the Russians to launch a preemptive strike at Tientsin or Shanghai. Further, he reported that a squadron of twenty-three Russian warships had left Vladivostok for a naval demonstration in Chinese waters and that seventy thousand Russian troops had begun to move toward the Sino-Russian border.[56]

The crisis eased almost as quickly as it had begun. Brandt advised Schering in April that international interests—and the presence of a large British naval force in northern Chinese waters—had persuaded both the Russians and Chinese to back down from their belligerent positions. The crisis had, however, convinced Brandt to petition the Admiralty to significantly increase the German naval presence in East Asia. Acknowledging that *Luise* would soon leave Chinese waters, he thanked Schering for a job well done "in the interests of the service."[57]

The end of the crisis allowed *Luise* to depart for Hong Kong several days later; there, Diederichs used the time to prepare her for the long journey home. His log recites a daily litany of preparations as *Luise*'s crew loaded coal and supplies, tuned engines, patched sails, and painted just about everything that did not move. Thanks to Diederichs's hard work, Schering soon cabled Berlin that he was ready for immediate departure, awaiting only appropriate orders. Much to Schering's frustration, however, no orders arrived. *Luise* remained in Hong Kong for more than two months without hearing from the Admiralty. The wait also made Diederichs's job more difficult, as Hong Kong's miserable weather began to erode *Luise*'s readiness. Throughout the month of May, high heat and humidity weakened the crew and caused spoilage of the ship's supply of fresh food, which Diederichs feared would cause significant health and dietary problems. Perhaps the worst blow to morale was that *Luise*'s mail from home had ended up in Singapore. The period's single high point occurred when Schering received unofficial news that Diederichs had been "frocked" to the rank of commander.[58]

June brought no relief. The crew's general health continued to decline in the face of hundred-degree heat and 100 percent humidity. These conditions, plus the lack of mail, continued to affect morale. As hard as Diederichs worked, the ship was no longer ready for sea at an instant's notice. Hong Kong's constant rain had forced him to strike *Luise*'s sails below in order to avoid their being water soaked. The damp air had also begun to rust metal and rot leather. Diederichs feared that this would adversely affect the breech mechanisms of *Luise*'s guns, for which he lacked parts.[59]

Circumstances suddenly changed on 1 July. Schering received cabled orders directing him to set sail for Germany, returning by way of the Cape of Good Hope rather than by Suez as originally anticipated. The orders further directed him to visit Madagascar, at the request of the German Foreign Ministry, to support the work of German diplomats there. Further orders, the telegram noted, awaited him in Singapore.[60]

Luise steamed out of Hong Kong harbor on 3 July. The delay in departure had cost Schering favorable winds, compelling him to proceed under steam. Further, the timing now meant that *Luise* would be sailing into typhoon season. Because *Luise*'s engines consumed coal at a prodigious rate as she steamed through the South China Sea, Schering halted briefly at Saigon, French Indochina, to coal.[61]

Moving now with some haste to escape adverse weather, *Luise* touched only briefly at Singapore. The German consul delivered Schering's additional orders, which clarified *Luise*'s new mission: to proceed to Tamatave, Madagascar, to assist the consul and show the flag.[62] The new route home also required Schering to hire a pilot in Singapore for the voyage south through the perilous waters of the Dutch East Indies. To escape the typhoon region as rapidly as possible, *Luise* proceeded largely under steam. Once beyond Sumatra, however, as the chances of typhoons diminished, Diederichs called out the crew to hoist sails, slowing the ship's pace but allowing *Luise* to conserve coal. He also used the period, as the crew's health improved, to undo the material damage to *Luise*'s rigging and machinery caused by the long stay in Hong Kong.[63]

Luise reached French-owned Mauritius, anchoring in the harbor of Port Louis, on 9 August. The local English community, anxious for news of the outside world, greeted *Luise* enthusiastically, believing her to be *Prinz Adalbert* with Prince Heinrich, Queen Victoria's grandson, aboard. Although disappointed, they nonetheless provided *Luise*'s crew with a pleasant liberty. The minute German community, a single firm and a handful of German nationals, likewise provided gracious hospitality. The German consul, a Scotsman, gave the crew a guided tour of the town, and the island's governor hosted a reception for *Luise*'s officers, even toasting His Imperial Majesty in German.

With favorable winds out of the east, Schering set sail for Madagascar, eighty miles distant. When the winds suddenly shifted, *Luise* had to tack well away from the island until Schering raised steam in two boilers in order to reach Madagascar the next day. Madagascar was an independent monarchy gradually falling under French colonial influence. Queen Ranavalona ruled a strife-torn island where intertribal rivalry produced a steady supply of slaves for African traders. The government was relatively unfriendly to all Europeans except the French, with whom they had had trade and diplomatic relations for some time. Although the island had no strategic value (it lacked a decent port), it did have extensive economic potential. The German consul, an employee of a Hamburg trading firm, had worked for some time to counter French influence. He hoped that a visit by a German warship would impress, or perhaps pressure, the queen's government and lead to more formal relations.

The small port of Tamatave was the center of the island's commerce. The small expatriate community numbered twenty-two Europeans, including four Germans, and five trading firms. Only six German ships had visited the island since the new year. One had recently gone aground in the high winds; her German crew of eight petitioned Schering for transportation to Cape Town. Following *Luise*'s arrival, Tamatave's governor arranged a formal dinner for Schering and his officers. Riding in sedan chairs carried by slaves, they journeyed uphill to Fort Tamatave. A band welcomed them at the front gate with what Schering described as a "hideous sounding" rendition of the German national anthem.

The ensuing conversations proved moderately productive. After a ritual exchange of toasts, Schering and the governor discussed the possibilities of closer ties. Although the governor could make no promises, he nonetheless agreed to pursue the matter actively with his government. He also agreed to dine aboard *Luise* on the following afternoon. That dinner never occurred. Later the same evening, weather conditions suddenly worsened: The wind freshened, the seaway increased, and the temperature dropped. As the crew prepared for a storm, Schering sent an officer ashore to advise the consul of his decision to put to sea. He hoped to return within twenty-four hours but could make no guarantees. *Luise* left the harbor under steam at dawn, needing the power to maneuver away from the hostile coast and easterly winds. After riding out the storm for twenty-four hours and with another typhoon approaching, Schering concluded that conditions precluded a return to the poor anchorage at Tamatave. He therefore set a new course for the Cape of Good Hope. *Luise*'s brief visit nonetheless proved successful, as representatives of the queen's government eventually signed the desired commercial treaty with Germany.[64]

A second storm struck *Luise* some days later. Heavy winds forced Diederichs to direct the crew in shortening sail. The work was dangerous, as waves caused the ship to heel over more than 30 degrees, throwing water over the command bridge and damaging the rudder. To the relief of the entire crew, *Luise* reached Simonstown, Cape Colony, before the ship could sustain greater damage. Since everybody was anxious to return to Germany as well, Schering decided to make only a brief visit, allowing Diederichs just enough time to make temporary repairs and load coal and provision.[65]

Reflecting this desire for homecoming, both Schering's reports and Diederichs's log become exceedingly succinct thereafter. Alternating sail and steam as weather and equipment permitted, *Luise* passed around the Cape of Good Hope and proceeded into the Atlantic Ocean. She passed the equator on 6 October and made landfall at the Cape Verde islands for coal and fresh provisions. Less than a month later, at dawn on 4 November, lookouts sighted Lizard Point, the southernmost point of England. Halting briefly at Plymouth for a last load of coal, *Luise* steamed into Wilhelmshaven at 0915 on 9 November 1880.[66]

EPILOGUE

Following *Luise*'s arrival, Schering found satisfying news. His repeated complaints about the chaotic command conditions on the East Asia station had finally produced results. A study commissioned by the Admiralty and endorsed by the Foreign Ministry recommended the creation of a larger, integrated squadron under the command of a flag officer to replace ships operating on an individual basis. Capt. Louis von Blanc, flying a commodore's broad pennant, formally constituted the East Asian Squadron, which initially included steam corvettes *Stosch* and *Hertha,* sail frigate *Elisabeth,* and gunboats *Wolf* and *Iltis,* in 1881.[67]

Meanwhile, Diederichs worked to deactivate *Luise*. In the reverse of actions two years before, the crew under his direction removed provisions, emptied coal bunkers, hoisted out guns, and cleaned ship. Diederichs's hard work allowed the chief of the Wilhelmshaven naval station to formally place *Luise* out of service on 20 November 1880.[68] As Diederichs himself prepared to go ashore to reunite with Henni and their children, a delegation from the crew stepped forward and saluted him. They presented him with a hand-carved model of *Luise,* carefully crafted to show every detail in miniature. As he saluted the quarterdeck and stepped ashore, he proudly carried the model to show Fritz (age eight) and Herman (three).[69]

Diederichs had little opportunity thereafter to enjoy his return. He was met with the news that his mother had recently died in Marienwerder, dampening the joy of his family reunion. And his orders awaited him: He was being assigned to a teaching post at the Marineakademie in Kiel.

4

Defending the Coasts: Diederichs and Strategic Planning, 1880–1890

Following the formal ceremony that placed *Luise* out of commission on 20 November 1880, Diederichs boarded the afternoon train at the Wilhelmshaven Hauptbahnhof and departed immediately for Kiel. His new assignment was a joint appointment as gunnery and torpedo instructor for both the undergraduate Naval School (*Marineschule*) and the postgraduate Naval War College (*Marineakademie*). In fact, for much of the next decade, Diederichs's work with the Marineakademie in particular would link him not only to the academic training of the naval officer corps but also to the initial development of strategic planning.

NAVAL EDUCATOR

When Diederichs reported for duty at the Dürstenbrook campus on 21 November, several weeks after the beginning of the fall term, he joined a small but seasoned faculty. Capt. Alfred Stenzel carried a heavy load, teaching naval history, naval tactics, and naval science, while Lt. Cdr. Louis Riedel was responsible for navigation and seamanship. Adjunct civilian professors from the University of Kiel continued to teach the non-naval courses in science and modern languages.[1]

Diederichs also discovered that the schools' structure and curriculum had changed since he had matriculated first at the Marineschule (1866–67) and then at the Marineakademie (1872–74). As chief of the Admiralty and founder of the Marineakademie, Albrecht von Stosch, an admiral since 1875, had implemented a new regimen for officer training in that year that now took fifty-four months from admission to active duty: a six-month orientation cruise to provide initial shipboard experience, a six-month stint at the undergraduate Marineschule, a six-month gunnery course aboard either SMS *Renown* (Wilhelmshaven) or SMS *Gefion* (Kiel), a two-year midshipman cruise to East Asia prior to commissioning, and a year's matriculation in an officers' refresher course at the Marineschule before active duty.[2]

Diederichs therefore taught three levels of students: midshipmen who spent a six-month term at the Marineschule, recently commissioned officers who attended a refresher course at the Marineschule, and older officers matriculating in the Marineakademie's postgraduate program. His thirty-three midshipmen had just completed a six-month training cruise (April to October) in the Baltic and North Seas to learn seamanship and ship-handling. He now taught them basic gunnery and ordnance courses and supervised their midshipmen exams in April. His refresher course counted thirty-six lieutenants, jg, who had just received their commissions after completing a two-year training cruise to East Asia and passing the lieutenant's exam. Diederichs had returned too late himself to participate in the examinations, but in later years he would proctor and evaluate the two-hour gunnery portion (oral and written) of the examination.

His refresher courses, during the eleven-month term that lasted from October to August, taught theoretical knowledge—such as the formulation of trajectory and range—and practical applications. Course requirements included six research papers: one on gunpowder, three on the technology of naval artillery, and two on the use and exercise of ships' guns. Successful performance on the final examination in September established an officer's seniority within his rank and led to more attractive postings.[3]

Stosch had added a third academic year to the Marineakademie, where Diederichs also held a joint appointment. The first year focused on general courses in logic, mathematics, chemistry, physics, and land and naval tactics and offered an optional course in international law. The second year concentrated on professional courses, including naval history, gunnery, steam engineering, naval design, nautical astronomy, coastal survey, and one optional sequence chosen from maritime law, the history of civilization, and health. Students in their third and final year continued professional courses in naval history, torpedoes, steam engineering, naval design, nautical astronomy, and geography, with optional courses in history, harbor construction, marine biology, and political economy. Students also studied one foreign language chosen from English, French, Danish, Russian, or Spanish.[4]

Diederichs taught the ordnance and gunnery course for the second-year class (eight lieutenant commanders and lieutenants, sg) and torpedoes for the third-year class (six officer students). He met with members of the second-year class at 0930 on Tuesday, Thursday, and Saturday for lectures on gunnery. He met with the third-year students at 0830 on Tuesdays for an hour of torpedo instruction and at 0930 on Monday, Wednesday, and Friday for advanced gunnery. Because he had not arrived in Kiel until late November 1880, he needed to cram four months of work into two.[5]

Diederichs based his gunnery courses on fairly standard issues. Although the fleet had recently begun conversion to breech-loaded guns, German warships still used muzzle-loading cannon fired in broadsides at close range. His torpedo courses focused on even more rapidly developing technology and reflected his recent service with the Torpedo Service and SMS *Luise*. From the Dürstenbrook campus, Diederichs could intersperse his technical lectures with occasional field trips aboard SMS *Gefion,* anchored nearby in Kiel fiord, and to the artillery and torpedo depots at Friedrichsort for more practical demonstrations. The Imperial Shipyard, across the fiord in Gaarden, likewise allowed his students to see firsthand the torpedo and gunnery developments he described.

Following his arrival in Kiel, Diederichs soon discovered that the Marineakademie, under the influence of Captain Stenzel, had become the navy's unofficial center of strategic thinking. (The *Torpedowesen* under Tirpitz had become a similar source for tactical ideas.) Stenzel, who had reported for duty at the Marineakademie in fall 1875, developed what Rolf Hobson calls the "Prussian School of naval thought," in which he systematically translated existing military strategies of land warfare, especially those of Karl von Clausewitz, into naval terms. In fact, Stenzel made "one long attempt to baptize Clausewitz with salt water," promoting the strategic value of the *Vernichtungsschlacht,* the "battle of annihilation" that would make the destruction of the enemy's fleet a primary goal. Commerce raiding—attacks against an enemy's merchant fleet and seaborne commerce—had only secondary value.[6] Although some of Stenzel's ideas anticipated those of Alfred Thayer Mahan and Alfred von Tirpitz (see chapter 5), Stenzel never developed Mahanian concepts such as sea power and command of the seas, nor did he ever fully develop the concept of a battle fleet or promote the navy as the agent of imperial expansion. His ideas nonetheless influenced the first stage of German naval planning with which Diederichs would soon become involved.[7]

The end of the academic year in late August 1881 brought Diederichs little rest. In September, Diederichs and the other commissioned faculty joined the fleet as umpires for the annual exercises. Diederichs observed the maneuvers' final phase, which consisted of simulated attacks against Kiel, from the squadron flagship *Friedrich Carl*. He had intended to return to Kiel for the next academic year, but his brief service at sea proved too much for his sometimes fragile health. Following consultations with Dr. Martini, the schools' staff surgeon, he formally requested a three-month convalescent leave. He and Henni took the boys to Italy in search of warmer weather and drier climes as a relief from Kiel's damp, cold winter. His recuperation was successful, allowing him to resume his duties in January 1882 at the beginning of the second term.[8]

THE ORIGINS OF OPERATIONAL PLANNING

Diederich's return to active duty at the beginning of 1882 occurred simultaneously with the outbreak of diplomatic tensions with Russia. Ironically, only a few months earlier, Germany and Austria-Hungary had joined Russia in the Dreikaiserbund in June 1881 in an attempt to reduce problems in the Balkans. Now, however, talk of a possible Franco-Russian alignment raised fears in Germany of a major war with Russia. The diplomatic crisis prompted the Kaiserliche Marine to develop a more formal program for operational planning in case of war.

Planning had originated in the 1860s during the Roon administration and continued through Stosch's early years. These initial attempts produced general policies on coastal defense, overseas operations, and offensive sorties to drive the enemy away from the coast. Stenzel had added offensive goals in terms of decisive battle, but hardly anything resembling specific operational plans existed to use in case of war. The Admiralty's files contained only one vague plan for war against France, dating from the mid-1870s, which called for a rapid strike on French naval bases and a blockade of France's Atlantic ports.[9]

Stosch therefore directed his staff to begin the more formal preparation of operational plans in March 1882. The responsibility for operational planning resided in the Admiralty's Military Department (*Militärische Abteilung*, or Department A) under the direction of Capt. Eduard von Knorr. The department had three sections: A1 (*Militärische Verwendung der Schiffe* [military utilization of ships]), which had responsibility for operations and operational planning; A2 (*Personalien*), which dealt with personnel matters, particularly the assignment of active and reserve officers during time of war; and A3 (*Militär-wissenschaftliche Angelegenheiten* [military intelligence matters]), which collected and evaluated information about other navies.[10]

The *Dezernent* [chief] of A1, Capt. Eduard Heusner, developed the first operational plan, or O-Plan, against Russia. Heusner anticipated that Germany would have naval superiority in the Baltic and therefore proposed an immediate attack on the Russian fleet at the outbreak of war. His goal, echoing Stenzel's recent ideas, was the destruction of the Russian fleet in a single decisive battle. If the Russians refused open battle and withdrew instead into their well-defended ports, the German fleet would blockade Russian forces with an inner barrier of mines supported by an outer screen of light warships. The fleet's armored frigates would deploy in the Gulf of Finland as a mobile strike force (*Angriffsflotte*) to intercept any Russian ships attempting to break out of the blockade.[11]

The chief of *Dezernat* A2, Cdr. Wilhelm Stubenrauch, drew up the accompanying mobilization plan. He assigned Diederichs to command SMS *Blücher,* a thirty-four-hundred-ton flush-deck corvette, if war broke out. *Blücher,* launched in 1877 as part of the *Bismarck* class, was familiar to Diederichs because he had overseen her refitting in 1878 as a torpedo testing ship. Diederichs's officers would include Lt. Cdr. Hunold von Ahlefeld as executive officer and Lt. Cdr. Adolf Becker as navigator, and Lieutenants (sg) Alfred Marschall-Viebrok, Hermann Lilie, and Adalbert von Colomb as divisional and watch officers.

Diederichs and *Blücher* would serve as part of Adm. Otto Livonius's Light Division. This unit included *Blücher*'s sister ship *Gneisenau* (three thousand tons, sixteen 150-mm guns) as flag, light corvette *Olga* (twenty-four hundred tons, one 150- and two 87-mm guns), *Aviso* (dispatch boat), *Grille* (five hundred tons, one 125- and two 88-mm guns), screw frigate *Arcona* (twenty-four hundred tons, nineteen 150-mm guns), and light corvette *Nymphe* (twelve hundred tons, seventeen 120-meter guns). The Light Division would screen the Angriffsflotte in its advance into Russian waters and then reconnoiter the Russian defenses. If the Russian fleet came out to meet the Germans in open battle, the Light Division would fight its smaller Russian counterparts and attempt torpedo strikes on the main Russian force. In case of blockade, the division would serve as the inshore squadron to watch Russian ports, protect the mine barrier, and provide early warning of an enemy sortie.[12]

Although the crisis waned by the end of the summer, Stosch decided to use the possible conflict as the basis for the annual maneuvers. Planning involved an "Eastern Power" (Russia) entangled in a conflict in the Balkans, with Germany as a belligerent. The Eastern Power would dispatch a naval squadron (four armored frigates) from the Baltic to the Mediterranean at the outbreak of the war with additional orders to attack and destroy the naval bases at Kiel and Wilhelmshaven en route to the Mediterranean. The mission of the defending squadron was to intercept the Eastern Squadron and prevent it from attacking Kiel. This squadron included a division commanded by Cdr. Alfred Tirpitz (*Blücher, Luise*, torpedo tenders *Ulan* and *Friedrichsort*) and a division commanded by Lt. Cdr. Paul Jäschke, fresh from Diederichs's lectures at the Marineakademie, consisting of four *Schütze*-class torpedo boats (fifty-five tons, two 350-mm torpedo tubes). The aggressor force would win if it successfully passed the Friedrichsort fortifications and entered the Kiel fiord; the defending force would prevail if it prevented the Eastern Squadron from entering the fiord. Stosch assigned Diederichs and the other faculty from the Marineakademie to serve as umpires for the exercises. The defending squadron established positions in Fehmarn Sound, which separated Fehmarn Island from the mainland near Lübeck, on the night of 10 September. Tirpitz deployed his ships in line abreast, while Jäschke's torpedo boats took up position on the north side of the sound with orders to attack the Eastern Squadron from the rear. As the aggressor squadron hove into view, Tirpitz's ships used searchlights both to blind and distract the "enemy" ships. The torpedo boats sneaked in undetected to "launch" torpedoes at a range of one hundred meters.

The defenders fell back to Kiel in the second part of the exercise. They now supported the Friedrichsort fortifications and protected a mine barrier in defense of the fiord's mouth. As the aggressor squadron steamed into view at dawn on 11 September and opened fire on the fortifications, the defenders advanced to attack. After-action reports differed as to the outcome. The aggressor commander described the defenders as ineffective, while *Luise's* commander claimed to have fired a successful broadside into *Friedrich Carl*. Diederichs and the other umpires declared the exercise a draw.

The aggressor squadron then steamed into the fiord, passed through an outer barrier of moored mines, and came under fire from shore installations at a range of two nautical miles. Jäschke's torpedo boat division again attacked the aggressor squadron from starboard aft but were driven off by a counter-barrage, claiming to have successfully fired their torpedoes before retreating in the face of gunfire. The umpires discounted the torpedo boat claims but declared that the coastal fortifications had successfully repelled the enemy attack. This concluded the exercise.

Perhaps reflecting his army background, Stosch's formal after-action analysis contained the greatest praise for the role of the Friedrichsort fortifications. He cited the defensive benefits of torpedo boats but failed to perceive any offensive value. His sole conclusion recommended the construction of torpedo-armed launches to be carried aboard battleships.[13]

IN DEFENSE OF GERMAN COASTS

Maneuvers accomplished, Diederichs returned to the Marineakademie to begin the new academic year. Rather than focus on the preparation of his lecture notes, however, he instead began to write a formal, if unofficial, memorandum evaluating both the recent war scare and the fall maneuvers. It is unclear whether Stosch solicited this document or Diederichs simply wrote it on his own. The fact that it now lies filed in Stosch's papers, without copies or indication of circulation, suggests that it was both unofficial and not widely read. In some ways, the memorandum is not particularly original; in other areas, it is quite progressive. It nonetheless seems to have affected both Diederichs's transfer to the planning office of the Admiralty in 1883 and the formulation of later memoranda on the further development of the navy.

Diederichs completed the fifty-page, handwritten memo and submitted it to Stosch in November 1882 under the title "Consideration of the Defense of German Coasts against Sea Powers which Attack Simultaneously from the

Baltic Sea and North Sea."[14] Inspiration for the document derives from several sources, including Diederichs's own professional experiences, the recent maneuvers, Stenzel, and Gen. Helmut von Moltke. In fact, Moltke, chief of the German General Staff, may have provided the strongest impetus. For a decade, he had identified France (revenge for Alsace-Lorraine) and Russia (suspicious of Germany's role in the Balkans) as Germany's likely foes and begun to draw up contingency plans for a two-front war.[15]

In any event, Diederichs's analysis of the August war plans and the September exercises led him to conclude that existing O-plans were inadequate and incomplete. The former failed to comprehend the full value of torpedoes; the latter had been designed without considering the possibility, and greater likelihood, of a two-front war against both Russia and France. Diederichs echoed Moltke's belief that Germany's next conflict would be that two-front war. He postulated that the two powers would launch a simultaneous attack against Germany's North and Baltic Sea coasts. Rather than passively await this assault, Diederichs proposed that the Kaiserliche Marine seize the initiative and counter with an aggressive defense. Diederichs also devised his proposals on the basis that Germany would not have to fight alone but would depend on active support from allies Italy and Austria-Hungary. He therefore expected Austrian forces to block a Russian sortie from the Black Sea and the Italian fleet to counter French forces based in the Mediterranean. This would leave Germany to face remaining French forces in the North Sea and Russian ships in the Baltic.

Germany would nonetheless face a substantial quantitative disadvantage, particularly if the French and Russian forces were ever able to combine their forces. Germany could send twelve armored ships—seven currently stationed at Wilhelmshaven and five at Kiel—against nineteen French and eight Russian battleships. Only seven of the twelve German armored ships, however, were capable of offshore offensive operations. The remaining ships—four armored corvettes and a monitor—would need to remain in the vicinity of their respective bases because of their limited operating ranges and their original design as coastal defense vessels. Enemy forces also had a qualitative advantage. France's capital ships included *Admiral Duperre* (11,000 tons, four 360-mm guns) and *Courbet* (10,500 tons, eighteen 240-mm guns).

Russia had *Petr Veliki* (10,500 tons, four 320-mm guns). Conversely, Germany's three largest warships included the aging armored frigate *König Wilhelm* (10,600 tons, eighteen 240-mm guns) and two *Kaiser*-class ships (8,800 tons, eight 260-mm guns). Among other ways to offset these disadvantages, Diederichs proposed the greater use of torpedo boats.

Diederichs anticipated that the enemy forces would use their superior strength to pursue three strategic goals. They would first blockade the respective German coasts—facing the French in the North Sea and the Russians in the Baltic—with the intent of disrupting German naval operations and coastal trade. Second, they would then seek to link up their forces for joint operations in the Baltic Sea. Finally, they would undertake amphibious landings at various points along the Baltic coast to move overland, first against Kiel and then Berlin.

To counter these potential threats, Diederichs proposed an aggressive two-front defense that contained echoes of Moltke's 1866 campaign against Austria and Hannover and foreshadowed Gen. Alfred von Schlieffen's later plan for war against France and Russia. In a kind of reverse Schlieffen Plan, Diederichs recommended a naval blitzkrieg against Russia in the Baltic and an aggressive defense against the French in the west: "Although it is important to deploy the sortie fleet (*Ausfallflotte*) in Wilhelmshaven and prevent or impede a blockade of our North Sea ports, the primary mission of the navy at the outbreak of the war is to establish control of the Baltic Sea with the bulk of our forces." This suggests an awareness of Napoleonic emphasis on mobility, perhaps translated through Stenzel, that would allow the fleet to defeat its foes in detail. Having defeated Russian forces, Germany could then transfer part of its Baltic squadron to the North Sea to join with the Ausfallflotte against the French. The key, Diederichs argued, was rapidity of attack; the element of surprise would contribute to the campaign's success particularly by preventing the linking up of French and Russian forces. This identification of Russia as Germany's initial foe reflected contemporary naval planning; the addition of France as a second enemy and the need to fight a two-front war is more novel.

Although the Baltic had the higher priority, Diederichs nonetheless recommended a preemptive strike against the French Atlantic bases at Cherbourg and Brest. He believed that the Germans could seize the initiative because they could mobilize their forces more quickly than their opponents. Following this attack, the German fleet could construct a barrier of mine fields or even establish a blockade to prevent French forces from leaving their bases. Additionally, German warships could block the narrow Straits of Dover to prevent a French penetration of the North Sea. "The French," he believed, "would have little ability to launch an effective counterattack if we were able to accomplish this plan." With the French unable to enter the North Sea and thus unable to support their Russian allies, German forces would have an easier time in the Baltic against Russia.

Diederichs constructed a series of possible Baltic scenarios. For example, if the Russian capital ships refused battle on the open sea and instead hid behind protective mine fields, the German Angriffsflotte would be "unable to destroy their armored ships with a major strike." In an ironic anticipation of later Japanese attacks against Russian forces at Port Arthur in 1904, Diederichs proposed a lightning-like raid by shallow-draft torpedo boats in a night attack. If surviving Russian warships then came out of their bases in pursuit of the Germans, the assault fleet would ambush them.

If the Germans were otherwise unable to destroy the Russian fleet, Diederichs then recommended a blockade. This would consist of mine barriers and an inshore squadron of torpedo boats and fast corvettes supported at a distance by the main force concentrated at the mouth of the Gulf of Finland. The size of the blockading squadron depended on Russian strength and the ability of Germany's North Sea squadron to deploy ships into the Baltic to support these operations.

After the anticipated defeat of the Russians in the Baltic, Germany would transfer its capital ships to the North Sea to confront the French threat. "We must keep enemy ships at a sufficient distance from our coastline," he wrote, "to allow our shipping unhindered access to individual harbors." Failure to keep the enemy away would also make German naval operations more difficult: "If the enemy succeeds in blockading our coastline, if he is allowed to overpower us or implement a strategic dispersal along our coasts, he will leave us with the sole alternative of annihilating his forces." That imperative derived from the obvious importance of the Jade basin and the Elbe and Weser estuaries, which would require a significant allocation of naval and financial resources. If the French were indeed able to enter the North Sea,

Diederichs recommended a multilayered coastal defense (warships, mines, and fortifications) supplemented with sorties by the armored ships of the Ausfallflotte and torpedo boats. This plan resembled Jachmann's 1870 strategy, now enhanced by a decade of technological developments.

Diederichs first anticipated that the French would seek to establish a series of offshore positions from which to attack specific sites (*Angriffsobjekte*) along the German coast. He presumed that the French would select these positions "at a sufficient distance from our coast" as to "command the estuaries of the larger rivers or provide disembarkation points suitable for landing on our coasts." He specifically identified British-owned Helgoland, which dominated the Jade basin and the river estuaries, as the primary site and Borkum, which controlled the Ems estuary, as a secondary site for French operations. Noting that French ships had sheltered in the lee of Helgoland during the Franco-German War, he proposed to barricade the island with minefields. He acknowledged that this might elicit an English protest but judged national security a greater priority than diplomatic nicety. He also noted that the Kaiserliche Marine needed to position its own ships at or near Helgoland to disrupt French operations. Borkum was more familiar territory to Diederichs because he had served nearby aboard *Natter* in 1870. Here he focused his defense on an inshore squadron of lighter ships, plus mines and coastal fortifications. He wrote, "We must establish defensive perimeters around our harbors that will prevent enemy attacks but not inhibit our own ability to sortie against the enemy." It was essential, he continued, to always retain the ability for sorties by either the Ausfallflotte or torpedo boats, fighting what he called a "little war" (*klein Krieg*).

The Ausfallflotte formed the core of Diederichs's plan for an aggressive defense and for asserting superiority in the North Sea. This sortie fleet would serve as a mobile strike force that would consist of large armored ships—he used the term *Schlachtschiffe,* battleships—and operate out of Wilhelmshaven. His tactics again resembled naval guerrilla warfare: "We should not launch these sorties against the enemy's main force of battleships but rather against the support ships that carry the enemy's provisions and coal." The ships would also range deep into the English Channel if necessary to prevent the shipment of supplies and reinforcements to the French forces in the North Sea and prevent movement into the Baltic.

To enhance these defensive arrangements, Diederichs emphasized the strategic importance of a canal that would link the Baltic and North Seas, allowing the German fleet to concentrate its forces in either sea without passing through the Baltic straits. Diederichs had seen firsthand the value of such a canal in 1870 when he transited the Eider Canal aboard *Natter*. The Eider Canal, however, was too shallow and narrow to allow the passage of deep-draft warships. Stosch himself had already proposed a new canal in his construction plan for 1873, but the lack of funds prevented any action. Now, however, the threat of a two-front war made a canal even more important strategically. Diederichs therefore recommended the construction of a new and larger sea-level canal that would link the Kiel fiord at Holtenau to the Elbe estuary at Brünsbuttel. Such a canal would allow warships to pass between the Kiel and Wilhelmshaven naval stations in fifteen hours at a steady five-knot pace.[16]

Perhaps Diederichs's most novel contribution dealt with the new torpedo technology, which had proved itself at the "Battle of Fehmarn Sound." Although his experience in the Torpedowesen and aboard *Luise* had shown him that *Fischtorpedos* "are intricate and complex" and thus prone to mechanical failure, he nonetheless believed that their strategic value "outweighs any misgivings." He therefore proposed a greater financial commitment to torpedo research and development. He further examined the tactical value of torpedo boats, which, he said, had assumed "outstanding importance." For example, he postulated an attack against a defended harbor or enemy fleet in which shallow-draft torpedo boats would use their greater speed and maneuverability to force their way through minefields or past other defensive barriers and attack with torpedoes and quick-firing guns. Other torpedo boats, mounting electric searchlights, could illuminate the battlefield for nighttime attacks.

Diederichs therefore recommended the design and construction of three new classes of torpedo boats. The first and largest class would be thirty meters long, carry both torpedoes and quick-firing guns (*Revolverkanonen*), and have a speed of eighteen to twenty-two knots. Their function would include escorting the main battle fleet, scouting enemy forces, and attacking enemy harbors. The second (medium) class would carry a similar armament, have a speed of sixteen to eighteen knots, and operate as an inshore squadron to provide coastal defense. The third (light) class would carry fewer weapons, have a ten- to twelve-knot speed, and escort coastal shipping.

Diederichs acknowledged two obstacles—one professional, one philosophical—to these plans. First, traditionalist members of the officer corps still resented such new and revolutionary warfare and weapons, as he had certainly learned during his days with the Torpedowesen. Then, anticipating arguments that would arise with regard to unrestricted German submarine warfare during World War I, he admitted that torpedo warfare might violate moral or conventional restrictions. He briefly examined the issue of whether the adverse ethical response to such horrific weapons might outweigh the strategic value of torpedoes but quickly concluded, pragmatically, that "effectiveness outweighed ethics." He cited the example of firearms in the fourteenth century, which had initially caused a significant moral aversion until proof of the new weapon's effectiveness eroded philosophical objection.[17]

Although novel and advanced in some respects, Diederichs's memorandum reflected certain conventional standards. It upheld current German naval strategy, anticipating naval war against second-rate naval powers such as Russia and France, but it made no mention of either Britain or operations outside home waters. There are vague references to decisive battles, perhaps under Stenzel's influence, but little language that suggests Mahan or Tirpitz a decade later. This is hardly a criticism, however, since German naval strategy had not yet evolved beyond the limited concept of coastal defense. William's "new course" and Tirpitz's "risk fleet" were still, after all, well in the future. In any event, it is difficult to judge the influence of Diederichs's memorandum, given how little evidence there is of its circulation beyond Stosch.

After submitting the memorandum, Diederichs returned to his primary duties as instructor in gunnery and torpedoes at the Marineakademie for the 1882–83 academic year. His lectures took on new urgency in light of the recent war scare, the summer's operational planning, and the fall's maneuvers and memorandum. The year nonetheless passed without incident, either at Kiel or on the broader diplomatic front.

FRIEDRICH CARL

At the end of the spring term of 1883, Diederichs received orders assigning him to *Friedrich Carl* as first officer for the summer maneuvers. He had served aboard *Friedrich Carl* (seven thousand tons, twenty-two 210-mm guns), an aging armored frigate, as a watch officer in 1872. He now reported aboard on 24 April 1883 at Wilhelmshaven to find that her crew had already begun to place her in service. One week later, he formally reported to her commanding officer, Capt. Friedrich Graf von Hacke, that *Friedrich Carl* was ready for sea.[18]

Rear Adm. Wilhelm von Wickede commanded the maneuver squadron. His ships included three armored frigates besides *Friedrich Carl*: *Kaiser* (flag), *Deutschland,* and *Kronprinz.* On the basis of the 1882 maneuvers and, perhaps, Diederichs's memorandum, he intended to incorporate a variety of exercises involving torpedoes and torpedo boats into the standard summer activities. He acknowledged, however, that he faced two linked obstacles: Many of his fellow officers still questioned the value of torpedoes, and, meanwhile, the fleet lacked personnel trained in their use. In any event, the two imperial shipyards had been busy since fall 1882 mounting torpedo tubes on his warships. He formally activated the training squadron in Wilhelmshaven on 13 May. Following a week of independent drills and operations, the squadron departed the Jade for the Baltic on 21 May.[19]

As first officer, Diederichs set about training *Friedrich Carl*'s crew. Because of the prevailing fiscal circumstances of the German navy, the ship's complement had spent the previous months ashore at the Second Matrosendivision in Wilhelmshaven. Now, Diederichs's primary task was to transform the crew, a mixture of seasoned sailors and raw recruits, into a single, cohesive unit. The ship anchored off the Torpedo Depot, Friedrichsort, to load torpedoes on 29 May and commenced torpedo drills in nearby Eckernförde on 1 June. Initial trials went well, all things considered—despite the comic aspects of having four armored frigates awkwardly maneuvering to simulate firing torpedoes at each other. Engineering, rather than technological, problems soon forced a halt to the exercises, however, as steam plants in *Kaiser, Deutschland,* and *Kronprinz* broke down. Diederichs's work as executive officer had borne fruit; Admiral von Wickede, squadron commander, remarked that *Friedrich Carl* alone operated without problems and commended officers and crew for their good work.[20]

Following repairs at Kiel, the squadron returned to the North Sea in July. Perhaps in acknowledgment of Diederichs's memorandum, the squadron spent a week in and around the Ems estuary. This allowed squadron officers to acquaint themselves with the defensive value of Borkum, the likely first target of a French attack, and the shallow and tricky waters of the Frisian Islands. Wickede next detailed *Kaiser* and *Friedrich Carl* to participate in joint exercises with two *Schütze*-class torpedo boats (fifty-six tons, two 360-mm torpedo tubes) in the Jade. Mechanical problems, fairly standard for the class, forced the temporary suspension of the drills and required Wickede to send the torpedo boats back to Kiel via the Eider Canal for repairs. Additional trials, both in the North and Baltic seas, proved equally disappointing. In his after-action analysis, Wickede complained that the boats broke down repeatedly, suffered equipment and hull damage even in moderate seas, and lacked adequately trained crews. So far as he was now concerned, the prognosis for regular and active use of torpedo boats was not good.[21]

When maneuvers ended in mid-September, *Friedrich Carl* returned to Wilhelmshaven. According to standard procedures, Diederichs spent the next two weeks preparing her for deactivation. As the crew disembarked and marched over to the barracks of the Second Matrosendivision, the officers scattered to new assignments. Diederichs himself received orders to assume duties as artillery director at the Imperial Dockyard in Kiel. Because his five months at sea aboard *Friederich Carl* had again revived his physical problems, he never reported to his new post. Instead, he requested and received a three-month convalescent furlough.[22]

CAPRIVI AND STRATEGIC PLANNING

Six months before Diederichs went on leave, the Kaiserliche Marine underwent a leadership change. Lt. Gen. Leo von Caprivi replaced Stosch as chief of the Admiralty in March 1883, continuing the practice of appointing *Marinegenerale* ("navy generals"). Known for his administrative and organizational skills, Caprivi came to the navy directly from the Ministry of War. Given his military background, Caprivi did little to change the navy's traditional missions, focusing particularly on coastal defense, during his tenure as Admiralty chief (1883–88). According to Tirpitz, Caprivi's conservatism was at least partially due to his constant fear that a two-front land war against France and Russia might break out every spring.[23] As Caprivi acquainted himself with naval issues, he presumably read Diederichs's earlier memorandum outlining the navy's role in such a war. This would explain why Diederichs received new orders in December 1883, which directed him to report to the Admiralty, where Caprivi assigned him as chief of Section (*Dezernat*) A1, Operations (*Militärische Verwendung der Schiffe*). Section A1 had dual responsibilities: the direction of ships on active service and operational planning. Diederichs's new post also allowed him to renew his friendship with Capt. Rudolf Schering, who had an office nearby as the director of the Admiralty's Central Secretariat. Caprivi's interest in Diederichs's earlier work probably accounts for his receiving the Order of the Red Eagle, Fourth Class, in the New Year's honors list on 20 January 1884.[24]

Diederichs's first task was to evaluate a draft document—"Memorandum concerning the Further Development of the Imperial Navy"—prepared by the Admiralty to set the strategic direction and construction program of the Caprivi administration.[25] Diederichs immediately recognized the document's content, since it resembled that of his own memorandum of November 1882 as well as existing naval doctrine. In fact, the basic premise of the Caprivi plan was coastal defense, subordinating all current activities and future developments to that end. Moreover, unlike Stosch's 1873 program, which had intended to direct the navy at least a decade into the future, Caprivi's proposals were more shortsighted, focusing solely on the near term.

The memorandum began with a statement referring to the navy's constant financial problems. Although the document described the navy as a "healthy young organism," it nonetheless complained that "an institution such as the German navy cannot live from hand to mouth." Echoing Stosch's earlier analysis, the document classified ship types according to anticipated missions: *Kreuzer* for overseas service, *Schlachtschiffe* (battleships) for limited offensive operations, and torpedo boats for coastal defense. Because the navy lacked adequate financial support, it could not afford to overlook a single technological initiative (more torpedo boats) and needed to set more careful spending priorities (fewer battleships).

Based on fiscal realities and expected missions, the Admiralty memorandum continued the navy's emphasis on coastal defense. This had the advantage, the document noted, of freeing the army for other duties and giving the navy a vested interest in every part of Germany's coasts. The memorandum even proposed giving the navy responsibility for coastal fortifications, which would require an attendant increase in budget, matériel, and personnel. To this end, the document proposed the construction of what would become the *Siegfried* class of coastal battleships (thirty-seven hundred tons, three 240-mm guns) and several categories of torpedo boats.

In fact, the memorandum placed a significant emphasis on torpedo boats. Torpedo boats were valuable economically and strategically to a second-rate naval power that could not afford a fully developed battle fleet. Even though torpedoes were "the most complicated weapon in existence," torpedo boats could make a major contribution to coastal defense. A large number of well-directed boats could harass a blockading force, particularly at night. The document noted, "The value of torpedo boats lies in their ability to suddenly appear out of the protection of night and fog, from the wake of battleships, or from a hiding place on the coast." Torpedo boats also possessed an economic value, using less coal and personnel than battleships. The memorandum therefore proposed the immediate construction of seventy torpedo boats (eighty to one hundred tons, three torpedo tubes) even if the new program required the navy to postpone the construction of armored ships and cruisers.

Caprivi's Admiralty memorandum revealed an ambivalent attitude toward battleships. Under regular circumstances, battleships would form the core of Germany's fleet. "The world position of the German Empire," the document noted, "depends on armored battleships and the security provided by a coordinated and effective high seas fleet." Elsewhere, the memo continued, "There is no doubt whatsoever that the German fleet could not make even modest claims to sea power without armored ships." Torpedoes, after all, would always remain secondary to the heavy batteries carried by battleships on the high seas: "Artillery still stands in the first line of decisive naval weapons." The problem with battleships, however, centered on a lack of funds. Because battleships were expensive to construct, man, and maintain, the memorandum recommended that the navy concentrate its limited funding on coastal defenses rather than on operations on the high seas.

Additionally, the memo contained an equally ambiguous appraisal of the emerging strategy of commerce raiding, or "cruiser war" (*Kreuzerkrieg*). Commerce raiding had recently come into vogue with the ideas of French Adm. Théophile Aube and his *Jeune École* or "Young School," which identified Britain as France's major foe. Because of the overwhelming superiority of the Royal Navy, Aube proposed that France avoid open battle but instead focus on destroying Britain's economic foundation through commerce raiding, supplemented by attacks on British ports and coastal trade by battleships and torpedo boats. His pragmatic motto: "Ruthlessly flee the strong, ruthlessly attack the weak."[26]

Because German naval planning still identified France and Russia as more likely foes, *Kreuzerkrieg* had only minimal value. Neither France nor Russia depended on overseas commerce to the extent that Britain did; commerce raiding had no great strategic advantage in a war against them. Moreover, the memo notes, the newer merchant ships could outrun their attackers: "While in old times the warship was able to carry a greater weight of sails and a larger crew, the modern merchantman now has an advantage in speed and maneuverability [over cruisers]." The document nonetheless failed to reject *Kreuzerkrieg* outright—helping to confuse German strategic thinking for another decade. In any event, cruisers lacked "battle value" in a European war against armored ships (i.e., battleships), whose primary purpose was to seize and maintain control of the seas. Cruisers, however, still performed a valuable service overseas, where they could show the flag, protect overseas interests, and "represent German honor with strength."[27]

Except for its standard emphasis on coastal defense, the memorandum provided no clear strategic direction for the further development of the German navy. It simply reiterated the underlying assumption that Germany would continue to confront France and Russia as likely foes. In terms of a construction program, it charted a rather equivocal middle course between battleships and cruisers, while hinting at an informal adoption of Jeune École, with its greater emphasis on torpedo boats. This confusing direction would last for more than a decade.

INTO THE HEART OF DARKNESS

With the Admiralty's attention focused on coastal defense and the likelihood of war against continental foes, little was left for Diederichs to do. His preoccupations soon shifted from strategic planning to another issue: imperialism in Africa.

Chancellor Bismarck had long opposed colonial adventures, preferring instead to focus on continental matters and the protection of his new German state. Thus, as he famously noted, "My map of Africa lies in Europe. Here is Russia, there is France, and here in the middle are we. That is my map of Africa." Yet, by 1884, German public opinion had come to demand colonies, particularly since unification had spurred the growth of German nationalism and the rapid expansion of German trade overseas. Bismarck himself had little choice but to convert to imperialism.

For obvious reasons, the navy now emerged as the "vanguard of imperialism." German warships quickly followed the course set by German traders in Africa, establishing three protectorates in 1884: Southwest Africa in April, Togo in July, and Cameroon in August. To consolidate and extend these acquisitions, the navy dispatched a flying squadron to Africa under the command of Rear Adm. Eduard Knorr. Therefore, when Zanzibar resisted similar encroachments early in the next year, Germany was ready: A naval show of force quickly persuaded the sultan to accept a German protectorate and the establishment of German East Africa in August 1885.[28]

One of the squadron's ships was SMS *Stosch* (three thousand tons, sixteen 150-mm guns), a flush-decked corvette of the *Bismarck* class. Her commanding officer, Capt. Georg von Nostitz, suffered a fatal heart attack on 5 August. Cdr. Richard Geissler, *Prinz Adalbert*'s first officer, assumed temporary command of SMS *Stosch* until Berlin could dispatch a more senior officer. When the news reached the Admiralty, Diederichs politicked with his superiors to secure the new post. Although the slot called for a full captain (*Kapitän zur See*), Diederichs was a senior commander, outranking Geissler by three and one-half years and thirty-three files on the commanders' list. He was also in the zone for promotion to captain. Moreover, he was well acquainted with the African operations, since his work for the last fifteen months had concentrated on planning support for that mission. His brief campaign was successful. An imperial order, dated 9 August 1885, relieved Diederichs of his post in the Admiralty and appointed him as *Stosch*'s new commanding officer. Diederichs knew, however, that his command would be brief. The Admiralty had already directed that *Stosch*, overseas since 1881, return home to await conversion as a training ship. Nonetheless, Diederichs said a quick good-bye to Henni and the boys, boarded a private steamer at Hamburg-Altona on 12 August 1885, and arrived at Zanzibar to assume command of *Stosch* on 7 September 1885, his forty-second birthday.[29]

Diederichs had barely begun to move into his quarters aboard *Stosch* when he received new orders. A recent, and brief, colonial conflict with Spain in regard to the Caroline Islands in the Pacific had convinced the Admiralty to provide security for the new colonies. The Admiralty therefore directed Commo. Karl Paschen to organize a new squadron, which would include *Stosch* (flag), *Prinz Adalbert,* and *Gneisenau* and proceed immediately to West African waters.

As the ships rounded the Cape of Good Hope, *Stosch* developed engine problems. Paschen promptly shifted his flag to *Prinz Adalbert* and ordered Diederichs to steam into Cape Town for repairs. By the time Diederichs and *Stosch* rejoined the squadron in the Bight of Benin in November, the crisis had ended. The Admiralty therefore directed *Gneisenau* to return to Knorr's command in East Africa and ordered *Stosch* and *Prinz Adalbert* to set course for home. After an uneventful voyage, the two ships reached Wilhelmshaven on 21 December 1885.[30]

AT HOME IN KIEL

Following *Stosch*'s deactivation ten days later, Diederichs joined Henni and the children in nearby Leer to celebrate a belated Christmas. The New Year saw him receive new orders to return to academic life at the Marineakademie in Kiel for the spring term. Anticipating another four-year tour in Kiel, Diederichs and Henni decided to plant roots. Tired of leasing apartments, which they had done for their entire married life, they also felt that the stability of a private home would benefit Fritz (now thirteen) and Herman (eight), who had spent their lives in a series of temporary residences.[31] They purchased a hillside lot at Reventlowallee 13, conveniently located within walking distance of the Marineakademie and with a beautiful view of the Kiel fiord, and began to build a house. Diederichs himself designed the house which cost thirty thousand marks to construct and furnish.

Much to his pleasure, Diederichs also found that his new superior was Capt. Rudolf Schering. Schering himself had just assumed a newly created post as head of the navy's various training commands—*Direktion des Bildungswesens der Marine*—while serving simultaneously as director of the two schools. Diederichs himself served as instructor of naval history and strategy, the post held earlier by Stenzel, and as deputy director of the Marineakademie. Since Schering was often absent, touring other naval training facilities, Diederichs acted as acting director—an appropriate post, particularly following his promotion to Kapitän zur See on 18 December 1886.[32]

Diederichs certainly had abundant material in the way of new experiences and available resources for his courses. His recent service aboard *Stosch* provided material for his lectures on recent naval history, while he drew from a large body of notes prepared earlier by Stenzel for naval strategy. For naval tactics, Diederichs used his copy of "Tactical Exercises for the Fleet," formulated by Capt. Hans Koester, which he had evaluated while still serving as *Dezernent A1* in 1885. This document, seen now, amply confirms Tirpitz's complaint that tactics had remained largely unchanged since the days of sail: It describes such traditional tactics as ship-to-ship action at near and distant artillery ranges and the use of rams, along with newer tactics using torpedoes.[33] But Diederichs and the navy now had to incorporate ideas arising from the Jeune École. Noting that modern cruisers now had the speed to overtake merchant ships, Caprivi admitted in June 1886 that cruiser war had strategic value after all. His somewhat hesitant endorsement of *Kreuzerkrieg*, particularly in a war against a far superior enemy fleet, confused German strategic planning for a decade in what Tirpitz later called the "ten lost years."[34]

By the end of spring term 1887, Diederichs's health again begun to cause problems. Kiel may have possessed beautiful scenery with the tree-clad slopes above the blue fiord, but it also had cold, damp winters with chilling winds off the Baltic Sea. In fact, both Diederichs and Henni suffered from occasional poor health. She had developed signs of arthritis early on, while he still regularly endured pulmonary problems. After consultations with naval physician Gutschow, whom Diederichs had first met at Yokohama in 1879, Diederichs again requested convalescent leave. The furlough, which lasted from 12 April to 20 July 1887, meant that Diederichs missed the first weeks of summer maneuvers in the North and Baltic Seas. Any disappointment arising from this circumstance quickly receded when Caprivi awarded him the *Dienstauszeichnungs-Kreuz* (Distinguished Service Cross) and assigned him to command the Third Division of the *Manövergeschwader* (maneuver squadron).[35] He hoisted his broad pennant aboard SM Armored Gunboat *Mücke* (twelve hundred tons, one 350-mm guns, two 350-mm torpedo tubes) on 16 August. The division included three other *Wespe*-class armored gunboats: *Viper, Salamander,* and *Camäleon.* Designed and constructed in the late 1870s, the gunboats provided inshore and mobile defense for the Jade and the river estuaries.[36]

The 1887 maneuvers were the largest in the history of the German navy. Vice Adm. Alexander Graf von Monts commanded the entire force, with Rear Admiral Paschen in charge of the North Sea squadron and Vice Admiral Blanc directing the Baltic maneuver squadron. Diederichs had already missed the ceremonial aspects of the maneuvers, which included a visit to the annual Cowes regatta in England and the start of construction on the new Kiel Canal. He had returned in time to participate in the strategic and tactical exercises in which the *Manöverflotte*'s two squadrons took turns simulating attacks against the other's bases (Kiel and Wilhelmshaven). At one point, the maneuvers produced an interesting picture of the Kaiserliche Marine's near future as Cdr. Alfred Tirpitz led the Fourth Division's fourteen modern torpedo boats in attacks against aging armored frigates *Friedrich Carl* and *König Wilhelm*.[37]

Diederichs's own experiences were equally mixed. *Mücke* and the other armored gunboats proved to be poor sea boats in the rough chop of the North Sea. Likewise, their gun crews could not fire the main 350-mm gun because high winds caused the boats' low freeboard to ship considerable amounts of water. The boats also lacked maneuverability and consequently were at a disadvantage in war games with the more agile torpedo boats. The experience confirmed that the class had little value beyond inshore and riverine defense.[38] When he resumed his teaching post at the Marineakademie at the conclusion of the maneuvers in September, Diederich incorporated the lessons learned into his lectures on naval strategy. His service again brought him to the attention of the crown. Kaiser Wilhelm I awarded him the Order of the Royal Crown, Third Class, in January 1888.[39]

At the end of the 1887–88 academic year, Diederichs received orders to direct an *Admiralstabsreise,* literally a "naval staff tour" but more like a working sea retreat for developing combat competence. Recently adopted by Caprivi, these trips were floating war games deliberately copied from the military *Kriegspiel,* which the Prussian army had used since 1810 to train staff officers, evaluate war plans, and improvise new strategies and tactics. The primary intention of the Admiralstabsreise, held in the spring, was to develop the strategic and tactical program for the ensuing summer maneuvers. The possibility of a two-front war with Russia and France was a standard subject.[40]

Diederichs boarded SMS *Falke* in Wilhelmshaven on 30 April 1888 and departed for two weeks of exercises in the North Sea. He brought with him all eight officers from the Marineakademie's second-year class to participate in the war games. Given his recent activities, Diederichs was the ideal officer to administer the games. The Admiralstabsreise's first phase simulated a series of defensive torpedo attacks against a fleet attacking Wilhelmshaven. The second phase tested elements of a new operational plan formulated in October 1887. Titled "Coastal War in the North Sea," the plan postulated a defensive war against a stronger and unnamed western power (France). The navy would concentrate its forces in the North Sea to defend the Jade Bight and the Weser and Elbe estuaries. Sorties by the aging *Ausfallkorvetten* and the armored gunboats of the *Wespe* class would undertake a war of attrition against superior French forces and prevent the passage of the aggressor forces into the Baltic Sea. When the exercises ended on 16 May, Diederichs disembarked for a three-month furlough combining a summer vacation with additional convalescent leave.[41]

He returned to active duty in time for summer maneuvers. On 15 August, he again hoisted his broad pennant in SMS *Mücke*. His command, now configured as the Fourth Division, an armored flotilla (*Panzerfahrzeugsflottille*), included the three other armored gunboats *Viper, Salamander,* and *Camäleon*. A technical problem slowed *Mücke's* activation when an officer from the *Torpedoversuchs-Kommission* had difficulty installing new torpedo technology. When the complications threatened to delay *Mücke's* participation in the maneuvers, the Admiralty simply ordered Diederichs and *Mücke* to proceed without the new torpedo armament.[42]

As expected, the exercises borrowed from Diederich's earlier Admiralstabsreise. The initial phase focused particularly on the defense of the Weser estuary and Wilhelmshaven. During one phase, the Third Division (SMS *Blitz* and fourteen torpedo boats) and Fourth Division sortied from Wilhelmshaven against an "aggressor" squadron consisting of the armored frigates and nascent *Schlachtschiffe* of the First and the Second Divisions. A second, similar exercise tested the value of the armored gunboats and torpedo boats in conjunction with the Jade coastal fortifications. The defending forces achieved some success but not without strategic and technological difficulty.[43]

After maneuvers ended in September 1888, Diederichs again returned to the Marineakademie to transform his recent experiences into course lectures. His contributions to the issue of defending Germany's coasts brought him to the attention of the army, which arranged for him to receive the *Festungs-Inspection* medal in the new year's list of royal and imperial honors.[44]

Later that spring, Diederichs received orders to direct another Admiralstabsreise. Accompanied by a Marineakademie class, he boarded SMS *Grille,* the former royal yacht, on 8 April 1889 for the two-week exercises. The program again involved the defense of German coasts with the addition, somewhat appropriately, of inshore operations along the North Sea coast. As usual, the floating war games anticipated the 1889 maneuvers. During the course of the exercises, *Grille* steamed through familiar waters for Diederichs, including the Frisian Islands and the Ems estuary.[45]

Diederichs had secured command of SMS *Sachsen* for the subsequent maneuvers. The lead ship of a new class of battleship, *Sachsen* displaced eight thousand tons and carried a primary battery of six 260-mm guns. Diederichs's first mission was to accompany the Manöverflotte to Portsmouth, England, to participate in the annual Cowes regatta. Seven German battleships escorted the new Kaiser Wilhelm II (see chapter 5) to England to visit his grandmother, Queen Victoria, and observe the regatta. The gathering of British naval might impressed the young emperor, who wore the uniform of a British admiral for the ceremonies. The fleet then returned to the North Sea to apply the principles developed during Diederichs's recent Admiralstabsreise. The emperor awarded Diederichs with the Royal Crown Order, Second Class, for his contributions to the exercises.[46]

Once again, Diederichs returned to the Marineakademie after the maneuvers, for what proved to be his final academic year. Before the end of the spring term 1890, he received new orders appointing him director of the *Kaiserliche Werft,* the Imperial Shipyard, at Kiel.[47] For the last six weeks of the term, he shuttled back and forth between the Marineakademie on the west side of the Kiel fiord and the shipyard on the east side. When the academic year ended, he assumed his new job full-time. As he cleaned out his desk at the Marineakademie, he could look back on a successful decade of service. He had developed a solid career in the navy's academic branch, earned a fine reputation as a war planner both from his 1882 memorandum and his tour with the Admiralty's war plans division, personally witnessed the initial foundation of Germany's overseas empire, and become fully involved in the fleet's strategic development through his courses at the Marineakademie and his direction of successive staff tours. He must have wondered what the next decade would bring.

5

The Kaiser's Navy: Diederichs and the New Course, 1890–1897

Diederichs's transfer from the Marineakademie to the Kaiserliche Werft coincided with the emergence of Kaiser Wilhelm II and his "New Course" (*Neue Kurs*), which intended to develop Germany into a world power. This period also witnessed the rise of Diederichs's junior colleague, Alfred Tirpitz, who now began to develop strategic ideas that would ultimately lead Germany to challenge the superiority of the British Royal Navy and threaten the security of the British Empire. Diederichs viewed these events with some misgivings, and his response to them that would eventually come to threaten his continuing naval service.

WILHELM II AND THE NEW COURSE

The new kaiser's paternal grandfather was Kaiser Wilhelm I of Germany; his maternal grandmother was Queen Victoria of Great Britain. His parents, Crown Prince Friedrich Wilhelm and Crown Princess Victoria, were liberal outcasts in conservative Germany. His difficult and traumatic birth on 27 January 1859 left him with a withered left arm and a temperament marked by a sense of inferiority. Educated by a succession of doctrinaire tutors under his grandfather's direction, Wilhelm became ideologically and personally estranged from his parents and developed an abiding ambivalence toward Great Britain, whose navy and empire he envied.

Wilhelm succeeded to the throne at the age of twenty-nine on 15 June 1888, upon the death of his father, Kaiser Friedrich III. Friedrich himself had ruled only briefly, assuming imperial office after the death of his father, Wilhelm I, on 9 March 1888. Historians still speculate about the course of German history if liberal Friedrich, already suffering from terminal throat cancer at the time of his succession, had led Germany into the twentieth century rather than his conservative son.

Once he assumed the throne, Wilhelm II discovered that he had to share power with Chancellor Otto von Bismarck. Bismarck had worked well with the grandfather, Wilhelm I, but could never get along with the grandson. The young emperor resented and resisted sharing power with the aging Iron Chancellor and tried to oust him from the day of his succession. In return, Bismarck briefly considered a constitutional coup d'etat in 1890 but, at the age of 75, decided that he no longer had the political will for such a fight. When he resigned on 20 March 1890, Wilhelm II appointed the more compliant Caprivi as Germany's new chancellor. Having rejected Bismarck, Wilhelm also rejected Bismarck's policies, using the nautical metaphors "dropping the pilot" and "steering a new course" to mark his new direction for Germany.

As emperor, Wilhelm surrounded himself with courtiers who shared his faults and penchant for mediocrity. After his experiences with Bismarck, he chose advisers who used flattery to steer his decision making. Thereafter, he often rejected reasonable advice if it went against his existing prejudices and opinions. Wilhelm was arrogant, emotional, inconsistent, romantic, anti-intellectual, and spoiled. In many ways, he was Louis XVI without Marie Antoinette.[1]

While on active duty, Diederichs never openly questioned the emperor's decisions or policies. Only after his retirement did he feel comfortable with offering criticism. He disliked Wilhelm's arrogance and despised the emperor's tendency to surround himself with sycophants. Diederichs deplored dishonesty and deception, two characteristics necessary for the flatterers and yes-men who populated the imperial court. Equally, he had no interest in the power and influence that came with such conduct. Diederichs preferred honesty and simplicity of thought and deed—elements, he eventually discovered, that were not welcome at the court. (See chapter 8.)[2]

The emperor may have had many vices, but he had one virtue. From an early age, he had developed an interest in naval matters. As a child, he had a full-rigged frigate that sailed the lakes around Potsdam and a large mock ship on the grounds of the royal palace. He enjoyed reading nautical fiction and non-fiction.[3] He first met Diederichs in 1869 during a cruise aboard royal yacht *Grille*. His younger brother, Prince Heinrich (1862–1929), entered the navy at fifteen, retiring as a grand admiral in 1918. When Queen Victoria made her German grandson an admiral of the fleet at the Cowes regatta in August 1889, Wilhelm wrote his uncle, Edward, Prince of Wales, "Fancy wearing the same uniform as St. Vincent and Nelson. It is enough to make me giddy."[4] After his coronation, Wilhelm broke a long tradition of the Hohenzollern "soldier kings" to make a naval officer his primary military adjutant.[5]

Accordingly, Wilhelm took seriously article 53 of the constitution, which placed the Kaiserliche Marine under his direct command. He therefore replaced Caprivi with Vice Adm. Alexander Graf von Monts as Admiralty chief in July 1888. After three successive generals (Roon, Stosch, Caprivi), Monts became the first naval officer to serve as the navy's senior administrator. (Caprivi returned to the army before succeeding Bismarck as chancellor in 1890.)

Following Monts's advice, Wilhelm decided to abolish the Admiralty in 1889 and replace it with a structure resembling the army's tripartite division. The emperor first created the Naval Cabinet (*Marinekabinett,* or MK) to advise him on personnel decisions and other naval matters. Capt. Gustav Freiherr von Senden-Bibran, a bachelor who possessed a lifelong devotion to the navy and an equivalent dislike for the British, became the first chief of the Naval Cabinet and held the post until 1906. The emperor then dissolved the Admiralty, which had existed since 1872, and divided its powers into operational and administrative branches. The *Oberkommando der Marine,* exercised operational command of the navy through its commander in chief, Vice Adm. Max von der Goltz, who served in the post from 1889 to 1895. Goltz and his staff prepared operational plans, developed strategy and tactics, and planned the annual maneuvers. The *Reichsmarineamt,* or RMA, the Imperial Naval Office, was a cabinet-level office headed by a state secretary, an active flag officer, who served as the navy's administrative head. He planned naval construction and maintenance programs, directed the procurement of naval material, and represented the navy in the Reichstag. Rear Adm. Eduard Heusner served briefly in the post until replaced by Rear Adm. Friedrich von Hollmann in April 1890. Tirpitz succeeded Hollmann in June 1897.

This tripartite division made for interesting service politics. Senden, as head of the MK, particularly as his seniority grew over the next decade, became the emperor's naval eminence grise. Of the other two naval authorities, the OKM was *prima inter pares* because of its operational and planning functions. The administrative RMA, which represented the navy in the Reichstag, nonetheless exercised significant influence because of its "power of the purse." Thus, an inevitable conflict developed over strategic differences throughout the 1890s. The fact that each of these three officers had immediate and individual access (*Immediatbericht*) to the emperor also increased the potential for intraservice rivalry. For example, Senden had a standing appointment to meet with Wilhelm, either in Berlin or Potsdam, on Tuesday mornings. Goltz, the OKM commander in chief, briefed the emperor on Monday mornings with a formal presentation (*Immediatvortrag*) on any number of subjects. The state secretary (Heusner, Hollmann, or Tirpitz, in succession) had his audience on Tuesday afternoons.[6]

KAISERLICHE WERFT

Meanwhile, Diederichs initially had observed these momentous events from his relatively quiet post at the Marineakademie. However, just as the clash between Wilhelm and Bismarck reached its climax in early 1890, Diederichs received the new orders appointing him as director (*Oberwerftdirektor*) of the Imperial Shipyard, Kiel. He succeeded Rear Adm. Viktor Valois, a longtime friend and correspondent, who had just gained appointment as commander of the Cruiser Squadron overseas. Diederichs did not even have a chance to finish the spring term, assuming his new duties at the Kaiserliche Werft on 10 March 1890. His new staff included Hafenbau-Direktor Georg Franzius, who held a joint appointment at the Marineakademie, and Cdr. August Thiele (married to Henni's sister Hanni), who served as information director.[7]

Opened in 1867, the Imperial Shipyard at Kiel contained facilities for the construction and repair of the navy's warships. Situated between Gaarden and Ellerbek on the southeast side of the fiord, the Kiel yard was the largest of the three *Kaiserliche Werften*. It included six full-sized docks for capital ships, three smaller construction docks, and nine slips for torpedo boats. Personnel, which eventually grew to more than sixty-three hundred white- and blue-collar workers, had access to day care, schools, and recreational facilities. As Oberwerftdirektor, Diederichs also had the responsibility for the development of Kiel as a commercial and military port, an experience that served him in good stead at Kiao-chou in 1897. (See chapter 6.)[8]

The new post required some family decisions, because the Diederichses still owned a house on Reventlowallee on the west side of the fiord. Although Diederichs could have commuted to work by steam launch every day, he and Henni decided instead to sell their house and move into an apartment in Gaarden, just outside the shipyard's front gate. In the ensuing transaction, they sold their house for thirty-five thousand marks, making a profit of five thousand marks over their original investment.[9]

The transition from an academic post to a technical command was not always easy for Diederichs. His immediate superior, Vice Adm. Eduard Knorr, chief of the Kiel naval station, noted in Diederichs's annual fitness report in January 1891 that he was somewhat out of place as *Werft* director. Knorr nonetheless praised Diederichs for his versatility, expertise, professionalism, and dependability. He further concluded that Diederichs would prove fully capable by the end of his tour and considered him quite qualified for flag rank.[10]

One major problem that Diederichs faced was the anarchic nature of German naval construction in the early 1890s. Because the Kaiserliche Marine still lacked a unified strategic vision, the Kiel shipyard simultaneously built *Siegfried*-class battleships (thirty-eight hundred tons, three 240-mm guns) for coastal defense and *Bussard*-class light cruisers (eighteen hundred tons, eight 105-mm guns) for overseas service. At the same time, private shipyards elsewhere in Kiel constructed *Brandenburg*-class battleships (10,700 tons, six 280-mm guns) for squadron warfare. From his second-floor office in the Werft administrative building, Diederichs could watch workers in the Germania shipyard in nearby Gaarden build the triple-screw *Kaiserin Augusta* (sixty-three hundred tons, four 150-mm and eight 105-mm guns), a new class of *Auslandskreuzer*.[11]

At the same time, Capt. Alfred Thayer Mahan, an American naval officer and historian, began to emerge as the severest critic of such strategic chaos. From his academic position at the Naval War College, Newport, Rhode Island, Mahan had in 1890 published *The Influence of Sea Power upon History,* which immediately caused a revolution in naval thought. Mahan argued that the primary goal of naval power was to gain command of the sea. This was best achieved, he believed, by using a concentrated battle fleet, consisting of battleships, to sweep one's enemy from the sea. He further contended that commerce raiding could not achieve this goal in part because it dispersed naval assets and required a global network of bases for logistical and technical support. Mahan's ideas quickly created a new standard for the measurement of power, as "world power" replaced "great power" in the lexicon of international prestige. Whereas continental territory and military size defined great-power status, now world power stood on three interdependent legs: naval power, overseas empire, and international trade. Mahan thus equated world power with sea power, which the Germans promptly translated into *Weltmacht und Seemacht.* In this melding of navalism and imperialism, sea power established and defended the colonial empire, whose revenues subsidized naval operations and whose territory supplied the navy with overseas bases.[12]

Kaiser Wilhelm soon became attracted to Mahanian ideas. The link between *Seemacht* and *Weltmacht* particularly appealed to the ambitious emperor. He later wrote a British friend, "I am just now not reading but devouring Captain Mahan's book and am trying to learn it by heart. It is a first class work and classical in all points."[13] Based on his reading, Wilhelm now sought a German Mahan. Coincidentally, on 6 April 1891, he hosted a formal dinner to honor retired Gen. Helmut von Moltke at the Kiel naval station. Wilhelm invited his officers to discuss existing naval conditions in the context of Mahanian principles. When no one offered any novel or unconventional thought, Wilhelm chastised them for their lack of originality. Only Capt. Alfred Tirpitz, chief of staff of the naval station, stepped up, as he later wrote, "to describe how I conceived the development of the navy."[14]

Tirpitz, in fact, had already begun to set his ideas to paper. In a memorandum entitled "Our Further Maritime and Military Development," he rejected the popular concept of the cruiser-based Jeune École and argued that battleships alone were capable of achieving victory on the high seas. He therefore rejected past operational planning, relegating plans like Diederichs's 1882 proposals to the naval dustbin, and simply ignored extracontinental considerations and traditional expectations for coastal defense. He argued further that the navy must immediately overhaul its training exercises, which still emphasized ship-to-ship action, and focus instead on evolutions necessary for squadron warfare (*Geschwaderkrieg*).[15] Tirpitz produced a second memorandum in late 1891—"Memorandum Concerning the Reorganization of the Armored Fleet"—that focused on naval readiness and again emphasized the strategic importance of the "open-sea battle" fought by battleships.[16] The two documents earned Tirpitz appointment as chief of staff to the OKM in January 1892 and a reputation as the Kaiserliche Marine's new strategic prodigy.

Wilhelm's conversion to battleships and a battle fleet was nonetheless incomplete. The emperor and Admiral Hollmann of the Reichsmarineamt continued to support a substantial role for cruisers and commerce raiding, compelling Tirpitz to complain that the RMA "was still working for a cruiser war; it even urged the Emperor in this direction."[17] Likewise, Senden, as chief of the Marinekabinett, also whispered in the emperor's ear on behalf of cruisers. This somewhat schizophrenic approach led to what Lambi refers to as "incompetent" naval planning, particularly since the battle for Wilhelm's soul between cruiser advocates and battleship proponents would continue for some years to come.[18]

Diederichs, too, was somewhat ambivalent about these trends. He had no great strategic attachment to cruisers or cruiser war but, on the other hand, was not obsessed with battleships, either. However, unlike Tirpitz, he preferred to factor both coastal defense and overseas operations into any new strategic formula. Moreover, Diederichs preferred to avoid naval and imperial policies that alienated Great Britain. He finally broke with Tirpitz once it became clear to him that Tirpitz identified Britain as Germany's primary foe and desired to construct a fleet accordingly.[19]

In any event, Diederichs had begun to consider the possibility of leaving the navy. Already unhappy with a variety of circumstances—health, professional frustrations, emerging strategic considerations—Diederichs became even more discontented in August 1891 when he learned that the emperor intended to transfer him to a lesser post at the Wilhelmshaven naval station. He immediately complained to Senden, whom he had known since the

Niobe cruise of 1865, that he resented the proposed transfer, which he interpreted as criticism of his current performance at the Kiel shipyard. He therefore intended to seek early retirement, using his chronic health problems as the excuse. Senden, who advised the emperor on personnel issues, immediately sought help from Tirpitz and Oldekop to persuade Diederichs to reconsider. Senden explained that the emperor's intention was not to punish Diederichs but, rather, to acknowledge his growing reputation as a professional troubleshooter who could fill a variety of disparate posts. When the campaign worked and Diederichs decided remain in the navy, Senden was relieved that he had proved reasonable and did "not throw in the towel" ("die Flinte ins Korn zu werfen"). The incident nonetheless revealed an intriguing element of Diederichs's character that would cause him problems a decade later. Senden complained to Tirpitz that Diederichs had shown himself willing to challenge the emperor's wishes. This bordered on disloyalty so far as Senden was concerned. "I find this appalling," he wrote, "and can explain his behavior only in that he assumed the reassignment was meant to be a hint [of no confidence]. God knows, Diederichs has no reason to assume this."[20]

Diederichs's next fitness report—January 1892—confirmed his versatility and effectiveness. Knorr noted that Diederichs "performs any duty well" and had developed the reputation as a talented officer with excellent skills and high character. Knorr again recommended him for promotion to flag rank. Hollman, who oversaw ship construction as state secretary of the RMA, added a note citing Diederichs for his "extremely capable" work as shipyard director.[21] Wilhelm affirmed these positive evaluations when he promoted Diederichs to rear admiral on 20 January 1892. Diederichs became one of fourteen flag officers, which included five vice admirals and nine rear admirals. (The Kaiserliche Marine did not get its first admiral, Goltz, until 2 September 1892.)[22]

To confirm that he truly merited promotion, Diederichs decided that a professional visit to shipyards in the United States would enhance his ability to administer the Kiel Werft. Since the emergence of Mahanian ideas in 1890, the U.S. Navy had recently experienced many of the same strategic and technological pressures as the German fleet.[23] Believing that he could learn much from his American counterparts, he requested a forty-five-day furlough to visit Washington, D.C., Chicago, and Newport, Rhode Island. Permission granted, he thereupon purchased a second-class ticket aboard SS *Normannia* of the Hamburg-America Line, departing from Hamburg on 11 May 1893.[24]

After a brief stop in New York to tour the navy yard there, Diederichs arrived in Washington late on the evening of 23 May. His official host was Cdr. French E. Chadwick, who had visited Germany in 1878 to evaluate naval training methods and had recently become chief of the Bureau of Equipment. In the room that Chadwick had arranged for him at the Metropolitan Club, Diederichs barely had a chance to unpack before he received an invitation from the British ambassador to attend a reception celebrating the birthday of Queen Victoria. Escorted by Commander and Mrs. Chadwick and accompanied by the German ambassador, Diederichs attended the reception at the British embassy.[25]

Once he had fulfilled his social obligations, Diederichs began the professional part of his visit. Guided by Chadwick, he spent several days visiting the facilities at the Washington Navy Yard. Although the yard no longer constructed warships, it had become the center for the design and development of naval ordnance with the opening of the Naval Gun Factory in 1886. There, Diederichs watched yard workers preparing to cast 8-inch guns for U.S. cruiser *Olympia,* then under construction at the Philadelphia Navy Yard.[26]

After taking a sightseeing tour of the American capital, Diederichs entrained for Chicago and the Columbian Exposition. The World's Fair celebrated both the discovery of America in the past and the development of new technology for the future. Diederichs examined a series of technological exhibits, including displays of Krupp guns and demonstrations of Worthington pumping engines, and toured the German village to see familiar arts and crafts.[27] Diederichs returned to the East Coast via Montreal, enjoying a respite from the spring humidity and large crowds of tourist-packed Chicago. He stayed overnight at the Windsor Hotel, where he dined in some comfort—a receipt notes that he paid $4.40 for dinner and wine—before proceeding to Newport, Rhode Island.[28]

Newport was the home of the two significant naval facilities: the Naval War College and the Torpedo Research Station. Chadwick had reserved a room for him at the Newport Reading Room, a men's club, and arranged for guided tours of the two naval institutions. The U.S. Navy had established the Naval Torpedo Station on Goat Island in 1869. Diederichs discovered that American torpedo development resembled its German counterpart. The Americans had evaluated a series of disappointing torpedo designs before adopting a Whitehead-licensed torpedo in 1891.[29] The Americans had opened the Naval War College in 1884 as a postgraduate academic facility for aspiring young officers. Mahan had held a position there—instructor in naval history and tactics—similar to Diederichs's at the Marineakademie. (Diederichs's visit would raise German interest in the Naval War College and lead to an OKM analysis of the American curriculum.)[30] He returned to Germany with souvenirs for Henni and their sons and reported for duty at the Werft on 24 June 1893. After duly reporting his findings to station chief Knorr, he then joined in preparations for the summer maneuvers.

Since 1891, the Kaiserliche Marine had kept its capital ships on permanent active status rather than deactivating them at the end of the annual maneuvers. Another decision had reconfigured this standing force as the eight-ship Maneuver Fleet (*Manöverflotte*), which consisted of two four-ship divisions.[31] The 1893 exercises, which as always simulated defense against attacks in the North Sea and Baltic, proved unsatisfactory because of obsolete tactics and the chaotic mix of German warships.[32] The emperor took at least one step to resolve this situation in October 1893, relieving Diederichs as director of the Werft and appointing him instead as the new chief of the Squadron's Second Division. (Vice Admiral Deinhard, the squadron commander, had retired; Rear Adm. Hans Koester, the former chief of the Second Division, replaced him.) Vice Adm. Viktor Valois, recently returned from overseas, congratulated Diederichs on his new post, hoping that he would find the "fresh air" of sea duty a refreshing change from the past several years of shore duty.[33]

Shipyard workers marked Diederichs's departure with a torchlight parade on 28 October. Accompanied by a marching band, several thousand workers wound their way through the shipyard to the Werft's administrative center. A chorus performed two appropriate pieces, and then the parade leader hailed Diederichs as an able leader with a "warm heart" who had shown great care and concern for the workers. In turn, Diederichs thanked the workers for their positive spirit, loyalty, and fidelity and wished them "health, joy, and prosperity." He concluded his remarks with a cheer—"Dreimal hurrah!"—for the emperor, whereupon the marchers dispersed to the patriotic notes of "Heil Dir im Siegerkranz," the Prussian anthem.[34]

TROUBLESHOOTER

Although Koester's First Division contained four *Sachsen*-class armored corvettes, Diederichs's Second Division reflected the haphazard nature of German naval construction of the previous generation. He flew his flag in armored frigate *König Wilhelm,* commissioned in 1869. His division also included two other armored frigates: *Deutschland* (1875) and *Friedrich der Grosse* (1877). His only modern ship was the brand-new battleship *Brandenburg* (10,500 tons and six 280-mm guns).[35] Although divisional command brought him new prestige, Diederichs's life became even more complicated in January 1894 when the navy re-appointed him as Oberwerftdirektor at Kiel. The two jobs now required him to shuttle back and forth between Kiel and Wilhelmshaven, the home port for the division.[36]

Diederichs spent the first six weeks of the new year at Kiel. He returned to Wilhelmshaven in time to welcome Kaiser Wilhelm aboard *König Wilhelm* on 20 February 1894. As officers and crew manned her side, the emperor came aboard to celebrate the twenty-fifth anniversary of *König Wilhelm*'s commissioning as the fleet's first capital ship. Retired Vice Adm. Wilhelm von Henk, her first commanding officer, led a contingent of naval and administrative officials to participate in the celebration. Kaiser Wilhelm autographed a formal photographic portrait for Diederichs to mark the occasion.[37]

Continuing his peripatetic assignments, Diederichs rejoined the division in April for a training cruise in anticipation of summer maneuvers. Exercises went well until *König Wilhelm,* with her eight-meter draft, went aground on one of the shifting mud banks of the North Sea's Frisian coast. *Deutschland* and *Friedrich der Grosse* succeeded in towing her off before the damage and embarrassment could grow too great. A few days later, *Brandenburg* slewed out of line after a boiler explosion. May brought more satisfying circumstances, including ceremonial visits to Norway and Scotland. To show the flag and give his crews a chance of liberty, Diederichs led the division to Oslo and Bergen before proceeding to Scottish waters. Diederichs himself took the opportunity to experience fine Scottish cuisine—haggis and oatmeal—during a visit to Kirkwall on Orkney Island, only a few kilometers from Scapa Flow. The division returned to Kiel in late May to load coal and provisions in preparation for annual maneuvers.[38]

Summer 1894 proved to be a watershed for the Kaiserliche Marine. From his position as chief of staff to the OKM, Tirpitz wrote his famous *Dienstschrift IX* in June. This document, "General Experiences from the Maneuvers of the Fall Training Fleet," used a critical evaluation of the ill-fated 1893 maneuvers as background for revised strategical and tactical lessons for the 1894 exercises. Echoing Mahanian concepts, Tirpitz identified command of the seas (*Seeherrschaft*) as the primary goal of naval operations. He therefore argued that "squadron war" (*Geschwaderkrieg*), rather than "cruiser war" (*Kreuzerkrieg*), provided the most effective means to this end: "As the history of all previous naval wars illustrates, it is the battle fleet that most completely fulfills the needs of offensive operations necessary to achieve a decisive victory in battle." Commerce raiding, he argued, had only limited value since the absence of a global network of naval bases undermined its usefulness and cruisers, dispersed throughout the world's seas, could not achieve *Seeherrschaft*—command of the seas—on their own. To achieve these goals, Tirpitz proposed the development of a fleet that would consist of seventeen battleships (two squadrons of eight each, plus a fleet flagship) and an additional six heavy and twelve light cruisers for reconnaissance and overseas service. For the first time, too, Tirpitz began to hint at the possibility of war against Britain, rather than Russia and France, as he called for the concentration of the battle fleet in the North Sea. Rather than divide limited funds between battleship construction and coastal fortifications, Tirpitz argued further, a battle fleet could provide the most effective form of coastal defense.[39]

Annual maneuvers began a few weeks later. Since the Tirpitz memorandum had not had time to circulate through all of the upper echelons of the naval command structure, the summer program continued the traditional focus on the defense of Germany's coasts in a two-front war. For example, in one exercise, Koester's First Division defended the North Sea coasts against a "western" (i.e., French) attack, while lighter units protected the Baltic coast against Diederichs's Second Division, which acted as the "eastern" (i.e., Russian) force. Although this basic plan was quite conventional, the program's instructions added a new element, tasking the North Sea battleships with achieving Seeherrschaft over the western force.[40]

Following the end of the maneuvers in late September, Diederichs disembarked from *König Wilhelm* in Wilhelmshaven for the last time. New orders assigned him to three months' temporary duty on Knorr's staff at the Kiel naval station. (Rear Adm. Karl Barandon replaced Diederichs as chief of the Second Division; Capt. Otto von Diederichsen replaced him as Oberwerftdirektor.) Diederichs learned, rather too quickly, that Knorr, an irascible old sea dog, was not the easiest superior to work for. Knorr preferred to work alone and had difficulty delegating authority. In any event, Diederichs's reputation as a troubleshooter and his successful tenure at the Werft, particularly in his relations with the workers, placed him in a good position to deal with a series of personnel problems that had developed during his absence.

Diederichs's temporary duty became permanent on 14 January 1895 when he secured appointment as the chief of the First Inspectorate (*Marineinspection*). The inspectorate administered the activities of the Kiel Matrosendivision and Werftdivision. The former directed the training of new seamen and provided cadre for active-duty ships. The latter had technical and logistical responsibility for activating ships.[41] Diederichs used this position to advocate the revival of the old system of Admiralty Staff Officer (*Admiralstabsoffizier*), a professional cadre of staff officers with whom he had served in the Torpedowesen in the 1870s. The ASO program, however, had gradually disappeared in the intervening years—a circumstance, according to Diederichs, that undermined the professional training of potential staff officers. He now proposed establishing an experimental program at the Kiel station to test his recommendations. When the proposals drew little response, he shelved the matter but would revive it several years later.[42]

As head of the First Inspectorate, Diederichs quickly became involved in the final stages of the construction of the new Kiel Canal. Prussian and German authorities had discussed the possibility of linking the North and Baltic Seas for centuries. A first step, the Eider Canal, had allowed shallow-draft vessels to move from the Kiel fiord to the Weser/Elbe estuary since the 1780s. Diederichs, who had transited the canal aboard SMS *Natter* in 1870, called for a wider, deeper canal in his 1882 memorandum. Successive Admiralty chiefs had also supported the idea until Caprivi finally secured Reichstag support in 1886. Construction began in 1887 as a workforce of nearly nine thousand began to move eighty-two million cubic meters of dirt. At completion in 1895, the ninety-six-kilometer canal was twenty-two meters wide and nine meters deep. The canal had obvious strategic value, allowing warships to pass from sea to sea without steaming around the Danish peninsula.[43]

Wilhelm formally opened the Kaiser Wilhelm Canal on 21 June 1895 with a formal parade of warships. He and Empress Victoria had boarded yacht *Hohenzollern* in Hamburg-Altona and proceeded through the canal in the van of a large line of German and foreign warships the day before. For the occasion, the Manöverflotte expanded to four divisions. Diederichs commanded the Fourth Division (Training Squadron, *Schulgeschwader*), which included four old *Bismarck*-class corvettes (*Stosch, Stein, Moltke,* and *Gneisenau*). The opening ceremonies were a kind of Diederichs family reunion. Diederichs himself hoisted his rear admiral's flag aboard *Stosch,* commanded by Henni's brother-in-law Capt. August Thiele. Cadet Herman von Diederichs, who had entered the Kaiserliche Marine in April, was also aboard. Lt. (jg) Fritz von Diederichs served aboard SMS *Mars,* Knorr's flagship. Henni herself watched the pageantry from specially constructed bleachers at the canal's Holtenau terminus. Thirteen other navies, including that of the United States, sent ships to participate in the formal program. That evening, Diederichs and Henni attended a formal banquet, hosted by the emperor in a hall designed to look like a sail frigate, using the figurehead and other artifacts from recently deactivated *Niobe,* Diederichs's former training ship, as decorations.[44] Diederichs remained in Kiel for the annual regatta. He was an avid sailor who took every opportunity to spend time under sail. At one point, Senden even remarked that the emperor intended to enlist Diederichs's services for the regatta competition as a member of *Hohenzollern*'s crew because of his early training under sail.[45]

For the maneuvers that followed, Diederichs received command of the Manöverflotte's newly created Second Squadron. This unit included the Third (four *Siegfried*-class armored gunboats) and Fourth (the *Bismarck*-class training ships) Divisions. In ensuing exercises, Diederichs won high praise not only for his command of the squadron during the course of new and complex tactical maneuvers but also for his aggressive leadership in the maneuvers' coastal defense element. During the initial phase of the maneuvers, Diederichs commanded the Second Division (four *Sachsen*-class sortie corvettes) in a mock battle against Koester's First Division (four *Brandenburg*-

class battleships). As the First Division attempted to penetrate the estuaries and simulate an attack on Wilhelmshaven, Diederichs intercepted the aggressor force, broke through the enemy's van, and blocked its assault. Knorr praised Diederichs's conduct, concluding, "I consider him to be fully qualified to command a squadron," a sentiment the emperor underlined in blue pencil.[46] Koester, whom Diederichs had defeated in the simulated battle, endorsed the commendation as well.[47]

CHIEF OF STAFF

After maneuvers ended in September 1895, the Kaiserliche Marine disbanded the Second Squadron and assigned Diederichs as chief of staff to Admiral Knorr at the Naval High Command.[48] The transfer returned Diederichs to Berlin for the first time since his service in the Admiralty's planning section in the mid-1880s. He looked forward to the new post at the OKM with some trepidation, however, having earlier working with Knorr at the Kiel naval station. He was fully aware of Knorr's reputation; the admiral was known to his colleagues as "Red Eduard" for his choleric personality.[49] Knorr had become commander in chief in 1895, inheriting Tirpitz from his predecessor. Knorr did not delegate authority well and disliked having to work with a chief of staff. When he and Tirpitz began to clash over both strategic and personality issues, Tirpitz requested to be relieved of his duties and arranged for a lengthy furlough. Diederichs filled the vacant position at the end of the summer, a few months later. As he feared, Diederichs too had problems with Knorr from the beginning of his new tour. He complained both to Tirpitz and to Felix Bendemann that Knorr often bypassed him when assigning duties to subordinates, regularly disregarded his advice, and tended to misuse his other staff officers.[50]

As chief of staff, Diederichs also faced the continuing strategic argument between proponents of battleships and cruisers. The first involved Tirpitz's continuing campaign for a battle fleet, while the second involved the development of the first operational plans for war against Great Britain. Knorr submitted a memorandum to Kaiser Wilhelm in November 1895 that called for a fleet consisting of twenty-five capital ships—seventeen battleships and eight *Siegfried*-class armored gunboats—which would give Germany narrow superiority over the combined Russian Baltic forces and French Atlantic fleet. Invited to comment, Tirpitz increased the number to twenty-seven warships—a figure, he believed, that would elevate Germany to the first rank of naval powers and to world power status. Accordingly, Wilhelm ordered Hollman in December 1895 to incorporate these figures in his planning for the navy's next Reichstag budget.[51]

Meanwhile, events in Africa suddenly exposed the weaknesses of the German fleet as an aspirant to global sea power. Armed and supported by Governor Cecil Rhodes of Britain's Cape Colony, Dr. L. S. Jameson led six hundred men in a filibustering raid into the independent Transvaal Republic in December 1895. Although Boer forces under President Paul Kruger quickly defeated the attack, the incident soon developed major international repercussions. After consulting with his senior naval and diplomatic advisers, Wilhelm telegraphed his congratulations to Kruger on 3 January 1896. The British, in turn, interpreted the Kruger Telegram as German interference in a matter involving their sphere of influence in southern Africa.[52] Although the diplomatic fallout of the Jameson Raid and the Kruger Telegram never approached a true war scare, Wilhelm nonetheless concluded that the incident demonstrated Germany's naval weakness. He therefore began a personal, if still somewhat equivocal, conversion to Tirpitz's battle fleet concept and the attendant desire to elevate Germany to world-power status. He asserted this claim in a speech two weeks later on 18 January 1896 to celebrate twenty-five years of a united Germany: "The German Empire has become a world empire."[53]

Two factions now warred for control of Wilhelm's soul. One faction, induced by the Jameson Raid and Kruger Telegram to raise the specter of war with Britain, called on the emperor to implement Tirpitz's battle fleet proposals and even appoint him as head of the RMA, which had authority over construction. The other faction, the incumbent Hollmann and Chancellor Hohenlohe, advocated caution, arguing that war with Britain was unthinkable and that the Reichstag was not in the political mood to appropriate substantial funds for increased naval construction. Tirpitz met with the emperor on 28 January 1896 to reiterate his proposals and to campaign for Hollmann's job. He essentially proposed the recreation of the Admiralty, abolished in 1889, as a "super-ministry" with paramount authority to implement his battle-fleet program. Because of the strategic significance of these ideas, he demanded first priority in fiscal planning and the subordination of other naval, diplomatic, and colonial agencies to his authority.[54] His time, however, had not yet come. More senior officers—Tirpitz was now thirteenth on the admirals list—resented his grab for power, while Wilhelm himself, who had originally abolished the Admiralty to give himself greater power, also took exception. When Hollmann succeeded in persuading the Reichstag to appropriate funds for four additional warships in March, Wilhelm decided to leave him in place at the RMA and exiled Tirpitz overseas to command the Cruiser Division in East Asia.[55] Senden broke the bad news to Tirpitz on 31 March that the emperor "has decided not to appoint you State Secretary at this time."[56]

These recent events also had significant impact on strategic planning. Although Knorr's November 1895 memorandum maintained the Kaiserliche Marine's traditional focus on a two-front war with France and Russia, Tirpitz's proposals combined with the Transvaal incident to raise the specter of war with England. Knorr therefore directed Diederichs to begin the development of war plans against Great Britain. Thus Diederichs came to play a second role in regard to operational planning. His 1882 memo had pioneered plans for a two-front war against France and Russia. Now, his service with the OKM involved him in the initial planning for war across the Channel. (Continuing this trend, he developed the first plans for war against the United States during his later tenure—1899–1902—at the Admiralstab, discussed in chapter 8.) Operational planning fell under the purview of the *Admiralstabsabteilung* (Admiral Staff Detachment). Four subdivisions focused on regional planning: A1 (overseas), A2 (Russia, Scandinavia, and Eastern Europe), A3 (Western Europe and the Mediterranean), and A4 (Great Britain and the British Empire). A fifth (A5) developed related tactics for experimentation during annual maneuvers.[57]

Cdr. August von Heeringen produced the initial draft—"Concepts for an operations plan of our warships in a war between Germany alone and Britain alone"—on 5 March 1896. He began with the discouraging statement that the Royal Navy badly outnumbered the German fleet, even with so many British warships dispersed throughout the world. He then speculated that the British would send their battleships to Germany's North Sea coast and their cruisers to fight a commerce war against German shipping. Germany could only counter these developments by a more rapid mobilization and a preemptive strike against British merchant shipping in the Thames. Heeringen hoped that this would draw out the few British warships that had completed mobilization, which the momentarily superior German forces could then defeat in detail. The author doubted that this would give Germany a final decisive victory or compel the British to sue for peace; rather, it would allow Germany a few more days to mobilize remaining forces, dispatch commerce raiders, mine the southern approaches to the North Sea, and ready coastal defenses for the inevitable British counterattack.[58]

Diederichs followed up with a more detailed memorandum on 23 April 1896. This second document combined elements from Heeringen's original March memorandum with Diederichs's own cautionary reservations about war with Britain. He immediately argued, for example, that it would be a "mistake bordering on a crime," if Germany fought alone in such a conflict. No preemptive strike or superior defensive position would counteract the fact that British naval superiority would inevitably lead to a German defeat. If the purpose of naval war were indeed to "subordinate the foe to our will" and thus achieve a decisive victory, Germany should never enter a war without at least a reasonable expectation of such a victory. Implicitly countermanding Tirpitz's battle-fleet doctrine, Diederichs contended that an alliance with other naval powers, rather than a larger fleet, would deter potential British aggression. He concluded initially that it would be better to not fight at all than to fight without a real chance of defeating the Royal Navy.

In any event, like Heeringen, Diederichs recommended a rapid German strike before the British could fully mobilize their superior fleet. He advocated a "simultaneous offensive," using mines to close English ports, combined with an attack by commerce raiders to disrupt coastal trade. The advantage of surprise would enable the German fleet to defeat whatever British ships they engaged. Thus, he wrote, "The highest principle of a defensive strategy must remain that our naval forces, so far as possible, engage in open battle. Our entire fleet must seize the first favorable opportunity to strike." He admitted that such a plan, if undertaken properly and effectively, would disrupt the British economy and thus force the English to sue for peace.

In examining possible British strategies, he added a second warning. Using examples drawn from his days as a naval history instructor at the Marineakademie, he cited British wars against France, Spain, Holland, and Denmark, concluding: "If England remains true to her history, she will seek to destroy our naval power." The reference to Denmark was particularly meaningful, suggesting a possible preemptive strike by British naval forces. On two occasions (1801 and 1807) during the Napoleonic Wars, the British had "Copenhagened" the Danish fleet without recourse to a declaration of war. Germany should therefore prepare for the possibility of a similar British attack if relations between the two states continued to deteriorate. He warned that Germany should not neglect coastal defense, which would play an important role in preventing a successful British strike, and therefore recommended a greater investment in coastal artillery and fortifications, particularly given the strategic importance of the river estuaries and coastal waters in the North Sea. In fact, he noted, Germany needed to strengthen coastal fortifications as a major priority since, in his view, the existing defensive network was incapable of fending off a British attack.[59]

Failing a preemptive British strike, Diederichs expected the British to "blockade our harbors and attack our maritime strong points." Citing Prussian naval operations in 1870 and alluding to his own 1882 memo, he reiterated the value of the Ausfallflotte, the sortie fleet, to counteract the British strategy. He recommended the allocation of a "significant element of our fleet" to break through the blockade or prevent attacks on the strategic river estuaries. Given probable British superiority, he contended further that "we must offer battle only in case of favorable conditions and at a time of our choosing." He made one optimistic point, suggesting that the German fleet would make up for its quantitative inferiority with its superior "warlike spirit" (*kriegerischen Geist*) which had permeated the German military culture since 1870.

He also evaluated warship types in relation to likely operations. Until Germany could construct more coastal fortifications, the Kaiserliche Marine would use battleships as the "first line of defense." He would then create a second defensive layer built around the fleet's existing coastal defense vessels (*Siegfried* and *Sachsen* classes). He even recommended the rearmament of the aging *Bismarck*-class corvettes, which he had commanded as the Schulgeschwader in 1895, to support the new and larger coastal defense ships. "These corvettes," he noted, "can support night combat not only with their guns but also with their searchlights." For a strategic reserve, he recommended the creation of a force consisting of auxiliary merchant cruisers and obsolete warships equipped with quick-firing guns. This would extend the service life of older ships and provide a means—"The cost for this is quite low"—of expanding the fleet. Finally, drawing on his experiences aboard *Natter* in 1870, he proposed the development of a new class of river gunboats to protect the Kaiser Wilhelm Canal and inshore waters, particularly the Frisian coast, and support coastal fortifications.[60]

As copies of his memorandum began to circulate among the other officers on the planning staff, Diederichs began to focus on planning the upcoming maneuvers. In late April, he assigned Heeringen to draft a program that would incorporate the possibility of war with Britain in both offensive and defensive exercises.[61] The need to both develop operational plans and prepare for maneuvers quickly tested the capabilities of the Admiralstabsabteilung, particularly in June when Knorr allowed the RMA to co-opt several officers from the OKM staff. Diederichs had complained as early as fall 1895 that his staff did not have enough officers to carry out its assigned tasks. Now, he had even fewer officers to do the work. Furthermore, to protest Knorr's administrative style, several officers had already requested transfers because of their own frustrations with the commander in chief. When Diederichs formally requested that Knorr restore the absentee officers to duty with the OKM, Knorr accosted him in the hallway of the OKM suite and bluntly asked him to make recommendations for his own successor. Stunned by this sudden turn of events, Diederichs submitted a short list of qualified officers. Without making an immediate decision on Diederichs's status, Knorr took a premaneuver furlough in late June. He returned in a more affable mood in July, asking Diederichs to stay on as chief of staff until spring 1897.[62]

1896 MANEUVERS

The 1896 maneuvers were important because they changed the face of German operational planning. Whereas earlier maneuvers had anticipated war against France and Russia, the 1896 exercises also incorporated the possibility of Britain as Germany's primary foe. The program nonetheless resembled the 1895 maneuvers, simulating an attack by an enemy fleet against the Jade/Weser/Elbe basin. Diederichs added a new element, proposing that the training ships participate in the maneuvers rather than leaving immediately on their training cruises. This would give the cadets and midshipmen an earlier introduction to naval tactics and strategy. This, he wrote, would enhance their characters and provide a stronger professional foundation for their entry into the officer corps.[63]

The first element of the maneuvers reflected earlier strategic considerations. The key element involved a French attack on the Elbe estuary at the western terminus of the Kaiser Wilhelm Canal. The plan used names of existing French warships and French strategic concepts and vocabulary. The significance of this operation was illustrated by the passage of fifty-two ships through the canal in thirty hours. The Manöverflotte, now renamed the First Squadron, rendezvoused at Wilhelmshaven on 9 August. The former Third and Fourth Divisions again formed a temporary Second Squadron. The program called for tactical exercises in Baltic waters during August followed by strategic maneuvers in the North Sea during the first two weeks of September. Following initial gunnery exercises near Helgoland, the entire force proceeded into the Baltic Sea by way of the Kaiser Wilhelm Canal. The fleet completed the initial, tactical phase of the maneuvers by 1 September.[64]

Kaiser Wilhelm briefly suspended the maneuvers on 7 September, Diederichs's fifty-third birthday, to celebrate the visit of Czar Nicholas II to Kiel. The Russian czar visited several new battleships and then received senior ranking German officers, including Diederichs, at Kiel Schloss on the evening of the eighth. The czar's visit, however, put the maneuvers off schedule. When the fleet had returned to the North Sea, Knorr notified Diederichs at 0600 on 11 September that he intended to alter the maneuvers program. Knorr had concluded that the area of operations, bounded by Helgoland and the Jade, had too little sea room to complete the exercises. He therefore decided to move both squadrons to the vicinity of Borkum. When Diederichs objected to this abrupt change on the grounds that it would cause great logistical dislocation and mean the loss of a day or two from a program that was already behind schedule, Knorr called him into *Blücher*'s chartroom and, in the presence of Knorr's aide, Lt. Cdr. Wilhelm Lans, berated him for his hesitation. According to Diederichs's account, the discussions grew more heated until Knorr spoke angrily. "Now, if I do not see this done at once, I will take over and do it myself." Diederichs responded in as calm a way as possible, "Your Excellency has already authorized the original instructions for these exercises." Knorr retorted, "Admiral von Diederichs, you made a similar remark some days ago. You seem unwilling to follow my orders."

Diederichs denied any such remark: "That is not what I believe happened, Sir." Knorr broke off his tirade at this point and abruptly left the chartroom to rejoin his staff on the flagship's signal bridge.

Two hours later, Knorr called Diederichs to his cabin to advise him that he could no longer work with him. Diederichs noted succinctly, "I accepted his decision, saluted, and left." He assumed that his dismissal would not become official until the end of the maneuvers and therefore continued to carry out his administrative duties, albeit "with some personal difficulty." With the end of the maneuvers on the 15 September, Diederichs submitted his final written report to Knorr. At that time, he attempted to explain his reasons for opposing the move to Borkum, but Knorr refused to listen and again noted his preference for a new chief of staff.[65]

In fact, an imperial directive relieved Diederichs as chief of staff on 10 October 1896 and appointed Rear Adm. Karl Barandon in his place. At the same time, Diederichs asked for and received a six-month furlough.[66] He described these events in a long, soulful letter to Tirpitz, now commander of the Cruiser Division in East Asia, who of course had experienced similar treatment at Knorr's hands. Diederichs attributed his problems with the commander in chief to his belief that Knorr had never provided him "with the support I needed to carry out my duties" or solicited his professional advice. He advised Tirpitz that he now intended to use his furlough to consider his professional options.[67]

Diederichs withdrew to his Berlin apartment to discuss the issue with Henni and a few close confidants. It was now possible that his service to the crown was over. He and Henni celebrated a quiet and bittersweet twenty-fifth anniversary on 14 November. Christmas was equally quiet and lonely, because Fritz, a senior lieutenant, was serving under Tirpitz aboard SMS *Irene* in East Asia and Cadet Herman was on a training cruise aboard SMS *Gneisenau* in the Mediterranean. At this juncture, no one could criticize Diederichs if he chose to retire and pass the family tradition of service into the hands of his two sons. After all, he had fulfilled his family's tradition, with thirty-two years of service to the crown. Perhaps it would be better to retire; after all, he had become quite frustrated with the emperor's "new course" and its attendant impact on the Kaiserliche Marine's strategic development. After all, as he wrote Tirpitz, "Our children are our future and our hopes."[68]

6

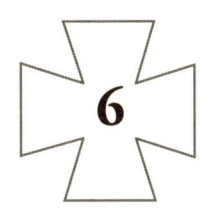

A Mailed Fist: Diederichs Takes Kiao-Chou, 1897–1898

"It was uncertain whether retirement or a new command would follow this furlough."[1] Thus begins Diederichs's personal account of the German navy's seizure of Kiao-chou Bay, China, in November 1897.

When Knorr dismissed Diederichs as chief of staff of the Oberkommando der Marine in October 1896, Diederichs requested and received six months' leave. He then withdrew to his Berlin apartment to consider his options and discuss his professional future with his wife. They had celebrated their twentieth-fifth wedding anniversary in November with both melancholy and trepidation. Diederichs knew that there were few positions available to a rear admiral fired from his last post. Admittedly, Tirpitz had survived his own dismissal as chief of staff in 1895 to become commander of the Cruiser Division in East Asian waters. No such redemption, however, appeared likely for Diederichs. Even though he was the senior rear admiral on the admirals list, there were no vacant posts for someone of his rank. Then came good news: In early January 1897 Senden notified him that

Knorr had written a positive fitness report to mark the end of the calendar year.[2] Although his future seemed bleak, he and Henni still had hope.

FAMILY PROBLEMS

Potentially tragic news soon darkened his mood. The navy notified him via telegram on the afternoon of 22 January that his Herman, an eighteen-year-old midshipman aboard SMS *Gneisenau,* had contracted typhus during a training cruise to the Mediterranean. With their son lying dangerously ill in an Alexandrian hospital, Diederichs and Henni immediately decided to go to Egypt. This decision came at great personal cost, since Henni was suffering intense pain from a recurrent bout with arthritis. Diederichs swung into action with his usual alacrity. He quickly learned that a British steamer, SS *Arcadia,* was scheduled to depart Brindisi, at the southern tip of Italy, for Egypt on the afternoon of 24 January. Because Berlin banks had already closed for the day, he borrowed travel funds from close friends and then packed for himself and Henni. Only hours after receiving the telegram, the couple departed for Italy on the evening train from the Berlin Hauptbahnhof. They changed trains in Bologna twenty-four hours later to catch a faster English mail train on the Calais-to-Brindisi run. Diederichs had to purchase the new tickets on the spot, dealing with the impediment of an avaricious Italian conductor who exchanged a hundred-mark note for eighty French francs. Diederichs justified the transaction, however, noting, "My overriding fear of missing the steamer left me no choice." The couple reached Brindisi in time, boarding SS *Arcadia* soon after noon on the twenty-fourth. The ship departed a few minutes later, steaming into the eastern Mediterranean on a course similar to that taken by SMS *Luise* twenty years before.

Although the steamer's accommodations were "filthy and inaccessible," the worried parents were willing to sacrifice comfort for speed. Because the steamer was not scheduled to stop at Alexandria, the couple had to disembark in Port Said on 27 January, backtrack to Cairo aboard the English mail train, and then board a small French steamer for the brief trip down the Nile Delta to Alexandria. When they arrived, anxious and exhausted, in the early morning hours of the twenty-eighth, Diederichs checked Henni into a hotel to rest and then took a hansom cab to the hospital. Although Herman's condition was still critical, the attending physician and *Gneisenau*'s chief surgeon advised Diederichs that his son was out of danger. Herman would nonetheless need to remain in the hospital for another two months to recuperate. When Diederichs returned to his hotel to tell Henni the good news, she "immediately relieved the tension of the previous few days with a mighty outpouring of tears."[3]

Diederichs remained in Alexandria for the next four weeks. He and Henni spent their days with Herman in his hospital ward and their evenings exploring Alexandria and Cairo. After a month of this routine, Diederichs decided to return to Berlin to resolve his future. Since his six-month furlough formally ended on 1 April, he needed to know if there were a position yet available to him in the navy or if he should simply retire. He therefore made arrangements for Henni to reside at the hospital during the remaining month of Herman's convalescence and then accepted Capt. Oskar Stiege's offer of passage to Italy aboard SMS *Moltke*. Diederichs disembarked at Messina, crossed the straits to Naples, and boarded a train for Berlin. He briefly interrupted his return trip at Baden-Baden to look for retirement real estate. In case he retired, he and Henni worried that Berlin's prices were too high for his pension and the weather too cold and damp for Henni's arthritis. They had agreed that Baden-Baden, with its mineral hot springs, would make a pleasant retirement home.

When he reached Berlin in late March, Diederichs learned that his professional salvation was at hand. During his absence, the battleship-cruiser debate had resurfaced. Kaiser Wilhelm had again reversed himself, converting to Tirpitz's battleship doctrine. The emperor had therefore decided to dismiss Hollmann as state secretary and recall Tirpitz from East Asia to replace him. That action finally created a vacancy for Diederichs to fill. His difficulties with Knorr had not ended his career after all. Senden now advised him that Wilhelm intended to appoint him as chief of the Cruiser Division. Diederichs immediately cabled the good news to Henni, who was preparing to leave Alexandria with Herman. Diederichs formally received notification of his new assignment on 1 April. When Henni and Herman reached Berlin on the tenth, they had much to celebrate: Diederichs's imminent return to active duty, Herman's recovery, and an anticipated reunion with Fritz, currently serving as a junior officer aboard SMS *Irene* in East Asia.

THE CRUISER DIVISION

Because his orders directed him to depart for Hong Kong on or about 1 May 1897, Diederichs had only four weeks to prepare for his new command. Although he had served twice previously in East Asia, he returned to the familiar offices of the OKM to immerse himself in the files of the Cruiser Division and review the history of German naval operations in the region. Prussian warships had operated in Chinese waters since 1860, remaining permanently after 1869 with the establishment of the East Asian station. The Treaty of Peking, signed in September 1861, allowed Prussian warships to operate in Chinese waters for the protection of German trade (Article 6) and missionaries (Article 10). Article 38 promised swift naval retribution for crimes committed against German nationals by Chinese subjects.[4]

As the region continued to grow in economic and strategic importance, the navy formed its first organic squadron for service in East Asia. Configured in 1881 as a flying squadron under the command of a flag officer, the new unit could show the imperial flag and the weight of German naval might in foreign waters, protect German nationals abroad, act as the vanguard of German imperialism, and undertake commerce raiding in wartime.[5]

Cruisers had long filled a vital service for the German navy. The *Auslandskreuzer* were fast and well-armed. The sudden appearance of a cruiser with her long-range guns was usually sufficient to enforce the will of an imperial power. Joseph Conrad's Marlow testified to the terrifying potential of a cruiser squadron in *Heart of Darkness*:

> Once, I remember, we came upon a man-of-war anchored off the coast. There wasn't even a shed there, and she was shelling the bush. . . . Her ensign dropped limp like a rag; the muzzles of the long six-inch guns stuck out all over the low hull; the greasy, slimy swell swung her up lazily and let her down, swaying her thin masts. In the empty immensity of earth, sky and water, there she was, incomprehensible, firing into a continent.[6]

Once Stosch's policy of *Infanterieismus* had been applied to a cruiser's crew and they were trained in infantry weapons and tactics, the ship could send naval infantry ashore to solve any colonial crises that her main battery could not resolve.

The navy established a second squadron to support the establishment of colonies in Africa. This squadron gained permanent status and designation as the Cruiser Squadron (*Kreuzergeschwader*) in 1885. Diederichs had briefly served with the squadron in fall 1885 when he held temporary command of SMS *Stosch*. Because the development of an African colonial empire took precedence over German naval operations in East Asia, the navy abolished the squadron in Chinese waters and reduced its presence there to a pair of gunboats and an occasional aging training ship. The Kreuzergeschwader itself continued to serve overseas until it returned to Germany for deactivation in 1893. Diederichs, in fact, had presided over its deactivation while director of the Imperial Shipyard, Kiel.[7]

The emergence of Sino-Japanese tensions in the early 1890s revived German naval interest in China. Influenced by its own imperialist aspirations, Japan sought to emulate Western powers in the dismemberment of the declining Chinese empire. The Japanese wanted Korea, a traditional tributary state long under Chinese control, to provide raw materials for Japan's growing industrialism and assuage the hunger of Japanese nationalism. The conflict resulted in the outbreak of the Sino-Japanese War in August 1894.[8]

Diederichs continued to read the files with growing interest. Kaiser Wilhelm, who believed that other European powers would use the crisis to expand their colonial spheres in East Asia, worried that Germany might miss an opportunity for imperialist adventure. He therefore created the Cruiser Division (*Kreuzerdivision*) under the command of Rear Adm. Paul Hoffmann on 25 September 1894. Hoffmann's new command included modern light cruiser *Irene* (five thousand tons, four 150-mm and eight 105-mm guns) and three aging small cruisers *Arcona* (twenty-six hundred tons, ten 150-mm guns), *Marie* (twenty-six hundred tons, ten 150-mm guns), and *Alexandrine* (twenty-six hundred tons, ten 150-mm guns). (New naval nomenclature designated eight-ship units as squadrons and four-ship units as divisions.) His orders directed him to protect German interests and examine possible sites for a German base in China.[9]

Following his arrival in East Asia in late 1894, Hoffmann quickly concluded that the Kreuzerdivision lacked adequate resources for the job at hand. He complained particularly that the three small cruisers, originally designed in 1875, were simply too old and obsolete to support his mission. He therefore asked the OKM for more modern replacements. Knorr responded in January 1895, dispatching heavy cruiser *Kaiser* (eighty-eight hundred tons, eight 260-mm guns) and light cruiser *Prinzess Wilhelm* (five thousand tons, four 150-mm and eight 105-mm guns) to replace *Alexandrine* and *Marie*. Knorr also assigned small cruiser SMS *Cormoran* (eighteen hundred tons, eight 105-mm guns) to independent operations in East Asian and Pacific waters.[10]

Hoffmann underlined the need for a German base in East Asia. He reported, for example, that both the Chinese and the Japanese governments had denied him access to logistical and coaling facilities in Shanghai and Nagasaki, respectively, following the outbreak of the war. These circumstances, he complained, had undermined the Kreuzerdivision's ability to protect Germany's expanding position in China. He therefore advised Berlin that the establishment of a German naval base in China was "absolutely necessary."[11]

THE QUEST FOR BASES

Diederichs knew from personal experience that Germany's warships on foreign station had long suffered from having no overseas naval bases, particularly since the advent of modern steam warships that required constant and sometimes technologically complex fueling and maintenance services. Although steam engines generated greater speed than wind-driven propulsion and provided more constant power, steam warships also required regular and reliable supplies of coal. A sail frigate, which carried spare masts and extra cordage, could make necessary repairs at sea. A modern cruiser, with steam boilers that rusted and propeller shafts that broke, needed continuous maintenance and ready access to repair facilities.

Fueling and maintaining steam warships posed only minor difficulties for ships within steaming range of Kiel or Wilhelmshaven but caused significant problems for ships in East Asia. Without a base, German warships depended on British (Hong Kong), Chinese (Shanghai), or Japanese (Nagasaki) facilities for technical and logistical support. A survey begun in 1869 identified several potential base sites, but the outbreak of the Franco-German War in 1870 deferred final resolution of the issue for a generation. Although German forces usually operated out of the port of Amoy in southern China, warship commanders complained regularly that the lack of a permanent base impaired naval operations.[12]

Now, Diederichs concluded, the decline of Chinese political independence and territorial integrity provided a new opportunity for Germany to acquire a base in Chinese waters. After all, imperialism continued to make major inroads in the Middle Kingdom. Britain had expanded its economic domination of China by developing Hong Kong and establishing a dominant position in Shanghai and the Yangtze Basin. France had solidified its presence in southern China with victory in the Sino-French War (1884–85) and the consolidation of its imperial presence in Indochina. Russia had made inroads into Chinese territory in Central Asia and continued to threaten Manchuria. Japan, too, sought an imperial foothold in China in emulation of its European peers.

Diederichs's assessment had strong support within German government. Kaiser Wilhelm himself argued that Germany should consider the immediate seizure of Taiwan as the new center of German naval operations in East Asia. He justified this act with reference to German trade with China: "We require a fortified site in China because our trade totals 400 million [marks] annually."[13] Admiral Hollmann, state secretary of the *Reichsmarineamt,* strongly presented the navy's case, arguing that "bases are an absolute necessity for overseas naval operations."[14] The new chancellor, Chlodwig von Hohenlohe, agreed, noting that the acquisition of Chinese territory would fulfill "the need for bases for our fleet and commerce which we have asserted for decades."[15] Even Foreign Minister Hermann von Marschall, who disliked any thought of imperial entanglement, nonetheless admitted that Germany would suffer national humiliation "if Germany alone of the Powers were to go away empty-handed from a partition of the Chinese Empire."[16] Eduard von Heyking, German ambassador to China, actively advocated naval action: "We cannot wait [to acquire a base], because our warships cannot swim about here forever like homeless waifs, and we run the risk of losing prestige because we have expressed wishes without pushing them through."[17]

The next step, Diederichs concluded, was to identify potential sites. A survey of naval and diplomatic officials produced a fairly expansive list of possibilities. These included Amoy, a port he had first visited in 1862 that was still the center of German naval operations in China; Chusan Island, south of Shanghai; Kiao-chou Bay and Wei-hai-wei on Shantung peninsula; Mirs Bay, north of Hong Kong; Swatow, centered between Amoy and Hong Kong; Montebello Island off the southern tip of Korea; and the Pescadore Islands, south of Japan.[18]

The Sino-Japanese War ended, however, before the Kaiserliche Marine could either select a site or undertake action. The Treaty of Shimonoseki, signed on 17 April 1895, forced China to acknowledge the independence of Korea and gave Japan a strong territorial position in China. The conclusion of hostilities convinced Marschall to reverse his earlier support for a German base in China. He now feared that new diplomatic tensions and complications would hinder German interests elsewhere or produce friction with other great powers. He therefore acted to discourage naval interest in a Chinese base.[19]

Subsequent events in China, however, quickly reminded Marschall and others of the necessity of German naval operations in East Asia. Western-sponsored Christian evangelism in China had long caused violent xenophobic reactions. When a new wave of violence broke out in September 1895, Wilhelm ordered the navy into action. He noted in particular, "Great unrest exists in the Shantung peninsula and it is there that our major action should occur." He directed Hoffmann to send some ships to provide protection for German mission stations and others to make a show of force "in the harbors of Shantung." He then ordered Hoffman to make all necessary preparations for the seizure of Wei-hai-wei.[20] Admiral Hoffmann, however, replied that executing Wilhelm's proposal would be complicated by new circumstances: The Japanese intended to occupy Wei-hai-wei as part of their spoils of war from the recently concluded war.[21]

Marschall promptly cautioned against unilateral action. He warned Wilhelm that any German action would no longer occur in a vacuum: "It is not possible to seek the acquisition of a coaling station without regard to Russian or English interests." He reminded the emperor that Britain continued to expand its spheres around Hong Kong, Shanghai, and the Yangtze Basin. Russia had made clear its interest in the Liaotung peninsula, which would preclude any German action in northern China. The Japanese occupation of Wei-hai-wei closed that avenue as well. Because these factors severely limited German options, the foreign minister pleaded with the emperor to avoid any precipitate act.[22]

The Kaiserliche Marine nonetheless continued to make its case for a base in China. Diederichs was also on more familiar ground as he began to review documents that he himself had prepared while chief of staff. The first file was a major document that Admiral Knorr had presented to the emperor in an *Immediatvortrag* on 8 November 1895, in which Knorr had used strategic and economic arguments to justify an East Asian base "as soon as possible." Because modern warships could not operate effectively without constant access to base facilities, he noted that the lack of a base impeded operations at a time when other naval powers were expanding their positions in the Far East. He also argued that the German economic presence in East Asia had grown so much in recent decades that a base was mandatory in order to fully protect German interests.

According to Knorr, the ideal base must have several necessary characteristics. These included a good harbor with deep anchorages and protection against wind and sea, defenses against land or sea attack, and a location near major shipping lanes and navigable rivers. Knorr preferred a central location, distant from the Russian sphere in northern China and from English possessions in the south. Such a site would place a German base between the Yangtze River, dominated by Shanghai, in the north and the Pearl River, controlled by Hong Kong, in the south. "Our base," he told the emperor, "must lie in the center of these points." Knorr personally preferred an island site, rather than one on the Chinese mainland, because it would be politically easier to acquire and militarily easier to defend. This would also isolate the site from unrest on the mainland. In fact, he cited the English model: "Everything depends on our creation of a German Hong Kong." In any event, Knorr identified four sites that met these criteria: Chusan, Amoy, Samsah, and Kiao-chou.

Chusan Island, within easy reach of the Yangtze delta, was his first choice. It possessed a good harbor and the potential to become a commercial center of "the first rank." Knorr admitted, however, that its acquisition could cause a diplomatic problem. The Anglo-Chinese Treaty of 1846 gave Chusan treaty-port status under international protection and therefore prohibited China from ceding it to a foreign power. Knorr nonetheless contended that a Chinese base was so important that Germany should consider ceding its Samoan claims to Britain in exchange for Chusan. He argued, "Samoa is merely Samoa, but Chusan gives us access to a proper share of Chinese wealth."

Amoy, which had served for a generation as Germany's unofficial trading center in Chinese waters, was by far Knorr's second choice. An island site like Chusan, Amoy possessed much of the same strategic potential, but it lacked access to a wealthy hinterland and lay too far south in the shadow of Hong Kong. Amoy's status as a treaty port and its proximity to Japanese-held Formosa would also create diplomatic problems.

Samsah, south of Amoy, stood third on Knorr's list. Although its current lack of development gave it little economic value, it did have potential. Knorr admitted that the navy had only general information about Samsah's bay, which had adequate maritime value, but noted that he had directed Admiral Hoffmann to reconnoiter the bay further. Another complication was the presence of American naval forces, which informally used the bay as the center of U.S. naval operations in Chinese waters.

Kiao-chou Bay was Knorr's fourth choice. Centered on the fishing village of Tsingtao on Shantung peninsula, this site had originally stood higher on the German navy's list. Because it was not a treaty port, its acquisition would not cause diplomatic repercussions. According to reports, it had a spacious harbor, proven inland coal reserves, and the potential for rail access to the Yellow River basin in northern China. Further analysis, however, suggested major flaws that led Knorr to conclude that Kiao-chou "has little potential as a base for our fleet in East Asia." It lay too distant from the Yangtze, lacked easy access to interior trade until expensive railroad construction could link it with the existing internal network, and possessed a shallow bay which, according to known information, iced over during the winter. Furthermore, neither Kiao-chou Bay nor Tsingtao possessed any modern maritime facilities, which would render its development "more costly than the construction of Wilhelmshaven."

Knorr feared that the opportunity to acquire a base might not occur again. Not only was China experiencing military and economic decline, but the other powers acknowledged that Germany "possesses an unassailable right based on legitimate interests and political necessity" to acquire a site in East Asia. He therefore closed with the insistence that Germany must act with "foresight and energy."[23]

As Diederichs knew from bitter experience, Knorr's hope for swift action was not forthcoming. The navy's senior officers could not agree on a single site. Wilhelm now campaigned for Wei-hai-wei. Admirals Hollmann (RMA) and Hoffmann (Cruiser Division) preferred Amoy. Admirals Knorr (OKM) and Senden (MK) advocated Chusan. Among the naval officers, only Diederichs supported Kiao-chou. Based on his own evaluation of the situation, he had concluded that Kiao-chou would best serve the navy's needs.[24]

While still chief of staff, Diederichs himself had taken the initiative in an attempt to persuade the Foreign Ministry to accept a German base in China. He particularly emphasized the navy's technical needs when he wrote Marschall in April 1896, "The difficulties confronting our ships in East Asian waters, arising from the use of modern ships abroad, continue to grow." Diederichs cited regular reports from Hoffmann that the lack of a base impeded German naval operations in East Asia. Hoffmann's ships had to depend on overextended English and Japanese coaling and repair facilities, which might not always be available during periods of conflict. Diederichs wrote strongly, "I cannot emphasize enough the need to free our warships as soon as possible from dependence on foreign facilities." He cited the recent example of SMS *Kaiser*, Hoffmann's flagship and only capital ship, which had recently struck an uncharted rock upon entering Amoy. Although *Kaiser* had sustained only minor damage, the ship was out of active service for twenty-two days because of the need to proceed to Hong Kong and then await access to repair facilities there. A German base would provide better access and improve operational readiness.[25]

Toward the end of his examination of files, Diederichs turned to the most recent message traffic with his soon-to-be predecessor, Rear Adm. Alfred Tirpitz. Tirpitz had replaced Hoffmann as commander of the Cruiser Division on 15 June 1896 with orders to "seek out a place on the Chinese coast where Germany could establish a military and economic base." Tirpitz's instructions specifically directed him to evaluate Chusan, Amoy, and Samsah Bay. The navy had dropped Kiao-chou from its list, according to Tirpitz, because it had little strategic value as a naval base and lay too far north of China's main economic regions.[26]

It had not taken long for Tirpitz to understand, as Hoffmann had, the operational difficulties arising from the lack of a base. He reported at one point that four of his five ships were either undergoing repairs in Hong Kong and Nagasaki or waiting for dockyard space to commence repairs. When the OKM ordered him to send his last ship to the Philippines, he complained, "The lack of a permanent base diminishes the squadron's [sic] effectiveness."[27]

Tirpitz undertook a lengthy examination and analysis of each site, but his two reports only clouded the issue. His first report, submitted on 5 September 1896, evaluated four potential sites. He cited specific difficulties related to Chusan because of existing treaties, which the British would uphold, and its proximity to Shanghai, where the British would not permit competition. Amoy remained a viable site, since Tirpitz had learned that neither British naval officers nor merchants would oppose the establishment of German sovereignty there. He made only brief but unfavorable reference, for economic reasons, to Samsah, which he had not yet visited. He spoke most favorably of Kiao-chou, citing its natural bay and access to coal reserves. Tirpitz concluded with the comment that he himself had not made up his mind about which site to recommend. He admitted a current preference for Kiao-chou but acknowledged that his attitude might change as he examined other sites, particularly Chusan, more closely.[28]

Tirpitz's report reached Berlin in October 1896 just as Knorr dismissed Diederichs from his position as chief of staff. Although it temporarily elevated Kiao-chou to the number one site on the navy's list, it did little to clarify the situation. Foreign Minister Marschall continued to oppose any action, fearing diplomatic problems with China and Russia. Admirals Hollmann, who preferred Amoy, and Knorr, who liked Chusan, doubted the navy's ability to occupy and hold Kiao-chou Bay against Chinese or European opposition. Admiral Senden, who had the ear of the emperor, also preferred Chusan. Diederichs, Kiao-chou's staunchest advocate, was no longer in a position to promote the site.[29] To make matters even more confusing, Tirpitz himself denied ever having recommended Kiao-chou. Although he later claimed in his memoirs to have been the guiding force behind the selection of Kiao-chou, Tirpitz wrote Senden in early 1897, "The remark in your letter that I had advocated Kiao-chou surprises me. . . . All I said was that we should not cross Kiao-chou off the list and merely wanted to get orders enabling me to carry out further investigation."[30]

Because of the confusion, the emperor now directed Knorr to clarify the

Kaiserliche Marine's position and identify a single site. Knorr responded in an *Immediatvortrag* on 28 November 1896 in which he identified Kiao-chou and Amoy as the two preferred sites. He reiterated many of the existing arguments for and against either site, concluding that Kiao-chou had the advantage in both strategic and economic considerations. He failed to clarify the situation, however, when he equivocally noted, "I prefer Kiao-chou," but also supported the "seizure of Amoy at a later time."[31]

Pursuant to this advice, Wilhelm directed Knorr to prepare an operational plan for the seizure of Kiao-chou. Knorr drew up a generic plan in December 1896 that called for the formation of a naval infantry brigade, drawn from the Kreuzerdivision's ships, to occupy Tsingtao, the fishing village at the mouth of Kiao-chou Bay. Wilhelm agreed to the plan pending selection of a date to commence operations. That date depended in turn on the occurrence of an event, as *casus belli*, that Germany could use to justify a move against Kiao-chou.[32]

Despite these preparations, neither Wilhelm nor the navy had committed fully to Kiao-chou. Knorr, in fact, decided in mid-December to send a senior naval engineer, Georg Franzius, to China to undertake a more formal survey of possible sites. Diederichs endorsed the decision for two reasons: First, such a survey would indeed clarify which site provided the best potential as a base and, second, he and Franzius were friends from their days together at Kiel. They had both served on the faculty of the Marineakademie, and Franzius had worked for Diederichs at the Kiel shipyard as director of the harbor construction division. Franzius reached China in early February, visiting each site, including Kiao-chou, in turn.[33]

Ironically, as Diederichs now discovered from reading the files, Franzius's mission had become quite timely. In a new report, dated 6 December 1896, Tirpitz reversed his previous recommendations. He disclosed a disturbing development from China, citing an article in the *North China Daily News*, an English-language newspaper published in Shanghai, which reported that China had agreed to lease Kiao-chou to Russia. Although he suspected that the story was incorrect, Tirpitz nonetheless recommended that the navy resume its search. He reviewed existing sites, reiterating existing technical and diplomatic concerns about Chusan, Amoy, Samsah, and Kiao-chou. Based on this evaluation, he concluded that the navy should reject all four sites and focus instead on an unspecified site in the Yangtze Basin. In the final analysis, he even began to question the very value of an East Asian base. He warned Berlin that "a smaller naval power such as Germany" might not have the capability to acquire and maintain a base against Chinese or European opposition. Perhaps fearing that naval adventurism in China would further detract from his battle fleet proposals, he even argued that Germany lacked adequate economic and strategic reasons to justify significant German naval operations in East Asia altogether.[34]

In the wake of Tirpitz's gloomy report, the German navy's quest for a Chinese base faltered. Wilhelm and Knorr suspended plans to seize Kiao-chou pending resolution of the new issues. The December report was also Tirpitz's last contribution to the Kiao-chou issue. The emperor had decided in early 1897 to recall him to Berlin to replace Hollmann at the RMA, with orders to commence the development of a German battle fleet. Once he returned to Berlin, Tirpitz lost interest in East Asia. As he sought to develop his battle fleet for operations "between Helgoland and the Thames," global operations and overseas bases became a distraction rather than a priority.

Diederichs was the third successive commander of the Cruiser Division with orders to find a base site in China. Hoffmann had not succeeded because of high-level indecision. Tirpitz was too preoccupied with his battle fleet and too easily dissuaded by other circumstances to act. Diederichs understood these problems and therefore departed for East Asia with two goals: persuade Knorr and other senior naval officers to accept Kiao-chou and overcome Foreign Ministry opposition to any action whatsoever. He therefore vowed, "I departed with the intention of forcing events if necessary."[35]

EAST OF SINGAPORE

Diederichs left Berlin by rail on 1 May 1897. He said his sad good-byes to Henni and Herman at the Hauptbahnhof. He was particularly worried about Henni and her chronic arthritis; her poor health would become the main topic of their ensuing correspondence. Still, the prospect of seeing his son Fritz in East Asia alleviated some of his sadness. Three days later, he boarded the North German Lloyd liner SS *Preussen* in Genoa for the voyage to East Asia. He traveled in the relative comfort of a second-class stateroom and took only four weeks, a far cry from his swaying hammock and six-month voyage aboard *Amaranth* in 1862. Diederichs went ashore briefly in Port Said, Egypt, to telegraph Capt. Hugo Zeye, flag captain in SMS *Kaiser* and acting chief of the Kreuzerdivision, to meet him in Hong Kong. Diederichs intended to take formal command of the division at that time before proceeding north to Shanghai, the center of divisional operations during summer months.[36]

East of Singapore, in the South China Sea, Diederichs enjoyed a postbreakfast conversation with a German plantation owner from Borneo and a Chinese diplomat returning from London. The setting could have been copied from Joseph Conrad's *Lord Jim:* "A calm and pressing humidity covered us and the sun shone on the reflecting waters as if it were shiny steel." From his lounge chair, Diederichs sighted a large bamboo tree trunk floating upright in the water. When he commented on its distance from land, the diplomat told him that, according to Chinese legend, the log was the rudder of a boat lost by God. Whoever sighted the rudder first could expect great fortune. The incident had quite an impact on the Chinese passengers, who continued to comment on Diederichs's auspicious experience for the remainder of the voyage. Diederichs himself concluded, "I can only assume that the acquisition of Kiao-chou fulfilled this omen."[37]

Diederichs reached Hong Kong on 31 May 1897. He moved ashore to the Mount Austin Hotel to wait for *Kaiser* and conveyance to Shanghai. Although he cabled Zeye upon his arrival, he received no response. This silence and the absence of any German warship mystified him. He nonetheless used the time for sightseeing, meeting with the German consul-general and surviving a wild rickshaw ride through crowded streets. He admitted to some difficulty in the hot, humid climate, as temperatures regularly climbed above ninety degrees. His comfortable accommodations, six hundred meters above Hong Kong Bay, provided at least some relief. He spent an evening as a guest of the German Club, where he met a retired naval surgeon who had formerly served aboard SM gunboat *Iltis*. The expatriate spoke highly of Admiral Hoffmann, the original chief of the Kreuzerdivision, but was meaningfully noncommittal about Tirpitz.[38]

After a week in Hong Kong, Diederichs finally received a telegram from Zeye, who had just arrived in Shanghai after a divisional rendezvous at Kobe, Japan. Boiler problems aboard *Kaiser* had delayed his return to Shanghai and would prevent him from coming to Hong Kong to meet Diederichs. He would, however, send another ship, as soon as one became available. Diederichs therefore decided to continue to Shanghai aboard SS *Preussen*. He cabled Zeye accordingly, requesting a rendezvous at Wusung, downriver from Shanghai at the mouth of the Yangtze River.[39]

When *Preussen* reached the Wusung roadstead on 10 June, Diederichs again failed to find a German warship awaiting his arrival. This violated naval protocol, which dictated that Captain Zeye himself be on hand to greet his new commander. Diederichs later referred to this incident as "an immediate crisis" and described Zeye's breach of protocol as "insulting." In the absence of official transport, a fuming Diederichs proceeded upriver to Shanghai aboard a commercial steamer and checked into a hotel. By way of a hotel employee, he sent a curt note to *Kaiser*, notifying Zeye of his arrival.

To his pleasant surprise, Diederichs discovered that Georg Franzius was staying at the same hotel. That evening, the two colleagues sat down to discuss the engineer's findings. Franzius, who had arrived four months earlier, had already surveyed possible base sites at Amoy, Chusan, and Samsah. He had interviewed Ambassador Heyking and then participated in the formal ceremonies marking Tirpitz's departure from the East Asian station in April. He then visited Kiao-chou Bay aboard *Kaiser* in early May. He had sighted an unidentified Chinese warship in the bay and also noticed signs that the Chinese had begun to improve Tsingtao's fortifications. Franzius spent a week undertaking a fairly extensive survey of the bay and updating the original nautical charts drawn up in the 1870s. Based on a comparison of the four sites, Franzius concluded that Kiao-chou Bay exceeded the other sites "in every respect." Diederichs, of course, agreed. He also reminded Franzius that Kiao-chou possessed strategic and economic value as well. (Following his return to Kiel in August, Franzius filed his formal report recommending Kiao-chou as the site for a German naval base. He credited Diederichs's "reasonable judgment" in influencing his recommendation.)[40]

While awaiting word from Zeye, Diederichs also learned from Franzius that service politics explained Zeye's inappropriate behavior. The flag captain was a loyal member of Tirpitz's "torpedo gang." The Tirpitz faction disapproved of any officer, like Diederichs, who had not openly and enthusiastically embraced the battle fleet. According to Franzius, Zeye also hoped to take credit for the selection of Kiao-chou. Rather than meet Diederichs at

Wusung as custom required, Zeye had delayed so that he could complete and post his own positive report on Franzius's investigations. Zeye hoped that he might gain personal acclaim for the anticipated acquisition of a naval base in China and feared that Diederichs's assumption of command would foil his ambitious plan.[41]

To show his irritation, Diederichs waited until 13 June 1897 to board *Kaiser* and assume formal command of the division. In the meantime, he had met with Flag Lt. Gustav von Ammon, one of his former students from the Marineakademie, who briefed him on current issues affecting the station. When Diederichs finally boarded *Kaiser*, Zeye, who now reverted to flag captain, at least observed proper protocol. The ships's bosun formally piped Diederichs aboard as a crewman hoisted his rear admiral's flag at the fore. Diederichs also met Cdr. Reinhold Brussatis, commanding officer of SMS *Cormoran*, independently attached to the East Asian station but serving under his divisional command. Diederichs was unable to meet the commanding officers of the other ships—*Irene, Prinzess Wilhelm,* and *Arcona*—which were in Chefoo for gunnery practice.

Escorted by *Cormoran*, *Kaiser* departed Shanghai on 15 June. Diederichs's first act was to make the obligatory pilgrimage to the *Iltis Denkmal,* the monument in southern Shantung province that marked the site where gunboat *Iltis* sank in a storm in July 1896 with a loss of seventy-one officers and men. German merchants in China had provided funds to erect a monument and construct a cemetery to mark the *Iltis* tragedy.[42]

Then Diederichs began his primary mission, which was to identify the best site for a German naval base in China. He visited each potential site in turn, disguising each visit as the standard duty of the division to show the flag on the East Asian station. *Kaiser* first steamed south to Chusan, the site preferred by Knorr, before reversing course and calling on several ports in northern Shantung. Diederichs deliberately bypassed Kiao-chou at this time. Some months earlier, Knorr had halted calls there, fearing that regular visits would signal German intention. This in turn could provoke the Chinese government into further developing Kiao-chou's defenses against possible Western imperialism.[43] In any event, *Kaiser* halted next at Wei-hai-wei, temporarily occupied by the Japanese, on 21 June. Having already discounted Chusan, Diederichs also doubted the value of Wei-hai-wei as a naval base, describing the bay's lack of protection from wind and sea as "completely unfavorable."[44] *Kaiser* raised anchor three days later and proceeded west to Chefoo. En route, a lookout sighted HMS *Immortalité,* commanded by Capt. Edward Chichester. Diederichs suspected that the British had sent Chichester to investigate the German presence in Wei-hai-wei, which the they intended to occupy after the Japanese departure. Diederichs, in fact, would meet *Immortalité* and Chichester "under rather unfriendly circumstances" in Manila during the summer of 1898.[45]

Kaiser and *Cormoran* now joined the other ships of the division at Chefoo. For the first time since he assumed command, Diederichs had the entire division together under his orders. A series of ceremonial visits greeted his arrival as he met with each of his ship captains in turn: Cdr. Georg du Bois (*Irene*), Cdr. Adolf Thiele (*Prinzess Wilhelm*), and Cdr. Gottlieb Becker (*Arcona*). The occasion also marked a family gathering of sorts. Diederichs's older son Fritz was a lieutenant, j.g., aboard *Irene.* Adolf Thiele's brother August, who commanded SMS *Stosch,* was married to Diederichs's sister-in-law, Hanni. In fact, Diederichs, Fritz, Thiele, and du Bois all sent birthday greetings to Henni to mark her forty-fourth birthday on 27 June.[46]

Leaving *Kaiser* behind to participate in divisional exercises, Diederichs left Chefoo aboard *Prinzess Wilhelm* on 1 July. Accompanied by Fritz and Flag Lieutenant Ammon, Diederichs proceeded west to Peking, where he intended to meet with Ambassador Heyking. On arriving at the Chinese capital, Diederichs wrote Henni to express a sense of awe: "I am here in the capital of the Chinese Empire!" He and Fritz had a momentary opportunity to play the tourist, contrasting the impressive architecture of the Manchu quarter and the beautiful artistry of Ming tombs with the "indescribable filth" of poorer quarters of the city. His host and escort was Frau Elisabeth von Heyking, whom he described as gracious and hospitable.[47]

Diederichs had several discussions with Heyking, focusing particularly on the base issue. Heyking complained at one point that Tirpitz had never fully advised him of the Kaiserliche Marine's intentions in East Asia nor had Tirpitz sought his advice as to possible base sites. Heyking also warned Diederichs to act carefully. The diplomat feared that any use of force by the German navy would accelerate China's decline into chaos. He formally requested that Diederichs use negotiations first, with force as a last alternative, if or when it came time to acquire a base site. Diederichs refused to make any promises. He advised Heyking in turn that force alone, rather than diplomatic persuasion, would succeed in convincing China to cede a site to Germany. He also told the ambassador that the navy had not yet committed itself to a particular site. He himself, however, preferred Kiao-chou, asserting that "Kiao-chou alone is the goal of my efforts."[48]

Later that day, 6 July, Heyking conducted Diederichs and Fritz to the Tsungli-Yamen, China's foreign ministry. Diederichs's account of his meeting with Chinese diplomats bristles with resentment. According to the Chinese world order, China was far superior to "outer barbarians" such as the Europeans. Ironically, this attitude collided with Diederichs's own ingrained European contempt for the "yellow races." Thus, Chinese officials wore "stupid looks on their faces" as they grudgingly greeted him in a conference room that had all of the comfort of a "third-class waiting room in a side hall." Diederichs had praise only for Li Hung-chang, the grand old man of Chinese politics, whom he described as a powerful figure "who revealed great intelligence and temperament." Speaking through an interpreter, Diederichs raised the issue of a more formal German naval presence in China. He told Li that German ships needed a site in Northern China, such as Kiao-chou, to support divisional operations. He added, in a response to a question by Li, that German ships could not depend on Hong Kong, which was too far away, and Shanghai, whose dockyards were too busy. In a carefully worded discussion of Kiao-chou, Diederichs elicited the information from Li that the Chinese intended to construct their own maritime facilities there, in part to prevent a European power from claiming the site. Li also denied, quite vehemently, that China had granted any sovereign rights to Russia in regard to Kiao-chou. Based on this conversation, Diederichs concluded that China would not willingly concede a port to Germany, confirming the need for forceful German action.[49]

Diederichs left Peking on 11 July. As he and his companions made their way to the coast to rendezvous with *Prinzess Wilhelm*, he closely observed the Taku forts, which guarded the riverine approaches to Peking. (German forces would advance through the area three years later during the Boxer Rebellion in 1900.) Before he embarked aboard *Prinzess Wilhelm*, Diederichs met the Chinese general who commanded the local garrison. The entire garrison turned out on dress parade, with flags and a gun salute in Diederichs's honor. Neither the troops nor the officers impressed Diederichs, who had begun to develop a negative view of Chinese military readiness. He noted, for example, that many officers were physically unhealthy and lacked military bearing. The troops themselves bore equipment that he described as "medieval" and seemed no match for modern German weapons. He noted further that the garrison contained only about one-third of its standard complement, with uniformed coolies standing in for the missing troops. He suspected that the troop commanders had simply pocketed the extra pay owed to the absent soldiers. He therefore surmised—correctly, as events would prove—that the garrison at Kiao-chou would suffer from similar weaknesses.[50]

Prinzess Wilhelm rejoined the Kreuzerdivision in Korean waters on 16 July, enabling Diederichs to continue his tour of the East Asian station. Accompanied by his staff, Diederichs briefly visited Seoul to personally assess the political situation in the "Hermit Kingdom" and examine the outside possibility of a Korean base site. His visit quickly convinced him that Korea was caught between the rock of Japan and the hard spot of Russia. He found little, in fact, to convince him that Korean waters had value to German naval operations. He immediately returned to his ships and set sail for Hakodate, the most important port on the Japanese home island of Hokkaido. Fulfilling a promise he had made earlier to Heyking, he left *Cormoran* behind to patrol the Yellow Sea and Gulf of Chihli.

While his other ships coaled in Hakodate, Diederichs pondered his next move. He had intended to take the division to Vladivostok, the primary Russian port and naval base in the Pacific, but problems with *Kaiser*'s engines convinced him to turn south to Yokohama instead, in the company of *Prinzess Wilhelm*. He directed *Arcona* to survey the Sakhalin Islands and then join *Irene* in a brief cruise in Russian waters along the Siberian coast.[51]

Advised that the repairs to *Kaiser* would take at least five weeks, Diederichs decided to use the time to catch up on personal and professional correspondence. He proudly wrote to his wife that Captain Du Bois, their son's commanding officer aboard *Irene,* had complimented Fritz for his demeanor and professionalism as a young naval officer. On a more personal note, Diederichs also acknowledged some health problems, largely gastrointestinal, which had temporarily restricted him to a diet of oatmeal. He hoped that he could resume a regular diet soon.[52] He was equally concerned with Henni's health. She suffered from an extreme case of arthritis that impaired her dexterity and occasionally required her to use a wheelchair. She had written him in late July that her medical treatments had become quite expensive, cutting severely into her living expenses. Diederichs, who banked part of his salary in Berlin for Henni and received the remainder through pay warrants drawn on East Asian banks, wrote that "your good health is worth any cost" and promised to wire her additional funds. He could always live on the expense account the navy provided him for entertaining foreign officers and dignitaries.[53]

Diederichs also used his time at Yokohama to draft his final conclusions in regard to base sites in China. He dictated a forty-page report, entitled "A Military and Political Report on the Situation in China," on 21 August 1897. Once his yeoman had produced a clean copy, Diederichs placed the report in a sealed container and had a divisional ship carry it to Hong Kong, where it was placed in a safe aboard a North German Lloyd liner bound for Germany.

Diederichs's report first addressed the strategic necessity of German naval operations in East Asia. Tirpitz had questioned that need in his December 1896 report. Diederichs now responded, asserting strongly that "German interests here are indeed sufficient to justify corresponding [naval] strength." In fact, he argued, "We must energetically pursue the development of this power." He advised his superiors that only a German naval base would enable the navy to support Germany's continued economic and diplomatic presence in China. He recommended swift action to carry out this goal before the great imperial powers—he specifically cited Britain and France—devoured China: "I believe that Germany must use renewed effort in the brief time remaining before the collapse of China to reverse the long weakness of German power here."

Based on his survey of potential bases, Diederichs again disagreed with Tirpitz to emphatically contend that Kiao-chou was the only valid site. He evaluated and rejected the other sites in turn: Amoy lacked broad economic potential, Tirpitz's preference for a site in the Yangtze Basin would engender British opposition, and Chusan would raise insoluble diplomatic complications. Kiao-chou, on the other hand, had great potential. In his memo he cited economic arguments—the navy's strategic needs were indisputable—including the value of a rail network into Shantung's coal district, with a link to the Peking-Hankow line. He warned, in fact, that Germany's economic interests in China might fail to expand hereafter unless Kiao-chou were developed as the center of future financial activities. He also played the religious card: Any increased German presence would provide additional protection for German missions in Shantung. He therefore concluded emphatically, "It is my firm belief that Kiao-chou provides the greatest fulfillment of our needs as a German base."

He acknowledged that the German acquisition of Kiao-chou could produce international repercussions and cautioned, "We must proceed carefully." He nonetheless discounted Russian claims to Kiao-chou, noting that Russia seemed more interested in developing a sphere of influence in Manchuria to protect the Trans-Siberian Railroad. Likewise, he contended, Britain would not oppose action, since a German Kiao-chou would provide a buffer between British and Russian spheres. The French, as well, had become so involved in their expansion of power in southern China that they paid no attention to northern China. Above all, Diederichs proposed energetic action. He feared that news of Germany's plans might leak out and give the Chinese an opportunity to reinforce the garrison at Tsingtao and develop stronger defenses. He also realized, however, that under current circumstances Germany could not move against Kiao-chou without a legitimate reason. Given the history of European imperialism in China, that reason would need to be some violent act perpetrated by the Chinese government or individual Chinese subjects against German nationals or strategic interests.[54]

With his paperwork complete for the time being, Diederichs again played the tourist. Ambassador Herman von Treutler invited him to stay at the embassy in Tokyo. The high point of his visit came on 6 September when he visited the Imperial Palace for an audience with the Meiji emperor, Mutsuhito. Diederichs had a much higher opinion of the Japanese than he did of the Chinese. After all, only thirty years after the restoration of the imperial throne, the Japanese had dragged themselves into the nineteenth century, creating a strong industrial economy and defeating China in the Sino-Japanese War. Later, on a tour of the vibrant Japanese capital, Diederichs purchased an ornamental wooden chest as a gift for Senden, which, he joked to Henni, could hold all the reports he had received from Diederichs.[55]

Work crews finally completed repairs on 29 September, allowing the flagship a brief shakedown cruise in Tokyo Bay. Diederichs and *Kaiser* then steamed south to Kobe, where the flagship's crew used the period for torpedo practice and minesweeping training. Diederichs went ashore, rented a horse, and make a quick overland trip to Kyoto, the traditional imperial and cultural capital of Japan. Although soaked by a sudden wind and rain squall, he nonetheless enjoyed his brief visit in the old imperial city, where he purchased souvenirs, including a tea set, for Henni. He paid a price in health, however, writing Henni that "the old pains have returned."[56]

After departing Kobe on 8 October, Diederichs continued his tour of Japanese ports. He visited Nagasaki next, where he met Adm. Sir Archibald Buller, commander in chief of Britain's East Asian station. The ceremonial visits they exchanged allowed Diederichs to tour HMS *Centurion* (10,500 tons, four 320-mm guns), Buller's powerful flagship. The two flag officers developed a strong professional friendship and correspondence thereafter. Diederichs then visited Kagoshima, on Kyushu's southern coast, where the local governor guided Diederichs on a tour of the port's modern maritime and industrial facilities.[57]

Kagoshima was Diederichs's last port of call on his "grand tour" of the East Asian station. His return to Shanghai aboard *Kaiser* on 20 October also marked the end of the division's summer patrol season. His ships would spend much of the winter undergoing necessary refits and repairs. Thus, his first task in Shanghai was to make arrangements and draw up a schedule for the winter work. Over the next few months, he intended to send *Irene* to Hong Kong and order *Arcona* to Shanghai for repairs. Once these two ships returned to active duty in November, he planned to send *Kaiser* to Nagasaki and repair *Prinzess Wilhelm* in Shanghai. In the meantime, he assigned *Cormoran* to Ambassador Heyking, who intended to visit the German community in the Wuhan (Wuchang-Hankow) megalopolis six hundred nautical miles up the Yangtze River. (*Cormoran,* with a shallow draft drawing only five meters, was an ideal ship for the Yangtze patrol.) Diederichs had once hoped to accompany Heyking, but divisional duties forced him to remain behind. Instead, Flag Captain Zeye and Flag Lieutenant von Ammon would accompany Heyking. Diederichs used this circumstance—the need to disperse his force between three different ports—to underline the problems associated with the lack of a German base in East Asia. He warned the OKM that, with his ships dispersed, he would have difficulty undertaking major missions.[58]

In fact, Kiao-chou, was never far from his attention. Although the OKM had prohibited visits to Kiao-chou, Diederichs now requested permission to take *Kaiser* and *Prinzess Wilhelm* to Kiao-chou for fall gunnery practice and then station *Prinzess Wilhelm* there during the winter months. This would accustom the Chinese to a German naval presence in the bay and lay the foundation for a later claim if necessary. Diederichs, who had not yet visited Kiao-chou, reminded Knorr that a personal evaluation of Kiao-chou was "urgently valuable" in his quest for a base site.[59]

Diederichs's request caused consternation in Berlin. Tirpitz, who was currently preparing a draft of his Fleet Law for submission to the Reichstag, feared that any adventurism in China, particularly if it failed or produced German casualties, would turn public and parliamentary opinion against his bill. He therefore complained that Diederichs's plan posed "the greatest danger" for Germany.[60] Senden, the emperor's senior naval aide, preferred Chusan as the site of a German naval base and therefore opposed Diederichs's request. He nonetheless acknowledged that he had recently spoken with Franzius, who evinced great surprise that the navy had not yet selected Kiao-chou.[61] Adm. Hans Koester, acting commander in chief during the absence of Knorr on sick leave, ignored both arguments. He understood full well the importance of overseas naval bases to global operations and therefore granted Diederichs permission to visit Kiao-chou later in the fall.[62]

Circumstances changed dramatically and quickly only a few days later. Diederichs's August report, carried to Germany in a sealed pouch aboard a North German Lloyd liner, reached Koester at the Naval High Command on 25 October. Koester promptly forwarded copies to Tirpitz at the RMA and to the new foreign minister, Bernhard von Bülow. He then presented the report to Kaiser Wilhelm in a formal audience on 1 November. Diederichs's forceful recommendation was the final argument that Wilhelm needed to make a conclusive decision. He now directed the navy to seize Kiao-chou when the opportunity arose.[63]

Meanwhile, in China, Diederichs had decided to take the initiative. He met with Karl Reyner, the local director of Carlowitz & Company, a major

German firm doing business in China, on 27 October. Acting in his extraordinary capacity as commander of the Cruiser Division, Diederichs signed a secret agreement with Reyner whereby Carlowitz would act as the Kaiserliche Marine's agent in the purchase of land at Kiao-chou. Because only Chinese subjects could own land outside treaty ports, Carlowitz agreed to work through "dummy persons." Diederichs committed the navy to compensating the firm in the amount of purchase costs and expenses, plus two years' interest. If Germany did not acquire the property and the government refused to compensate the company, Diederichs agreed to personally cover the costs, estimated at ten thousand marks, himself. Reyner and Diederichs signed the agreement in the presence of the consul-general on 28 October 1897.[64]

Events now seemed to move more rapidly. Cdr. Reinhard Brussatis, *Cormoran*'s commanding officer, cabled Diederichs on 31 October that a Chinese mob had assaulted German officers and insulted the imperial flag in Wuchang. Brussatis and four officers had boarded *Cormoran*'s steam launch for a quick visit to Wuchang from Hankow the day before. As the launch approached the Wuchang pier, a mob of approximately five hundred Chinese attacked the boat's passengers with rocks and paving stones. The attack bruised but did not seriously injure several crewmen. Brussatis and his officers, armed only with sidearms, landed and attempted to walk inland but turned back when the mob attacked a second time. The officers retreated to the launch and then returned to *Cormoran*. Brussatis promptly reported the incident to Ambassador Heyking, who lodged an immediate note of protest with Viceroy Chang Chih-tung, and cabled Diederichs.[65]

Diederichs immediately sought to use this incident as the justification for the seizure of Kiao-chou. He cabled Berlin, requesting permission to move against Kiao-chou "in pursuit of our further goals."[66] In turn, Koester forwarded the request to Tirpitz and Bülow for their opinion and advice. Their responses convinced Koester, however, that the incident did not warrant the occupation of Kiao-chou. Tirpitz feared that such an act would disrupt his plans to seek parliamentary approval for his battle fleet, while Bülow worried that Russia would object to Diederichs's actions. Tirpitz and Bülow both preferred caution to action, accepting Ambassador Heyking's alternate recommendation to demand the punishment of the ringleaders and a formal apology by the Chinese government. Koester therefore telegraphed Diederichs to take no action but, rather, to let Heyking deal with the incident diplomatically.[67]

Fearing that Berlin would miss "this wonderful opportunity," Diederichs appealed the decision and again requested permission to move against Kiao-chou. He directed Cdr. Otto von Burski, *Kaiser*'s acting commander, and Commander Thiele aboard *Prinzess Wilhelm* to begin preparations for an assault on Kiao-chou. His impatience only increased when Admiral Buller asked him why the Germans had not acted more forcefully in response to the Wuchang incident.[68] When he received no response by noon on 5 November, he wrote, "My hopes for energetic action from Berlin now dwindled."[69]

PROCEED IMMEDIATELY TO KIAO-CHOU

Additional events again intervened, however. Diederichs received a new, more frightening telegram from Heyking on 6 November: "German Catholic missionaries wire from south Shantung that one member murdered, one missing, home plundered."[70] Succeeding telegrams advised Diederichs that members of a xenophobic group—the *Ta Tao Hui* (Society of the Great Knife)—had murdered two German Catholic priests in a village in southern Shantung province on 1 November. The priests had belonged to the Society of the Divine Word, a German order that had begun work in Shantung province in 1880. Kaiser Wilhelm had assumed personal responsibility for the protection of the society's missionaries a decade later.[71]

Sensing his opportunity, Diederichs again sought permission to move against Kiao-chou. He justified intervention on the grounds of the original Sino-Prussian Treaty of 1861, which allowed the German navy to intervene on behalf of endangered German nationals. He therefore telegraphed Berlin, "Catholic missionaries murdered Shantung. Shall compensation for this with *Cormoran* incident be used in the sense of my cable of 3 November?" Receiving no response, he repeated his request more adamantly on 7 November: "May incidents be exploited in pursuit of further goals?"[72]

The deafening silence from Berlin signified a brief period of governmental indecision. Upon receipt of Diederichs's first Kiao-chou cable, Chancellor Hohenlohe had advised caution, preferring a diplomatic, rather than a military, solution.[73] Wilhelm, however, shrugged off the advice and decided on direct action: "The energetic intervention of our fleet must produce abundant vengeance for this [massacre]."[74] He was even more poetic in a message to Foreign Minister Bülow:

> Thousands of German Christians will breathe a sigh of relief in the knowledge that German warships are present [in China]. Hundreds of German merchants will shout for joy when they learn that Germany has finally won an imperial foothold in Asia. Hundreds of thousands of Chinese will begin to tremble when they feel the mailed fist of the German empire on their necks. And the whole German people will be happy that their government has done a manly deed.[75]

Now that he had made a decision, Wilhelm dispatched one more cable. He addressed this one to Diederichs: "Proceed immediately to Kiao-chou with the entire squadron. Occupy suitable sites and seize the area as compensation for the missionaries. Keep the objectives of your trip secret."[76] Diederichs, who received the telegram on 8 November, immediately acknowledged receipt of his orders: "Will proceed immediately against Kiao-chou with greatest energy."[77] Diederichs had achieved his hopes for moving on Kiao-chou: As Diederichs noted in his memoir, "With this order, the responsibility for action now passed to me."[78]

Although Diederichs had promised to move quickly, he faced several obstacles before he could implement his orders. His primary concern was a momentary lack of warships. He had only heavy cruiser *Kaiser* and light cruiser *Prinzess Wilhelm* currently available. Small cruiser *Cormoran* (nineteen hundred tons, eight 105-mm guns) was steaming down the Yangtze from Wuchang but would not arrive in Shanghai for several days. Steam-sail corvette *Arcona* remained docked at Shanghai for an annual refit; dockyard workers would not complete repairs until 24 November. Light cruiser *Irene* required more substantial work; a Hong Kong dockyard would not finish repairing engines, relining propeller shaft casings, and replacing crankshaft bearings until 30 November.

Diederichs believed that he would need every ship under his command to take and hold Kiao-chou. Although he acknowledged that the Sino-Japanese War had decimated the Chinese fleet, the Chinese still had several cruisers that could inflict extensive damage with their 210-mm guns and torpedo boats and gunboats that could launch hit-and-run attacks against his ships. After all, he had no friendly bases to repair battle damage, and international law would limit his access to neutral facilities. He therefore contacted his absentee captains and ordered them to complete their respective tasks as soon as possible and proceed to Kiao-chou independently.[79]

A second problem was secrecy. Diederichs feared that other European powers would intervene or the Chinese would quickly reinforce Tsingtao if his mission became known. He therefore made no public comment on the missionaries' murders as he prepared his ships for sea. When a reporter for the *North China Daily News* asked him for an explanation, he responded that he intended to take *Kaiser* north to Kiao-chou for the previously announced gunnery exercises and send *Prinzess Wilhelm* and *Cormoran* south to Samsah Bay to commence antipiracy patrols. In the meantime, he quietly hired Chinese interpreters, purchased riding and pack horses, and leased steamers to carry coal, provisions, and building supplies.[80]

Diederichs confronted an additional problem from a somewhat unexpected quarter. Heyking, who had returned to Shanghai on 9 November, asked Diederichs to postpone action until he could return to Peking and seek an audience with Chinese diplomats. Heyking preferred alternative compensation for the murder of the missionaries, including the judicial punishment of the alleged murderers and the payment of financial reparations. Diederichs, however, refused to postpone his operations, arguing that any delay would only allow the Chinese to reinforce Kiao-chou or other European powers to foil German plans. He therefore advised Heyking that he intended to move as swiftly as possible to implement his imperial orders.[81]

With preparations complete, Diederichs directed Captain Zeye to weigh anchor and proceed to sea soon after dusk on 10 November. To maintain his subterfuge and the facade of peaceful intent, Diederichs directed *Prinzess Wilhelm* and *Cormoran* not to leave until the following day. The two ships would rendezvous with *Kaiser* at sea on the day after and strike targets on and around Kiao-chou Bay on 14 November. As *Kaiser* prepared to stand into danger, Diederichs posted a final note to Henni: "We depart soon for the long-waited exploration of a northern port." He closed with an enigmatic reference to their upcoming anniversary: "My thoughts will be with you on the fourteenth."[82]

At sea, Diederichs discussed his intentions with the divisional staff in *Kaiser*'s flag quarters on the morning of 11 November. Much to his frustration, Flag Captain Zeye promptly proposed postponing the assault until Tuesday, the sixteenth, to give Ambassador Heyking a final opportunity to reach a diplomatic solution in Peking. Flag Lieutenant von Ammon recommended Monday, the fifteenth, to avoid battle on the Sabbath. Because of "the imminent danger of intrigue" by other powers, Diederichs advised his staff officers that "we [can] not afford to lose a single moment" and confirmed the operations for Sunday, the fourteenth.[83]

Diederich's three ships rendezvoused at sea at dusk on 12 November. *Prinzess Wilhelm* and *Cormoran* had departed Wusung at 1040 hours on the eleventh, turning south until out of sight of land before reversing course to the north. The two ships exchanged regular signal-light messages during the night of 11–12 November to remain on station and avoid missing the rendezvous with *Kaiser*. Lookouts aboard *Prinzess Wilhelm* sighted columns of smoke to the north at 1745 on 12 November, with *Kaiser* heaving into sight at 1800. The three ships then formed line ahead with the flagship in the van and proceeded toward Kiao-chou.[84]

Diederichs called Captains Thiele (*Prinzess Wilhelm*) and Becker (*Arcona*) aboard *Kaiser* at a midnight conference to brief them on his plans. The attack would commence at dawn on the fourteenth with a naval bombardment. *Kaiser* and *Prinzess Wilhelm* to stand offshore to shell Chinese positions in and around Tsingtao. *Cormoran*, with her shallow draft, would steam into Kiao-chou Bay to provide inshore fire support. Following the bombardment, divisional boats would embark Captain Zeye and the naval brigade, drawn from the larger crews of *Kaiser* and *Prinzess Wilhelm*, and land them directly on the beach on the seaward side of Tsingtao.

The division arrived off Tsingtao soon after dawn on 13 November. The three ships cleared for action but made no other aggressive moves. When their arrival provoked no defensive response from ashore, Diederichs concluded that his secretive preparations had succeeded. He went ashore in his admiral's barge under the guise of a friendly visit, to which he was entitled under the terms of an earlier Sino-Prussian treaty. Captain Zeye, who had visited Kiao-chou with Franzius in May 1897, acted as his guide. They landed at a long pier, where Diederichs observed a new fort still under construction.

Diederichs entered Tsingtao to reconnoiter the area and examine Chinese readiness. The local garrison consisted of approximately three thousand regular troops, under the command of General Chang Kao-yüan. Half of these troops garrisoned Tsingtao while the other fifteen hundred manned four outlying forts and an artillery battery. (Diederichs's combined crews numbered fewer than eleven hundred officers and men.)

Although the Chinese had a numerical advantage, the Germans had qualitative superiority. The Chinese troops carried obsolete German *Jägerbuschen* M/71 rifles rendered largely unusable by rust. Diederichs's own naval infantrymen carried modern Mauser rifles, 8-mm machine guns, and 37-mm field artillery. A brief visit to the garrison's powder magazine produced similar intelligence. Diederichs noted only a few small kegs and wooden chests holding loose powder grains of "doubtful value." Diederichs believed further that the four Chinese forts had limited defensive potential. Surrounded by shallow ditches, the forts had four-meter-high earthen walls and narrow wooden gates. Diederichs suspected that the narrowness of the gates would hinder the movement of troops out of the forts and thus impede their ability to deploy against the German assault. The earthen walls would likewise provide little protection against his ships' guns. Based on these initial observations, he concluded that the Chinese forces were completely unaware of the impending German attack and equally unprepared to defend their positions.

Diederichs determined that the only serious threat to his forces came from the garrison's gun battery. This fortified position consisted of fourteen 8-cm Krupp guns dating from the 1870s. Their short range—fifteen hundred meters—presented only minimal danger to Diederichs's ships, which could stand offshore and bombard the emplacements with *Kaiser*'s 260-mm or *Prinzess Wilhelm*'s 150-mm guns. The Chinese artillery, however, commanded the proposed landing site and could thus disrupt Diederichs's amphibious assault. He therefore decided to modify his landing plan, proposing to disembark his forces directly onto the pier rather than on the narrow beach under the guns of the Chinese battery. On closer inspection, however, he noticed that the Chinese gunners had inexplicably rendered their guns inoperable by removing the breech blocks. He now concluded that the German attack against the unprepared Chinese would be a farce.[85]

Sunday, 14 November 1897, dawned clear and cool with a slight easterly wind. *Cormoran,* with her shallow draft, steamed into the inner bay to bring the forts and powder magazine directly under her 105-mm guns. *Kaiser* and *Prinzess Wilhelm* cleared for action at 0600, manned main batteries, and hoisted out boats to transport the amphibious force—30 officers, 77 petty officers, and 610 seamen—ashore. Although Diederichs knew that the Chinese gun battery presented no threat, he still worried that the Chinese could disrupt his landing force with small arms. The first wave therefore moved quickly to the pier and began to disembark its troops. The second wave, including Diederichs and his staff officers, followed moments later.[86]

To the beat of patriotic Prussian marches performed by *Kaiser*'s band, the force formed up into two columns at the foot of the pier. Diederichs, on horseback, and one detachment marched into Tsingtao in the direction of the main garrison and the artillery battery, while Zeye led the other to occupy the outlying forts and powder magazine. A special unit advanced into the center of town to destroy the garrison's telegraph line, which denied General Chang the ability to communicate with his superiors. The Chinese, who were used to visits by foreign warships, were caught by surprise when the German troops landed. Two Chinese battalions—approximately six hundred troops—mustered into formation at the main fort but made no attempt to prevent the German advance.

Although Diederichs was momentarily unsure whether the Chinese would actively oppose his operations, the lack of an aggressive Chinese response convinced him that his plans had succeeded. In Shanghai, his ability to keep the expedition secret had prevented the Chinese from being aware of his plans and given his forces the advantage of surprise. In Tsingtao, the speed and effectiveness of his maneuvers—his forces had achieved their primary objectives by 0815—had denied Chang to opportunity to effectively respond. Diederichs now concluded, "I now had him completely in hand."[87]

Once his forces were in position, Diederichs sent Ammon forward to make contact with General Chang. Ammon carried a written ultimatum that demanded an immediate Chinese withdrawal from Tsingtao and its environs. Chang greeted Ammon politely and promptly extended a formal invitation to Diederichs to join him for dinner. Somewhat nonplussed, Ammon requested the general's forbearance and presented him with Diederichs's ultimatum and the proclamation announcing the occupation of Kiao-chou. Chang requested time to consider the demands and withdrew into his headquarters. As German patrols posted copies of the proclamation at various sites in Tsingtao, Diederichs awaited developments. A trio of mounted Chinese messengers eventually appeared with an invitation for Diederichs to meet Chang in the garrison's *Yamen,* or headquarters. Diederichs declined, asserting his superior military position, and instead invited Chang to meet him within the German lines.

Chang appeared at 1000 with a mounted escort. Diederichs advised him that he intended to occupy the entire Kiao-chou region as compensation for the murder of the two German missionaries. He therefore demanded that the Chinese withdraw their forces immediately or face destruction by a superior force. Chang initially refused to withdraw, telling Diederichs that to act without permission would "cost him his head." He requested additional time to consider his options and, if necessary, prepare his troops for evacuation. He noted that many members of his garrison had lived in Tsingtao for some time and had numerous dependents and possessions that would make withdrawal difficult and slow. Diederichs stood firm, believing that he needed to handle Chang "with strength if I were to continue to dominate negotiations." When Diederichs continued to threaten Chang with the stick of naval bombardment while offering him the carrot of honorable withdrawal, Chang finally agreed. Moments later, Chinese troops began to evacuate their remaining fortified positions and withdraw to the north. Diederichs's sailors quickly moved in to replace them.

As the landing detachment raised the imperial German flag and *Prinzess Wilhelm* fired a twenty-one-gun salute, Diederichs formally proclaimed the German occupation of Kiao-chou at 1420 hours on 14 November 1897. He announced to his mustered troops and a few curious residents that he had occupied Tsingtao in order to establish a permanent foothold for German sovereignty and culture on Chinese soil. He assured his Chinese listeners that Germany continued to be a good friend to China and that the occupation was not intended as a hostile act but rather as compensation for the deaths of the German missionaries. He warned, however, that he would punish anyone who tried to impede the German action.[88]

Diederichs established his headquarters in Chang's former office. His signalmen quickly repaired the severed telegraph line and established a signal office next door. Moments later, with service restored, the German telegrapher began to receive messages. To his surprise, he discovered that the first two incoming cables were addressed to Diederichs himself. The encoded telegrams—sent from Berlin—had come separately via Shanghai and Chefoo. Because the code book was still aboard *Kaiser,* Diederichs sent Ammon back to the flagship to retrieve it. In the meantime, he dispatched a brief telegram in the clear to Berlin: "Executed orders. All quiet."[89]

When Ammon returned with the code book and deciphered the telegrams, their content stunned Diederichs. The cables, duplicate messages sent by the OKM, canceled his original orders and directed him to suspend operations against Kiao-chou pending negotiations with the Chinese government. If he had already occupied Tsingtao, the new orders directed him to not assert German sovereignty over Kiao-chou but rather consider his presence to be temporary.[90] Diederichs responded succinctly, "Proclamation already published. Refers to occupation [*Besetzung*], not seizure [*Ergreifung*]. Revocation not possible."[91] The telegram left Diederichs in a state of "understandable tension." He feared that Berlin had lost its collective nerve and wondered what circumstances—diplomatic or political—threatened to undo his achievements.[92] Another telegram, however, soon resolved his anxiety and reaffirmed his actions: "Congratulations on occupation. Proclamation remains in effect."[93]

Diederichs's rapid actions had made the acquisition of Kiao-chou an accomplished fact. His decision to occupy Kiao-chou on 14 November, rather than delay until the fifteenth, had borne fruit. He happily wrote Henni, "By the time you receive these pages, you will have already learned from the newspapers that the German flag was raised over Chinese soil at a location whose occupation I have actively worked for since my time as chief of staff in Berlin."[94]

Praise now began to roll in. Wilhelm acknowledged Diederichs's accomplishments by promoting him to vice admiral. Senden wrote, "You must now be swimming in bliss with the sudden and unexpected fulfillment of your wish."[95] Hoffmann, former commander of the division, applauded Diederichs's long-term commitment to Kiao-chou and then advised him that a "craven" Foreign Ministry had nearly blocked Diederichs's "final coup."[96] Koester likewise praised Diederichs for his devotion to the base issue and his triumphal success at Kiao-chou.[97] The one flag officer who did not offer congratulations was Tirpitz, who saw Diederichs's actions as a threat to his Navy Bill.[98]

It was only later, in fact, that Diederichs learned just how close Tirpitz and others had come to stopping his mission. His initial telegram, notifying OKM of the murder of the German missionaries, had caused great consternation among those who feared the domestic and diplomatic repercussions of any move against Kiao-chou. Foreign Minister Bülow and State Secretary Tirpitz had exerted pressure on Wilhelm to suspend the operation and send the cable that stunned Diederichs at his moment of triumph. But Diederichs had moved so quickly and effectively that the emperor had little choice but to reverse that order and approve what Diederichs had already done. Diederichs had reason to complain that the "timid behavior" of Tirpitz and Bülow had nearly ruined his mission. Any delay, he noted, would have been disastrous. He underlined this point with additional evidence: The weather on the fifteenth brought rain, fog, and heavy seas, all of which would have made an amphibious landing virtually impossible.[99]

THE MAILED FIST

Although Diederichs had now succeeded in his initial mission to plant the German flag on Chinese soil, he still needed to strengthen his position if he were to ensure German sovereignty over Kiao-chou. In many ways, the more difficult part of his mission was still ahead. After all, he still faced two challenges: developing Kiao-chou as a German naval base and defending the new possession against the possibility of Chinese counterattack. The need for new security arrangements was first on his mind, particularly when he learned that the Chinese had activated several German-built torpedo boats, including *Fei Ying* (eight hundred tons, two 105-mm guns, three 360-mm torpedo tubes) and had dispatched light cruiser *Fu Ch'ing* (twenty-two hundred tons, two 210-mm guns) to confront the Germans at Kiao-chou. Although these warships did not present a major threat to Diederichs's forces (*Kaiser* alone displaced eighty-eight hundred tons and carried a main battery of 260-mm guns), they could cause significant damage with hit-and-run attacks at a time when, after all, Diederichs lacked immediate access to repair facilities.[100]

Although SMS *Arcona* rejoined the Division on 17 November, Diederichs immediately requested additional reinforcements from Germany. He specifically asked for modern heavy cruiser *Kaiserin Augusta* (sixty-two hundred tons, twelve 150-mm guns) to supplement his division and a battalion of regular naval infantry to garrison Tsingtao.[101] Knorr approved both requests. He promptly cut orders dispatching *Kaiserin Augusta,* currently in the Mediterranean, to East Asia and ordered the formation of a new unit, the Third *Seebattalion,* drawn from existing units of the First and Second Battalions. Knorr also convinced Kaiser Wilhelm to reconfigure and reinforce Diederichs's current four-ship *Kreuzerdivision* to become the eight-ship *Kreuzergeschwader,* the Cruiser Squadron. Thus, Diederichs's existing command—*Kaiser, Irene, Prinzess Wilhelm,* and *Arcona*—became the new squadron's First Division, while Knorr created a new Second Division to include heavy cruisers *Kaiserin Augusta* and *Deutschland* (eighty-eight hundred tons, eight 260-mm guns), light cruiser *Gefion* (forty-two hundred tons, ten 105-mm guns), and *Cormoran*. Knorr told the emperor that the presence of the Cruiser Squadron in East Asian waters would give the Kaiserliche Marine much greater versatility to respond to new political or military developments.[102]

Kaiser Wilhelm enthusiastically concurred with these recommendations. He first promoted Diederichs to vice admiral, both as a reward for Kiao-chou and as a rank commensurate with his new squadron command. He then appointed his own brother, Rear Admiral Prince Heinrich of Prussia, to command the Second Division. When *Deutschland* and *Gefion* departed German waters on 15 December 1897, Kaiser Wilhelm toasted their mission with an evocative phrase: "Should anyone seek to hinder you in the proper exercise of our legitimate rights, go for them with a mailed fist."[103]

Closer at hand, Diederichs took measures to ensure the security of Tsingtao itself. Although he had limited confidence in his flag captain, he nonetheless appointed Captain Zeye as military governor of Kiao-chou. Diederichs created a standing garrison of approximately four hundred officers and men, drawn from *Kaiser* and *Prinzess Wilhelm,* and assigned *Cormoran* to provide inshore fire support. Work crews strengthened Tsingtao's fortifications, mounted 37-mm artillery on field carriages brought ashore from the division's ships, and repaired the original 88-mm shore battery. Diederichs formally designated an occupation zone extending approximately twenty kilometers outward from Tsingtao and ordered Zeye to disarm and expel any Chinese troops remaining within the area.

When it came to developing Kiao-chou as a naval base, Diederichs drew on several past experiences. He had taken civil engineering courses at the Marineakademie twenty years earlier and had developed an amateur's interest in architecture when he designed a house in Kiel in 1885. More recently, of course, he had spent four years at the Kiel shipyard. He now brought these skills to work on the new facility. He assigned Lt. (sg) Ernst von Bibra, seconded from *Prinzess Wilhelm,* the task of overseeing the project. He directed Bibra to hire native work crews, which, he noted, allowed his own seamen to carry out the duties aboard ship, while providing financial benefits to a depressed region that suffered from high unemployment. SS *Longmoon,* a civilian steamer Diederichs had chartered in Shanghai, arrived on 15 November with a load of building supplies.[104]

Diederichs needed haste since the full onset of winter and the arrival of reinforcements would test his new plans. In fact, workers repaired and expanded Tsingtao's existing barracks as temperatures soon dropped to zero, driven by brutal winds out of the north and northwest. The native workers converted several of the lightly constructed Chinese barracks, which often lacked doors and had only paper windows, into more permanent and substantial quarters. They cut and set windows to provide light, installed stoves and cupboards, constructed bunk beds and flooring, dug latrines, cleaned and decked wells, constructed stables, repaired roofs, improved streets, erected lighting, and established a new telegraph office.

Diederichs also kept his regular crews busy. Divisional navigators charted soundings, placed buoys, prepared landing stages, and dredged an anchorage in preparation for the construction of permanent dockyard facilities. Diederichs himself reorganized the local customs service, developed a series of property regulations, and began to transform Tsingtao from a Chinese village into a German city. Minor irritants occasionally occurred. Though Diederichs had hired native Chinese in Shanghai as interpreters, they spoke only the Ningpo dialect, while the local residents spoke Shantung. Also, Diederichs's men soon discovered that the local garrison had taken all the cooking utensils with them when they withdrew. This forced German cooks to prepare meals aboard ship and transport them ashore to provide warm food. Occasional problems notwithstanding, the course of progress allowed Diederichs to send positive reports back to Berlin.[105]

More severe difficulties developed elsewhere. General Chang now became a source of intrigue and complications. Diederichs had initially offered to convey Chang to Shanghai, but the Chinese general had refused, fearing punishment by his superiors in Peking. Diederichs had therefore granted him permission to remain in Tsingtao with his family, believing that Chang might prove useful as a hostage against hostile acts by his former troops. In fact, when reports reached Diederichs that a large body of Chinese troops had refused to leave the occupied zone, Chang agreed to ride out to their location and order them to lay down their arms and leave the occupied area. Before he left Tsingtao on the afternoon of 16 November, Chang gave Diederichs his word and promised to return to Tsingtao as soon as he had completed his mission.

Diederichs himself left Tsingtao on 18 November, *Cormoran* and *Arcona* to explore the inner bay. As the two warships steamed deeper into the bay, Diederichs received a message from Commander Thiele that Chang had broken his word, joined his former troops, and begun preparations to attack the German positions. Diederichs promptly ordered Zeye to prepare a force to move out and arrest Chang but not to leave until Diederichs could return to Tsingtao. When *Cormoran* and *Arcona* reached Tsingtao soon after dawn on 19 November, Diederichs found that Zeye had already marched out with the bulk of the garrison, leaving Tsingtao largely unprotected from an overland attack. Angry over Zeye's insubordination and recklessness, Diederichs immediately ordered Captains Brussatis and Becker to disembark landing detachments from *Cormoran* and *Arcona* to reinforce the forces remaining in Tsingtao. Meanwhile, Zeye quickly caught up with Chang and placed him under arrest. When Zeye and Chang returned to Tsingtao late in the afternoon of 19 November, Diederichs confined Chang to the pier fort and reprimanded Zeye, "who seemed very pleased with his 'success,'" for disobeying orders.[106]

Diederichs resumed his earlier mission to tour the inner bay on 20 November. He particularly wanted to visit the town of Kiao-chou, which lay at the western end of the bay and served as the district capital. *Cormoran* and *Arcona* disembarked his landing force, which numbered two hundred officers and men and light artillery, about four kilometers from Kiao-chou town. When the overland route proved too rough for wheeled vehicles, Diederichs decided to leave his two 37 mm guns behind and proceeded with a single machine gun for fire support. The column reached the gates of the walled city in mid-afternoon. Diederichs observed that the outer walls had deteriorated considerably and that the main city gate lacked a guard. After posting the proclamation, Diederichs spoke with the district's acting magistrate, a junior mandarin. He appeared cooperative and agreed to obey Diederichs's instructions. Diederichs noted that the inhabitants appeared resentful of the German presence but presented no outright resistance.

The detachment then moved into a small temple to spend the night. Although the magistrate had provided firewood, a sudden cold snap caught Diederichs and his men with only minimal protection against the bitter weather. The officers were quartered in the main shrine, which housed religious statues. The enlisted men slept around a giant campfire in the courtyard. Diederichs rolled himself up in his greatcoat and slept on the cold stone floor. He noted that an innovative junior officer slept more comfortably after discovering that "Chinese saints also perform miracles." The officer had stripped "the grim figure of its silken extravagance and fell asleep under the colorful covering." After a comfortable night's sleep, the "rested and robust officer restored the idol to its former splendor and went about his daily duties." Diederichs noted that everyone, except the aforementioned officer, spent an uncomfortable night.

Diederichs met with a delegation of municipal officials before his departure on 21 November. The senior official acknowledged German sovereignty with Confucian references, referring to himself as "your younger, ignorant brother Liu [who] bows low to the earth before you." Lacking sufficient troops to garrison the town, Diederichs warned his "younger brother" to abide by German occupation policies. The detachment marched back to the anchorage, reembarked aboard *Arcona* and *Cormoran,* and returned to Tsingtao later in the evening.[107]

Diederichs returned to discover that old dangers and new intrigues threatened the German position at Tsingtao. "The behavior of General Chang and his troops," he noted, "again proved annoying." Intelligence reports had produced information that a Chinese force, numbering fifteen hundred troops of "good quality," had begun to fortify positions at the northeast boundary of the occupation zone near the town of Zankau. Li Ping-heng, the governor of Shantung, had ordered additional troops to proceed there as well. Diederichs therefore directed Captain Zeye to take command of a new expeditionary force and expel the Chinese troops from German-occupied territory. The detachment, which numbered approximately 350 troops, departed on 27 November. Diederichs gave Zeye, "who burned eagerly for glory," careful instructions to avoid bloodshed if possible. Diederichs simply wanted to expel the Chinese troops from the occupation. He did not want a full-fledged war with China. He therefore accompanied the column for the first few hours in order to restrain Zeye's aggressiveness.[108]

Diederichs returned to Tsingtao to prepare additional defenses against the Chinese threat. Accompanied by Becker, as acting garrison commander, he rode around Tsingtao to examine existing defensive positions. He shifted units, identified fields of fire, ordered the development of new artillery positions, and called more sailors ashore to serve as naval infantrymen. Early on the afternoon of 28 November, he also received formal notification of his promotion to vice admiral and appointment as commander of the Cruiser Squadron. To mark the event, *Prinzess Wilhelm* fired a fifteen-gun salute as *Kaiser* hoisted Diederichs's new flag to the fore. The salute, however, frightened some of Tsingtao's native residents, who thought that the anticipated attack had begun.[109]

Meanwhile, Diederichs had lost contact with Zeye. Chinese units had maneuvered around the expeditionary force and interdicted Zeye's line of communication back to Tsingtao. Additional Chinese troops—Diederichs estimated the number at three hundred—had infiltrated deeper into the occupation zone and taken up positions on the high ground above Tsingtao in sniping range of the German garrison. Intelligence reports also noted that large numbers of Chinese troops had begun to move into Shantung from neighboring provinces. To compound matters, the Chinese cut the telegraph line linking Tsingtao to the outside world.

Diederichs responded to these threats with a general alert. He moved *Kaiser* and *Prinzess Wilhelm* closer to shore to bring the Chinese troops into the range of his main batteries. He also ordered his captains to arm their cutters and launches with machine guns to patrol the shallow waters and inlets near Tsingtao. Diederichs dispatched *Cormoran* into the inner bay to attempt to make contact with Zeye through signal light and flag hoist and to provide inshore fire support. Diederichs even hired a Chinese messenger, at an "exorbitant" fee, to ride out with a coded message. The money was wasted, however; the messenger soon returned, complaining that Chinese soldiers had prevented his passage. With tensions rising, German sentries reported mysterious lights emanating from Chang's former quarters and then almost opened fire on a column of unarmed Chinese laborers coming into Tsingtao from a nearby village at dawn on 30 November.

Even under house arrest, Chang chose this time to renew his intrigues. A search of his personal property on 31 November turned up four letters secreted in his rice supplies. One letter, dated two only days earlier, reported on the movements of Zeye's column. A second, from Viceroy Li Hung-chang, detailed the current military measures undertaken by the Chinese to recover Kiao-chou. A third, from Governor Li Ping-heng, ordered Chang to continue to undermine the German occupation of Kiao-chou. At this point, Diederichs decided to place Chang under close arrest aboard *Prinzess Wilhelm,* where Thiele confined him to the midshipmen's quarters. Diederichs then asked Heyking to arrange with the Tsungli Yamen in Peking for Chang's repatriation. Diederichs released him on the afternoon of 3 December but only after Chang, who left with a small escort, had once again given his word of honor. Chang later claimed, Diederichs learned, that he had acted honorably throughout the crisis, whereas Diederichs had acted dishonorably. Chang even claimed that Diederichs and an honor guard, dressed in full dress uniforms and wearing Bavarian dragoon helmets, had escorted him out of Tsingtao to the martial tempo of a ship's band. Chang's departure, no matter how commemorated, relieved one of Diederichs's major problems.[110]

A resumption of communications with Zeye soon solved another problem. Contacted by signal lamp from *Cormoran,* Zeye eventually reported that he and his force had located the Chinese forces encamped at the foot of Mount Lau-schau on 1 December. As Zeye's column advanced into view, the Chinese troops began to evacuate their positions and move north. Rather than simply escort them out of the occupied zone as Diederichs had directed, Zeye ordered an attack. When a field artillery section from *Kaiser* fired two salvos into the retreating Chinese ranks, they broke and ran. The skirmish cost three Chinese killed in action and dozens wounded but no German casualties.[111] Although Diederichs later described Zeye's actions as "insubordinate, arbitrary, and reckless," the skirmish caused the Chinese to begin a general withdrawal throughout the occupied zone.[112] When the expeditionary force returned to Tsingtao on 10 December, Diederichs nonetheless castigated Zeye for his disregard of orders. Diederichs had originally directed him to avoid bloodshed, fearing that a bloody confrontation with Chinese forces would imperil Heyking's negotiations with the Tsungli Yamen, incite foreign intervention, and encourage the antiannexation faction in Berlin.[113]

Heyking, in fact, had twice requested—8 and 10 December—that Diederichs suspend operations in order to allow negotiations to proceed without impediment. Following consultations with Diederichs and the Foreign Ministry in Berlin, Heyking had presented a series of demands to the Chinese government on 20 November. These included the outright cession of Kiao-chou Bay (China had made no similar territorial concessions since Britain acquired Hong Kong in 1842) and the right to construct railroads and mine coal in Shantung. Formal negotiations began on 27 December and continued intermittently into the new year. Whenever the

Chinese grew unhappy with the nature of the negotiations, they would simply refuse to see Heyking or suspend discussions. When this happened, however, Heyking would notify Diederichs, who would then turn up the heat in Kiao-chou, and that would usually produce a Chinese return to the table in Peking.[114]

Diederichs felt that the German position became more secure as December continued. *Irene* had arrived from Hong Kong on 3 December, further strengthening Diederich's force. The withdrawal of Chinese forces from the occupied zone in mid-month also reduced tensions. This allowed the squadron to celebrate a cold but joyful Christmas. While a single scanty Christmas tree with handmade decorations broke the gloom, squadron officers distributed small gifts and winter clothing contributed by German expatriates in Japan and Shanghai. Diederichs, at least, could celebrate with family members. Fritz, who came by civilian steamer from Hong Kong, joined Diederichs and Thiele for Christmas celebrations. Both were scheduled to rotate back to Germany in February.[115]

Diederichs noted that the gift of winter clothing was particularly welcome. Heavy winds out of the northwest, as well as sandstorms, struck at least twice a week. Diederichs wrote Henni that the bitter cold of the Kiaochou winter made the cold weather in Kiel seem downright spring-like by comparison. The cold chilled his bones so much that he could not even remain warm in his flag quarters aboard *Kaiser*, making him feel older than his years. The thermometer hovered around freezing, with a typical day being clear and cold with little snow. On the more positive side, Diederichs reported that the local climate seemed considerably more favorable than once thought. Winter at least allowed him to confirm a salient point about Kiaochou Bay; although ice had appeared in shallow areas of the bay, it presented no barrier to navigation.[116]

The winter weather had also begun to affect the health of the squadron's men. The first fatality came on 29 December when Seaman Buthmann died of a heart attack with complications from double lobar pneumonia. The report of his death cited the "cold and unclean Chinese quarters" in which he had lived while ashore as another contributing factor. Seamen from *Kaiser* buried their comrade on 2 January 1898 in a new cemetery on a plot of land near the pier fort. The squadron chaplain officiated at the funeral.[117]

Diederichs had cause for celebration with the arrival of *Kaiserin Augusta*, commanded by Capt. Leopold Köllner, on 30 December. The cruiser also carried Capt. Felix Stubenrauch, who replaced Captain Zeye, due for rotation home, as flag captain and military governor on 31 December. Diederichs marked Zeye's departure with relief, noting that "my worries of belligerent overzealousness then vanished."[118]

Diederichs also enjoyed a visit from his British friend Admiral Buller, who arrived off Tsingtao aboard HM Battleship *Centurion* on 14 January 1898. Diederichs described Buller, with whom he had developed a close professional friendship, as "highly esteemed along the entire coast." Diederichs was inland when *Centurion* arrived but hurried back to Tsingtao to greet Buller. When he went to board *Centurion* after dusk for the standard ceremonial visit, he scrambled up the ship's companionway to find neither a petty officer nor side boys. He wandered the decks looking for Buller's flag cabin until a marine sentry finally challenged him. Diederichs noted that such "failure of discipline . . . was not uncommon on the Chinese station." In any event, the two admirals enjoyed a meal of pheasant prepared by Buller's steward. In the course of their conversation, Buller acknowledged the value of the German position in Shantung as a buffer between British and Russian positions. The British themselves had begun to consider the establishment of a naval base at Wei-hai-wei to further counter Russian expansionism.[119]

With holidays behind him, Diederichs quickly discovered that the new year also brought new problems. Raids by Chinese soldiers in the northern and western quarters of the occupation zone compelled Diederichs to place garrisons in the towns of Kiao-chou and Chi-mo. He dispatched a hundred officers and men from *Kaiser* to Kiao-chou on 8 January and sent a second force, fifty men from *Prinzess Wilhelm*, to Chi-mo. Even more troubling, intelligence reports now estimated that more than ten thousand Chinese troops remained poised along the border of the occupation zone, preparing to attack during the Chinese New Year, which would begin on 22 January. Additional information reported the passage of Chinese warships southward in the direction of Kiao-chou Bay. Diederichs also noted that additional incidents of xenophobic violence against German missionaries and Chinese Christians had occurred in southern Shantung.[120]

Diederichs himself had personally witnessed Chinese preparations. During an excursion on horseback near Tsingtao, he had sighted two well-dressed Chinese observing the main German positions through binoculars from a hill north of town. When he approached, the two men quickly mounted horses and rode north. Captain Stubenrauch reported that a Chinese interpreter working for the Germans had overheard a conversation in an opium den to the effect that a military mandarin, dressed as a coolie, had already reconnoitered the Tsingtao camps. Other reports cited the infiltration of all three towns by soldiers in civilian garb. Diederichs now concluded from these and other reports that the Chinese would simultaneously attack German positions in Tsingtao, Kiao-chou, and Chi-mo under cover of the crowds and fireworks displays that would fill the streets in celebration of the Chinese New Year.

Diederichs took immediate precautions. He convened a midnight meeting aboard *Kaiser* on 21–22 January with his commanders to plan a response. Because he anticipated a simultaneous attack from sea and ashore, he ordered his squadron gunnery officers to replace the high-explosive shells used against land targets with armor-piercing shells for ship-to-ship combat. He detailed *Cormoran* to stop and search all seagoing junks in the immediate vicinity of Tsingtao and ordered that all ships arm cutters and launches for inshore patrols. Diederich also dispatched two hundred additional men and two machine guns, commanded by Brussatis, to reinforce the garrison at Chi-mo, fifty kilometers away. The gravity of the situation required Brussatis to make a forced march. Diederichs therefore directed that each seaman carry only minimal gear: a rifle and 180 rounds of ammunition, one day's rations, a warm coat, a pair of light shoes, and a pair of socks per man. The force took four horses for its officers and two pack mules to carry the machine guns. Because Diederichs did not want to repeat the mistakes of Zeye's expedition in December, he gave Brussatis specific orders to expel small units from the occupied zone but to avoid contact with larger elements. He also directed Brussatis to return to Tsingtao immediately if "a reconnaissance reveals the presence of such large Chinese forces that an attack against our position is imminent."[121]

Much to the relief of all concerned, Brussatis did not encounter any Chinese troops on their march to Chi-mo. Following his arrival, he immediately fortified positions at strategic points in the town and established observation posts on high ground outside. He also sent out scouting parties in an attempt to locate Chinese troops. He reported to Diederichs on 24 January that he had discovered no Chinese troops within forty li—thirty-six kilometers. He also advised Diederichs that local officials had assured him that the Chinese government wanted to resolve the matter quickly and peaceably.

Diederichs was celebrating this seemingly good news at supper with Fritz, who had returned from Shanghai to say good-bye before his scheduled rotation back to Germany, when Diederichs's steward interrupted their meal with a second, more disturbing message. Someone had killed a German sentry, Seaman Johann Heinrich Schulze, who had guarded Chi-mo's main gate late in the previous evening. Brussatis speculated that the killing might foreshadow a Chinese attack, particularly since a search for the killer had turned up five chests containing a hundred rifles in a house near the garrison's barracks. The incident, combined with infiltrating soldiers and hidden guns, seemed to confirm Diederichs's own suspicions of a general assault during the Chinese New Year.

Anticipating the attack within the next twenty-four hours, Diederichs placed all forces on alert. Small-arms fire crackled through Tsingtao with great regularity during the night of 24 January and early morning hours of the twenty-fifth as German sentries, unsettled by the incident at Chi-mo, fired at every unidentified sound and movement. Ships anchored in the roadstead used their searchlights to intermittently illuminate the shore while disembarking their reserve forces to reinforce the garrison ashore. *Cormoran* and the small-boat patrols reported the discovery of armed junks in the inner bay later in the day. Nightfall brought a new round of suspicious movements and nervous sentries.

After a second night of great tension and little sleep, sunrise on 26 January brought welcome relief. SS *Darmstadt,* transporting nearly twelve hundred men of the Third Naval Infantry Battalion, steamed into the Tsingtao roads and dropped anchor. The squadron's small boats promptly converged on *Darmstadt* to transfer the infantrymen ashore. Within hours the battalion had relieved Diederichs's own forces of the responsibility of providing a garrison for Tsingtao, with detached companies assuming the defense of Kiao-chou and Chi-mo. Relieved by the regular naval infantry, the squadron's landing detachments returned to their ships. Diederichs assembled a formal parade on 27 January to welcome Maj. Kopka von Lössow and the battalion and, coincidentally, celebrate the emperor's birthday. Ten days later, SS *Crefeld* arrived with a three-hundred-man naval artillery company and a battery of field guns.[122]

Diederichs still had one more issue to resolve. Chi-mo's chief magistrate reported the arrest of Schulze's alleged murderer on 31 January. An investigation conducted by local officials concluded that the motive was financial rather than political. The suspect, who confessed his crime under intense questioning, was a well-known troublemaker who had attempted to rob the seaman. Based on the Sino-Prussian Treaty of 1851, which allowed German authorities to try Chinese subjects accused of crimes against German nationals, and his own proclamation of martial law on 14 November 1897, Diederichs ordered Brussatis to convene a court-martial to try the suspect. The court, which convened on 1 February 1898, used the defendant's confession as the primary evidence against him. As presiding judge, Brussatis found the defendant guilty and sentenced him to death. Diederichs rode to Chi-mo on 2 February to observe the execution. The local magistrate requested that Chinese authorities carry out the execution in accordance to Chinese custom, rather than German law, in order to prevent unrest and disorder. Diederichs agreed and transferred the prisoner to Chinese custody. A Chinese executioner beheaded the murderer in the presence of Diederichs and local officials later that afternoon.[123]

The two events—the arrival of the Third Battalion and the execution in Chi-mo—marked the end of Chinese resistance to the German occupation of Kiao-chou. As a sign of good faith, the Chinese withdrew their naval and land forces that had threatened Tsingtao. In return, the Germans made a significant concession at the Kiao-chou negotiations in

Peking. The Germans had originally asked for the outright cession of Kiao-chou; they now accepted a leasehold instead. The reduction of tensions also allowed Diederichs to cancel martial law within the occupation zone on 14 February and order the squadron to stand down from combat status on the eighteenth.[124]

Ambassador Heyking and Viceroy Li Hung-chang signed the ensuing convention in Peking on 6 March 1898. The agreement granted Germany a ninety-nine-year leasehold on an area fifty kilometers around Kiao-chou Bay (approximately 520 square kilometers). Section I allowed Germany to develop and fortify a naval base at Tsingtao, fulfilling a goal that had existed within the German navy for thirty years. Section II provided an economic foundation for the new base, granting Germany the right to construct railroads and mine coal within the leasehold. Once the German Reichstag ratified the treaty on 8 April 1898, Kaiser Wilhelm formally established the Kiao-chou protectorate by imperial decree on 27 April. He placed it under the direct jurisdiction of the RMA and appointed Capt. Karl Rosendahl as governor.[125]

These arrangements ended Diederichs's personal responsibility for Kiao-chou but not his personal interest. After all, he wrote Fritz, the acquisition of Kiao-chou "fulfilled my purpose in the navy." Not incidentally, Kiao-chou also rehabilitated his career, in jeopardy on his dismissal from the OKM in 1896. Given this proprietary interest, it is perhaps not surprising that Diederichs complained about Kiao-chou's becoming an RMA responsibility. Diederichs feared that Tirpitz, preoccupied with his battle fleet, would simply ignore the development of Kiao-chou—a perception that provided significant tensions between the two officers at a later date.[126] He also complained to Henni that, according to Senden, Captain Zeye had begun to claim the credit for the selection of Kiao-chou as the site of a German base in East Asia. Since Zeye was a member of Tirpitz's "torpedo gang," Diederichs believed that Tirpitz had instigated this false claim in order to bask in the popular glow surrounding the occupation of Kiao-chou. He angrily conjectured that Tirpitz, for all of his success and ambition, would never rise to the level of Helmut von Moltke, Diederichs's hero and the army general responsible for German victories in the wars of unification.[127]

Meanwhile, with Kiao-chou securely in German hands, Diederichs could attend to personal issues. His most pressing concern was Henni's continuing poor health. His worries increased in part because of the lengthy delays in their correspondence. Their letters often took as much as six weeks to reach each other. Even then, she would not always bother him with news of her health. For example, he had written her somewhat poignantly in January, "The most recent post brought no news of you and although you write often I am always sad to not hear from you."[128] She did write him in March that she had begun to consider the possibility of going to Wiesbaden for controversial and expensive treatments for her arthritis. The only good news she had to report was that Fritz had arrived home in European waters and would soon visit her in Berlin. He responded with a draft for three hundred marks to apply to her medical treatments and a hope that he would return himself to a new post in Berlin in the fall.[129] In response, Henni wrote that visits by friends and acquaintances saved her from depression caused by her illness and Diederichs's long absence. She particularly appreciated regular calls by Frau Anna Knorr, who kept her abreast of the latest naval news and gossip. Henni was proud to report that, according to Frau Knorr, the emperor had spoken a hearty and resounding "well done" when he first learned of Diederichs's successful move against Kiao-chou. Henni could happily add that spring had finally come to Berlin: "Spring weather today—fifty-four degrees!"[130]

Another issue, which produced greater and greater frustration, was the absence of Rear Admiral Prince Heinrich of Prussia. Heinrich, who had left Germany in December 1897, was due to arrive at Tsingtao with SMS *Deutschland* and SMS *Gefion* in February 1898. Diederichs anxiously awaited Heinrich's arrival so that he could send ships into dockyards for necessary repairs and liberty, commence a regular patrol schedule throughout the East Asian station, and provide protection for Kiao-chou. He could not fulfill these three missions without Heinrich's ships. Prince Heinrich, however, refused to cooperate, preferring instead to undertake a triumphal tour of Asian ports. When he finally arrived in Hong Kong in early March, he advised Diederichs that he first intended to tour the southern part of the station and then visit Shanghai before arriving in Kiao-chou on or about 10 April.

Frustrated, Diederichs decided to send *Cormoran* and *Irene* to Shanghai for refits immediately and then dispatch *Kaiser* and *Prinzess Wilhelm* to Nagasaki as soon as Heinrich arrived in Tsingtao. Once repairs were completed, Diederichs intended to assign *Cormoran* to patrol Chinese waters and send *Irene* to the Philippines, where the outbreak of a Filipino insurgency threatened German nationals and interests in Manila. He also wanted all ships to commence extensive gunnery and torpedo drills in anticipation of the summer patrol season. Diederichs himself intended to make a long-postponed visit to Batavia, Dutch East Indies.

A second message only increased Diederichs's frustrations. Prince Heinrich had now decided to prolong his stay in Shanghai, postponing his arrival in Kiao-chou until late April, and then leave almost immediately for a state visit to Peking. A third communication cited Heinrich's intention to remain even longer in Shanghai, further postponing his arrival at Tsingtao until early May. Although he was Heinrich's superior officer, Diederichs had little choice but accept these royal decisions. He nonetheless wrote bitter letters to Henni, complaining that the prince's selfishness impeded squadron operations and prevented Diederichs from granting relief and liberty to the ships and crews of the First Division.

When Prince Heinrich had still not arrived by the beginning of May, Diederichs shifted his flag to *Prinzess Wilhelm* on the fourth and dispatched *Kaiser* to Nagasaki for repairs. He would follow soon after, if ever Heinrich reached Tsingtao. When Heinrich arrived, belatedly, on 5 May, Diederichs again postponed his departure in order to attend a series of receptions on land and aboard ships for the imperial prince. Although patient and calm in Heinrich's presence, Diederichs continued to speak of his frustration with Heinrich's selfishness and egotism.[131]

As he prepared to depart aboard *Prinzess Wilhelm* for Nagasaki, Diederichs wrote a final letter to Henni from Tsingtao. He told her that Prince Heinrich had requested an escort of three ships to accompany him to Peking. Diederichs had bluntly denied the request, reminding Heinrich that the squadron had more important duties, including visits to Batavia and Manila. The outbreak of the Spanish-American War on 25 April and the American victory at the battle of Manila on 1 May made this last mission even more important. Heinrich would just have to make do with *Deutschland* and *Gefion*. When Prince Heinrich complained about the inadequacy of his escort, Diederichs advised him flatly that "the Philippines must remain first in our sights."[132]

The 1866 crew. Otto von Diederichs stands fourth from right, near Plüddemann and his long-time friend Hoffmann. Thomson sits on the floor.
Bundesarchiv-Militärarchiv, Freiburg

Midshipmen attending the Marineschule in 1881. Cdr. Otto von Diederichs is seated on a chair, fourth from left. Prince Heinrich von Preussen, younger brother of Kaiser Wilhelm II, sits to his left.
Bundesarchiv-Militärarchiv, Freiburg

Diederichs family circa 1885. *Left to right:* Henni, Fritz, Herman, Friedrich, and Otto.
Bundesarchiv-Militärarchiv, Freiburg

Kaiserin Augusta, German cruiser, 1892–1919.
U.S. Naval Historical Center, Washington, D.C.

Rear Adm. Ernst Otto von Diederichs, oil painting, 1896.
Courtesy Gisela von Diederichs

Left to right: Cadet Herman von Diederichs, Lt. (jg) Friedrich von Diederichs, and Rear Adm. Otto von Diederichs, circa 1896.
Bundesarchiv-Militärarchiv, Freiburg

Diederichs in civilian clothes at a temple in Kiao-chou, November 1897.
Bundesarchiv-Militärarchiv, Freiburg

Formal parade marking the arrival of the 3d Naval Infantry Battalion, Tsingtao, Kiao-chou Territory, 27 January 1898. Diederichs and naval officers are on the left; Major von Lossow is on the right.
Bundesarchiv-Militärarchiv, Freiburg

Entrance to Diederichs's quarters ashore at the Tsingtao garrison headquarters, 1898. Diederichs is fourth from left.
Bundesarchiv-Militärarchiv, Freiburg

Vice Adm. Otto von Diederichs in his quarters aboard SMS *Kaiser*, 1899.
Bundesarchiv-Militärarchiv, Freiburg

SMS *Kaiser*.
U.S. Naval Historical Center, Washington, D.C.

Otto von Diederichs, circa 1900.
Bundesarchiv-Militärarchiv, Freiburg

SMS *Irene*.
U.S. Naval Historical Center, Washington, D.C.

Officer portrait, *left to right:* Lt. (jg) Herman von Diederichs, Adm. Otto von Diederichs, and Lt. (sg) Fritz von Diederichs.
Courtesy of Gisela von Diederichs

7

The Philippines: Diederichs and Dewey at Manila, Summer 1898

With Kiao-chou behind him, Diederichs could now write Henni that another issue required his attention: "I believe that we cannot ignore the Spanish-American War."[1] He believed that the outbreak of war between Spain and the United States again provided Germany with an opportunity to obtain a base in Asian waters. Alerted to the conflict while still at Kiao-chou, Diederichs used the brief voyage to Nagasaki aboard *Prinzess Wilhelm* in early May to review current intelligence on the issue. Although he had initially intended to visit Manila in July after his mission to Batavia, he now decided that the Philippines required his more immediate attention.

Diederichs drew an immediate and obvious comparison between Spain and China. Spain, once one of Europe's greatest imperialist powers, had become largely impotent by 1898. The vestigial Spanish empire itself teetered on the edge of dissolution as rebellions rent both Cuba and the Philippines. The United States, on the other hand, was young, vigorous, and expansive.

"Manifest destiny" had become the new American slogan as the Yankees were poised to take their first steps toward imperialism across the Caribbean and the Pacific.

The Philippines, he fully understood, had great strategic potential. The archipelago formed the eastern flank of the South China Sea within striking distance of Singapore (1,650 nautical miles) and Hong Kong (650 nautical miles). A Philippine base would also allow German warships to interdict the primary sea lanes through the South China Sea and command the Pacific's western approaches at the Luzon Straits. Looking eastward, the Philippines' position on the western edge of the Pacific basin would open up that entire ocean to German naval and colonial forces.

As Diederichs knew, it was Cuba, the last major Spanish colony in the Western Hemisphere, that provided the primary cause of the Spanish-American conflict. When the outbreak of a colonial revolt in 1895 elicited a brutal and bloody Spanish response, U.S. public opinion, inflamed by yellow journalism, supported first the rebellion and then the "splendid little war" against Spain that followed in April 1898. Citing their support for a fellow European monarchy, German diplomats had initially attempted to mediate Spanish-American differences. German favoritism continued once the war broke out. Kaiser Wilhelm himself anticipated a Spanish victory: "The *hidalgo* will certainly cut Brother Jonathan to pieces, for the Spanish Navy is stronger than the American." This predilection for Spain, according to Foreign Minister Bülow, "was well known to our fleet in the Far East."[2]

In fact, American forces quickly defeated Spanish units in the first major battle of the war. Commo. George Dewey and his Asiatic Fleet had destroyed Spain's primary forces in the Philippines at the battle of Manila on 1 May 1898. Although Diederichs spoke contemptuously of American claims to a decisive victory, given the fact that the Americans had better and bigger ships than the Spanish, he nonetheless believed that the battle marked the end of Spanish sovereignty in the Philippines. Furthermore, he anticipated that the upstart United States would ultimately defeat Spain—no longer a "stout-hearted land"—on all fronts. He expected that the war would result in the partition of the Philippines, which, he thought, would give Germany the opportunity to make territorial gains in Southeast Asia.[3] Tirpitz, as always, raised a dissenting voice, fearing that any overseas adventurism would threaten the development of his battle fleet. Until he could complete that program, he advised the Foreign Ministry, "the Spanish-American war had come too soon" as an opportunity for German expansion.[4]

In many ways, Dewey's victory had come too soon for the United States as well. American strategic planners had expected success in Cuba and the Caribbean but had given little thought to the Philippines and the Pacific. Although Dewey had sent his marines ashore to occupy the Cavite naval base and destroy the underwater cable linking Manila and Hong Kong, he lacked the land forces necessary to capture and hold Manila itself. He therefore decided to blockade Manila until reinforcements could arrive from the United States. Meanwhile, the McKinley administration equivocated about the fate of the Philippines. American public opinion was equally ambivalent. Few Americans even knew the archipelago's location. Mr. Dooley, Finley Peter Dunne's fictional Irish-American curmudgeon, spoke for many Americans when he said that he wasn't sure if the Philippines were islands or canned goods and could not decide what to do with them: "An' what shud I do with the Ph'lipeens? Oh, what shud I do with thim? I can't annex thim because I don't know where they ar-re. I can't let go iv thim because some wan else'll take thim if I do."[5]

The U.S. Government may have been hesitant but Germany was not. The acquisition of Kiao-chou had by no means ended the Kaiserliche Marine's quest for overseas bases. Thus, the outbreak of the Spanish-American war and the American victory at Manila now presented Germany with a new opportunity to expand its overseas presence and enhance the projection of German sea power. Knorr, in fact, had recently reminded the emperor, "I believe more than ever in the indisputable axiom that the German Navy currently requires a number of bases in all the seas for the further development of its overseas-warfare capability."[6] He therefore sought to use the Spanish-American conflict to renew the navy's search for bases. Like Diederichs, he anticipated the end of Spanish sovereignty in the Philippines. He therefore recommended that the navy commence immediate preparations "for the annexation of a portion of the Spanish possessions in East Asia if the opportunity presents itself."[7]

Using criteria first developed for the evaluation of Chinese sites, Knorr identified Luzon as the most favorable site for a German base. Manila Bay, in particular, offered one of the Pacific's best anchorages. Fortifications on Corregidor Island commanded access to the bay and provided excellent defensive potential. The Spanish had already constructed naval facilities at Cavite, eight miles from Manila. Mariveles Bay, northwest of Corregidor at the mouth of the bay, provided a small but protected anchorage. Another potential site was Subic Bay, seventy nautical miles up the coast. Subic Bay already had a small naval depot at Olongapo and a strong defensive position at Isla Grande, which guarded the bay's entrance. Knorr cited the port of Iloilo and Cebu plus Mindanao Island as secondary choices.[8] Kaiser Wilhelm agreed: "I am determined when the opportunity arises to purchase or simply take the Philippines from Spain—when her 'liquidation' approaches."[9]

Such opportunism led John Hay, the American ambassador to the United Kingdom, to complain, "There is to the German mind something monstrous in the thought that a war should take place anywhere and they not profit by it."[10] Hay's analysis—shared by many Americans—accurately reflected German public opinion, which also viewed the Spanish-American war as an opportunity for imperial and naval expansion.

It was therefore convenient, although not coincidental, that Diederichs, the hero of Kiao-chou, commanded Germany's most power naval force outside of home waters, only a few days away from the Philippines under steam. This became particularly important when Rear Admiral Prince Heinrich wrote from Hong Kong in April 1898 that a German merchant from Manila had told him that the Filipinos would soon win the rebellion and would then "gladly place themselves under the protection of another European power, preferably Germany." He also detached SMS *Gefion* for a quick visit to Manila to investigate the matter.[11] In fact, Consul Friedrich von Krüger in Manila corroborated Heinrich's report, writing that the Filipinos would accept a German prince on a Filipino throne once they gained their independence from Spain.[12] Interestingly, *Gefion*'s visit to Manila mystified the American consul in Manila, O. F. Williams, who wrote to Dewey that the presence of the German warship had an "import of which I have been unable to learn."[13]

Given the circumstances, Diederichs was quick to see the possibility for a second Kiao-chou, particularly when Krüger notified him that two German nationals had disappeared in northern Luzon. The missing Germans were engineers who had fled a mining region in the interior of northern Luzon when the insurrection threatened their lives. They had succeeded in reaching a coastal town, from which they were able to communicate their plight to Krüger, but he had now lost contact with them. He therefore requested that Diederichs dispatch a warship to the Philippines to protect "local German interests."[14]

When Diederichs cabled Berlin for permission to send a ship to Manila, Knorr ordered him to send not one ship but two. These orders proved to be a problem for Diederichs. As always, his ships were either dispersed throughout the station or under repair. He had already assigned *Cormoran* to patrol Chinese waters and *Arcona* to guard Kiao-chou. Much to his frustration, when he arrived in Nagasaki aboard *Prinzess Wilhelm*, he discovered that the Mitsubishi Dockyard and Engine Works had not yet completed *Kaiser*'s repairs and could therefore not begin a refit for *Prinzess Wilhelm* for several more weeks. The Second Division, with *Irene* attached, was with Prince Heinrich on his tour of Chinese and Japanese ports. In any event, Diederichs decided to dispatch *Irene* to Manila immediately, with *Cormoran* to follow a few days later. Since he intended to visit Manila himself, he also recalled *Kaiserin Augusta* from the Second Division for temporary use as his flagship.[15]

A SYMPATHETIC DEMONSTRATION

Irene arrived off Manila early in the afternoon watch on 6 May 1898. As she steamed slowly past the anchored American squadron, her crew fired an eleven-gun salute to Commodore Dewey's broad pennant while her band played an American national air. She then steamed over to Manila and anchored among a contingent of foreign warships, including French cruiser *Bruix* and English cruiser *Immortalité*. *Irene*'s commanding officer, Cdr. August Obenheimer, paid the customary ceremonial visit to Dewey aboard USS *Olympia* on 7 May. Dewey told Obenheimer that his instructions called only for the defeat of Spanish forces in the Philippines and that he lacked the troops to capture Manila. Obenheimer inferred from the conversation that the United States had no plans to annex the archipelago.[16]

Obenheimer took several steps to protect German nationals in Manila.

He first established a signal post—manned by a yeoman and a signalman—at the German consulate to provide early warnings of events ashore. Based on discussions with Krüger and the German community, he then developed formal plans to evacuate German nationals from the line of fire, chartering four small steamers to embark refugees if necessary. When SMS *Cormoran* joined *Irene* off Manila on the ninth, Krüger immediately requested that Obenheimer, as senior officer, send *Cormoran* to northern Luzon to locate and evacuate the missing German mining engineers. Although concerned for the two nationals, Obenheimer declined the request, at least temporarily, telling Krüger that he needed both ships close at hand because of the greater threat at Manila.[17]

Irene's mission was peaceful and humanitarian, but her presence at Manila caused the first of a series of problems with American forces. As *Irene* steamed past Cavite on 6 May, her band had played the American national anthem. The Spanish pilot aboard her, however, took the tune for the Spanish coronation march. He told the story to a reporter from *El Commercio,* Manila's leading newspaper, which published an article about the warship's arrival under the headline "Sympathetic Demonstration." Spaniards throughout the islands applauded the story exuberantly, believing that the Germans had come to their aid against the United States. British Consul E. H. Rawson-Walker, who had represented American interests since the outbreak of hostilities, promptly passed word of the incident to Dewey.[18]

Dewey, who believed the worst about *Irene*'s actions, had already developed an anti-German reputation. Disparaging his future Spanish opponents in 1897, he pondered the possibility of a more honorable war against Germany: "It is indecent to fight against Spain anyhow. Now, if France would come in too, we could save face, but best of all if Germany would come in. If only Germany could be persuaded to come in."[19] Dewey and Diederichs became embroiled in the first of several crises in March 1898, when Diederichs refused to surrender a German-born seaman who had deserted USS *Olympia* and now served aboard a German warship. Cdr. Nathan Sargent described the incident "as the first of many disagreeable occurrences which seemed fated to arise whenever American and German ships found themselves together."[20] Only a few days later, Prince Heinrich antagonized Dewey over an unintentional breach of naval protocol.

Although Heinrich apologized for the slight, Dewey remained angry. When the two met again on the eve of Dewey's departure for the Philippines, Heinrich joked, "I will send my ships to Manila to see that you behave." Dewey, in the presence of *Olympia*'s Capt. C. V. Gridley and Consul Rounseville Wildman, replied humorlessly, "I shall be delighted to have you do so, Your Highness; but permit me to caution you to keep your ships from between my guns and the enemy."[21] According to Sargent, Dewey nonetheless preferred Heinrich to Diederichs: "Had [Heinrich] been in command later at Manila instead of the German admiral with whom Commodore Dewey had to deal, much inconvenience might have been saved us and much bad feeling might have been averted."[22]

German activities at Manila did little to allay Dewey's suspicions. Cdrs. Obenheimer and Brussatis formally called upon Governor General Basilio Augustin y Davilo and Adm. Patricio Montojo y Passaron in Manila on 10 May. "Augustin thanked me repeatedly," Obenheimer reported, "for the support shown him by the German navy and by the Germans in Manila during the dark and troublesome days that Spain had to endure." Augustin requested that the German ships not salute the Spanish flag because any shot fired in the direction of Manila would cause panic in the city; the Spaniards could not return the salute in any event because their guns were already loaded with live shells. Obenheimer in turn offered medical supplies and the services of his ship's surgeon, which the beleaguered Spaniards gratefully accepted.[23]

Dewey, who viewed the meeting with great suspicion, concluded that the Germans and Spaniards had now begun to conspire against him. His distrust of the Germans only deepened when a Manila newspaper reported that Prince Heinrich was speeding to the relief of the Philippines with seven German warships. He would then join *Irene* and *Cormoran* to attack Dewey's squadron in conjunction with Spanish forces. Following a visit by several junior German officers to Manila's battlements on 13 May, a Hong Kong newspaper reported that the insurgents had seen the German officers over their sights but had not fired on them. Another Manila newspaper claimed that Obenheimer had made a public speech in Manila in which he told the Spanish that the Germans would join them to fight the Americans.[24]

Dewey's uncertain strategic position only compounded his German problem. Although Admiral Montojo had lost his main forces on 1 May at the battle of Manila, he still commanded twelve gunboats, ten small gun vessels, and three armed merchant cruisers.[25] These small warships could not confront Dewey's cruisers in open battle but could inflict substantial damage on the American squadron through surprise hit-and-run attacks. Dewey, after all, lacked a naval base for logistical and technical support—a factor that ironically resembled Diederichs's position against Chinese forces at Kiaochou six months earlier. An even greater threat developed in June when a Spanish squadron left Atlantic waters to reinforce Spanish forces in the Philippines. The relief force, scheduled to arrive in mid-July, included armored cruisers *Carlos V* (nine thousand tons, two 280-mm guns) and *Pelayo* (ninety-eight hundred tons, two 320-mm and two 280-mm guns) that easily outgunned *Olympia*'s 8-inch guns. Although the squadron eventually turned back and returned to Spain, the American secretary of the navy, John D. Long, advised Dewey that he believed the Spanish ships intended to join German warships in an attack on Dewey.[26]

The constant threat of Spanish attacks required the American squadron to maintain constant, and nervous, vigilance readiness. At one point, USS *Concord*'s log noted, "About 9:30 [P.M.] went to quarters owing to false alarm of a supposed boat which proved to be a piece of wreckage." The crew later remained at general quarters all night long because of anticipated surprise attacks.[27] On another occasion, an unidentified steam launch suddenly appeared near the American anchorage. Fearful that this signaled a Spanish torpedo attack, Dewey ordered one of *Olympia*'s 6-lb mounts to fire on the craft. When the launch heaved to, its abashed coxswain unfurled a rain-soaked German flag. He explained that he carried a message advising the Americans that a German warship planned to leave Manila Bay that night.[28] Dewey remained suspicious of these incidents, worrying that the Germans were covertly testing American readiness as the first step in their support of a Spanish attack. He therefore ordered his captains to douse all lights at dusk to avoid illuminating friendly ships. His captains regularly complained thereafter that neutral warships in the Manila roadstead indiscriminately used their own lights after dark. The officers worried that those lights, which occasionally lit up the American ships, made the squadron more vulnerable to Spanish attack.[29]

Dewey also suffered from limited and irregular communication with his superiors. When the Americans captured the Manila terminus of the Manila–Hong Kong submarine cable on 1 May, the British-owned Eastern Extension Telegraph Company refused to accept Dewey's messages because of contractual obligations to the Spanish government. Dewey therefore destroyed the cable. Lacking direct cable connections, Dewey had to send a ship to Hong Kong to dispatch and receive cables via the Hong Kong–San Francisco line. The entire process required a week or more, further isolating Dewey from his superiors. Dewey was reticent, in any event, to communicate with Washington. His telegrams—about fifty of them—were brief, succinct, and supplicatory. He rarely mentioned his conflict with the Germans and then appended no details. When President McKinley later asked him why he had never discussed his German problem with the Navy Department, he responded that "it seemed best that I look after myself, at a time when you had worries of your own."[30]

Isolated from his superiors and threatened by Spanish forces, Dewey also had to contend in early June with a sudden resurgence of his German problem. The North German Lloyd liner *Darmstadt* appeared in Manila Bay on 6 June carrying more than fourteen hundred German seamen. Dewey later complained in his autobiography that he had no advance warning of the event or adequate explanation for *Darmstadt's* arrival. He only knew that the Kaiserliche Marine trained its seamen as naval infantry for amphibious operations. When Dewey questioned the purpose of these forces, Obenheimer hurriedly assured him that the liner's presence was both harmless and necessary. Obenheimer explained that, for those warships on foreign station, the German navy customarily relieved an entire ship's crew and half her officers every two years; the navy usually leased a North German Lloyd or Hamburg-American Line steamer to transport the relief crews to the transshipment site.[31]

Darmstadt, carrying relief crews for the Cruiser Squadron, had departed from Kiel in early May en route to Tsingtao. When she arrived in Singapore, Diederichs redirected her to Manila to transfer replacements for *Irene* and *Cormoran*. To explain this change in procedure, *Darmstadt's* captain secured a letter of introduction to Dewey from the American consul in Singapore. Although Dewey later claimed in his autobiography that *Darmstadt* remained, ominously and for unknown reasons, in Manila Bay for another month, the liner actually departed for Tsingtao on 9 June.[32]

In any event, *Darmstadt*'s departure gave Dewey no respite from his German problem. As the McKinley administration continued to equivocate in regard to the Philippines' future, German interest in acquiring a Filipino base continued. Fearing that a final American victory in the Philippines would block a permanent German presence, Kaiser Wilhelm discussed the situation with Foreign Minister Bülow, who supported a German move into the Philippines. Tirpitz, on the other hand, now opposed such action, worrying that any foreign adventure would impede implementation of his new Fleet Law.[33] Faced with this split among his advisers, Wilhelm turned to Diederichs for information and advice. He ordered Diederichs to proceed to the Philippines with additional ships to obtain a "clear and correct picture" of the situation. Knorr forwarded the order to Diederichs on 2 June with an additional directive, "Develop a personal appraisal of the Spanish position. Protect German interests with the squadron."[34]

Diederichs moved immediately to comply with his orders. Since repairs on *Kaiser* were still unfinished, he recalled *Kaiserin Augusta*, the only available ship with flag quarters, to Nagasaki for the voyage to Manila. He also ordered *Kaiser* and *Prinzess Wilhelm* to follow him as soon as their repairs were completed. He particularly needed *Kaiser* because *Kaiserin Augusta* had no additional space for his squadron staff. He intended to proceed to Manila with only his new flag lieutenant, Lt. Cdr. Paul von Hintze, leaving the remainder of his staff in Nagasaki with *Kaiser*. He also devised new orders for *Darmstadt*, whose contract allowed her only a brief time on station. After transferring the crews to *Irene* and *Cormoran* (6–9 June), she was to rendezvous with the ships of the Second Division in Tsingtao (16–19 June). Rather than send her to Nagasaki to transfer crews for *Kaiser* and *Prinzess Wilhelm* and then on to Manila for *Kaiserin Augusta*, he ordered her to proceed directly to Manila to complete the final transfers (Mariveles Bay, 26–30 June).[35]

Thus, the gathering of five German warships at Manila in summer 1898 derived from two innocent and legitimate reasons, not an aggressive plan to seize the Philippines. The Filipino insurrection and Spanish-American conflict justified a ship or two to observe the conflict and protect German interests, while the need to transfer relief crews was made easier by Manila's central location. Diederichs also expected that Manila would fall quickly to American forces, making the need for his ships' presence to be quite brief. He made his decision based solely on pragmatic grounds. He had no idea that an extended and extensive German presence at Manila would aggravate Dewey and cause a major German-American crisis.[36]

Diederichs had welcomed the opportunity to go to Manila, since he had spent the previous six months on tense, active duty at Kiao-chou. He also used the occasion to send a letter to Henni, timed to arrive by her forty-fifth birthday on 27 June.[37]

Diederichs apparently brought to Manila no prejudices against the United States. He had certainly enjoyed his 1893 U.S. visit, both personally and professionally. He had corresponded with Dewey but had not met him before June 1898; he had had good relations with his predecessor, Adm. Frederick McNair. But his attitude seems to have changed after the events of the summer of 1898.

Diederichs departed Nagasaki aboard *Kaiserin Augusta* on 10 June. When he reached Corregidor on the morning of 12 June, he found no sign of an American blockade: "No ships, as far as we could ascertain, guarded the entrance."[38] He noted, in fact, that at no time did an American ship challenge or even approach the German cruiser. Not surprisingly, he wondered if a blockade really existed. Unchallenged, *Kaiserin Augusta* proceeded into the bay, steamed past Dewey's anchored squadron at Cavite, where he sighted the masts and yardarms of the sunken Spanish ships, exchanged salutes with *Olympia,* and anchored in the Manila roadstead.[39]

The ritual of ceremonial visits began immediately. Dewey, recently promoted to rear admiral but still junior to Diederichs, made the customary visit to Diederichs aboard *Kaiserin Augusta* in the morning; Diederichs returned the call aboard *Olympia* later that afternoon. These first meetings sowed the seeds of later discord. Dewey advised Diederichs that the Americans expected substantial reinforcements in the next few days which would, in concert with insurgent forces, finally allow him to launch a land assault on Manila. Dewey also admitted that the United States had not yet decided whether to retain the Philippines but did reserve "the right of possession through conquest."

The conversations soon turned tense, however, as Dewey registered his displeasure with the size of the German force at Manila. He contended that limited German economic interests in the archipelago in no way justified the presence of three powerful warships and a transport carrying fourteen hundred seamen. Diederichs responded that his orders called for him to make a personal analysis of the situation, that the Germans did have extensive economic interests in the Philippines, and that the nature of the Kaiserliche Marine's contract deadline with the North German Lloyd Line required a rapid transfer of crews, which justified not only the current presence of German ships for transshipment but also the impending arrival of several others.[40]

Dewey registered a second complaint in his ghost-written memoirs. He accused Diederichs of making a belligerent response—"I am here, Sir, by the order of the Kaiser!"—which he interpreted as an imperious and belligerent explanation of the presence of the large German force at Manila. Although Diederichs later admitted that he had probably used the remark, which was a stock phrase used by officers serving on foreign station, he denied that he had intended anything confrontational.[41] Ironically, although their conversations had become somewhat heated, Diederichs described Dewey in positive terms in his report of the incident: "The admiral, who is in his sixties, acts lively and energetically. He is very civil and makes a calm and assertive impression."[42]

The meetings also left Diederichs in a confused state. First, he concluded from the American ambivalence toward the Philippines that Germany might still gain a foothold there. Moreover, during their initial discussion, Dewey made no reference to the existence of a blockade. Since the Americans had never communicated the formal existence of a blockade to either Diederichs or Consul Krüger, Diederichs concluded that no blockade existed. He would later argue that this factor rendered moot Dewey's complaints about alleged German blockade violations.[43]

Diederichs went ashore on 13 June to pay a formal call on Governor General Augustin, who, hoping that the Germans would intervene on Spain's behalf, immediately asked Diederichs if he carried any special instructions. When Diederichs said no, the governor explained that he had cabled his superiors in Madrid to advise them that he could not hold the Philippines without "outside help." Diederichs quickly dissuaded him from believing that Germany would provide this external aid and asked that he advise his officials and forces accordingly. Diederichs feared that rumors of possible German intervention, rampant throughout Manila society, would raise doubts about the innocent nature of the German presence. He advised Augustin that he intended to defuse these rumors by carefully proving German neutrality.

Augustin returned the call at the German consulate later that afternoon. The governor told Diederichs at that time that he intended to negotiate an armistice with the insurgents. This would allow Spanish forces to focus their entire strength against the Americans. Even though Diederichs had already declined one request to intervene, Augustin formally asked him to at least mediate the truce with the insurgents. Diederichs again declined to intervene, citing the lack of instructions from his government and the need to uphold German neutrality in the complex issue. Diederichs did quote Dewey to Augustin, that the Americans had still not decided to annex the Philippines in case of an American victory. In a prophetic statement, Augustin responded with the belief that the Filipinos would resist an American takeover.[44]

Dewey later claimed that Diederichs's meetings with Augustin on 13 June proved the existence of a German-Spanish conspiracy. He also insisted that no other neutral officer had called on senior Spanish officials. Diederichs rejected the first charge as wholly untrue and disputed the second, citing visits to Augustin by French and Japanese admirals. Capt. Edward Chichester, commander of HMS *Immortalité,* and British Consul H. W. Rawson-Walker had also met with Augustin and Montojo. Dewey nonetheless argued that others also suspected the Germans of nefarious intent. He wrote, "One foreign consul [presumably, Rawson-Walker] in Manila, I know, had orders from his government to report the actions of the Germans in cipher."[45] Diederichs seemed almost to enjoy this troublemaking role. When describing these events to Fritz, he noted with some humor, "The situation here is quite intriguing and no one knows what the German admiral intends!"[46]

Between the two meetings with Augustin, Diederichs briefly toured Manila. He noted scenes of great disarray and chaos. Without wares to sell, shopkeepers had closed their shops, while large crowds on the verge of panic milled around the city's many squares. He also noted that the municipal authorities had cut down many trees in the city's parks and along the city's thoroughfares, either to provide fuel or fire zones in case of assault. Wherever he went, the Spanish population greeted him in a hopeful manner, believing that he and his warships would indeed provide the salvation they sought.[47]

Diederichs could offer Augustin some solace. Following their meetings on 13 June, Augustin asked Diederichs to negotiate the release of his family (Señora Augustin and five children, ranging in age from seven to fifteen), held under house arrest by the insurgents outside of Manila. Diederichs immediately agreed, gained permission from Dewey to contact the insurgents, and then arranged the release of the family. The Augustin family arrived in Manila on 27 June after two days and nights in a six-oared open boat. Diederichs reported, "Frau Augustin herself steered the craft when the helmsman became incapacitated." She proudly showed her sunburned and insect-bitten arms to the German officers who rescued her.[48]

Continuing his examination of the situation in Manila, Diederichs met with delegates from the German community at the consulate on 15 June. They advised him that the end of Spanish sovereignty would actually benefit the Philippines because the Spanish authorities had long practiced political oppression of Filipino natives and unfair trade restrictions on foreign merchants. The delegates nonetheless evinced some pessimism about the future of the Philippines. They doubted both that the native Filipinos could create an effective government and that Germany would have an opportunity to play a major role in a post-insurgent state. None welcomed an American role, but some saw hope in the possibility of some British involvement.[49]

Germany's presence in the Philippines increased on 18 June when *Kaiser* arrived from Nagasaki. Her arrival into Manila after dark only added to Dewey's suspicions. Although Dewey dispatched a steam launch to intercept the warship, *Kaiser* failed to heave to and proceeded to anchor in the Manila roadstead instead. When Captain Stubenrauch formally visited *Olympia* the next morning, Dewey personally complained that *Kaiser* had violated his blockade. Stubenrauch responded that he had not intended to run the American blockade. His Spanish pilot had not mentioned a blockade and neither he nor his lookouts had seen the American signals to heave to.[50]

The arrival of light cruiser *Prinzess Wilhelm* on 20 June completed the German contingent in the Philippines. Now Diederichs could evaluate the status of the American blockade, which, he wrote, the Americans had never formally announced and at most practiced "rather loosely." Occasionally, one of Dewey's smaller ships—patrol gunboats *Concord* or *Petrel,* and revenue cutter *Hugh McCulloch*—provided initial contact with incoming ships at the mouth of the bay. Likewise, a light cruiser intermittently patrolled the inner bay. None of these patrols was consistent or regular. This apparently haphazard performance explained the unhindered entrance of German or other ships as well as Diederichs's complaint that the Americans had not maintained an effective, and therefore legal, blockade.[51]

In any event, the scene was now set for a potential German-American naval confrontation. Diederichs had five warships and qualitative superiority: flagship *Kaiser* (eighty-eight hundred tons, eight 260-mm guns), heavy cruiser *Kaiserin Augusta* (sixty-two hundred tons and twelve 150-mm guns), medium cruisers *Irene* and *Prinzess Wilhelm* (five thousand tons, four 150-mm and eight 105-mm guns each), and light cruiser *Cormoran* (eighteen hundred tons, eight 105-mm guns). Dewey, on the other hand, commanded six warships and had quantitative superiority: heavy cruiser *Olympia* (six thousand tons, four 200-mm and ten 127-mm guns), light cruisers *Baltimore* (forty-four hundred tons, four 200-mm and six 157-mm guns), *Boston* (thirty-two hundred tons, two 200-mm and six 157-mm guns), *Raleigh* (thirty-two hundred tons, one 150-mm and ten 127-mm guns), and patrol gunboats *Concord* (seventeen hundred tons, six 150-mm guns) and *Petrel* (nine hundred tons, four 150-mm guns). The American squadron also had revenue cutter *Hugh McCulloch* and former Spanish small gunboats *Callao* and *Leyte.*

John T. McCutcheon, a reporter for the Chicago *Record* attached to Dewey's squadron, described the large German contingent as "a more imminent menace than the Spanish fleet reported approaching through Suez."[52] But if the Germans had truly had aggressive intent, Diederichs could have brought in the remaining ships of Prince Heinrich's Second Division: heavy cruiser *Deutschland* (eighty-eight hundred tons, eight 260-mm guns), light cruiser *Gefion* (forty-two hundred tons, ten 105-mm guns), and corvette *Arcona* (twenty-six hundred tons, ten 150-mm guns).

Meanwhile, Germany was not the only neutral power represented by warships in the islands. Capt. Edward Chichester and armored cruiser *Immortalité* (fifty-six hundred tons, two 240-mm and ten 150-mm guns) followed gunboat *Linnet* (eight hundred tons, two 175-mm guns) into Manila Bay in early May and remained until late August. British light cruisers *Iphigenia* (thirty-four hundred tons, two 150-mm guns) and *Bonaventure* (forty-four tons, two 150-mm guns), plus gunboats *Swift, Pique, Rattler, Plover,* and *Pygmy,* joined him at various times during the summer. Adm. Philippe de la Bedolliéré's French contingent included armored cruiser *Bruix* (forty-seven hundred tons, two 180-mm and six 147-mm guns), protected cruiser *Pascal* (four thousand tons, four 160-mm guns), and the aging barbette ship *Bayard* (six thousand tons, four 240-mm guns). Admiral Nomura brought protected cruisers *Akitsushima* (thirty-one hundred tons, four 150-mm guns), *Naniwa* (thirty-seven hundred tons, two 260-mm guns), *Matsushima* (forty-two hundred tons, one 310-mm and twelve 120-mm guns), and *Itsushima* (forty-two hundred tons, one 310-mm and eleven 120-mm guns) to represent Japanese interests in the archipelago. Even an Austro-Hungarian sloop *Frundsberg* (fourteen hundred tons, four 150-mm guns) arrived for a brief visit in July. Dewey, however, complained only about the German presence.[53]

This roster of neutral warships is somewhat deceiving because none of the foreign contingents was ever present in its entirety at any one time. For example, Diederichs regularly rotated his ships to Mariveles Bay for relief or coaling. He sent *Irene* to visit Dagupan in Northern Luzon and then to Subic Bay. *Cormoran* left Manila to visit Cebu, Iloilo, and Piegan. Because of these developments, Diederichs rarely had more than two or three ships together in Manila Bay at once. On 26 June 1898, for example, only *Cormoran* lay anchored in the Manila roadstead. *Irene* had not returned from Dagupan; *Kaiser, Kaiserin Augusta,* and *Prinzess Wilhelm* lay anchored in Mariveles, coaling and transshipping relief crews and supplies from *Darmstadt*. Dewey, in contrast, reduced his force only once, sending USS *Baltimore* to sea in mid-June to search for an overdue American convoy outward bound from San Francisco.[54]

Ashore, new entanglements also developed. Augustin again asked Diederichs to intervene in the Spanish-Filipino conflict. He advised Diederichs on 22 June that the Spanish government had ordered him to place

Manila under international control rather than surrender the city to the insurgents. He therefore requested that Diederichs formally take charge of the city. Once again, however, Diederichs declined, citing the American presence and his own lack of instructions. Augustin then approached the other neutral commanders, who also refused his request. Dewey, who still lacked sufficient troops to occupy Manila, denounced the Spanish proposal and warned the neutrals not to consider it.[55]

The incident nonetheless allowed Dewey to single out the Germans for criticism. He claimed that German officers regularly went ashore to conspire with their Spanish counterparts and that German ships saluted the Spanish flag but ignored the American ensign. German sailors occupied the Pasig lighthouse for several days and then, without permission, landed at Mariveles to take possession of the vacated quarantine station. Diederichs himself had supposedly taken up residence ashore in "a large house which had been the quarters of the Spanish officials."[56]

Diederichs, in his own account of the summer's incidents, refuted or explained these charges. He noted, for example, that other neutral officers had met ashore with Spanish officials. The Spanish had also requested that no warship render a salute because any gunfire, no matter how ceremonial, would frighten Manila's inhabitants. He admitted that German sailors had briefly occupied the Pasig lighthouse but only during the process of bringing lighters downriver, for use in the transfer of *Darmstadt*'s relief crews, and then with Dewey's permission. Diederichs acknowledged his temporary residence at Mariveles, while coaling *Kaiser* from collier *Drachenfels* on 26 and 27 June. Because Mariveles possessed no modern equipment, the crew required two days of hard manual labor to replenish *Kaiser*'s bunkers. Rather than contend with coal dust and its adverse impact on his pulmonary problems, Diederichs arranged to stay ashore on the advice of his staff surgeon. Diederichs's Chinese cook found refuge for him in the former quarters of the quarantine station's chief medical officer. Given Manila's constant heat and humidity, Diederichs was relieved to spend two days and nights "in complete peace and comfort" ashore. He also noted that other neutrals, including the British, used Mariveles to coal their ships.[57] Such incidents, no matter how innocent or explainable, nonetheless increased Dewey's suspicions.

Oddly enough, as Dewey's suspicions increased, Diederichs's expectations of a more direct German role in the Philippines declined. He had concluded by late June that the Spanish would lose the archipelago "unless another power comes to their aid." Although he had little interest in promoting German intervention, he nonetheless cited continuing American ambivalence toward the Philippines. He reiterated both Dewey's remark that the United States reserved the right of "possession through conquest" and the McKinley administration's indecision in regard to the archipelago's future. He also discounted Consul Krüger's earlier report that the Filipinos would accept a German monarch or protectorate. In talks with insurgent leaders, he had received no hint of such interest and attributed the earlier speculation to the wishful thinking of a few individuals. Instead, he noted that the Filipinos intended to establish an independent native government. He cited nationalism, illustrated by the popular motto, "The Philippines for the Filipinos," as the primary cause of the rebellion and doubted that the Filipinos would submit passively to new foreign domination after independence. He did, however, see a slight advantage, but little opportunity, in Filipino independence, advising German support for the Filipinos "so that we can come to their aid when the inevitable crash of self-government comes and they ask for our help." However, he also cited an informal survey of European expatriates who preferred a casual English economic presence to more direct German or American political sovereignty.

Diederichs also admitted that his relations with Dewey were less than friendly. He reported that new rumors claiming that German forces would help Spain retain the islands had reached Dewey. The presence of five warships lent credence to these rumors and heightened Dewey's suspicions. Diederichs therefore believed that the departure of several ships, following the completion of crew transfers, would alleviate German-American tensions. Diederichs even had a few kind words for the Americans who, he noted, "proceed in a businesslike manner under well-trained commanders" even if they had begun the war "unprepared by European standards."[58]

Diederichs's private and more forthright opinions, communicated in his personal correspondence, further confirm a lack of interest in turning Manila into another Kiao-chou. In fact, his personal priority, the security of Kiao-chou, made him anxious to return with his squadron to the Chinese coast.

Since his orders required him to remain in the Philippines until the fall of the city, he complained to Henni about the slow pace of American reinforcements. He feared, in fact, that he might have to remain at Manila another two or three months, when he much preferred to make the long-postponed visit to Batavia and then return to Kiao-chou. He happily reported the imminent arrival of twenty-five hundred American troops in early July, which he hoped would suffice to allow the Americans to capture Manila and permit him to leave Filipino waters.[59]

Whatever his hopes may have been, Diederichs's plans for his departure and an attendant reduction of German forces came too late to reduce tensions. His presence at Manila had already become widely known in Germany and the United States. A writer for the *Marine-Politische Correspondenz* noted, "[the fact that] the same officer who took possession of Kiao-chou is in command of the squadron guarantees energetic action at the right moment."[60] An editorial for the semiofficial *Norddeutsche Zeitung* similarly justified his presence because war threatened the "life and property of German merchants in the Philippines."[61] Needless to say, Ambassador James White cited these and similar comments when he reported to the U.S. State Department that many Germans hoped that Diederichs would create a new Kiao-chou in the Philippines. He recommended that the USN reinforce Dewey's naval contingent in the archipelago.[62] White's consular peers in Southeast Asia shared his fears. Consul O. F. Williams, writing from Cavite, noted that the Germans were "making asses of themselves as usual." Consul Rounseville Wildman (Hong Kong) charged that the Spanish "would have surrendered without bloodshed [except] for these [German] mischief makers."[63]

For all of this, the worst was yet to come. Dewey's "German problem" was on the flow, not the ebb. Through accident or design, *Irene*, his original nemesis, would turn crisis in June into confrontation in July.

THE PERILS OF *IRENE*

Although Diederichs had lost hope by late June that Germany might still gain a foothold in the Philippines, he nonetheless dispatched his ships throughout the islands to examine potential sites and, not incidentally, protect German interests. Thus, he sent *Cormoran* south to visit Cebu and Iloilo in the Visayan islands, and *Irene* north to Dagupan, a small port in Lingayen Gulf, to look for the missing German mining engineers. Two successive incidents involving *Irene* set off the next round of German-American tensions.

The first incident began, seemingly as all would begin, innocently. Because of the threat posed to the American squadron by reinforcements dispatched from Spain, Dewey had sent USS *Baltimore* to locate and escort a convoy of troop transports due in from San Francisco. *Baltimore* rendezvoused with the convoy several days out to sea on 25 June.[64] Meanwhile, American revenue cutter *Hugh McCulloch,* carrying Dewey's flag lieutenant Thomas M. Brumby, steamed out past Corregidor on 27 June to patrol the approaches to Manila Bay and await the convoy's arrival. The cutter had already intercepted HMS *Pygmy* when another warship steamed into view from the north. Lookouts quickly identified the ship as SMS *Irene,* returning from Dagupan. Obenheimer had not located the missing German nationals but he had evacuated Spanish noncombatants—four women and ten children—endangered by the Filipino insurrection.

McCulloch hoisted the international signal B-N-D—"Halt. I have something to communicate. Close."—and launched a cutter to intercept *Irene.* Even though the German warship had been in Philippine waters for six weeks and Brumby had visited her several times, he boarded the cruiser to formally ask her identity. Obenheimer welcomed Brumby aboard but then asked him what pressing matter required him to halt and board *Irene.* Brumby initially declined to specify his purpose but then responded that the American squadron awaited the return of *Baltimore* and the arrival of the convoy. At this point, Obenheimer formally protested that such a circumstance did not warrant *McCulloch's* use of the BND signal or the interception of *Irene.* Brumby returned to *McCulloch,* which resumed her patrol, while *Irene* steamed into Manila Bay.[65]

Without immediate reference to *McCulloch's* actions, Diederichs decided to dispatch *Irene* to survey Subic Bay a few days later. Situated on Luzon's west coast sixty nautical miles north of Manila, Subic Bay had superb potential as a naval base, offering a fortified entrance at Isla Grande, protected anchorages, and an existing naval depot at Olongapo.[66] The proposed reconnaissance assumed new dimensions on 1 July when Consul Krüger advised Diederichs that insurgents had recently occupied Olongapo. Krüger feared that a new rebel offensive would threaten German nationals in the area and asked Diederichs to expedite plans for a survey of the bay. The consul also informed him that IJNS *Matsushima* had visited the bay several days earlier and assisted in the evacuation of Olangapo's Spanish residents and garrison, which consisted of several hundred Spanish regulars and native soldiers, to Isla Grande. Civilian craft had conveyed the garrison's dependents and Olangapo's civil officials to the island as well. Because an insurgent blockade had cut off Spanish food supplies, Governor Augustin now asked Krüger to request that Diederichs replenish the island's stores.[67]

Diederichs immediately declined Augustin's request but ordered *Irene* to proceed to sea at dawn on 5 July to undertake a general reconnaissance of Subic Bay. Diederichs formally assigned three tasks to *Irene:* to seek out and evacuate any German nationals from the path of the rebel offensive, to survey potential anchorages to shelter the squadron in case of a typhoon, and, not forgetting the cruiser squadron's prime directive, to explore the bay's military value. Although Diederichs had rejected Augustin's request to supply the Isla Grande garrison, he did approve humanitarian intervention when he directed Obenheimer to call "at such places where women and children are endangered, take them on board, and convey them to Manila."[68] This latter gesture had an unintended result, leading to a new German-American confrontation.

Irene steamed out of the Manila roadstead at dawn on 5 July, reaching Subic Bay in the forenoon. Obenheimer immediately sighted an approaching steam launch flying a Spanish flag. The craft, manned by a crew of ten and armed with a revolving cannon in the bow, comprised Isla Grande's sole naval force. The launch's commander confirmed Krüger's information that insurgent attacks had forced the Spanish garrison at Olongapo to evacuate its positions and withdraw to Isla Grande. The insurgents had demanded that the garrison surrender or face bombardment from an armed merchant ship. Almost immediately, *Irene*'s lookouts sighted the insurgent ship, *Companie de Filipinas,* approaching the island from the direction of Olongapo. Obenheimer knew from several sources that *Filipinas*'s native crew had mutinied, murdered their Spanish officers, and then mounted several artillery pieces taken from the Olongapo naval depot. *Filipinas* hauled up near the island and sent a boat across to *Irene*.

The insurgents notified Obenheimer that they had just demanded the surrender of the Spanish forces on Isla Grande. If the Spanish troops refused to capitulate, the ship would bombard the island. In response, Obenheimer rebuked the rebel officer for showing the insurgent flag at sea, since any military act carried out under the flag constituted an act of piracy under international law. The rebel officer immediately assured Obenheimer that he would cancel his attack, returned to his ship, and steamed back to Olangapo. Obenheimer's yeoman, Ernest Heilmann, later wrote, "I was convinced that this interference was the salvation of the little garrison on Grandy Island."[69] Citing Dewey as his source, Captain Chichester recorded a slightly different version, in which Obenheimer had prevented the insurgent attack by "informing the Rebel Leader that the Germans were friends of Spain and would not allow the Spaniards in that place to be molested and that if [the insurgents] persisted in trying to land they would be shelled by *Irene*."[70]

Obenheimer himself went ashore on Isla Grande early in the afternoon. He spoke with the senior Spanish officer, who informed him that the island garrison housed approximately five hundred troops in addition to civil servants, dockyard employees, a large number of women and children, and several priests. The garrison lacked adequate supplies of food, water, and munitions. As directed by Diederichs, Obenheimer offered to evacuate the garrison's dependents and noncombatants to Manila but declined to offer provisions or any other material aid. Neutrality laws allowed him to offer medical supplies for the Spanish wounded. Thus, when the garrison commander requested *Irene*'s support against the rebel assault, Obenheimer again refused. He promised to return to Isla Grande at the conclusion of his mission to evacuate the garrison's noncombatants.

Irene then steamed over to Olongapo navy yard, which the insurgents had now occupied. A military band welcomed Obenheimer ashore and the local insurgent commander gave him a tour of the dockyard, which had significant potential as a naval base. Obenheimer observed that, situated on a peninsula that bisected Olongapo's inner and outer harbors, the dockyard had spacious quays and sufficient open space for expansion. Obenheimer duly asked his host about the presence of German nationals in the area. As *Irene* lay anchored for the night off Olongapo, her watch officer recorded only a single incident: *Filipinas* weighed anchor and proceeded out of the harbor soon after midnight.

Irene visited Subic town, in the bay's northwest corner, on 6 July. Several boats flying flags of truce greeted the ship, welcoming the Germans in the name of Aguinaldo's provisional government and inviting them to enjoy the hospitality of a visit ashore. When Obenheimer asked his new hosts about the presence of German nationals, they advised him to visit a town in the interior where several European refugees had been reported. Accompanied by two rebel leaders, Obenheimer mounted a borrowed horse and began the two-hour journey inland to the town of Castillejos. He found several hundred Spanish troops in detention but no German nationals. Obenheimer returned to Subic, boarded *Irene,* and steamed over to Isla Grande at dusk. At dawn on the seventh, *Irene*'s boats evacuated Isla Grande's noncombatants: seven women, twenty-one children, a badly wounded soldier, and a Catholic priest.[71]

As far as Obenheimer was concerned, his mission to date had been peaceful and without incident. All that would soon change. Unbeknownst to him, *Filipinas* on 6 July had steamed to Cavite, where her commander immediately complained to Aguinaldo that the Germans had prevented, without provocation or justification, his attack on Isla Grande. Aguinaldo in turn appealed to Dewey, his erstwhile ally, who immediately ordered light cruiser *Raleigh* and gunboat *Concord* to prepare for departure. Dewey gave orders to Capt. J. B. Coghlan, *Raleigh*'s commander, to proceed to Subic Bay and investigate *Irene*'s alleged interference.[72]

The American warships reached Subic Bay soon after dawn on 7 July just as *Irene* completed the evacuation of Isla Grande's noncombatants. Heilmann, who was with Obenheimer on *Irene*'s navigating bridge, noted that the sudden arrival of the American ships caught the Germans by surprise:

> When the two ships were first sighted I saw a rather puzzled look on the Captain's face. It was evidently his intention to transfer his passengers quietly, and without publicity from [the American] quarter.
>
> At this stage, the women and priest were sitting on the poop deck, while the children were running about, now on the poop and now on the

forecastle, I heard the Executive [Officer] ask the Captain: "Would it not be better if we send all the Spaniards below decks until the ships have passed?" To which the Captain, after a short silence, replied: "No, I will be responsible for this."[73]

Raleigh, preparing to bombard the Spanish entrenchments on Isla Grande, had cleared for action but had not gone to general quarters. *Concord*'s crew remained at cruising stations. Both ships passed to starboard of *Irene* a few moments later, went to battle stations, and, as *Irene* disappeared over the horizon, commenced firing their 6-inch guns on the Spanish positions. The Spanish forces immediately hoisted a white flag and surrendered.[74] *Irene* reached Manila Bay later in the afternoon. Obenheimer sent the evacuees ashore and then reported aboard *Kaiser* to Diederichs.[75]

Diederichs's ensuing report to the Naval High Command said little about the episode with the American warships. He focused instead on the illegal actions of the insurgent ship *Filipinas* and comments by rebel leaders soliciting German support for an independent Philippines. He nonetheless decided to end *Irene*'s service in the archipelago. He advised the OKM that *Irene* had not yet had the opportunity to train her new crew, both because of her service at Manila and because of the debilitating weather of a Manila summer. He may also have concluded that *Irene*'s involvement in the BND and Isla Grande incidents would foster a new round of German-American antagonism. In any event, he ordered Obenheimer to proceed to Kiao-chou and relieve SMS *Arcona.* He then transmitted orders to *Arcona* to reconnoiter the Caroline and Mariana Islands, where American forces had reportedly captured Guam. After coaling at Mariveles, *Irene* steamed north out of the archipelago on 9 July.[76]

Irene's adventure prompted Diederichs to question the navy's practice of relieving crews on foreign station. *Irene*'s new personnel, who made up approximately half of her regular complement, had arrived in East Asia with only minimal training. The protocol called for them to finish their training aboard ship. It was this second stage that had proved so difficult for *Irene*'s new crew. "Current basic training procedures," Diederichs wrote, "do not adequately prepare new crews for ship duties." Diederichs recommended that seamen-recruits receive more thorough training—the role, after all, of the

Matrosendivision in Kiel and Wilhelmshaven—before assignment to active duty with the fleet. Diederichs also acknowledged that using Manila for transshipment had both complicated his responsibilities and created new problems: "I fear that the results of these circumstances will haunt the squadron for some time to come." He concluded, "Although imperial needs are certainly paramount, there must nonetheless be a better procedure for manning ships on foreign station."[77]

Press reports of *Irene*'s actions unleashed an immediate editorial uproar in the United States. The *New York Times*, for example, described *Irene*'s actions at Isla Grande as an unfriendly act that bordered on a "breach of peace."[78] The Detroit *News* perceived a pattern of German expansionism: "No doubt the Kaiser has his eye on the Philippines, but in that respect the Philippines do not differ from the remainder of the earth's surface."[79] The St. Paul *Dispatch*, citing the strength of Diederichs's squadron, belligerently postured, "If Wilhelm wants to test his navy, let him do it." The Atlanta *Constitution* wrote that "if Germany persists in the arrogance which has thus far marked her course, she will walk out of the Philippines with an empty satchel and a sore heart." The Detroit *Tribune* was more clement, noting that the "Monroe Doctrine does not apply to the universe. . . . There are times when the other fellow is entitled to have something to say." The *New York Evening Post* agreed: "We have no interest in preventing Germany from acquiring a coaling-station in the Philippines."[80] The German press, of course, defended *Irene*'s actions. For example, the Berlin *Lokal Anzeiger* countered the American charges with the editorial response that no "reliable account of the affair has yet been received, but it is certain that if the German vessel interfered at all, it was for the protection of people who have a right to be protected."[81]

Contrary to press reports, eyewitness accounts of the German-American "confrontation" at Isla Grande agreed that the reality of the affair was quite innocent. Obenheimer's official report stated succinctly, "While departing from the bay, the SMS *Irene* passed two American ships, presumably *Raleigh* and *Concord*, which approached in a state of battle readiness and, as we lost sight of them, steamed into the bay."[82] *Raleigh*'s log merely noted, "At 6:45 we passed a German cruiser which came out of Subig [sic] Bay."[83] *Raleigh*'s commander stated in his official report, "Upon arrival off that bay at 7:00 A.M., 7th, a German man-of-war was met coming out. She steered as wide of us as she could and proceeded toward Manila Bay."[84] Dewey made no mention of alleged German interference in a letter to his son, writing only that "*Raleigh* and *Concord* captured an island yesterday in Subig [*sic*] Bay with several prisoners."[85]

Nor did Diederichs make mention of the incidents in his private correspondence. He was more concerned with Henni's continuing health problems and service politics in Berlin. He also acknowledged his own physical maladies, citing the summer heat and humidity that caused him great physical discomfort and brought back his respiratory problems.[86] He did refer to the BND incident in a letter to Fritz, describing *McCulloch*'s actions simply as "confused." In addition, his view of the American character had become more cynical: "They calculate every act in dollars and cents." He nonetheless acknowledged that the Germans were partly at fault for the tensions at Manila—a factor that would diminish, he hoped, with the departure first of *Irene* and then of other warships following crew transshipment. He also blamed the English as another source of tensions, criticizing them for alleged "mischief" and wondering if their forces would actively intervene on behalf of the Americans. He joked, with some seriousness, that he might need to stay longer at Manila just to observe the perfidious English.[87] He wrote a similar comment to Henni: "The English are behind everything you have read in the papers."[88] Henni had also read the press reports. She cited several German newspapers that had begun to anticipate the establishment of a new Kiao-chou in the Philippines. She wondered if this meant something new, given his earlier letters in which he had doubted Germany's ability to gain a foothold there. Her greater concern, however, was about his health; he had acknowledged a return of rheumatism. She hoped that he could soon leave Manila's unsafe and unhealthy conditions. Her own health had recently improved, particularly since she had begun new therapy (hydrotherapy and mud baths). She also reported that Fritz had begun to consider seeking a transfer to the Naval Infantry. "The navy," she wrote, "is not the same for him as for you."[89]

IF GERMANY WANTS WAR

Admiral Dewey, however, was less sanguine about the crisis. In a deliberate attempt to show his displeasure with German actions, he transferred to

McCulloch on 5 July and steamed slowly but meaningfully around two German warships anchored in Mariveles Bay.[90] The arrival of *Filipinas* on the sixth with reports of alleged German interference in Subic Bay convinced him not only to dispatch warships to Isla Grande but also to develop a formal protest to register with Diederichs. Thomas Brumby, his flag lieutenant, visited Diederichs in *Kaiser*'s flag quarters on 8 July to present Dewey's litany of complaints. Brumby first advised Diederichs that Dewey had tried to make the blockade as painless as possible to visiting neutral warships but that a continuous pattern of German transgressions might now compel Dewey to enact a more stringent blockade. In response, Diederichs agreed that Dewey had indeed conducted the blockade in "the mildest way possible" and denied "any intention of interfering in the least with Admiral Dewey's operations." He promised to restrict nighttime movements by his ships but nonetheless asserted an occasional right to move around after dark. Brumby concluded in his official report, "I was convinced of [Diederichs's] sincerity and personal probity."[91]

Diederichs formally responded to Dewey's complaints in a letter carried to *Olympia* by his flag lieutenant, Lt. Cdr. Paul von Hintze, on 10 July. Although the letter attempted to explain alleged blockade transgressions, the gist of Diederichs's response was an official protest of the BND incident in which *McCulloch* had stopped and boarded *Irene* on 26 June. Diederichs argued that international law did not permit the search of or visits to neutral warships wishing to enter blockaded ports and that *McCulloch* had used the BND signal improperly.[92]

According to Hintze, Dewey appeared conciliatory after reading Diederichs's letter. In fact, Dewey blamed the incident on the inexperience of the *McCulloch*'s commander: "You see, the *McCulloch* is not a man-of-war, she is but a revenue cutter, maybe the captain has made there some mistake in signaling." Hintze then reminded Dewey that *Irene* had been in Philippine waters since early May, "a fact known to practically everyone." *McCulloch* could merely have identified her through her flag or silhouette and then have communicated with her through a flag hoist or signal lamp without recourse to stopping or boarding her. Growing somewhat more agitated, Dewey responded that he had the right to board any ship, whether man-of-war or merchant ship, "to make the inquiries necessary to establish the ship's identity."

The discussion now grew more heated. According to Hintze, Dewey grew steadily more angry during the interview, finally blustering, "Why, I shall stop each vessel whatever may be her colors! And if she does not stop, I shall fire at her! And that means war, do you know, Sir? And I tell you, if Germany wants war, all right, we are ready!"[93]

Hintze, who noted in his official report that he quietly slipped away as Dewey began to repeat the phrase "if Germany wants war," concluded that Dewey's angry outburst arose from a combination of mistrust of German intentions, rumors of alleged German activities, and press exaggerations of German actions in the archipelago. Diederichs, whose opinion of Americans continued to decline through the summer, added his own evaluation of Dewey's outburst:

> I attached little value to blustering remarks made in a condition of extreme excitement and complete loss of self control . . . and still less to his threats. I thought both were excusable considering the immaturity and rudeness of the American nation which has had neither the time nor material progress to teach its sons tact and good manners.

When he read the dispatch in Berlin, Wilhelm concurred, glossing, "Well said. Correct."[94]

The exchange of flag lieutenant visits solved none of the growing tensions between Deiderichs and Dewey but instead engendered an active correspondence offering differing interpretations of blockade procedures. Dewey began the exchange on 11 July with reference to the BND incident. He first noted that neither Brumby nor *McCulloch*'s captain could immediately identify *Irene* or her ensign because she had approached the cutter bow on, turning parallel to *McCulloch*'s course only at the last moment. Although the cutter had launched a boat to intercept *Irene*, Brumby hoisted BND because *Irene*'s high approach speed implied that she did not intend to stop. Moreover, *Irene*'s arrival surprised the Americans, who believed she lay anchored in Mariveles Bay. In any event, Dewey wrote, enemy warships often hoisted neutral colors as a legitimate *ruse de guerre*. Dewey therefore argued that boarding a neutral warship in order to elicit her identity was correct, since his status as blockader assured him that right.[95]

Diederichs's response, delivered to *Olympia* later that day, took exception to Dewey's contention. It did not matter whether *McCulloch*'s lookouts could not immediately identify *Irene,* Diederichs argued, since international maritime law permitted a blockading warship to halt and board only those neutral merchantmen suspected of carrying contraband of war. No such right—*droit de visite*—extended to warships flying a neutral flag.[96]

Dewey continued the exchange with a response on the morning of 12 July. He denied that he had ever claimed the *droit de visite* but stated that he did reserve the right to communicate with any warship passing through his blockade. The incoming vessel itself might wish to receive relevant information, especially if entering a blockaded zone at night. In any event, the blockading squadron permitted neutral warships to enter a blockaded port only as a matter of international courtesy, not right.[97]

Before responding to Dewey's second letter, and to buttress his own case, Diederichs polled his fellow neutral commanders. Admiral de la Bedolliéré, commander of the French contingent, agreed that a warship's peculiar silhouette and ensign adequately identified her; the possible use of false colors in no way justified any extraordinary method of identification. Captain Saito of IJNS *Akitsushima* cited the actions of Japanese officers during the Sino-Japanese War of 1894–95 who followed a practice similar to Diederichs's proposal—communication for purposes of identification but no boarding. Captain Ziegler, commanding officer of the Austrian frigate *Frundsberg,* considered the entire matter academic, since he planned to depart for Yokohama immediately.[98] Only Captain Chichester, the senior British officer, failed to agree totally with Diederichs's stance. Visiting Diederichs aboard *Kaiser* on 12 July, he argued that international law did permit the boarding of warships for identification. He nonetheless admitted that searching such a warship was "inadmissible and resentable." After much prompting, he also acknowledged to Diederichs that he himself would shoot any foreign boarding officer who "does not take my word" for proof of identity.[99]

Diederichs now responded to Dewey's letter. Although he acknowledged Dewey's right to communicate with any neutral man-of-war entering harbor, Diederichs continued to resist Dewey's claim to the right to board incoming warships for purposes of identification. He cited the opinions of the other neutral officers and again justified his arguments on the ground that a warship's unmistakable configuration distinguished her from merchant ships and that her flag signaled neutrality. The possible use of false colors as a ruse of war, he maintained, made no difference.[100]

Although he considered his position just and proper, Diederichs nonetheless sought to prevent further ship-to-ship confrontations. He therefore established formal procedures dealing with the identification of neutral warships. His captains could permit the traditional ceremonial visit, mutually undertaken by ships' captains, as well as boarding for purpose of identification at night only or when darkness prevented visual identification of a warship's shape or national ensign. However, he refused to allow daytime visits for purposes of identification and notified his subordinates that German ships had the right to refuse such visits. He concluded, rather belligerently, "If force is used, respond with force."[101]

Dewey also sought to reduce the possibility for future confrontations. He ordered his captains to "exercise great care" when visiting warships coming into Manila Bay. Boarding officers were only to ask the ship's identity, her captain's name, and her last port of call.[102] Dewey nonetheless considered the use of force. Oscar King Davis, a reporter aboard *Olympia,* overheard Dewey discuss contingency plans with *Raleigh*'s J. B. Coghlan. The two officers considered a preemptive strike against the *Kaiser,* whose 260-mm guns outranged and outgunned anything in the American squadron. Their biggest problem was how to fire shells accurately enough to penetrate *Kaiser*'s armored gun deck and disable her guns.[103]

The catharsis of the Diederichs-Dewey correspondence seemed to lessen German-American tensions. When Dewey sent Diederichs a gift of some frozen mutton from a newly arrived transport, Diederichs returned the gesture by presenting Dewey with a live calf that he had just received from Hong Kong. Dewey responded to the gift with a gracious note: "Thank you very much for your most acceptable present, just received. I hope to enjoy the change in food greatly."[104] "Thus," Diederichs wrote, "a dead sheep and a live calf formed something of the nature of a sacrifice on the altar of friendship."[105] The mutton truce soon allowed Diederichs to report that his relations with Dewey had become "formal but not unfriendly."[106] Dewey agreed, writing Consul Wildman in Hong Kong: "The Germans are behaving better and I don't think there is the slightest intention on their part to interfere at present. What they may do later remains to be seen."[107]

As calm returned, Diederichs could pause to evaluate the reasons for German-American tensions. He tended to play down the influence of his squadron's actions in the Philippines: "I do not believe that the source of difficulty with Admiral Dewey is as much the actions of His Majesty's ships as it is [American] mistrust toward Germany which has existed since the beginning of the Spanish-American War." He nonetheless acknowledged the negative impact of the presence of a vice admiral and five German warships. He also cited the constant, if innocent, movement of German nationals between sea and shore, which had "caused an already existing suspicion to grow because of the impulsive prejudice of the American squadron commander." Finally, Diederichs blamed the "accusations, harassment, and incitement of Englishmen and the English press in East Asia."[108]

Diederichs submitted a second report, predicting the future of the Philippines. He concluded that the Americans would now claim the archipelago by right of conquest. Given the growing American presence, he doubted that harm would come to German nationals, as had happened in China in November, and allow him to recreate another Kiao-chou. Moreover, he assumed that political expediency would lead the insurgents to cast their lot, albeit temporarily, with the Americans. Once the United States moved to establish political sovereignty in the Philippines, however, he predicted that "the United States will not be spared a war against the natives."[109]

THE FALL OF MANILA

Sufficient American reinforcements had finally arrived by early August. The U.S. Expeditionary Force, commanded by Maj. Gen. Wesley Merritt, numbered eleven thousand regular and National Guard troops. Naval reinforcements included the cruiser *Charleston* (thirty-seven hundred tons, two 8-inch guns) and the monitor *Monterrey* (forty-one hundred tons, two 12-inch and two 10-inch guns). The Spanish garrison, which contained nearly fifteen thousand regular and volunteer troops, also prepared for the final battle. When Governor General Augustin cabled a pessimistic report to Madrid, his superiors relieved him and in late July replaced him with Maj. Gen. Fermin Jardenes. Diederichs immediately offered Augustin and his family refuge aboard a German warship. Augustin sent his family aboard the *Kaiserin Augusta* but decided to remain behind himself, to share the fate of his comrades in the city.[110] The Americans sent Jardenes a formal ultimatum on 7 August, giving him forty-eight hours to surrender. Dewey and Merritt then scheduled their attack for 0900 on 10 August. When Jardenes asked for additional time to consult with his superiors, Dewey and Merritt declined. Jardenes then asked the neutral consuls to intervene and dissuade the Americans from attacking, but they too demurred.

Dewey notified the neutral commanders of the ultimatum and requested that they shift their ships from the bombardment zone within a prescribed period. The German refugee flotilla had now grown to four steamers—*Elcano, Herminia, Banan,* and *San Nicolas*—which carried more than two hundred German nationals and an equal number of Spanish refugees from Manila. Convoyed by *Kaiserin Augusta,* the four ships steamed to Mariveles Bay on the morning of 9 August. They remained there under the protection of the *Cormoran,* which was coaling from the collier *Trinidad,* while the *Kaiserin Augusta* returned to Manila. Dewey duly thanked Diederichs for sending the German ships elsewhere rather than placing them near Cavite, where five British, three French, and one Japanese refugee vessels remained anchored in the crowded roadstead. British warships *Immortalité* and *Iphigenia* and Japanese cruisers *Naniwa* and *Matsushima* anchored near the American squadron as well. *Kaiser, Prinzess Wilhelm,* and *Kaiserin Augusta,* which carried Augustin's family, took up positions near the French *Bayard,* carrying Admiral Montojo's wife and family, and *Pascal* northwest of the mouth of the Pasig River. Diederichs noted dryly that the German warships "lay with steam up in order to be prepared for any situation."

The American deadline passed on 10 August with little action. *Concord* and *Petrel* steamed over toward the Pasig River, where they anchored, but the remaining American units made no aggressive moves toward the city. The Americans had decided to postpone their attack, Diederichs learned, because Merritt's troops were not yet ready to launch an assault. He wondered how this could be, since many of the American troops had served in the Philippines since late June. The delay, he noted, also irritated Dewey's sailors, who had to remain under steam and cleared for battle for several more days. Consul Krüger used the brief respite to meet with Dewey to discuss several minor issues. Dewey was pleasantly affable, blaming his poor relations with Diederichs on the press, which had used rumor, innuendo, and falsehoods to widen the German-American schism.[111]

Following another exchange of notes with the French consul as intermediary—the Americans calling for surrender, Jardenes asking for more time—Dewey and Merritt scheduled the assault for 0900 on 13 August. The final battle, as it happened, would be little more than a sham. Through the French consul, the belligerents had confidentially agreed to fight an honorable, but brief, battle: Dewey's ships would fire a few broadsides, Merritt's troops would fire a volley or two, and the Spanish forces, their honor intact, would surrender.

As Merritt's troops advanced against the Spanish entrenchments on the morning of 13 August, Dewey's ships formed into two columns and steamed out of the Cavite anchorage. The British and Japanese warships, stationed nearby, saluted the American flag, while *Immortalité*'s band played Dewey's favorite march, "Under the Double Eagle." *Immortalité* and *Iphigenia* weighed anchor, steamed over toward the German and French ships, and dropped anchor. When *Iphigenia* blocked Diederichs's view of the developing battle, he ordered Stubenrauch to shift *Kaiser*'s position to a better vantage point. The American warships opened fire at 0930. Ninety minutes later, Diederichs wrote, "The American flag flies over the city."[112]

Strangely enough, the fall of Manila produced two more sources of German-American tension. Later press and historical accounts claimed that Captain Chichester had placed his warships between Diederichs and Dewey to prevent a surprise German assault on the preoccupied American ships.[113] Such charges were, however, ludicrous. Diederichs had only three ships left at Manila; Dewey had eight. The German ships had steam up but were anchored and not cleared for action. The *Kaiser*'s change of position was the only action taken by a German ship that day.[114] Chichester made no mention of alleged German intentions, noting only, "On the American Squadron weighing, this ship [*Immortalité*] and the *Iphigenia* weighed and proceeded to an anchorage north of the Pasig River to watch the proceedings."[115] Neither Dewey nor his captains reported any suspicious German action, either.[116] The alleged incident nonetheless served to further erode German-American relations.

Then there was the matter of former Governor General Augustin. Accompanied by Consul Krüger, Augustin had boarded the *Kaiser* on the morning of the battle to request transportation to Hong Kong for himself and his family. Krüger had already secured American permission for Augustin's departure, so Diederichs readily agreed. Since Diederichs had decided to dispatch the *Kaiserin Augusta* to Hong Kong to notify Berlin of Manila's fall, Augustin simply joined his family aboard the cruiser, which got under way soon after dusk on 13 August. When the ship arrived at Hong Kong on the fifteenth, Augustin and his family quietly transferred to steamer *Prinz Heinrich* for the voyage to Spain.[117] Assuming that the Americans would make their own official and public announcement of Manila's surrender, Diederichs had also ordered the cruiser's commander to keep the news of the city's fall and Augustin's whereabouts secret. Captain Köllner therefore told a British officer that Manila still fought on and that his ship carried only Spanish noncombatants and the squadron's mail. When someone recognized Augustin as he boarded SS *Prinz Heinrich,* Consul Wildman angrily confronted Consul Wilhelm Rieloff, who continued to deny that the German cruiser had transported Augustin to Hong Kong. Köllner finally admitted the truth when Commo. Swinton Holland, commander of the British naval forces at Hong Kong, asked him directly. Holland noted in his report that neutral Germany's aid to an official of a belligerent state was "unusual and peculiar, raising much comment by the press, and generally condemned by public opinion."[118]

Press response was most heated in the United States. A *New York Times* editorialist noted that the Germans could have reduced the outcry over the Augustin incident merely by acknowledging his presence aboard *Kaiserin Augusta.* He complained, "But then it is not the object of the German Navy to save exasperation. Rather it seems to be the object of that navy to produce exasperation."[119] Mr. Dooley, imagining a letter from his "Cousin George" to President McKinley, had similar sentiments:

> In pursooance iv ordhers that niver come, to-day th' squadhron undher my command knocked th' divvle out iv th' fortifications if th' Philippines, bombarded th' city, an' locked up th' insurgent gin'ral. The gov'nor got away be swimmin' aboord a Dutch ship, an' th' Dutchman took him to Ding Dong. I'll attind to th' Dutchman some afthernoon whin I have nawthin' else to do.[120]

Press reaction also came to the attention of the German Naval High Command. Admiral Knorr immediately cabled Köllner, still in Hong Kong, to demand an explanation. Köllner responded, "The transfer took place under the orders of the squadron commander and with the permission of the Americans."[121] The anglophobic Senden accused the English of manufacturing the adverse press coverage while explaining the incident simply as a "casual series of misunderstandings." He nonetheless recommended that Diederichs make a public statement explaining the incident.[122] Diederichs did explain to his superiors that he had decided to keep the matter confidential because he believed it was the Americans' prerogative to announce their own victory and Augustin was by then a private citizen who deserved his privacy.[123]

These issues notwithstanding, Manila's fall ended the need for Diederichs's presence in the Philippines. He therefore made preparations to commence the long-postponed visit to Batavia (Jakarta), Dutch East Indies, to celebrate the coronation of Queen Wilhelmina of the Netherlands. Before departing, Diederichs dispatched *Cormoran* to Iloilo and Cebu, where German nationals still resided, and left explicit instruction for Captain Köllner, who would remain with *Kaiserin Augusta* as the senior German naval officer, to continue to protect German national and interests in the archipelago. Diederichs's departure was not without incident. When U.S. monitor *Monadnock* (four thousand tons, four 10-inch guns) finally arrived at Cavite from San Francisco on 16 August, she saluted Dewey's flag but not the flags of the other three admirals—Diederichs, de la Bedolliéré, and Nomura—present at Manila. Now choosing to stand on protocol,

Diederichs made a point of protesting the slight to Lieutenant Brumby, who excused it on the grounds that the monitor's captain was probably unaware of proper saluting procedure.[124]

After three months at Manila, Diederichs finally departed on 21 August. When *Kaiser* encountered two American troop transports soon after passing Corregidor, American sailors climbed their ships' shrouds to cheer the warship, but they quieted suddenly when they recognized *Kaiser*'s German identity. In his ensuing report interpreting the events of the summer, Diederichs mentioned the incident and his assumption that the Americans had initially taken *Kaiser* for a British warship. He wrote almost contemptuously of the American naval record in the Philippines, doubting that either the initial naval battle at Cavite on 1 May or the staged bombardment of Manila on 13 August would in any way advance naval science or strategy. He particularly belittled the American squadron's marksmanship. Although press accounts of the Cavite battle had praised Dewey's gunnery, Dewey himself had commented to Diederichs that his ships had actually fired quite poorly; Dewey attributed it to his crews' inexperience and lack of practice. Nor had American gunnery improved by 13 August; *Immortalité*'s gunnery officer commented to Diederichs that the bombardment had produced "a damned-bad shooting, rather a poor performance after having had us wait for fifteen weeks." Diederichs had equal contempt for Merritt's troops. Although well trained and in excellent physical shape, they lacked discipline and, he believed, could never stand up to a European army. He derogatorily noted that many carried personal mail tucked into their turned-up shirt sleeves and wore toothbrushes as hat ornaments. Thus, their inept assault on Manila came as no surprise to him.[125]

The summer's controversy certainly took some time to abate. When *Irene* returned to Manila in November 1898, a minor press furor erupted when she failed to salute Dewey's flag upon entry into the Manila roadstead. Then, three months later, when hostilities between U.S. and Filipino forces broke out in February 1899, rumors quickly spread through Manila and East Asia that Dewey had detained *Irene,* allegedly discovering a large cache of weapons intended for the Filipinos. Although Obenheimer quickly refuted the story, the American press continued to speak suspiciously of German actions in the Philippines.[126]

Vestigial German interest in the Philippines, however, evaporated after the United States and Spain signed the Treaty of Paris on 10 December 1898. Spain surrendered all claims to Cuba and ceded the Philippines, Puerto Rico, and Guam to the United States in return for twenty million dollars.[127] These events certainly pleased Mr. Dooley, who had worried that if the United States did not acquire the Philippines, then "Schwartzmeister down th' street, that has half me thrade already, will grab thim sure."[128] Germany looked elsewhere, however, and negotiated the purchase of the Caroline, Palau, and Mariana (less Guam) Islands from Spain for $4.2 million.[129]

Diederichs offered his own conclusions about the tense summer in a letter to Fritz. With some bitterness, he blamed part of his problems on the "lies" printed by the British and American press about his "misunderstandings" with Dewey. He nonetheless admitted to partial responsibility for the tensions, acknowledging that the presence of an "unnecessarily large number of our ships at Manila" provided the Americans with some grounds for suspicion, no matter how unwarranted. He and his ships still had a legitimate purpose for their visit to the Philippines, both to observe the war and protect German interests. Furthermore, Manila was in fact a convenient site for the transfer of relief crews, even though this caused an additional set of tensions with Dewey. All, he reminded Fritz, occurred because of orders from Berlin. He concluded ultimately that Dewey had simply overreacted, particularly to the now famous confrontation with Hintze aboard *Olympia*.[130]

Diederichs wrote a similar analysis to Henni. He blamed the controversy on the American press, which seemed unwilling to let the issue die, and the British, who had "political motives" for promoting a decline in German-American relations. He particularly blamed Dewey, "who I thought was a gentleman," for inciting the American press. Moreover, he believed that Dewey had received poor advice from his "dear English friend," Captain Chichester, to challenge Diederichs's legal presence in Manila. Diederichs concluded, "The incident ended quickly and His Majesty expressed full confidence in my actions. At least I thought the incident had ended."[131]

Dewey, of course, had different, if contradictory, perceptions. As

Admiral de la Bedolliéré prepared to leave Manila in mid-August, he paid the customary last visit to *Olympia.* When he complimented Dewey on his handling of the entire summer's affairs, Dewey, pointing across the bay to the anchored German warships, responded, "Oh, yes, I made one [mistake]. I should have sunk that squadron over there."[132] Yet, in May 1899, Dewey told Consul General Rieloff in Hong Kong that his "so-called differences" with Diederichs derived from "stupid newspaper gossip." According to Rieloff, Dewey also spoke in the "friendliest manner" in regard to Diederichs.[133] But as he returned to the United States in 1899, Dewey casually mentioned to a fellow American, "Our next war will be with Germany." The American, an occasional stringer for the New York *Herald,* promptly reported the remarks to his newspaper. The ensuing article created an instant uproar, including formal protests from the German ambassador in Washington. Although Dewey regretted the remark, he never repudiated it.[134]

AFTER THE FALL

Following the fall of Manila, Diederichs dispersed his ships throughout the station in a return to standard duties. *Cormoran* and *Kaiserin Augusta* left the Philippines to join *Deutschland, Gefion,* and *Irene* in Chinese waters. *Kaiser* steamed west to the Dutch East Indies, leaving only *Prinzess Wilhelm* to protect German interests in the Philippines. He intended to rotate individual ships through Manila thereafter. Thus, *Prinzess Wilhelm* remained until relieved by *Arcona* in October. *Irene* then replaced *Arcona* in November. *Kaiserin Augusta* replaced *Irene* soon thereafter, remaining at Manila until the declaration of American sovereignty in March 1899.[135]

Relieved of responsibility for Manila, Diederichs could now carry out his long overdue plans to visit the Dutch East Indies. His new mission was to represent Germany at celebrations marking the coronation of Queen Wilhelmina of the Netherlands. After a somewhat leisurely ten-day voyage, *Kaiser* arrived at Batavia, Java, on 30 August. Diederichs was glad to return to sea, where salt-laden breezes lowered the temperature after the hot and humid summer in Manila.[136] Accompanied by Hintze and Stubenrauch, he went ashore at Batavia on 1 September, taking a suite in the Hotel de Nederlanden. The German officers attended a variety of formal functions, including dinners, parades, and a memorial service in the Willemskerk on 6 September hosted by Governor General A. D. Heringa. Diederichs also took time to meet with members of the German community, who sponsored a *Festessen* in his honor on the tenth. He and Captain Stubenrauch exchanged ceremonial visits with several Dutch naval officers, including the rear admiral commanding the Dutch naval forces in East Indies waters. The Dutch admiral wrote him that the "officers of the Royal Navy of the Netherlands hold the Imperial German Navy in high esteem."[137]

Following his departure from Batavia, Diederichs spent a few days surveying possible sites for coaling depots elsewhere in the East Indian archipelago. With Dutch permission, he examined sites on Sumbawa to the east of Batavia and Sumatra to the west. Diederichs complained in his ensuing report to Knorr that the legacy of Manila continued to haunt him. Wherever he went, his mission provoked some interest in the Singapore press, which accused him of unspecified mischief.[138]

Kaiser paused long enough in Singapore for Diederichs to read new allegations in the local papers and post a birthday letter to Fritz. The navy had just assigned Fritz, who turned twenty-six on 10 October, as a watch officer aboard SMS *Oldenburg*. Since Fritz had spoken at length to both Diederichs and Henni about his desire to look to a career elsewhere, the assignment disappointed Diederichs, who had hoped that Fritz would receive an appointment as a flag lieutenant to a senior officer. Such duty, he believed, demanded social and diplomatic talents that might, if necessary, provide Fritz with the background for an alternative career, perhaps in the diplomatic service. Diederichs nonetheless reminded his son of the family tradition of service to the state, not in some blind obedience to the dynasty but rather as a way of serving others. He thanked Fritz for his own birthday wishes and reported that his health had improved once *Kaiser* put to sea from Manila Bay. He admitted, however, that he had begun to feel the effects of each passing year now that he himself had turned fifty-five.[139]

Kaiser halted briefly at Hong Kong in late October. Diederichs planned a quick tour of the station before *Kaiser*'s annual refit. He spent a few days in ceremonial and tourist activities. In an ironic reminder of Manila, he hosted Captain Chichester aboard *Kaiser* for a formal dinner. He then proceeded to

Amoy, where he wrote a lengthy letter to Henni. He expected replacement by 1 April 1899 but did not know to what post he would return. At some point, he also intended to make a final pilgrimage to the *Iltis* monument. He appended a list of goods he would send home via steamer, including souvenirs and photographs. He would write again from his next port of call, Fuchow, in Samsah Bay, where *Kaiser* would show the flag and take annual gunnery practice.[140]

His next letter began with a rather caustic comment: "You will know what happened to *Kaiser* from the newspapers." As *Kaiser* steamed into Samsah Bay on 15 November 1898, she ran aground on uncharted rocks. Diederichs immediately cabled Prince Heinrich to proceed south with *Deutschland* to provide assistance. Instead, the prince dispatched *Arcona* and *Cormoran* but stayed behind in Shanghai. With some difficulty, the two smaller ships succeeded in towing *Kaiser* off the rocks and into deep water. Diederichs took *Kaiser* to Hong Kong for immediate repairs before boarding a private steamer to Tsingtao, where he made *Prinzess Wilhelm* his acting flagship.[141]

The incident sparked a bitter conflict between Diederichs and Prince Heinrich. When Diederichs demanded an explanation for his disobedience, the prince excused his decision on the grounds that he needed to remain behind in Shanghai to participate in events marking the formal dedication of the *Iltis* monument. Diederichs, who considered court-martialing the prince, complained about Heinrich's insubordination in a letter to Senden. For whatever reason, Senden showed the letter to Kaiser Wilhelm, Heinrich's brother.[142]

With his ships again dispersed throughout the station for winter repairs, Diederichs turned to his correspondence with Henni. Their letters again focused on personal issues, particularly their respective health conditions and his anticipated return to Germany in the spring. Henni wrote a wistful letter on 13 November, the eve of their twenty-seventh wedding anniversary and the first anniversary of the occupation of Kiaochou. She had not seen Otto for eighteen months and hoped that they would be able to celebrate their next anniversary together. She could at least report that she had already received anniversary greetings from Fritz and Herman and that she expected a visit from a longtime friend Rear Adm. Felix Bendemann, currently director of the *Admiralstababteilung* in the OKM. During his visit, Bendemann cast some light on Diederichs's future assignment. Under prodding by Tirpitz, the emperor had begun to consider the abolition of the OKM, which would probably force Knorr's retirement in the spring. Although reorganization would enhance Tirpitz's own power at the Imperial Naval Office, it would probably result in a new post for Diederichs as well.[143]

The new year also brought some loving admonition from Henni. She wrote in January 1899 that several newspapers had reported additional details of his conflict with Dewey in Manila. She castigated him for not telling her more details, although she assumed that he had deliberately withheld the information because of her poor health. She also warned him to expect bitter intraservice politics when he returned to Germany since, in her opinion, Senden was as ambitious and power-hungry as Tirpitz. In fact, Fritz had recently cited his own disgust at these circumstances as one of his reasons for leaving the navy.[144]

Henni had additional service gossip to relate later in the month. Frau Anna Knorr had told her that Admiral Knorr hoped to postpone his retirement, and perhaps forestall the abolition of the OKM, until Diederichs returned later in the spring. Knorr anticipated that his departure might unleash Tirpitz on a new grab for power but that Diederichs's return home would stem the tide. Meanwhile, Senden had taken a lengthy furlough in order, according to Frau Knorr, to avoid any conflict with the ruthless Tirpitz. Much to Henni's pride in her husband, Frau Knorr had also told her that the emperor regularly praised him for his actions in the Philippines.[145]

In the meantime, Diederichs learned more about his professional future. Senden informally advised him that the emperor had in fact decided to abolish the Naval High Command, placing some of its existing responsibilities in a new office, the Admiralty Staff. Wilhelm intended to appoint Diederichs as chief of the new office. Rear Admiral Prince Heinrich would serve as acting chief of the Cruiser Squadron until a permanent commander could come out from Berlin.

With all this information in mind, Diederichs began his final tour of the East Asian station. He had, for the most part, enjoyed his service there—with Kiao-chou as the high point and Manila as his nadir—but looked forward to returning to Henni and a new future in Berlin. He recommended that they rendezvous in Freiburg im Breisgau, if her health permitted, to examine potential retirement sites. He paid a final visit to Tsingtao in April to direct the squadron's spring gunnery practice before. As *Kaiser*'s band played martial airs, the bosun lowered Diederichs's flag in a formal ceremony on 14 April 1899, ending his tenure as squadron chief. Temporary command then shifted to Prince Heinrich aboard *Deutschland*. Diederichs took a private steamer to Hong Kong where he boarded (as he noted somewhat wryly) the North Lloyd liner *Prinz Heinrich* on 22 April for the return voyage to Germany.[146]

8

Constant Strife: Diederichs and the Admiralty Staff, 1899–1902

Diederichs's return voyage aboard SS *Prinz Heinrich* was uneventful. After a month at sea he disembarked at Naples on 24 May 1899 and boarded a train for Germany. He had hoped that Henni might meet him at the quay, but her poor health prevented her from leaving Berlin. He briefly interrupted his rail trip north first to visit Freiburg im Breisgau and then Baden-Baden. He and Henni had discussed the possibility of retiring to either site. Freiburg, nestled in the mountains of the Black Forest (and current home to the *Marinearchiv*), was the more beautiful of the two, but Baden-Baden offered easier access to medical facilities and mineral hot springs important to Henni's recuperation. When Diederichs arrived in Berlin a few days later, Henni met him at the train station. They had been separated for twenty-five months. Their reunion was a joyful one, particularly when Fritz, serving aboard SMS *Oldenburg*, and Herman, recently commissioned aboard SMS *Brandenburg*, arranged leave to join them in Berlin.[1]

Diederichs quickly discovered that much had changed since he had left

Berlin in May 1897. While Kiao-chou and Manila occupied his attention in East Asia, momentous events in Berlin had changed the structure and mission of the Imperial German navy. The two most significant events were the passage of the first Navy Law (*Flottengesetz*) in March 1898 and the reorganization of the navy's command structure in March 1899. Both events had propelled Tirpitz to the pinnacle of naval authority. Although Diederichs's correspondents had kept him apprised of these issues, nothing prepared him for the actual impact of Tirpitz's assumption of power. Likewise, Diederichs seemed to have had no idea, as he prepared to assume his new post, that he would soon become involved in a political struggle with Tirpitz. As Diederichs reveled in the twin joys of family reunion and popular acclaim for his success at Kiao-chou, he could not have suspected that his rejuvenated career would run aground on the hidden shoals of service politics within three years.

REORGANIZATION

Like any other bureaucratic entity, the Kaiserliche Marine was subject to internal political problems and rivalries. In fact, one of its more compelling administrative concerns was the presence of ambitious and power-hungry officers who sought to increase their personal power at the expense of the broader institution. The German phrase for this is *Ressorteifer,* a term, not easily translated, that refers to the zealous pursuit of bureaucratic empire building.[2] Tirpitz had now become the most persistent practitioner of *Ressorteifer.* He first showed symptoms of this malady while chief of staff at the OKM (1892–95) when he led the crusade to convince Kaiser Wilhelm to change the navy's strategic orientation from cruisers to battleships. His campaign caused the first in a series of intraservice conflicts with officers, particularly Admiral Hollmann at the RMA, who disagreed with him and brought about his temporary banishment to East Asia. When Kaiser Wilhelm changed his mind—a not unusual event—and converted to the battleship doctrine, he recalled Tirpitz to Berlin in 1897 to replace Hollmann as state secretary.

Once he became head of the RMA, Tirpitz moved immediately to construct both his political empire and his battle fleet. He believed that he alone of the navy's senior officers should lead the fleet on this new course and that his ideas alone should provide strategic direction for the navy's future development. His motto, "Ziel erkannt, Kraft gespannt"—"Identify your goal and pursue it relentlessly"—epitomized the Machiavellian principle that the ends justify the means and underlay his tendency toward empire building.[3] He began construction at the RMA, in a post he would hold until 1916, by surrounding himself with his "torpedo gang." About a dozen officers who had originally served with him at the *Torpedowesen* now joined him at the RMA. These included Capt. August von Heeringen, director of the Zentrabteilung; Rear Adm. Wilhelm Büchsel, head of the *Marinedepartment;* Capt. Eduard von Capelle; Capt. Hugo Zeye, fresh from Kiao-chou; and Captains Hugo Pohl, Max Fischel, and Friedrich Ingenohl.[4]

Tirpitz presented his initial fleet plan to the emperor on 15 June 1897. The obvious mission of the new battle fleet, a point he reiterated several times, was to confront Great Britain, which he described as Germany's "most dangerous naval foe at the present time." He therefore proposed the concentration of the German fleet "between Helgoland and the Thames" rather than its dispersal on overseas operations. Because the "military situation against England requires battleships," he recommended that battle fleet contain nineteen battleships, along with support elements. Although he discounted the value of cruisers and *Kreuzerkrieg,* he at least recommended the construction of three heavy cruisers and nine light cruisers for foreign service. He intended to complete this program by 1905 at a cost of 480 million marks. Because of the strategic importance of his plan, Tirpitz also advised the emperor that he needed complete and absolute authority for the RMA to implement his program, even if this came at the administrative and structural expense of the other naval authorities.[5] It was this final factor that would lead directly to conflict with Diederichs.

The Tirpitz plan elicited little support from the navy's senior officers. Tirpitz, in fact, accurately complained that his fellow admirals lacked enthusiasm for his fleet plans.[6] When Knorr objected to Tirpitz's proposals in regard to cruisers, Tirpitz ignored further communications from the OKM. He also convinced Wilhelm to order the OKM to halt its resistance and cooperate with the RMA.[7] Admiral Hans Koester, chief of the Kiel naval station and former commander of the First Squadron, complained that such rapid fleet expansion would create an immediate personnel problem—*Deckungsfrage,* or "coverage question"—since the navy would need to divert officers from other important posts to man the new ships. He protested further that the plan would absorb too much of the navy's limited resources—both financial and material—and thus undermine naval preparedness.[8] Rear Adm. Iwan Oldekop, currently *Inspekteur des Bildungswesen,* worried that the Tirpitz plan would absorb much of the navy's limited budget and thus leave little financial support for officer training. The attendant personnel shortages would also make it less likely that officers would leave active duty to matriculate at the Marineakademie.[9] Diederichs, who had followed the debate from East Asia, feared that Tirpitz would use the plan to place himself at the summit—"an der Spitze"—of the navy's command structure. Anticipating what would become a major strategic issue, Diederichs also suspected that the Tirpitz plan would set Germany on a fateful collision course with Britain.[10]

Tirpitz nonetheless moved ahead with his proposals. He had transformed the proposals into a draft bill and prepared to submit it to the Reichstag when Diederichs's Kiao-chou report reached Berlin in late October. Because Tirpitz feared that any naval misadventure would cause the Reichstag to reject his bill, he adamantly opposed Diederichs's campaign for Kiao-chou, even after the German missionaries were killed a few days later.[11] Ironically, the seizure of Kiao-chou actually helped the bill. Foreign Minister Bernhard von Bülow, who opened the debate on 6 December, made a positive reference to Kiao-chou to great applause: "We no longer choose to exist in shadow but we now demand our place in the sun."[12] Although the debate, often personal and rancorous, continued into the new year, a majority of the Reichstag members eventually voted to pass the bill on 26 March 1898. Kaiser Wilhelm signed it into law on 10 April 1898, only days after the Reichstag had ratified the Kiao-chou treaty.[13]

The passage of the Navy Law fulfilled only part of Tirpitz's scheme. He next argued that he needed the paramount position within the *Marinebehörde* in order to more effectively implement the law. Among other things, this would give him control of the navy's limited budget, which would allow him to focus all spending on his battle fleet. Secondly, he wanted to suppress all opposition—administrative and strategic—to his program. Both issues would cause conflicts with other senior naval officers in general and Diederichs in particular later on.

Buoyed by imperial and parliamentary support, Tirpitz moved immediately against the Naval High Command. Although he had initially supported the abolition of the Admiralty in 1889 and the ensuing tripartite division of naval administration, he now preferred to recreate a central naval authority. Within a month of taking office in June 1897, Tirpitz began a campaign to usurp the power of Knorr and the OKM.[14] Some months later, after the passage of the Navy Law, Tirpitz submitted concrete proposals to the emperor. He first offered the emperor a "most gracious," if hypocritical, apology "that these organizational questions have surfaced now." He nonetheless argued that Germany's status as a "great sea power" and even the "existence of our Fatherland" depended on fulfillment of his program. Because a divided command hindered this goal, he asked that the emperor allow him to essentially recreate the Admiralty. He specifically cited the OKM's responsibility for operational planning and the direction of ships on foreign station. He agreed that these two elements belonged in the hands of a single agency but argued that the RMA should possess that authority. Because the RMA was responsible for the development of the battle fleet, Tirpitz should also direct the fleet's operational planning. Furthermore, since the RMA provided logistical support for ships on overseas service, he might as well direct those operations, too. Finally, to maximize his authority to develop the battle fleet, he demanded political status equivalent to the minister of war, with paramount authority over any issue that affected "the advancement of general maritime interests."[15]

Although Diederichs himself had suffered at Knorr's hands, he was nonetheless sympathetic to his former boss. In the privacy of letters to Henni from East Asia, he criticized the emperor for allowing Tirpitz to undermine Knorr and chided Senden for not playing a stronger mediating role. Diederichs firmly believed that administrative reorganization, with an attendant increase in Tirpitz's authority, would hurt the navy.[16]

Capt. August Thiele, now commander of the First Matrosendivision in Kiel, concurred, complaining that the passage of the Navy Law had now made Tirpitz "der grosse Mann" and that the new proposals would now allow him to completely dominate the navy. He anticipated the early retirement of several officers—Karcher (chief of the Wilhelmshaven naval station), Hoffmann, and others—if Tirpitz continued his anti-OKM campaign.[17] Vice Adm. Guido Karcher complained to Diederichs that Tirpitz was making a power grab that would give the state secretary inordinate power and increase the authority of the RMA at the expense of the other branches. His parliamentary victory in favor of the Fleet Law had already made him insufferable, and now, Karcher believed, Tirpitz would not be satisfied until "he alone possesses everything." All feared that reorganization would have an adverse effect on the navy.[18]

Tirpitz had, in fact, overreached himself. Knorr and other senior officers persuaded the emperor to reject these proposals in June 1898. Tirpitz, who had learned a valuable political lesson from Bismarck, promptly offered his resignation, which Kaiser Wilhelm refused.[19] Diederichs was following these events closely from his post in the Pacific, with Henni as his primary source of information. She in turn learned the details from Frau Knorr, who resented Tirpitz's attack on her husband's position and authority. According to Henni, the issue preoccupied not only senior naval authorities but also the press and Reichstag into mid-summer, when much of the German leadership, both civilian and military, left Berlin for holiday. Thus, Henni could write in late July 1898 that "In Berlin Alles beim alten, d. h., um Sommerschlaf" and that Knorr would thus remain in office at least through autumn; she referred to rumors that the emperor would then recall Diederichs to replace him.[20] Preoccupied with events in Manila, Diederichs by no means enjoyed the thought of this new can of worms. If he were able to choose his own assignment, he preferred to return either as commander of the First Squadron or chief of the Kiel naval station. He was not particularly interested in a post that would put him in constant conflict with Tirpitz.[21]

Oldekop wrote to Diederichs in August 1898 that Tirpitz continued to use his popularity with the emperor to assert his dominance of the RMA at the expense of the OKM. Oldekop believed that Tirpitz truly intended to recreate the Admiralty, whose original chief, Stosch, Tirpitz heartily admired. Oldekop saw no little hypocrisy in this attitude, given Tirpitz's earlier support for the tripartite division of naval power in 1889. Knorr, he feared, was losing the battle to retain his job and maintain an independent OKM. Oldekop further complained that Senden played a neutral and cowardly role in order not to damage his own authority as chief of the Marinekabinett.[22]

Although Tirpitz may have lost the initial skirmish, he refused to surrender. He maintained a drumbeat of memoranda and letters to the emperor, citing the strategic importance of the battle fleet to Germany's national security (and Wilhelm's prestige). The emperor finally capitulated in December

1898 and signed a service-wide decree soliciting proposals for the reorganization of the naval command structure. He made only two reservations: The commanding admiral or his successor would still direct ships on overseas duty, and station chiefs would maintain responsibility for the assignment of officers to ships and maneuvers.[23] Tirpitz revised his earlier proposals accordingly and submitted them to the emperor early in the new year. Knorr, who saw the writing on the wall, retired on 7 March 1899.[24]

One week later, on 14 March, Wilhelm formally abolished the Naval High Command. He then transformed the OKM's Admiral Staff Detachment into the freestanding Admiral Staff of the Navy (*Admiralstab der Marine*), headed by a new *Chef des Admiralstabes,* under the direct authority of the emperor. Wilhelm assigned three specific duties to the new Admiralty Staff: the formulation of war plans, the operational direction of ships on foreign station, and the coordination of naval relations with Germany's diplomatic partners, Austria-Hungary and Italy. The chief of the new Admiral Staff also gained *Immediatstellung,* the right of immediate access to the emperor. Wilhelm also granted independent command status and imperial access to the naval commands formerly under OKM authority. These included the commanders of the two naval stations, the inspector of the training service (*Bildungswesen,*) and the commanding officers of the First Squadron and the Cruiser Squadron.[25]

The impact of reorganization was significant for the naval authorities. Tirpitz had achieved partial success. The reforms confirmed his position as *primus inter pares* but left him somewhat frustrated. Although reorganization had the effect of making Tirpitz the most powerful naval authority, he was still not satisfied. He had failed to gain authority over operational planning or ships on foreign station. Furthermore, the expansion of *Immediatstellung* allowed too many officers to outflank his authority and appeal directly to the emperor.

Reorganization had nonetheless produced advantages for Tirpitz. The abolition of the Naval High Command fragmented planning, yielding operational planning to the Admiralty Staff and the development of tactical initiatives to the First Squadron. This separation of powers, often rendered absolute by poor communication between the various elements of the *Marinebehörde,* created a power vacuum happily filled by Tirpitz and the RMA. Even Kaiser Wilhelm acquired greater power, as the reorganization brought more elements of the navy under his direct command and allowed him to bypass both ministerial and parliamentary oversight. But it was Tirpitz who had essentially divided and conquered. Walther Hubatsch notes, "The newly decreed reorganization finally gave Tirpitz the freedom of action that he had long sought as state secretary of the RMA."[26]

With Knorr out of the way, Tirpitz moved to silence his other critics and foes. He had never abided dissent well, requesting as early as June 1897 that the emperor suppress internal naval opposition to his Navy Law.[27] Now, a momentary revival of the heretical *Jeune École* caused him again to muzzle dissent. Diederichs's old comrade Vice Adm. Victor Valois, retired since 1896, published *Seemacht, Seegeltung, Seeherrschaft* (roughly translated as "naval power, prestige, and control") in 1899. Valois reiterated the strategic value of cruiser war against Britain, whose Achilles heel was its merchant marine.[28] Capt. Curt Maltzahn, instructor in naval history and tactics at the Marineakademie, raised similar issues in a draft manuscript entitled *Seekriegslehre* (*Lessons of Naval Warfare*), in which he questioned the basic principles of Tirpitz's Dienstschrift IX and the battle fleet and praised cruisers and commerce raiding in a conflict with a stronger naval foe. Tirpitz attacked both authors on the grounds that their heterodoxy had strategic and financial implications. The adoption of commerce raiding and the construction of cruisers would undermine his emphasis on a battle fleet and reduce the funds available to construct battleships. He therefore persuaded the emperor to ban publication of Maltzahn's book and restrict the right of active officers to speak out in public.[29] Wilhelm decreed, "I have every intention of developing My Navy thoroughly and quietly and I, therefore, do not want public opinion to mistake the basic principles of My Navy." The decree concluded, "This order is directed simultaneously to flag and staff officers and is to remain in strict confidence."[30]

The primary victim of Tirpitz's pogrom was Vice Adm. Iwan Oldekop, Diederichs's closest friend and Maltzahn's senior officer as *Inspecteur des Bildungswesen*. Oldekop had actively opposed the fleet law, both because of the personnel "coverage" problem and reorganization and because of its devolution of power to Tirpitz. Now, insofar as Tirpitz was concerned, allowing Maltzahn to promote heretical ideas was Oldekop's third strike, particularly when he expressed his opinion that Tirpitz's campaign would have a chilling effect on the members of the officer corps. Oldekop foresaw that the bright young officers, like Maltzahn, who studied and taught at the Marineakademie would now be much less willing to speak their minds. He even cited the case of Maltzahn's famous predecessor, Capt. Alfred Stenzel, who was forced into retirement for his unpopular ideas. When Oldekop attempted personally to resolve the issue with Tirpitz, the state secretary refused to discuss the Maltzahn case and instead appealed directly to the emperor without ever hearing Oldekop's side. The result was the September decree that forbade public discussions of heterodox ideas. Based on these circumstances, Oldekop felt that he had no other choice by November 1899 but to retire. In a prophetic statement, he warned Diederichs to avoid intraservice conflicts with Tirpitz, who jealously held the ear of the emperor, and his empire-building proclivities.[31]

THE ADMIRALSTAB

As Tirpitz prepared the next step of his empire building, Wilhelm recalled Diederichs from East Asia to serve as chief of the Admiralty Staff. The emperor temporarily appointed Rear Adm. Felix von Bendemann, formerly chief of staff at the OKM, to fill the post until Diederichs's return. Trading places, Bendemann would then become the new commander of the Cruiser Squadron in East Asia.[32] Bendemann remained in office long enough to oversee the structural development of the *Admiralstab*. Most of the staff officers who had served with the OKM's Admiral Staff Detachment simply transferred over to the Admiral Staff. These included Capt. Alfred Breusing as staff director; Cdr. Gustav Bachmann as director of the Central Bureau; and Cdrs. Raimund Winkler, Karl Dick, and Max (von) Grapow, Lt. Cdrs. Wilhelm Souchon, Hermann Alberts, Johan Kaplen, and Gottfried Freiherr von Dalwigk zu Lichtenfels, and Lt. (sg) Walter Freiherr von Keyserling.[33] Bendemann's initial task was to establish direct contact with Diederichs and the Cruiser Squadron, since the Admiral Staff now had operational authority for overseas operations.[34] Bendemann also arranged to assign Commander Grapow to temporary duty with the Army General Staff. Grapow, the first naval officer ever to serve with the General Staff, spent April and May studying its structure and work.[35]

After his furlough in late August, Diederichs began to prepare himself for his new post. Since his new work would involve operational planning, he first requested permission to postpone reporting for duty with the Admiralty Staff so that he could observe the annual maneuvers. During his absence in East Asia, maneuvers, long focused on the defense of Germany's coasts against attacks by Russia and France, more and more anticipated a war against Britain instead. Since he had worked with the development of operational plans against Britain while chief of staff at the OKM several years earlier, he wanted to reacquaint himself with the new strategic developments. However, in September, Diederichs requested another postponement in order to seek temporary duty with the Greater German General Staff. Diederichs's goal, which would cause a political confrontation with Tirpitz, was to transform the fledgling *Admiralstab* into a naval version of the General Staff. The emperor granted Diederichs's request, directing him to report to the General Staff on 1 October 1899.[36] Although Grapow was the first naval officer to serve with the General Staff, Diederichs was the first flag officer to do so.

Diederichs had long admired Gen. Helmut von Moltke (1800–91), who had directed the General Staff from 1858 to 1888. Moltke was an author and novelist who was fluent in several languages. Diederichs often quoted Moltke's personal motto, "An officer should be more than he appears," to Fritz and Herman, advising them to improve themselves both professionally and academically. He admired the work that Moltke had done with the General Staff and now thought to emulate that accomplishment as well.[37]

Moltke's administrative and structural reforms elevated the prestige and effectiveness of the Prussian-German General Staff and enabled it to lead the army through the successful wars of Germany unification (Denmark, 1864; Austria, 1866; France, 1870–71). Moltke was also responsible for the further development of the *Kriegsakademie,* whose postgraduate curriculum trained staff officers to deal more effectively with the new and more complex technology of modern warfare. He also directed the development of operational plans for a two-front war against France and Russia, producing ideas that later influenced Diederichs's own 1882 plan.

When Diederichs joined the Greater German General Staff on temporary duty in October 1899, it had grown to include more than three hundred officers. Headed by Gen. Count Alfred von Schlieffen, it included 115 staff officers, an additional 120 officers matriculating at the Kriegsakademie in preparation for service as staff officers at regimental, divisional, and corps levels, and approximately ninety already serving as staff officers with regular army units. This relatively large number of officers was necessary because of the various missions of the General Staff, which included operational planning, intelligence gathering and analysis, administration of annual maneuvers and staff rides, and the study and writing of military history.[38]

Diederichs sought permission to work with the General Staff in order to study its structure and function for later application to the Admiralty Staff. He perceived the General Staff as a useful model for reform proposals, particularly since it combined many of the functions now held separately by the Admiralty Staff, RMA, and the other naval commands. He chose a precarious moment for recommending reforms that would essentially recreate the Naval High Command; Tirpitz had just secured the abolition of the OKM. Diederichs recommended structural and administrative reforms when he wrote Tirpitz in November 1899; he envisioned an Admiralty Staff that could simultaneously develop war plans, gather intelligence, and train officers in historical and current military ideas. In his enthusiasm for his new post, Diederichs seems not to have foreseen that his plans would involve him in a bitter intraservice rivalry with Tirpitz.[39]

What remained unclear after the naval reorganization was the Admiralty Staff's specific status as a member of the naval establishment and its exact relationship to Senden's *Marinekabinett* and Tirpitz's *Reichsmarineamt*. Tirpitz had, after all, campaigned to break up the OKM as a means of increasing his own authority. He certainly did not want the *Admiralstab* to become a disguised revival of the OKM and a coequal naval branch. As events will therefore show, he fought to maintain the Admiralty Staff in an inferior and subordinate position. Yet, the fact that Wilhelm appointed Diederichs, a vice admiral, as the chief of the new Admiralty Staff strongly suggests that the emperor, at least, intended the new institution to possess some power.

ADMIRALSTAB AT WORK

His temporary duty with the General Staff concluded, Diederichs formally assumed the duties of chief of the Admiral Staff on 20 December 1899. When he moved into his new office at Königgrätzstrasse 32, he found a request from Tirpitz to evaluate the impact of the Navy Law on operational planning as it related to Britain and the United States. Tirpitz had already begun to develop a second fleet bill based on the argument that even the current program, to be completed by 1904, would still leave Germany at a disadvantage.[40] Diederichs's response, which he presented to the emperor in January 1900, painted a bleak picture in case of a war against Britain. Diederichs noted that the fleet created by the Navy Law would still leave the Royal Navy with sufficient superiority to simultaneously attack German overseas commerce and blockade German ports. Echoing his original operational plan from 1896, Diederichs noted that Germany's only hope lay in an immediate attack before the British could mobilize their forces. In the event of a protracted conflict, however, Britain would surely win. Moreover, Diederichs anticipated the later Anglo-German naval race, which broke out after Tirpitz's second Navy Law, when he concluded that Britain would match any new German naval construction. He further projected that such competition would harm both navies, since neither could afford the attendant cost in funding, personnel, and material.

Diederichs was marginally more hopeful in his analysis of American forces. He used Mahanian terms—"The paramount goal of naval powers is command of the seas"—to argue that Germany's only hope for victory lay in an immediate attack on New England ports which, if successful, would compel the United States to sue for peace. Only such an attack could prevail, because Germany did not have sufficient forces either to blockade the entire American coast or undertake *Kreuzerkrieg* against the American merchant marine. He pointed out that neither the United States nor Germany had sufficient "secure bases" for supporting extensive overseas operations. He also noted that the American naval buildup, which had begun even before the war with Spain, had produced an American navy superior to the current German fleet. He therefore concluded that "[W]ar in 1904 will produce little success under current circumstances." If Germany were to confront either foe at a later date, Diederichs expected that the "fleet must first be doubled for war" to thirty-eight to forty battleships.[41]

Having developed this memorandum, Diederichs next turned to operational planning, the Admiralty Staff's single most important function. In a presentation to the emperor in February 1900, Diederichs reviewed the current course of contingency plans. Since the navy had first begun to develop war plans in the early 1880s, planning had focused on the possibility of a two-front naval war against France and Russia. In fact, the current plan in the files of the Admiralty Staff differed little from Diederichs's 1882 memorandum, proposing a lightning-like strike against French Atlantic ports, combined with an initial defensive operation against the Russians in the Baltic.

Diederichs reviewed for the emperor the existing plans for war with Britain, which he himself had begun to develop in 1896 while chief of staff at the OKM. He personally opposed the new strategic direction that identified Britain as Germany's primary foe, advising the emperor that the current plan had "little chance for success" against Britain. Citing potential British reaction to the second Navy Bill, currently before the Reichstag, he warned Wilhelm that an expanded German fleet, with its implicit threat to the British empire, could easily throw Britain into the arms of the French and Russians.

Finally, Diederichs advised the emperor that his staff had also begun to develop the first war plans against the United States (unaware, as it happened, that his worthy opponent, George Dewey, had returned from the Philippines to develop operational plans against Germany). Diederichs concluded his briefing with an argument on behalf of coastal defense. Perhaps in anticipation of another conflict with Tirpitz's policies, Diederichs also questioned the state secretary's decision to suspend plans to further develop coastal fortifications in favor of a forward defense by the battle fleet. For almost twenty years, since his 1882 memorandum, Diederichs had championed the value of fixed coastal defenses.[42]

Diederichs presented the first operational plan for war against the United States in an audience with the emperor on 26 February 1900. The plan had its origins in a series of special projects developed by Lt. (sg) Eberhard von Mantey while a student at the Marineakademie in Kiel. The plan that Diederichs proposed called for an all-out offensive against the East Coast of the United States, using every existing German capital ship, including the armored frigates. The fleet would stage out of European waters, refueling in the Azores before securing a Caribbean base in Puerto Rico. At that point, the German force would proceed north to attack either Boston or New York. In consultation with Gen. Alfred von Schlieffen of the army's General Staff and based on information supplied by Lieutenant (sg) von Rebeur-Paschwitz, the naval attaché in Washington, D.C., Diederichs and the Admiralty Staff continued to refine the plan for several years.[43]

The Admiralty Staff's second major mission was the direction of overseas operations. Diederichs had found himself on familiar ground when he dispatched operational orders to the *Kreuzergeschwader*, now commanded by Rear Adm. Felix Bendemann, in January 1900. In case of war with the United States, the Cruiser Squadron would remain in East Asian waters with orders to move aggressively—"Take every favorable opportunity to inflict damage on the enemy"—against American forces in the Philippines in order to protect Kiao-chou and German trade. Cruisers on other stations would proceed immediately to East Asia to reinforce the squadron. Diederichs also proposed the establishment of coaling depots along the route between European waters and Kiao-chou. He identified potential sites in German Southeast Africa, the Red Sea, and the Malacca Strait.[44]

Another of Diederichs's responsibilities was the coordination of naval operations and planning with Germany's diplomatic partners—Austria-Hungary and Italy—in the Triple Alliance (*Dreibund*). Unlike Tirpitz, who focused first and foremost on Britain, Diederichs continued to consider the possibility of a two-front war against France and Russia. He therefore convened a meeting of the allied navies in late November 1900 to develop proposals for joint naval operations. In a draft agreement initialed on 5 December 1900, Diederichs anticipated that the Italian and Austrian navies would operate against Russian and French forces in the Mediterranean while German warships would attempt to prevent the link-up of French and Russian forces in either the North Atlantic or the Baltic Sea. Although each allied fleet would operate independently, the agreement proposed the creation of a supreme allied headquarters, under German command, with responsibility for the strategic direction of all three fleets. Diederichs also developed plans for joint operational planning, intelligence gathering and analysis, an exchange of officers between naval staffs, and the development of a joint signal book with recognition signals.[45]

ROUND ONE: REORGANIZATION

Based on his experiences with the General Staff and his initial work with the Admiralty Staff, Diederichs concluded early in his tenure that the Admiralstab needed to reorganize its structure and augment its personnel. After all, as chief he was required to develop operational plans, direct overseas operations, coordinate allied operations, and plan various training exercises. To fulfill these missions, he had only seven other naval officers and four civilian clerks.

Adm. Hans Koester, commander of the Kiel Naval Station, actually raised the issue with the emperor in January 1900. He complained that the Admiralstab, under Bendemann, had slowed its preparation of operational plans in general and stopped work altogether on war plans against Russia. He noted, further, that the Admiralstab had still (under Diederich) failed to incorporate elements from the original Navy Law in the preparation of war plans against France and the United States. They had developed only defensive plans in case of war with Britain, a step back from the initial proposals made by Diederichs in 1896. Koester feared that the Admiralstab's seeming inability to fulfill its mission endangered national security.[46]

When the emperor asked Diederichs to explain this problem, he immediately drafted a lengthy response. He endorsed Koester's analysis, citing the lack of staff as the reason for the slowed planning and admitted that no plans currently existed "which meet with Your Majesty's approval." He reminded the emperor that the General Staff, which had a much larger contingent of officers, had to develop only a single operational plan: against France and Russia. "The navy," he noted, "requires more diverse plans since we must assess every sea power in the vicinity of our coasts." More recently, the Admiralstab also had had to consider the growing naval threat of the United States and Japan.

Diederichs proposed two specific solutions: an increase in the number of officers assigned to the Admiralstab and the creation of a separate intelligence section within it. Enlargement would allow it to fulfill its missions, particularly the development of war plans, more effectively. The establishment of an intelligence section would further aid the development of contingency plans, since his officers needed to gather, correlate, and evaluate current political, diplomatic, and military information—naval intelligence—on potential foes in preparation for the development of operational plans.[47]

Diederichs presented a second, more formal *Immediatvortrag* to the emperor later in February 1900. He strongly emphasized the idea that a weak and ineffective Admiralstab undermined the broader work of the navy, asserting that its lack of officers impeded "the rapid growth of the navy." He therefore argued that "the harvest would bear more fruit" if additional officers were assigned to the task of operational planning. He also cited the rapid turnover of staff directors—four in the previous six years—as an additional impediment to operational planning. (This problem would continue, as the Admiralstab had nine chiefs between 1899 and 1916, while the RMA had only Tirpitz.) Diederichs complained, too, that past operational planning had suffered from excessive "ballast," focusing too much on individual plans and too little on broader strategic linkage and coordination. In an unwittingly prophetic conclusion, Diederichs stated, "The decisions that Your Majesty now makes regarding operational planning will have great impact on future conflicts and will depend on Your Majesty's confidence in the Chief of the Admiralty Staff."[48]

Kaiser Wilhelm responded positively to Diederichs's presentation and invited him to develop his ideas more formally. Problems developed, however, when he forwarded his proposals to Tirpitz at the RMA. Blinded by the emperor's support—or forgetful of the emperor's equivocal personality—Diederichs now made a tactical mistake. He failed to understand that his proposals, no matter how appropriate and necessary, put him on a collision course with Tirpitz. Diederichs understood too late that Tirpitz would not abide a challenge either to his own dominant authority or the paramount priority he had attached to his own fleet development plans.

In any event, Diederich wrote to Tirpitz in March, "His Majesty the Emperor has acknowledged the need to further develop the Admiralty Staff." He particularly identified two areas of concern: a lack of personnel, which impeded operational planning and therefore naval readiness, and the need for an intelligence service, whose existence would enhance operational planning. To resolve these problems, he proposed four solutions in turn: an increase in the Admiralstab's complement, the creation of a subordinate intelligence section, the creation of an elite corps of staff officers to serve with other commands, and the transfer of the Naval War College to Berlin and its placement under the authority of the chief of the Admiralstab.

Diederichs particularly emphasized the importance of a separate intelligence section. He reiterated the necessity to gather pertinent information, through an analysis of journals and monographs as well as personal reconnaissance by naval attachés, and evaluate it for usefulness in operational planning. He had formally requested the assignment of two additional line officers and two civilian clerks to the new office. He ultimately envisioned a larger bureau, consisting of separate intelligence and counterintelligence divisions, directed by a senior captain. He also proposed that this office acquire the authority to coordinate the activities of the various naval attachés and establish an intelligence liaison with the Foreign Ministry to use information supplied by German diplomats abroad.

Diederichs's proposal regarding the Marineakademie proved more controversial. Again borrowing from the model of the General Staff, Diederichs planned to revive the practice of creating Admiralty Staff officers, educated at the Naval War College and under the direction of the Admiralty Staff, who would serve in various operational and technical commands. (He himself had served in an earlier version of this corps in the 1870s.) He likewise intended to reform the Naval War College on similar lines, modifying its curriculum to reflect staff issues rather than the more traditional emphasis on strategic, tactical, and technical developments. He would also assume greater responsibility for the selection of officers who applied to attend the Marineakademie and would have first priority on their employment after matriculation. He proposed that the transfer of the school from Kiel to Berlin occur during the summer in order to commence operations by the beginning of the academic year in autumn 1900. He particularly intended that these graduates serve subsequently as chiefs of staff and staff officers for the independent commands and as instructors at the Naval War College in naval strategy, tactics, and history.[49]

Tirpitz was not receptive to Diederichs's proposals, which now threatened his own plans. Tirpitz had never intended that the initial Navy Law "create the fleet in its ultimate form."[50] Instead, he had already begun in 1899 to prepare proposals for a second law. This presented his famous "risk fleet," which he ostensibly intended as a deterrent against attack. Any enemy fleet—such as Britain's—attacking Germany's new and stronger force would imperil its status as a world power. Tirpitz's intent, however, was hardly defensive, since he intended that this larger fleet serve as a tool of a "grand overseas policy [eine grosse überseeische Politik]" against Britain.[51]

Tirpitz introduced the new bill in the Reichstag in January 1900. With characteristic resourcefulness, he used Diederichs's own memorandum from 20 January 1900 to justify the further expansion of the fleet. In the course of parliamentary debates, he specifically cited Germany's existing naval inferiority both to Britain, as Germany's "strongest adversary" and potential foe, and to the United States.[52] Passed on 14 June 1900, the second Navy Law expanded the battle fleet to thirty-eight battleships: two fleet flagships, four squadrons of eight battleships each, and four more in reserve. The new law also included three heavy cruisers and seven light cruisers for overseas service. German shipyards would construct three battleships per year, replacing obsolete ships when necessary, with all construction to be completed by 1920.[53]

So far as Tirpitz was concerned, the new fleet law and Diederichs's proposals for the enlargement and expansion of the Admiralstab were mutually exclusive. First, he believed that fleet expansion should have principal priority in the management of the navy's limited personnel and finances. Further, Tirpitz asserted that he needed paramount authority within the navy's command structure in order to more effectively carry out his expansion program. Thus, even Diederichs's modest plans threatened Tirpitz's program.

Diederichs, who lacked excessive ambition and disliked institutional politics, never intended to embroil himself and the navy in a jurisdictional dispute with Tirpitz. He sought to expand the size and scope of the Admiralty Staff solely in order to enhance its own effectiveness in carrying out its diverse functions. Fritz von Diederichs described the problem: "Each of these men stood in the way of the other. For personal and professional reasons, Tirpitz sought to restrain the newly created Admiral Staff, while the other demanded recognition of his rightful authority."[54]

A second major factor that worked against Diederichs was his opposition to the new law. Many of the same officers—including Diederichs, Koester, and Hoffmann—who had questioned the intentions or content of the first law now criticized the second. Tirpitz, who already had a strong track record of punishing or purging opponents, brought this "disloyalty" to the attention of the emperor, who felt frustrated by the resistance of so many officers to the new program. Diederichs, the source of both opposition and alternative programs, would hardly win points either with Tirpitz or the emperor.[55]

Tirpitz now responded to Diederichs's plan. He agreed with the concept in principle—"The further development of the fleet requires a corresponding expansion of the Admiralty Staff"—but questioned whether it was possible at present. Since, he admitted, the second law would produce an even greater *Deckungsfrage* than the first, Tirpitz opposed any increase in the size of the Admiralstab. Furthermore, he resisted any increase in its authority which, he feared, might threaten implementation of the two fleet laws and his own power. He therefore forwarded Diederichs's proposals to the various commands with a negative endorsement.[56]

Response was immediate and critical. Vice Adm. August Thomson, commander of the First Squadron, acknowledged the validity of Diederichs's ideas but agreed with Tirpitz that the navy's limited personnel resources could not be stretched to increase the size of the Admiralty Staff or create a specific intelligence-gathering office. He adamantly rejected the transfer of the Naval War College to Berlin as "neither necessary nor desirable," describing the proposal as a "hazardous experiment."[57] Admiral Koester, commander of the Kiel naval station, echoed Thomson's evaluation, accepting the eventual need of a larger *Admiralstab* but stating, "The Front's current lack of officers, however, makes such changes impossible" and rejecting any change in the status of the Marineakademie.[58]

This lack of support for Diederichs's proposals and Tirpitz's own preoccupation with the development of the battle fleet allowed the state secretary to simply table the issue. Still a novice at bureaucratic infighting, Diederichs failed to campaign for his proposals and instead blamed Tirpitz for the lack of progress. Just as Tirpitz argued that the new fleet construction should have a priority on funding and personnel, Diederichs also complained that fleet expansion would absorb too much of the navy's limited budget and thus deny him enlargement of the Admiralty Staff.[59] He wrote Bendemann, now in command of the Cruiser Squadron in East Asia, that Tirpitz had begun to work behind the scenes to undermine his proposals and sabotage the work of the Admiralstab. He feared that Tirpitz intended to assimilate the staff and its functions into the RMA. He wrote angrily, "My authority flows out to anyone who wants it. This will unleash a disaster." Only half in jest, Diederichs invited Bendemann "to return immediately and take back the Admiralstab."[60]

Diederichs also complained that the emperor had made no attempt to respond to his proposals. The problem, he believed, was imperial inattention. The romance of new battleships and the Boxer Rebellion, which broke out in China in June 1900, distracted Wilhelm through the spring and summer of 1900. With the emperor simply ignoring any other naval issue. Diederichs wrote Bendemann in August, "I can only gain the Emperor's attention with great difficulty."[61] As long as the problem continued, as long as his office struggled with too many tasks and too few officers, Diederichs feared, the Admiralty Staff would produce only inadequate results. Caught between Wilhelm's indifference and Tirpitz's stonewalling, he grumbled that the navy coddled the battle fleet while neglecting operational planning. He bitterly compared the disparity in fiscal allocations to Spanish architecture, which he described as "a beautiful brick facade with no real building behind it because there is no material for further construction."[62]

As the issue remained ignored and unresolved through autumn, Diederichs continued to worry that the navy would suffer accordingly. In fact, the navy already had felt its effects; he admitted that his conflict with Tirpitz had undermined naval operations in Chinese waters. While he had responsibility for operational direction of the Cruiser Squadron, Tirpitz controlled the unit's logistical support. The lack of cooperation and communication between the two senior officers meant that the Cruiser Squadron suffered accordingly. He apologized to Bendemann for this problem and concluded mournfully, "This issue cannot continue much longer without leading to an open clash."[63]

Even trivial matters, he noted, alienated Tirpitz. For example, Tirpitz wrote a bitter note that Diederichs had failed to notify him of the *Dreibund* conference in November and December 1900. Tirpitz had learned of the conference through an accidental meeting with several foreign officers. His lack of knowledge, he wrote, placed him in an "embarrassing situation." Tirpitz therefore wrote Diederichs, "I must assume that this was an inadvertent oversight and expect that Your Excellency will prevent a similar situation hereafter."[64] By Christmas, the constant friction with Tirpitz had induced Diederichs to again consider retirement. He wrote Bendemann that he and Henni could "joyfully go to Baden-Baden," where they had now decided to build a retirement home, and leave the political travails of Berlin behind.[65]

ROUND TWO: ENLARGEMENT

Diederichs returned to the fray in January 1901, again raising the issue of enlargement at his weekly audience with the emperor. Diederichs reminded Kaiser Wilhelm that he had made his original proposals almost a year earlier in February 1900. At that time, Wilhelm had granted tentative approval and instructed Diederichs to develop the ideas more fully in consultation with the chief of the Naval Cabinet and the state secretary of the imperial Naval Office, the RMA. Senden had responded favorably, but Tirpitz had not responded at all. Acknowledging his frustrations, Diederichs advised the emperor that the "urgent necessity to further develop the structure of the Admiralty Staff" compelled him to proceed without counsel from Tirpitz. Diederichs's foremost priority remained the formation of an intelligence section, which would enhance operational planning. "The lack [of intelligence]," he said, "could have disastrous results." He cited the recent example of the Boxer Rebellion in China, which had caught the Cruiser Squadron largely unprepared. In order to operate in the Yellow Sea and send a naval brigade inland to relieve the besieged diplomats in Peking, Admiral Bendemann had had to borrow charts from the Russians and maps from the British. An intelligence section, Diederichs argued, would have such resources already at hand. He therefore proposed, with "great urgency," the formation of an initially small bureau of two line officers, a reserve officer for clerical duties, and a cartographer-photographer. He believed that this staff could operate with an annual budget of 150,000 marks. "It would be a tragic thrift," he told the emperor, "if we spent millions for the naval armaments but failed to spend thousands to contribute to the full and effective work of the Admiralty Staff." Diederichs assumed that Tirpitz would approve these recommendations, particularly since he expected that the fleet laws would generate "political tensions with the fleets of our most likely adversaries (England, America, France)." If the emperor granted his request, Diederichs promised to pursue the development of an intelligence office with the "undivided energy" of the entire Admiralty Staff.[66]

A few days later, Diederichs made specific personnel proposals for the 1902 fiscal year. In order to develop the Admiralty Staff along lines similar to the General Staff, he formally requested a total of thirty-two officers and eighteen civilian clerks. This was a significant increase from the eight officers and four clerks he initially administered. The new table of organization would include one vice admiral (chief), two captains and ten commanders as departmental heads, eleven lieutenant commanders as assistants, one lieutenant (sg) as adjutant, one naval engineer as technical adviser, and six reserve officers as general assistants.[67] These additional officers would allow him to properly staff a reorganized structure, including two new offices: Section K

(*Kriegsgeschichtliches Dezernat*), to study naval history, and Section N (*Nachrichtenbüro*), to gather and evaluated naval intelligence. An increase in the staff would also allow him to divide operational planning into two sections: Section A for Europe (*Europäische Abteilung*)and Section B for the rest of the world (*Aussereuropäische Abteilung*). The European Department consisted of A1 (Germany), A2 (Russia, Scandinavia, Austria-Hungary, and the Balkan states), A3 (France, Italy, Portugal, Spain), A4 (Great Britain, Belgium, Netherlands), and A5 (strategy and tactics). The Extracontinental Department consisted of B1 (general), B2 (South America), B3 (Asia), B4 (Africa, Australia, Pacific ocean), and B5 (North and Central Americas, Caribbean).[68]

Much to his dismay, Diederichs soon learned that he had not succeeded in convincing the emperor. Senden notified him that the emperor had tentatively decided to accept the formation of an intelligence section but would probably reject Diederichs's other proposals. According to Senden, the emperor had concluded that current funding, primarily dedicated to Tirpitz's battle fleet, would not allow the expansion of the Admiralty Staff on such a grand scale. Senden held out some hope, noting that the emperor would at least consider the proposals for inclusion in future budgets. In any event, he would not make a final decision until he had discussed Diederichs's proposals with Tirpitz. Senden had even more bad news. The emperor had also denied Diederichs's proposal to assign reserve officers to the Admiralty Staff, as an alternative means of expansion, and rejected Diederichs's request to move up, by six months, the scheduled assignment of two additional officers to the staff.[69]

Tirpitz met with the emperor in February 1901 to assert his "significant misgivings" about Diederichs's plans. Although he acknowledged that the growth of the navy would require the expansion of the Admiralty Staff at some future time, that time was not now. In any event, so far as Tirpitz was concerned, the Admiralstab was adequately staffed. Thus, Diederichs "moves too quickly with his proposals." Because the second Navy Law would create two additional battleship squadrons, the *Seeoffizierkorps* could simply not spare any officers for the Admiralty Staff. "The employment of the fleet," Tirpitz argued, "has first priority and therefore the expansion of the Admiralty Staff immediately assumes secondary importance." Tirpitz also rejected Diederichs's use of the General Staff as a model, arguing that Diederichs failed to understand the differences between management of war at sea and war on land. "A sea voyage," he noted, "is not like riding a horse." Tirpitz even implied strongly that the strategic importance of fleet expansion should render the Admiralty Staff subordinate to the RMA, asserting that a "separate Admiralty Staff must assuredly await the development of a larger fleet." In the same hostile vein, Tirpitz rejected Diederichs's plan for the Marineakademie, echoing Thomson's phrase that any meddling with the school was a "hazardous experiment." Tirpitz concluded succinctly: "I therefore recommend that the Admiralty Staff suspend its plans for organizational expansion until that future time when conditions and circumstances are more propitious."[70]

Having now heard from both Diederichs and Tirpitz, Wilhelm seemed to equivocate. Perhaps under Senden's influence or prodded by Koester (who had his own problems with Tirpitz), Kaiser Wilhelm made no immediate decision. He had at least begun to understand the negative impact of the continuing argument between two senior officers. He therefore advised Tirpitz, through Senden, that he wanted the conflict resolved as soon as possible so that the Admiralty Staff could return to its primary function of operational planning. Although he understood that its expansion would be difficult under current circumstances, he nonetheless instructed Tirpitz to consider its personnel needs in order to produce "an effective and competent institution."[71]

But Tirpitz did not relent. Determined to persuade the emperor, Tirpitz repeated his arguments in another audience in early March. He particularly attacked Diederichs's plan to move the Naval War College to Berlin and reorganize it to train staff officers. Tirpitz—of all people—actually accused Diederichs of empire building, arguing that the school needed to remain in Kiel and retain its original purpose in order to maintain its independence and avoid assimilation by the Admiralty Staff. He emphatically rejected the establishment of an elite corps of staff officers; he argued that the current shortage of line officers, combined with the further development of the fleet (with its own higher priority personnel needs), precluded the assignment of additional officers to the Admiralty Staff. He acknowledged the value of such a corps but believed that it would become more feasible with the fuller implementation of the fleet laws after 1904. He rejected outright Diederichs's request for additional staffing, arguing that the growing fleet had priority for new officers. He supported only one element of Diederichs's proposals: "I agree with the need to establish an intelligence bureau and attach it to the Admiralty Staff." He therefore proposed the addition of funding in the 1902 budget to pay for it. Tirpitz concluded his remarks with a plea to reconfirm the RMA's dominance in naval administration, "As Your Majesty's Imperial Naval Office continues to implement the Naval Law in regards to the creation of the fleet in subsequent years, I must respectfully emphasize that the Imperial Navy Office alone maintains responsibility for the further development of the naval officer corps."[72]

Following the presentations by both officers, Wilhelm made an initial decision granting Diederichs a partial victory. In a formal decree dated 16 March 1901, the emperor formally authorized the establishment of the *Nachrichtswesen* and its inclusion in the 1902 budget. As Diederichs had proposed, the new office would consist of a four-man staff with an annual budget of 150,000 marks.[73] Although Wilhelm assigned the new department to the Admiralstab, Tirpitz did not surrender gracefully. He instead launched another campaign aimed at attaching the new section to the RMA. The renewed conflict soon began to infect the various naval commands. Tirpitz drew on his supporters from the "torpedo gang"; Diederichs gained support from the less influential anti-Tirpitz crowd (Koester, Bendemann, with nods from the retired Valois and Oldekop). Senden, who sympathized with Diederichs but had jurisdictional aspirations of his own, stayed outwardly neutral and attempted to mediate the crisis.[74] He complained at one point to Bendemann that "Tirpitz and Diederichs remain in constant strife." Senden nonetheless sympathized with Diederichs, because he himself had lost political battles to Tirpitz. In fact, as Senden wrote, Tirpitz's victims were numerous: "Niemand will T[irpitz] sein Butter nehmen" ("No one wants Tirpitz to take his butter").[75]

ROUND THREE: COASTAL DEFENSE

A second, simultaneous issue—coastal defense—now began to merge with the original conflict over enlargement. Although the army would provide funding and material for coastal fortifications, the navy had gained primary responsibility for coastal defense in an imperial decree on 15 January 1894.

Initial planning identified two major areas of concern. The first was the German Bight, the triangular area between Helgoland, the Jade, and the Elbe estuary. The second was the Ems estuary and the Frisian Islands, with Borkum as its central defensive focus. When Britain emerged as a possible foe in 1896, coastal defense gained an even higher spending priority for both army and navy. Two years later, however, Tirpitz denounced coastal-defense planning when he argued that any naval investment in coastal defense would only slow development of his battle fleet. Tirpitz argued that his battle fleet would also be able to defend Germany's coasts adequately.[76] His argument resembled a Mahanian principle: "The best coast defense is the navy; not because fortifications are not absolutely necessary, but because beating the enemy's fleet is the best of all defenses."[77]

Tirpitz, as always, influenced Wilhelm to follow suit. The emperor decreed in January 1899 that the importance of the battle fleet outweighed that of coastal defense and thus vetoed any appropriation for the latter in the next fiscal year. In May, Bendemann asked for additional clarification, since the now-abolished OKM had formerly possessed jurisdiction over the matter; in June, Wilhelm assigned responsibility for coastal defense to the commanders of the Baltic and North Sea naval stations.[78] When Diederichs became chief of the Admiralty Staff six months later, he refused to let the issue die. He was particularly concerned for Germany's North Sea defenses, identifying the Jade and the Ems as the two most vulnerable areas. Instead, he contacted the German General Staff to elicit support for a new campaign in support of coastal defense. Over the next year, he maintained a regular correspondence with the army concerning the availability of coastal defense artillery to emplace in new or existing fortifications.[79] He forwarded this correspondence to the RMA but, as always, had difficulty obtaining a response from Tirpitz.[80]

Diederichs cited new strategic circumstances to justify a formal briefing on coastal defense to the emperor on 11 January 1901. The navy had originally prepared its defensive plans based on the premise of a war with France and Russia. In fact, Diederichs believed, the first Navy Law would produce a fleet sufficient to deter or defeat France and Russia. He now feared, however, that the Tirpitz's aggressive naval policies in the second law would drive Britain into the Franco-Russian camp and spark an Anglo-German naval war in the North Sea. Thus, Germany would face an even greater threat in the west than from the south and east. These new strategic factors obviously affected coastal defense, an issue that Tirpitz had neglected to Germany's detriment. Diederichs also accused Tirpitz of sabotaging his efforts to coordinate coastal defense with the army. He then walked a narrow line toward strategic heresy when he warned the emperor, "This circumstance will continue so long as the further development of the fleet claims all resources."

He was particularly concerned with the defense of the Ems estuary and the Frisian Islands. He was intimately familiar with the area, having served there aboard *Natter* in the Franco-German War and having returned on several occasions. In fact, his experiences compelled him to remind the emperor that the Frisian Islands possessed "great military significance because they would offer to our foe a well-protected anchorage and a defensible base for operations by hostile fleets against our coastline." He deemed the region so important, in fact, that he directed an *Admiralstabreise* there in summer 1900 to examine the operational requirements needed for the defense of the Frisian islands. The staff tour had focused specifically on the possibility of a British seizure of Borkum as the first step toward an attack on either the Ems estuary or to support operations farther north in the Bight. Diederichs concluded from the exercise that Germany's North Sea coast possessed inadequate defenses against a "massive, energetic, and continuous offensive" by Britain.

As a first step toward reversing this dangerous condition, Diederichs recommended that the navy designate Borkum as an official *Stützpunkt* (strong point) and develop it accordingly. He recommended, for example, the construction of permanent and extensive fortifications containing 280-mm guns and 210-mm mortars. He would also use minefields to protect seaward approaches and 100-mm and 150-mm batteries to command possible landing sites. He further proposed the establishment of a permanent naval station in the Ems estuary with logistical and technical facilities to support a minimum task group of four armored gunboats and four large torpedo boats. Finally, he recommended the creation of a joint planning commission to consist of delegates from appropriate army authorities (matériel), the RMA (finance) and the Admiralty Staff (operations).[81] As part of his campaign, Diederichs consulted Gen. Helmut von der Goltz, the army's inspector general for artillery, who estimated that the fortification of Borkum would cost

8,130,000 marks, of which the navy would pay 6,830,000 marks and the army 1,300,000 marks.[82]

Diederichs also studied defensive considerations for the German Bight in the north. The Bight was particularly important since it included the Elbe (Hamburg) and Weser (Bremen) estuaries, the Jadebüsen (Wilhelmshaven), and the western approach to the Kaiser Wilhelm Canal at Brünsbüttel. Because this area assumed such importance, he argued that it needed full defenses both at sea and on land. He therefore rejected Tirpitz's policy that the fleet alone could defend the region, arguing that the state secretary had "completely overlooked" the value of coastal artillery in fortified positions. So far as Diederichs was concerned, the most effective form of coastal defense was a mixture of fortified positions on land and mobile forces at sea.[83]

The joint campaign by Diederichs and Goltz proved momentarily effective. Wilhelm directed Diederichs in March to prepare formal proposals in regard to coastal defenses.[84] Tirpitz, however, went to the emperor and extracted the right to make the final evaluation of Diederichs's proposals. He also used the opportunity to present his own arguments in favor of a distant defense at sea by the battle fleet, which rendered stationary land defenses unnecessary. Since Wilhelm always seemed to follow the advice of the last person to speak with him, Tirpitz was gradually able to persuade the emperor to reject Diederichs's proposals one more time. As the tide turned against him, Diederichs complained to Bendemann that Tirpitz's ability to block improvements in coastal defenses would make Germany more vulnerable to enemy attack.[85] With tensions increasing again between the two admirals, Senden wrote Bendemann, "Tirpitz and Diederichs live in constant strife."[86]

Likewise, Tirpitz, the master *Ressorteifer,* prevailed again with his arguments in support of the battle fleet. Wilhelm published an imperial decree on 24 June 1901 that granted priority—both in personnel and matériel—to fleet expansion rather than naval operations or coastal fortifications. Given the strategic importance of the battle fleet, Wilhelm identified Tirpitz and the RMA as the primary authority responsible for the implementation of the navy laws. He therefore directed Diederichs to cease efforts to expand the Admiralty Staff and warned him not to "supersede the regular jurisdiction of the Imperial Naval Office" without imperial permission.[87] The imperial directive produced a temporary armistice in the conflict, prompting Senden to write Bendemann, "Tirpitz and Diederichs are on furlough. I will enjoy their absence."[88]

Diederichs may have lacked Tirpitz's skills at bureaucratic infighting, but he was no less committed to his ideas. After all, the principle of *Ziel erkannt, Kraft gespannt* applied to him as well. He therefore refused to accept defeat, even though he had now sustained two successive political setbacks (fleet enlargement and coastal defense) at Tirpitz's hands. He wrote an articulate defense of the independence of the Admiralstab and a blistering attack on Tirpitz's empire building to Senden in July. Diederichs first criticized the concentration of naval power that had existed in the Admiralty before 1889, noting that a unified command structure had "proved ineffective in the Stosch period and stifled necessary development in the Caprivi era." He argued that a comparable concentration of power in Tirpitz's hands would produce similar problems now, particularly since Tirpitz had ignored strategic and operational considerations in his haste to construct a battle fleet against Britain. Rather than a strong RMA and a weak Admiral Staff, Diederichs told Senden that he preferred the balanced tripartite structure that had existed between 1889 and 1899. This, he said, compared to the effective army system, which had a similar division of power between the Ministry of War, the General Staff, and the Military Cabinet. This system had already proven quite effective, most recently in the Franco-German War of 1870–71. Since the navy already possessed two equivalents in Tirpitz's RMA and Senden's Marinekabinett, Diederichs again proposed the expansion of the Admiral Staff to a position analogous to the German General Staff. Collective decision making, rather than a concentration of authority in the hands of one individual, was more likely to increase chances of effective decisions and reduce the possibility of error. He concluded, "I therefore believe that the RMA alone should not make important decisions that affect major military and technical issues, or that lead to the rapid development of the navy."[89]

THE FINAL ROUND

The summer truce did not last long. Flushed with victory in the matter of coastal defense, Tirpitz returned from his furlough in August to launch a broad offensive against the independence and authority of the Admiralty Staff. Citing his paramount responsibility for the implementation of the navy laws, Tirpitz now attempted to insert himself and the RMA into operational matters. He argued, for example, that the RMA should direct the disposition of ships on foreign station since his office made the logistical and technical arrangements to support those ships. Among other things, Tirpitz hoped that this change in procedure would allow him to prevent overseas misadventures, as he saw it, like the seizure of Kiao-chou and the incident at Manila, both of which, he believed, could have undermined his battle fleet plans. Diederichs interpreted Tirpitz's move as the first step in a broader campaign to usurp full control over operational planning and the probable abolition of the Admiralty Staff. He suspected that Tirpitz would next argue that the strategic implications of the battle fleet warranted the RMA's assumption of responsibility for operational planning.

Diederichs had come to believe that Tirpitz's preoccupation with battleships and the battle fleet would limit the navy's strategic alternatives and steer Germany on a dangerous course toward greater conflict with Britain. More and more, he saw himself and the Admiralty Staff as the only force that could stop Tirpitz's dangerous plans. He therefore wrote Bendemann in August 1901, "I see more clearly day by day how essential an independent Admiralstab is to the navy." Likewise, Diederichs feared that if Tirpitz gained control over operational planning he would stifle any strategic and tactical ideas, as he had earlier done with Valois and Maltzahn, that did not support his battle fleet. This would dangerously weaken the naval officer corps by muzzling junior officers who might show creativity and independence. In fact, citing "guilt by association," Diederichs now worried about the future careers of junior officers who served with him on the Admiralty Staff.[90]

This particular conflict had actually begun months earlier. Diederichs had convinced the emperor in February 1901 to detach SM Gunboat *Luchs* (eleven hundred tons, two 105-mm guns) from the East Asian station and transfer her to the west coast of South America. Diederichs worried that the continuing absence of a warship in the region would prove "unfavorable," leaving German interests seriously unprotected and prevent Germany from offering "an alternative to American influence."[91] He was therefore stunned to discover in February that Tirpitz had countermanded those orders and directed *Luchs* to remain in East Asia. With withering politeness, he asked Tirpitz for an explanation. Why, and on whose authority, had the state secretary of the RMA usurped the authority of the Admiralty Staff to direct overseas operations?[92] Tirpitz responded with equally cool succinctness that the battle fleet had first priority in all fiscal decisions and allocations. Thus, his office lacked the financial ability to support a warship in South American waters.[93] Diederichs fired back, without the usual respectful salutations, that His Majesty the Emperor had authorized the assignment on several occasions and therefore reiterated his request for material and logistical support for *Luchs*'s transfer.[94]

Dissatisfied by this exchange and unhappy with the threat to his authority, Diederichs complained to Kaiser Wilhelm on 1 April 1901. Diederichs respectfully reminded the emperor that the original imperial decree (14 March 1899) had granted operational control to the Admiralty Staff. Now, however, Tirpitz usurped that authority on the basis of his responsibility for arranging logistical and technical support for ships on foreign station. "The confusion fostered by this [division of authority]," he noted, "causes constant problems." Diederichs also pointed out that Tirpitz's fiscal obsession with spending money only on the risk fleet endangered strategic interests overseas. After all, South America had become a major point for German emigration and trade. Thus, a German ship needed to show the flag along the South American coast on a regular basis. In any event, how expensive could the issue be? A gunboat would require less cost than a light cruiser, while still offering the same strategic and diplomatic advantages.

Diederichs then cited a second violation of his authority. Rear Admiral Bendemann, chief of the Cruiser Squadron, had successfully solicited financial and logistical support from the RMA in March 1901 to commission a small auxiliary warship for service on the upper Yangtze River. Tirpitz not only failed to notify the Admiralstab of these arrangements but had also bypassed Diederichs to give operational instructions to Bendemann for the use of the craft. This, according to Diederichs, was a regular problem. Tirpitz often made logistical accommodations for ships on foreign station that deliberately interfered with operational matters and then withheld such "wholly necessary" information from the Admiralty Staff. Diederichs argued that such capricious tactics had already begun to undermine the effectiveness of overseas operations.[95]

Diederichs broadened his criticism to include Rear Adm. Wilhelm Büchsel, Tirpitz's deputy and director of the RMA's General Naval Section (*Allgemeine*

Marinedepartment). Büchsel, who had entered the navy with Diederichs and Tirpitz in 1865, was a devoted member of the "torpedo gang." Diederichs complained that Büchsel regularly made arrangements for crew transshipments without consulting the Admiralty Staff. Diederichs would dispatch operational instructions to the Cruiser Squadron, only to discover that ships were momentarily unavailable because of the need to exchange crews. When Diederichs asked Büchsel to provide prior notification of such arrangements, Büchsel refused, citing the RMA's authority to make such plans.[96]

The conflict continued into the fall. Diederichs proposed sending either a gunboat—SMS *Panther* (eleven hundred tons, two 105-mm guns)—or two small torpedo boats to Maracaibo, Venezuela, in October 1901. The Venezuelan government had refused to repay loans owed to German banks and had begun to harass German businessmen. Tirpitz vetoed the plan for the usual reasons: The navy currently lacked the resources—financial, personnel, and material—to support either proposal.[97]

Although Kaiser Wilhelm intervened and agreed to dispatch *Panther* to the Caribbean after all, Diederichs grew exceedingly more frustrated in his conflict with Tirpitz. Meanwhile, Tirpitz maintained a steady flow of memoranda and proposals asking the emperor to grant him operational command of ships on foreign station. Diederichs, who had no patience with courtly politics and ritual, withdrew into the minutiae of operational planning, essentially conceding the field to Tirpitz. His respect for both Wilhelm and Tirpitz, whom he once referred to as a "crafty Muscovite," continued to decline. On one occasion, he and Tirpitz arranged for a joint audience with the emperor to discuss their differences. As his carriage arrived at the palace at the appointed time, he saw Tirpitz depart. The state secretary had deceived him deliberately, arriving early to present his case to the emperor alone.[98] The only bright point during this dark period was his promotion to full admiral on 27 January 1902, second on the admirals list after Adm. Gustav Koester.[99] Promotion, however, was little consolation for his continuing conflict with Tirpitz.

The final blow fell in spring 1902. Diederichs complained to Senden in late March that Tirpitz continued to undermine his operational authority over ships on foreign station.[100] Diederichs decided to take his case directly to the emperor. He met with Wilhelm on 3 April 1902 to request that the emperor affirm the independence of the Admiralty Staff and compel greater cooperation from Tirpitz and the RMA. He particularly cited Tirpitz's practice of withholding information vital to operational planning. Policy dictated that Diederichs, as chief of the Admiralstab, send and receive all service memoranda and other materials through the RMA. Tirpitz, however, often refused to provide the necessary channels for communication, frustrating Diederichs's need to gather information from agencies such as the Foreign Ministry and the Colonial Office. Wilhelm, as always, made no immediate response but instead forwarded the request to Tirpitz at the RMA. For obvious reasons, Tirpitz resisted Diederichs's proposals, which he saw as a dangerous declaration of Admiralty Staff independence. Tirpitz therefore rejected the proposal with the reminder that the emperor had given him paramount authority with the navy's command structure.[101]

When Wilhelm failed to respond to his initiative, Diederichs raised the issue again on 16 April at his next audience with the emperor. His ostensible purpose was to present his weekly *Immediatvortrag,* a briefing on a visit by SMS *Habicht* (one thousand tons, five 125-mm guns) to Cape Town, South Africa. During the course of his presentation, Diederichs concluded that the emperor no longer had confidence in him or his ability to continue to serve as chief of the Admiralstab. At the end of the audience, he asked the emperor for permission to consider retirement.[102]

Diederichs now withdrew to his office to consider his professional future. His choices were simple but difficult. He could continue to fight for the independence of the Admiralstab, but his political will to maintain the fight had begun to erode. The battle fleet seemed to trump every card he played. He had won a minor victory with the intelligence section but had otherwise lost to Tirpitz on the more significant issues of enlargement and coastal defense. Now, it appeared, he was losing the battle on overseas operations. Senden, who could always be counted on to take the easy way out, advised him that it was his duty to please the emperor; "one ought to dance to his tune." Similarly, unlike Tirpitz, who had his "torpedo gang," Diederichs had no large corps of devout followers. He certainly had supporters—Koester, the Thiele brothers, and a few others—but, with the exception of Koester, none was in any particular position of power or influence and none had Wilhelm's ear to the extent that Tirpitz had.

Constant Strife, 1899–1902   255

His other option was to seek early retirement. He discussed the issue with Henni as well. She reminded him that he had considered retiring in 1896, following his dismissal from the OKM, and had regularly discussed retirement in their correspondence during his tenure as chief of the Cruiser Squadron. He had fought the good fight. He could certainly look back on a career of professional achievements. He had fulfilled his family commitment to serve the state, during an active career that had now lasted for almost thirty-seven years. And, of course, both he and Henni continued to suffer from physical problems. He also spoke with Fritz, a senior lieutenant on the staff of the Kiel naval station, and Herman, also a senior lieutenant and executive officer of *S 94*. According to Fritz, "After all that my father had experienced during his tour at the Admiralty Staff, he now looked for an opportunity to leave the service without provoking excitement."[103] Based on these considerations and after a month of contemplation, Diederichs decided to retire. He formally asked the emperor on 17 May 1902 to grant him a three-month furlough as terminal leave in preparation for retirement.[104]

Tirpitz did not even wait for Diederichs to make up his mind. Less than a week after Diederichs's last audience with the emperor, Tirpitz recommended Vice Adm. Wilhelm Büchsel as Diederichs's successor. Büchsel, who had entered the navy in 1865 with Tirpitz and Diederichs, was a charter member of the "torpedo gang." His current post was as Tirpitz's primary deputy in the RMA where, among other things, he supervised the administration of Kiao-chou. (One of his assistants was none other than Capt. Hugh Zeye.)[105] Tirpitz called Büchsel a "deserving naval officer," cited his experience in administration, and contended that Büchsel would work effectively with his naval peers (that is, Tirpitz). Tirpitz also suggested that his appointment would reduce tension between the two authorities and, in subtle criticism of Diederichs's tenure, improve the efficiency of the Admiral Staff.[106]

Diederichs briefly returned from his furlough in early August. He formally transmitted his request for retirement to the emperor on 9 August 1902. Ten days later, on 19 August, Kaiser Wilhelm responded with an official decree, announcing Diederichs's retirement and acknowledging that he would remain forever renowned in the chronicles of German naval history for his actions at Kiao-chou.[107] Based on a complex formula, Diederichs received credit for thirty-seven years and twenty-five days (calculated from 6

September 1865 to 30 September 1902) of active duty, with an additional bonus of five years, eight months, and seven days for service overseas. The total of the two amounts (forty-two years, nine months, two days) produced an annual pension of 11,592 marks (approximately three thousand dollars at contemporary exchange rates). In a final insult, Tirpitz, as state secretary, formally confirmed Diederichs's pension.[108]

Contemporary commentators concluded that it was Diederichs's unwillingness to pursue *Ressorteifer* that led to his fall from power. Gustav Bachmann, who served first as Diederichs's adjutant at the Admiral Staff and then became chief during World War I, referred to Diederichs's departure not as retirement but rather as dismissal (*Verabschiedung*), citing Diederichs's refusal to curry favor with the emperor as the cause of his downfall: "He simply had no patience for courtly etiquette [*Hofformen*] and alienated the emperor with his stubborn attitude."[109] Fritz von Diederichs, upon examining his father's papers, used the same term—*Verabschiedung*—and cited a similar cause: "This happened after my father had shown courage 'even in the face of princes' by openly and vigorously defending the untenable position of the Admiralty Staff."[110]

In many ways, Diederichs was the "last, best hope" of preventing the complete domination of the navy by Tirpitz. Once Diederichs left the scene, there was little interest in confronting Tirpitz. The navy's two senior admirals, Gustav von Koester (Kiel) and August Thomson (Wilhelmshaven), had little direct influence with the emperor in these issues. Vice Adm. Gustav von Senden-Bibran, in Diederichs's own words, would only do what was good for Senden. Vice Adm. Felix Bendemann supported Diederichs but was isolated in East Asia as commander of the Cruiser Squadron. The next three senior vice admirals—Prince Heinrich of Prussia, Volkmar von Arnim, and Wilhelm Büchsel—endorsed Tirpitz's program and therefore had little interest in supporting Diederichs's. In fact, as Diederichs feared, the independence of the Admiralty Staff quickly became a fiction as five of the next seven chiefs came from Tirpitz's "torpedo gang."[111] Thus, with Diederichs's departure, Tirpitz could claim that final victory. The navy was now his to lead and develop in his own image.

9

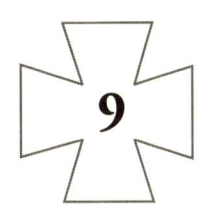

Watching from Afar: Diederichs in Retirement, 1902–1918

Diederichs and Henni decided to retire to Baden-Baden. Henni had convalesced there in 1897, once describing the city as "hot in summer, foggy in fall, and always expensive."[1] Nonetheless, the resort's famous mineral hot springs and unsurpassed medical facilities appealed to them both as their health problems continued. On returning from East Asia in 1899, Diederichs had visited Baden-Baden to survey retirement property. He and Henni visited it again during his final furlough from the Admiralty Staff in the summer of 1902. In the small and picturesque suburb of Lichtenthal, they discovered that a Cistercian abbey dating from the thirteenth century had property for sale on nearby Leisberg. The Diederichses purchased a view lot, overlooking the valley and only a mile or two from downtown Baden-Baden. Following his retirement, Diederichs designed and directed, as he had the family home in Kiel almost twenty years earlier, the construction of an airy and spacious villa. He and Henni temporarily leased an apartment in Baden-Baden at Maria-Viktoria-Strasse 12 until they moved into their new home, which they named "Kleiner Leisberg," in September 1903.[2]

Diederichs thus watched from afar as Tsingtao and Kiao-chou developed as a German naval base and maritime center. Over the next few years, naval engineers designed and built two large artificial harbors in Kiao-chou Bay with berths for sixty ships, a dry dock, a rail line, a machine shop, an armory, and a chandlery. The dockyard constructed a dozen small craft and patrol boats to support the navy's operations. The navy also developed "Fortress Tsingtao," with guns as large as 240-mm coastal artillery and 280-mm mortars in fortified positions. The new base, whose naval personnel soon numbered twenty-four hundred, became the permanent home port for the Cruiser Squadron. Over the next sixteen years, Tsingtao truly became "the Kiel of the Far East."[3] Meanwhile it had rapidly developed as the center of German trade in China. More than nine hundred steamers, carrying 1.3 million tons of cargo valued at thirty-five million marks, visited Tsingtao in 1913. Kiao-chou's railroads counted eight hundred kilometers of track and provided a direct rail link to Peking and the Yangtze basin. Mining companies produced five hundred thousand tons of coal annually. A combination of good weather, German order, and the Germania Brewery's famous "Tsingtao" beer quickly made the city a popular vacation spot for Europeans.[4] To mark Diederichs's role in the acquisition of Kiao-chou, the navy commissioned a commemorative inscription to be carved on a stone cliff overlooking Tsingtao: "For him who won for Kaiser and Reich the land all around, let this rock be named Diederichs's stone [*Diederichsstein*]."

Even from retirement, Diederichs maintained his interest in naval and political issues. As he watched the evolution of the fleet, his fear that Tirpitz's plan would alienate Britain ripened. Friedrich von Diederichs noted, "My father disagreed with our foreign policy, especially with the intensity with which Tirpitz directed naval policy against England."[5] Diederichs wrote to Capt. Paul von Hintze, his former flag lieutenant in East Asia, in January 1903 that imperial policies threatened "to squander the strength of the German Reich." He likewise complained that Büchsel, his successor, had halted all attempts to reform or restructure the Admiralty Staff, hindering operational planning and thus undermining the navy's ability to fight a war effectively.[6] Diederichs nonetheless admitted that he was relieved to be out of naval politics. He again wrote Hintze, "I only hear about the Navy from what I read in the newspaper. That suffices for now. House, garden, and woods are enough for me. Current political problems give me ample reason to enjoy the life I have here!"[7]

As tensions arising from imperial policies continued to increase, Diederichs wrote a more anguished, and dangerous, letter to Fritz in February 1904 in which he questioned the very legitimacy of the Hohenzollern regime. So far as he was concerned, Wilhelm and his advisers, Tirpitz and Bülow in particular, had driven Germany to the point of financial ruin and political collapse. Diederichs believed that Germany's only hope lay in a massive reform movement like the one that followed Prussia's disastrous defeat by Napoleon in 1806. He worried, however, that entrenched conservative and authoritarian political interests would block necessary reforms. Inevitably, such economic and political problems had also affected Germany's defense posture, making her less prepared for, and thus more vulnerable to, a sneak attack.[8] Frustrated by the misrule of Kaiser Wilhelm, Diederichs and Henni made a momentous decision. Ending four generations of service to the Hohenzollern dynasty, Diederichs decided to relinquish his Prussian citizenship in November 1904 to swear allegiance to the grand duke of Baden instead.[9]

Diederichs's fear that Germany had become exposed to a surprise attack was not altogether unfounded. The new threat was, in fact, a realistic one, and stemmed from Britain's growing dislike of Tirpitz's battle fleet. It had become abundantly clear to the British, beginning with Tirpitz's first navy law in 1898 and accelerating with the second navy law in 1900, that Germany had evolved into a substantial naval threat. In fact, even popular culture played a role, particularly with the publication of Erskine Childers's espionage novel, *The Riddle of the Sands,* in 1903. The novel's plot, which involved fictional German preparations for the invasion of Britain, inflamed British public opinion and produced demands for increased defense spending.[10]

The British responded to these tensions, in part, with the appointment of Adm. Sir John Fisher as First Sea Lord in 1904. Fisher immediately reoriented the Royal Navy's original aspect—France and Russia—to focus on Germany instead. He recalled warships from overseas to create a larger and more powerful Channel Fleet, countering Tirpitz's decision to concentrate the German fleet between Helgoland and the Thames. Fisher also gained a substantial technological lead in the naval race with Germany when he directed the construction and launching of HMS *Dreadnought* (eighteen thousand tons, ten 305-mm guns) in 1906. Powered by high-speed turbine engines, *Dreadnought* was the first all–"big gun" battleship, immediately becoming the archetype of battleship design thereafter. Fisher also pioneered the development of the first battle cruiser, HMS *Invincible* (seventeen thousand tons, eight 305-mm guns), in 1908, by which he intended to outgun contemporary cruisers and outrun modern battleships. Tirpitz responded quickly to Fisher's initiatives, launching the first German dreadnought, SMS *Nassau* (twenty-thousand tons, twelve 280-mm guns) in 1908 and the first battle cruiser, SMS *Van der Tann* (twenty-one thousand tons, eight 280-mm guns) in 1909. Moreover, Tirpitz persuaded the Reichstag to pass a supplementary law, or *Novelle,* in 1908 that increased annual battleship construction from three ships to four. With British opinion turning angrily against Germany, Fisher twice—in 1904 and in 1908—proposed using Britain's current naval superiority to "Copenhagen" the German fleet, that is, to launch preemptive strikes against the Kiel and Wilhelmshaven naval bases as the Royal Navy had done against the Danish navy in 1801 and 1807.[11] Diederichs watched these events with growing trepidation. Writing to Hintze in November 1907, he compared German naval development, which had provoked intense rivalry in Britain, to the "poisoned fruit" of children's fairy tales. He expressed specific regret for the decline in relations with Britain and worried that Kiao-chou would become one of the many victims of a future Anglo-German conflict.[12]

    Simultaneous Anglo-German diplomatic differences also developed. Alienated by German imperial and naval policies, Britain turned to France in 1904, resolving long-standing colonial differences, to form the Entente Cordiale. With France then acting as mediator, Britain resolved similar problems with Russia in 1907 to complete the formation of the Triple Entente. According to noted German historian Fritz Fischer, this left Germany encircled and compelled Kaiser Wilhelm to assume an even more aggressive posture to avoid destruction ("Weltmacht oder Niedergang"—roughly, "world power or decline"). Wilhelm sought to challenge British support for the entente by engineering international crises in Morocco, resulting first in the Algeciras Conference in 1905, and then by sending SMS *Panther* to the region in 1911. Britain proved true to her new allies, however, and the incidents succeeded only in producing greater Anglo-German antagonism. Kaiser Wilhelm, who liked to fish in troubled waters, made matters worse in his infamous interview with a correspondent from the London *Daily Telegraph* in October 1908. As he awkwardly attempted to assure the British people of his affection and friendship, he succeeded only in making himself appear foolish and untrustworthy. The interview had a similar negative effect on German public opinion, embarrassing the emperor and undermining confidence in his leadership.[13]

Although Diederichs had always been careful to avoid open criticism of his political and naval superiors while on active duty, his attitude changed after his retirement. He wrote two anguished letters to his son Fritz at the end of 1908 that portrayed not only his disgust at the current situation but also his fears for Germany's future. In the first letter, Diederichs openly criticized Wilhelm's "new course," whose biggest flaw, he maintained, was its lack of clear objectives. Successive chancellors and advisers had failed to curtail the emperor's bellicose actions. Moreover, the growing costs of the battle fleet, authorized by the supplementary law of 1908, had begun to undermine the financial health of the state. Sadly, he believed, Wilhelm's disgraceful *Daily Telegraph* interview had "failed to open the eyes of the [German] people sufficiently" to the dangers inherent in the emperor's policies and leadership. On the contrary, it had produced a situation in which "our enemies delight in our weakness," as they watched Germany "drift inevitably into catastrophe." He hoped that "Germany will meet a better fate than what I fear. May God grant it." (He closed on a somewhat more cheerful note: "I send you a few marks for Christmas for your expenses. Increase your investment in the chocolate industry with the remainder.")[14]

The second letter, written on the afternoon of Christmas Day, 1908, continued in a similar vein. Diederichs commented on anonymous charges raised in a recent issue of *Marinerundschau*, the navy's semiofficial journal, that Tirpitz's *Reichsmarineamt* had badly bungled procurement and construction policies for the new battle fleet. "Waste," he noted, "(and every rivet that is tossed aside is waste) only robs us of the means to wage war." So far as he was concerned, the problem was not a new one. After all, he charged, Tirpitz and his minions had certainly made "serious mistakes and committed hair-raising deeds in the past." He returned to the dominant issue: that

Tirpitz continued to concentrate on the battle fleet to the detriment of other potential weapons and strategies—submarines, which Tirpitz disdained, and coastal defense, which Tirpitz ignored. He again closed with a light note, thanking Fritz for a Yuletide gift of sausages and pastries.[15]

Diederichs's mood improved somewhat in 1909. In response to birthday greetings from Fritz, he could note positive results from his annual medical exam: "The ambitions are great but the ability is weak." He had recently taken his first ride in an automobile, which he compared to a typhoon. He repeated this analogy as he admitted his amazement with modern technology, particularly the extraordinary inventions of the Wright brothers in the United States. Airplanes and automobiles, he wrote, were almost inconceivable to someone trained in sailing ships. Diederichs made only a single reference to current issues, commenting negatively on French public opinion whose demand for *revanche* (revenge) for the loss of Alsace-Lorraine during the Franco-German War of 1870–71 was the latest threat to European peace.[16]

Diederichs's quiet retirement to Lichtenthal changed suddenly in early 1914, on the publication of George Dewey's autobiography. Ghostwritten by Frederick Palmer, the book provoked a significant controversy in Germany when it vehemently criticized Diederichs's conduct at Manila in 1898. Dewey's accusations drew on many of the same rumors and falsehoods—centering particularly on Diederichs's allegedly belligerent use of the phrase, "I am here, Sir, by the order of the Kaiser"—that had circulated at the time. The controversy even led to questions in the German Reichstag, where several delegates defended Diederichs and his actions.[17] Likewise, German newspapers entered the fray to criticize Dewey in turn for his book's alleged flaws and falsehoods and to note that Diederichs intended to respond to the charges in the March 1914 edition of the navy's professional journal, *Marinerundschau*.[18] Retired Vice Adm. Paul Hoffmann advised Diederichs to ignore any criticism arising from Dewey's book, given the source of the accusations, noting that he had also used the formulaic "I am here, Sir," while commanding the Cruiser Division during the Sino-Japanese War (1894–95).[19]

The Great War, the catastrophe that Diederichs had long feared, broke out only months later, in August 1914. The war caused Diederichs and Henni an immediate and personal crisis when they learned that their older son Fritz had been arrested in London and charged with espionage. Fritz had officially resigned his commission in November 1913 but continued to work for the navy in an "unofficial" capacity. Capt. Walter Isendahl, director of the *Admiralstab* intelligence section, had recruited him as an agent in March 1914.[20] Fritz had arrived in England in late July with instructions to gather information on British naval readiness. He checked into a London hotel, unaware that British counterintelligence agents had already marked him as a German spy. When Britain declared war on Germany on 4 August, the Metropolitan Police promptly arrested him at his London hotel. A British court eventually reduced the charges to violation of immigration laws and interned him for the remainder of the war at Knockaloe, an internment facility on the Isle of Man.[21] Fritz himself believed that the British had decided not to execute him because of their respect for his father.[22] The truth, however, probably lay more with a British decision that the evidence was simply insufficient to warrant such a drastic punishment.[23]

News of Fritz's arrest stunned his parents. Retired admiral Paul Hoffman wrote to commiserate and console, hoping that the British would not lock Fritz up, with his sunny ("*Sonnenfrisch*") personality, in some cold, dark watchtower.[24] Diederichs himself used all his influence to find a way to free Fritz, persuading the German government to seek assistance from neutral diplomats. Based on these contacts, the British initially agreed to exchange him in late 1914 for a captured British general but, for unclear reasons, the agreement fell through. Additional contacts, again through neutral sources, attempted to secure his expatriation first in 1916 and then again in 1918, but the British now refused because of Fritz's status as a former naval officer. Fritz remained in British custody for the remainder of the war, not returning to Germany until 1919.[25]

A second blow occurred a few weeks later, when Japanese and British forces landed near Tsingtao in September 1914 and besieged the German positions. Outnumbered and cut off from reinforcements, the Kiao-chou garrison surrendered on 7 November 1914. To add insult to injury, the Japanese occupiers promptly defaced the *Diederichsstein* monument. Recalled to European waters, the Cruiser Squadron survived only a month longer. Vice Adm. Maximilian Graf von Spee, who had served under Diederichs's command in East Asia some fifteen years earlier, died with his ships at the Battle of the Falklands on 7 December 1914.[26]

The war, in many ways, confirmed Diederichs's criticism of Germany's imperialist and navalist policies. Tirpitz's "risk fleet" did not deter the British but instead aroused English eagerness for war. The furious construction program and the ensuing Anglo-German naval race that began in 1898 produced thirteen *Dreadnought*-class battleships and three battle cruisers by the outbreak of war in 1914. The Royal Navy, on the other hand, numbered twenty-one battleships and four battle cruisers. Fearing in fact that he would lose his fleet in battle to a superior foe, Wilhelm kept his battleships at anchor at their Wilhelmshaven and Kiel bases. Tirpitz's vaunted *Geschwaderkrieg* thus gave way to the scorned *Kreuzerkrieg* and *Kleinkrieg* ("small war") as the Kaiserliche Marine's few successes derived from commerce raiding by a handful of cruisers, such as SMS *Emden,* and a few score of submarines. The failure of the High Seas Fleet to perform as intended proved Winston Churchill's prewar contention that the German navy was a "luxury" fleet that Germany could ill afford. Although Tirpitz ultimately accepted the value of submarines, particularly in an economic war against Britain, the failure of his risk fleet to achieve a German victory led to his resignation in March 1916.[27]

Two months later, the *Hochseeflotte* made its most serious attempt to strike a decisive blow at the British Royal Navy. The battle plan called for German battle cruisers to entice British battle cruisers into an ambush off Jutland, where German battleships would destroy them. Instead, the British ambushed the ambushers. Although the Germans sustained a tactical victory by sinking a greater number of British capital ships, the High Seas Fleet returned to its bases for another long period of inactivity.[28]

Life at "Kleiner Leisberg" became more difficult for Diederichs and Henni as the war continued. Henni, saddened by Fritz's imprisonment and weakened by continuing health problems, died on 17 December 1917 at the age of sixty-four, a month after their forty-sixth anniversary. Diederichs survived her by only a few months, dying on 8 March 1918 at seventy-four. Herman, currently serving in the RMA's Construction Department in Berlin, attended both funerals. Following his father's wishes, he had Diederichs's body cremated, with the ashes interred in a mausoleum at the Baden-Baden Hauptfriedhof.[29]

It was perhaps a blessing that Diederichs did not live to see the final destruction of the navy he had served for so long. When senior naval commanders decided to send the High Seas Fleet out to a final apocalyptic battle on 30 October 1918, enlisted crews mutinied rather than proceed to sea for the alleged "suicide sortie." The mutiny quickly spread ashore to Wilhelmshaven and Kiel and even farther inland, ending only with the armistice.[30] Once the war ended, the victorious allies, led by the British, demanded the surrender of the *Hochseeflotte*. Under the guns of the Royal Navy, the German fleet steamed over to Scapa Flow and internment on a day remembered grimly as only *Der Tag*, 21 November 1918. Rather than relinquish their ships to the British according the provisions of the Versailles treaty, German crews acknowledged final defeat when they scuttled ten battleships, five battle cruisers, and fifty smaller warships on 21 June 1919.[31]

It lay with Iwan Oldekop to write the final eulogy for Otto von Diederichs. In a letter to Herman von Diederichs in March 1918, he mourned their mutual loss: Oldekop had lost his "best and oldest friend," while Herman had lost his father. Oldekop noted that his friendship with Diederichs, begun aboard SMS *Niobe* in 1865, had endured for more than fifty years. During that time, they had participated in major events as the navy evolved from sail to steam and matured from a coastal defense force to a *Hochseeflotte*. At the same time, Prussia had transformed itself into Germany and developed from a continental force to a world power. Throughout, Diederichs had served the navy and the state with duty, honor, integrity, and loyalty. Oldekop concluded his letter to Herman quite simply: "You can be proud of your father."[32]

Notes

ABBREVIATIONS

AKO	Allerhöchste-Kabinetts-Ordre (Imperial Decree)
BAMA	Bundesarchiv-Militärarchiv (Federal Military Archives), Freiburg, Federal Republic of Germany
N	Nachlass (papers)
RM	Reichsmarine
HMSO	Her Majesty's Stationery Office, London
LC	Library of Congress, Washington, D.C.
NARA	National Archives and Records Administration
PAAA	Politisches Archivs des Auswärtiges Amtes (Foreign Ministry Archives), Bonn, Germany
PRO	Public Record Office, London
RG	Record Group

Chapter 1. With Duty and Honor, 1843–1867

1. Personalbogen [Personnel File], BAMA, N 255/1.
2. Otto's older son, Friedrich (Fritz), wrote a brief biography of his father for inclusion in the family records; see BAMA, N 255/1, "Kurzbiographie von Otto von Diederichs." For the christening, see BAMA, N 255/1, Geburts- und Taufschein (certified copy), 8 March 1917.

3. Frau Gisela von Diederichs graciously showed me the original patent and coat of arms, as well as providing additional family information, in Baden-Baden in 1994.
4. F. F. A. von Diederichs, *Die Systeme der Staatswissenschaften von Say, Jacob und Politz nach ihren Hauptmomenten und mit besonderer Rücksicht auf die sogenannte Nationalökonomie: Nebst Ideen zur neuen, sachgemässen Begründung und Behandlung der berührten Materien* (Cologne: Bachem Verlag, 1833).
5. For genealogical and family details, see "Kurzbiographie," BAMA, N 255/1; *Gothiasches Genealogisches Taschenbuch der Adelige Häuser* (Gotha: Justus Perthes, 1939), 114–15; and Deutschen Adelsarchiv, *Genealogisches Handbuch des Adels: Adelslexikon,* ed. Walter von Hueck (Limburg am Lahn: C. A. Starke, 1974), 2:473. Christoph's older brother (and Otto's great-uncle), Karl Diederichs, received a similar patent in 1817 as mayor of Herford. Karl's son, Eduard von Diederichs, secured a commission in the Prussian Army and rose to the rank of major general.
6. Diederichs's academic reports, BAMA, N 255/1.
7. James Russell, *German Higher Schools: The History, Organization and Methods of Secondary Education in Germany* (1905), 124.
8. Friedrich von Schiller, "An die Freude," *Schillers Gedichte*, 51.
9. See academic reports, BAMA, N 255/1.
10. George Paulsen, *German Education: Past and Present* (1908), xiv. Prussia had instituted this practice in 1814 during the *Befreiungskrieg* [War of National Liberation] against the French. See also Steven Clemente, *For King and Kaiser! The Making of the Prussian Army Officer, 1860–1914* (1992), 28–33.
11. Plehwe to Frederick von Diederichs, 28 December 1861, BAMA, N 255/1. For the examination's content, see Henry Barnard, *Military Schools and Courses of Instruction in the Science and Art of War* (1872), 297–302.
12. Alfred von Cronsaz, *Die Organization des Brandenburgischen und Preussischen Heeres seit 1640* (1873), 2:37, 43. The Ostpreussisches Füsiliers, which consisted of three battalions, was brigaded with the Second Rhenish Infantry and the Twenty-eighth Landwehr as the Thirtieth Infantry Brigade.
13. Physician's note, BAMA, N 255/1.
14. BAMA, N 255/1, Diederichs, holographic note, folio 60; see also Interior Ministry to Diederichs, 26 June 1862. A second document, dated 29 July 1862, provisionally relieved Diederichs of military liability for 1863 and 1864 pending completion of his sea service. He needed to fulfill the obligation by 1 May 1865 or face civil punishment.
15. The Admiralty finally adopted the new policies in June 1864. See *Verordnung*

über die Ergänzung der Offizier-Corps der Königlichen Marine, 16 June 1864, BAMA, RM 1/143.
16. Herman Melville, *Moby-Dick* (New York: Bantam, 1967), 11.
17. "Kurzbiographie," BAMA, N 255/1.
18. Diederichs, holographic note, folio 60, BAMA, N 255/1.
19. Diederichs later compared this voyage to a trip made thirty-five years later in which he enjoyed the luxury of a stateroom aboard a modern passenger liner; see Diederichs to Henni von Diederichs, 4 May 1897, BAMA, N 255/4.
20. For conditions in China, see, for example, Peter Ward Fay, *The Opium War, 1840–1842* (1975); John Fairbanks, *Trade and Diplomacy on the China Coast: The Opening of the Treaty Ports, 1842–1854* (1953); Jonathan Spence, *God's Chinese Son: The Taiping Heavenly Kingdom of Hong Xiuquan* (1996); Immanuel Hsü, *The Ili Crisis: A Study of Sino-Russian Diplomacy, 1871–1881* (1965).
21. Willi A. Boelcke, *So Kam das Meer zu Uns: die Preussisch-Deutsche Kriegsmarine in übersee, 1822–1914* (1981), 235–37.
22. Service Record, 13 May 1865, BAMA, N 255/1.
23. Eberhard von Mantey's *Deutsche Marinegeschichte* (1926) remains the classic study of German naval history. Mantey (1869–1940) was a career naval officer who served variously in the Naval History Department and Naval Archives Branch of the *Admiralstab*. See also Lawrence Sondhaus, *Preparing for Weltpolitik: German Sea Power before the Tirpitz Era* (1997); and Hans Georg Steltzer, *Die Deutsche Flotte: ein historischer überblick von 1640 bis 1918* (1989). Steltzer titles this chapter "Preussen ohne Seemacht."
24. Die Entstehung der Preussische-Deutsche Flotte, October 1881, BAMA, RM 1/1845. The small craft, none of which remained in service after 1819, displaced only sixty-five tons each and carried two 24-lb guns; Erich Gröner, *German Warships, 1815–1945*, vol. 1, *Major Surface Vessels*, revised and expanded by Dieter Jung and Martin Maass (1982), 127.
25. Hans Jürgen Witthöfft, *Lexikon zur deutschen Marinegeschichte*, vol. 1 (1977–79). See also, Sondhaus, *Weltpolitik*, 1–6.
26. Departments 2 and 3 were the Artillery and Engineers, respectively. See Prussia, Kriegsmarine-Oberkommando, *Ranglisten der Königlich Preussischen Marine aus den Jahren 1848 bis 1864* (1894), 1.
27. Die Entstehung der Preussische-Deutsche Flotte, BAMA, RM 1/1845.
28. Paul Heinsius, "Anfänge der Deutschen Marine," in *Die Erste Deutsche Flotte, 1848–1857*, ed. Walther Hubatsch (1981), 13–27.
29. Rolf Güth, *Von Revolution zu Revolution: Entwicklungen und Führungsprobleme der Deutschen Marine, 1848–1918* (1978), 22–25.

30. For the administrative evolution of the navy, see Denkschrift über die Organisation der oberen Marinebehörden, 1848–1871, BAMA, RM 1/1849; and Walther Hubatsch, *Der Admiralstab und die Obersten Marinebehörden in Deutschland, 1848–1945* (1958), 17–18, 220. For personnel developments, see Prussia, Kriegsmarine, *Ranglisten der Königlich Preussischen Marine aus den Jahren 1848 bis 1864* (1894), 2–3. Prince Adalbert held the substantive rank of lieutenant general and inspector general of artillery.
31. Four Prussian midshipmen served aboard USS *St. Lawrence* from November 1848 to July 1849; see "Notes regarding assistance desired by Germany from the United States in forming a Navy, 1848–1849" in Record Group 45, Subject File VI-8, Relations between the United States and Germany, 1849–1910, National Archives, Washington, D.C.
32. Die Entstehung der Preussische-Deutsche Flotte, BAMA, RM 1/1845.
33. For the history of the Frankfurt fleet and the Danish war, see Mantey, *Marinegeschichte,* 48–55, and Steltzer, *Deutsche Flotte,* 45–82.
34. Liste der Offiziere nach dem Stande vom 1 Mai 1850, in Hubatsch, *Deutsche Flotte,* 105–6; and Das Entstehen der heutigen Deutschen Marine aus der ehemähligen Preussischen Flotte von 1848–1852, BAMA, RM 1/1849.
35. Die Entstehung der Preussische-Deutsche Flotte, BAMA, RM 1/1845.
36. Denkschrift über die Organisation der oberen Marinebehörden, 1848–1871, BAMA, RM 1/1849; Witthöft, *Lexikon,* 1:10–11; Hubatsch, *Admiralstab,* 22–23, 220–23; *Rangliste aus 1848–1864,* 13–14.
37. Quoted in Hubatsch, *Admiralstab,* 23–24.
38. Mantey, *Marinegeschichte,* 56–70.
39. Denkschrift über die Organisation der oberen Marinebehörden, and Der Flottengründungsplan von 1863 und seine Abänderungen und Ausführung bis zum Jahre 1872, BAMA, RM 1/1849. See also Paul Koch, "General von Roon als Marineminister," *Marine-Rundschau* 14 (1903): 397–401; and Hubatsch, *Admiralstab,* 25–26, 224–26. The last chief of the Admiralty (1858–61) was Karl Anton Fürst von Hohenzollern-Sigmaringen, whose son, Leopold, inadvertently provided the cause of the Franco-German War of 1870–71.
40. Mantey, *Marinegeschichte,* 73–80.
41. Alfred von Tirpitz, *My Memoirs* (1919), 1:1.
42. Plan zur Gründung der Preussischen Kriegsmarine, 17 June 1865, BAMA, RM 1/2873; Plan zur Erwerbung der Preussische Kriegsmarine von 1865, BAMA, RM 1/1849.
43. Die Entstehung der Preussische-Deutsche Flotte, BAMA, RM 1/1845. See also Gerhard Koop and Erich Mulitze, *Die Marine in Wilhelmshaven* (1997), 7–13;

Michael Salewski, "Kiel und die Marine," in *Geschichte der Stadt Kiel*, ed. Jürgen Jensen and Peter Wulf (1991), 272–86.

44. See Prussia, Marine Ministerium, *Liste der Königlich Preussische Marine pro 1866* (1866).

45. For the development of the Seekadetten-Institut, see Admiralität, RM 1/741, Manteuffel to Friedrich Wilhelm III, 19 April 1855, and AKO, 13 May 1855. For the school's curriculum and training regimen, see Admiralität, RM 1/202, Nachweisung des Königlichen Seekadetten-Institut, 25 January 1865. See also Karl Peter, "Seeoffizieranwärter-Ausbildung in Preussen-Deutschland von 1848–1945," undated manuscript, Militärgeschichteforschüngsamt, Freiburg.

46. Die Entstehung der Preussische-Deutsche Flotte, BAMA, RM 1/1845. See also Lawrence Sondhaus, "'The Spirit of the Army' at Sea: The Prussian-German Naval Officer Corps, 1847–1897," *International History Review* 17 (1995): 459–84.

47. Verordnüng über die Ergänzung der Offizier-Corps der Königlichen Marine, 16 June 1864, BAMA, 1/143; Entwurf zu Grundzügen der Einrichtung der Marineschule, 29 December 1864, BAMA, RM 1/202.

48. Marineministerium to Oberkommando, 11 February 1865, BAMA, RM 1/202. During the Danish War of 1864, according to Tirpitz, the "influx of these uneducated sea-dogs from the merchant service of those days brought many a joke into our mess; we called them Hilfsbarone, and they included some remarkable characters." See Tirpitz, *Memoirs*, 1:2–4.

49. Adalbert to Roon, 24 April and 6 May 1865, BAMA, RM 1/143.

50. Verordnung über die Ergänzung der Offizier-Corps der Königlichen Marine, 16 June 1864, BAMA, RM 1/143.

51. Heldt to Bothwell, 26 August 1865, BAMA, N 255/1.

52. Hans Hildebrand, Albert Röhr, and Hans-Otto Steinmetz, *Die Deutschen Kriegsschiffe* (1982), 5:14–15.

53. Batsch to Marineministerium, 30 June 1865, BAMA, RM 1/1614; Marineministerium to OKM, 15 September 1865, BAMA, RM 1/2460.

54. Entries for 6 and 7 September 1865, BAMA, N 255/43. Diederichs continued the practice of keeping a personal log during gunnery training aboard SMS *Gefion* (1866) and as first officer aboard SMS *Luise* (1878–80) for a mission to East Asia.

55. Kadetten-Institut to OKM, 27 May 1865 and 6 November 1865, BAMA, RM 1/186.

56. Entries for 9–15 September 1865, BAMA, N 255/43.

57. Entries for 16–20 September 1865, BAMA, N 55/43.

58. Entries for 21–28 September 1865, BAMA, N 55/43. For the development of the Kiel naval base, see AKO, 24 March 1865, RM 1/736; AKO, 29 December 1865,

RM 1/1850. See also, Michael Salewski, "Kiel und die Marine," in *Geschichte der Stadt Kiel,* ed. Jürgen Jensen and Peter Wulf (1991), 272–86.
59. Entries for 24–27 September 1865, BAMA, N 255/43.
60. Entries for 3–7 October 1865, BAMA, N 255/43.
61. Entries for 20–21 October 1865, BAMA, N 255/43.
62. Entries for 23–24 October 1865, BAMA, N 255/43.
63. Peter, *Seeoffizieranwärter-Ausbildung,* 114.
64. Entries for 23–30 October, 1–3 November 1865, BAMA, N 255/43. Diederichs's log also contains sketches of several kinds of cannons and the list of commands for firing a 32-lb gun.
65. Entries for 6 and 16 November 1865, BAMA, N 255/43.
66. Entries for 30 November and 1 December 1865, BAMA, N 255/43.
67. Nachweisung der an Bord SM Brigge *Rover* und *Musquito,* 14 September 1865, BAMA, RM 1/2460; see also entry for 3 December 1865, BAMA, N 255/43.
68. Entries for 24 and 25 December 1865, BAMA, N 255/43.
69. Entries for 28 and 29 December 1865, BAMA, N 255/43.
70. Batsch to OKM, 4 December 1865, and Batsch to OKM, 21 December 1865, BAMA, RM 1/2460.
71. Entries for 1 and 6 January 1866, BAMA, N 255/43.
72. BAMA, RM 1/2461, Batsch to OKM, 22 January 1866, BAMA, RM 1/2461; see also entries for 12 and 15 February 1866, BAMA, N 255/43.
73. The book, *Ein Strauss für Schleswig,* inscribed "Ehrengeschenk der Matrose Ottos von Diederichs," is in BAMA, N 255/34. See also entries for 26 February to 22 March 1866, BAMA, N 255/43.
74. Entries for 28 February, 8, 10, 14, and 22 March, and 1 April 1866, BAMA, N 255/43. Batsch used the opportunity to catch up on his correspondence; see Batsch to OKM, 22 February and 18 March 1865, BAMA, RM 1/2461.
75. Entry for 11 April 1866, BAMA, N 255/43.
76. Batsch to OKM, 9 April 1866, BAMA, RM 1/2461.
77. Batsch to OKM, 27 April 1866, BAMA, RM 1/2461; entries for 25 April to 7 May 1866, BAMA, N 255/43. Tirpitz describes the events in his *Memoirs,* 1:6–7. He noted that "we youngsters were disappointed in our joyful anticipation of a fight" once the crisis ended.
78. Entries for 11–14 May 1866, BAMA, N 255/43. For the content of the examination, see Verordnung über die Ergänzung der Offizier-Corps der Königlichen Marine, 16 June 1864, BAMA, RM 1/143.
79. Entries for 20 and 21 May 1865, BAMA, N 255/43. For Diederichs's examination results, see Zeugniss der Reife zum Seecadett für den Matrosen 2te Klasse Ernst Otto von Diederichs, 23 June 1866, BAMA, N 255/1.

80. AKOs, 17 and 24 June 1866, BAMA, RM 1/2827.
81. Hildebrand, *Die Deutschen Kriegsschiffe*, 2:133–35. The war created a major dilemma for Diederichs's good friend, Midshipmen Iwan Oldekop, who received similar orders. Oldekop, a Hanoverian subject, reported aboard *Gefion* even though Hanover entered the war as an Austrian ally.
82. Entries for 23 June to 4 July 1866, BAMA, N 255/43. See also Mantey, *Marinegeschichte,* 84–85.
83. Diederichs's personnel records were later updated to show that he would receive seventeen months' service credit for sea duty for the thirty-four months of merchant marine experience from June 1862 to May 1865; see Stosch to station chief, 26 October 1874, BAMA, N 255/1.
84. Organisation der Marineschule, 15 May 1866, BAMA, RM 1/205; Marineministerium, 5 September 1866, BAMA, RM 1/203.
85. Entry for 30 October 1866, BAMA, N 255/43.
86. Adalbert to Navy Ministry, 18 October 1866; Liebe to OKM, 24 October 1866, BAMA, RM 1/203.
87. Liebe to OKM, 8 and 9 December 1866, BAMA, RM 1/203.
88. AKO, 13 July 1867, BAMA, RM 1/2827.
89. Zeugniss der Reife zum Offizier für den Seekadett Ernst Otto von Diederichs, 18 August 1867, BAMA, N 255/1.
90. For Diederichs's assignments, see Personalbogen, BAMA, N 255/1. For organizational details on the Matrosendivision, see Organisation-Reglement für die Stammdivision der Flotte der Ostsee, 10 January 1868, BAMA, RM 31/1.
91. AKO, 27 August 1867, BAMA, RM 1/2827.
92. "Kurzbiographie," BAMA, N 255/1.
93. "Mit der Dummheit kämpfen Götter selbst vergebens," from Schiller's play about Joan of Arc, *Die Jungfrau von Orleans,* act 3, scene 6.

Chapter 2. Training for Preparedness, 1867–1878

1. Alfred Stenzel, *Kriegsführung zur See: Lehre vom Seekriege* (1913), 18. Stenzel adapted this dictum from Karl von Clausewitz. See particularly, Rolf Hobson, "The German School of Naval Thought and the Origins of the Tirpitz Plan, 1875–1900" (1996).
2. Hildebrand, *Kriegsschiffe,* 141–42; MacLean to OKM, 31 December 1867, BAMA, RM 1/2476. Diederichs did not maintain a personal log aboard *Musquito* as he had in his previous service on *Niobe* and *Gefion*.
3. Mantey, *Marinegeschichte,* 87–94.
4. Übungsbericht SMS *Musquito* von 16 Dezember 1867 bis 1 Juni 1868, undated, BAMA, RM 1/2477.

5. Flottenweiterungsplan von 1867, BAMA, RM 1/1849; Hildebrand, *Kriegsschiffe,* 3:142.
6. Personalbogen, BAMA, N 255/1. For information on the Matrosendivision, see Prussia, *Organisation und Dienstbetrieb der Kaiserlich Deutschen Marine* (1901), 26–28.
7. Personalbogen, BAMA, N 255/1; Hildebrand, *Kriegsschiffe,* 2:135
8. Personalbogen, BAMA, N 255/1; Gröner, *Warships,* 42–43.
9. Witthöft, *Lexikon,* 2:153.
10. Gröner, *Warships,* 84; Hildebrand, *Kriegsschiffe,* 3:26.
11. Jachmann to OKM, 26 June 1869; Ratzeberg to OKM, 26 July 1869; Marine Station der Ostsee to OKM, 16 August 1869, BAMA, RM 1/2529.
12. Personalbogen, BAMA, N 255/1. For promotion policies, Verordnüng über die Ergänzung der Offizier-Corps der Königlichen Marine, 16 June 1864, BAMA, RM 1/143.
13. Übungsbericht SM Brigg *Musquito* von 1 Juni 1869 bis 1 Juni 1870, undated, BAMA, RM 1/2477.
14. See particularly Michael Howard, *The Franco-Prussian War: The German Invasion of France, 1870–1871* (1962); Otto Pflanze, *Bismarck and the Development of Germany* (1963); and David Wetzel, *A Duel of Giants: Bismarck, Napoleon III, and the Origins of the Franco-Prussian War* (2001).
15. Adalbert to Naval Ministry, 26 July 1870, BAMA, RM 1/529; Bericht über die Verteilung unserer Seestreitkräfte in einem Kriege mit Frankreich, 13 July 1870, BAMA, RM 1/2317.
16. Adalbert to Naval Ministry, 26 July 1870, BAMA, RM 1/529; Jachmann to Falckenstein, 18 February 1871, BAMA, RM 1/532.
17. Adalbert to Naval Ministry, 26 July 1870, BAMA, RM 1/529; Gröner, *German Warships,* 1:132–33; Hildebrand, *Kriegsschiffe,* 5:9.
18. Jachmann to Naval Ministry, 31 October 1870, BAMA, RM 1/531.
19. Jachmann to Falckenstein, 18 February 1871, BAMA, RM 1/532.
20. Prussia, General Staff, *The Franco-German War, 1870–1871,* part 1, *History of the War to the Downfall of the Empire,* vol. 1, *From the Outbreak of Hostilities to the Battle of Gravelotte,* trans. F. C. H. Clarke (London: HMSO, 1874), 76–80.
21. Prussia, General Staff, *The Franco-German War, 1870–1871,* part 2, *History of the War to the Downfall of the Empire,* vol. 2, *From the Battle of Gravelotte to the Downfall of the Empire* (London: HMSO, 1876), 424–25.
22. Prussia, General Staff, *The Franco-German War, 1870–1871,* part 2, *History of the War against the Republic,* vol. 1, *From the Investment of Paris to the Re-Occupation of Orleans* (London: HMSO, 1880), 285–87. See also Mantey, *Marinegeschichte,* 95–104; Steltzer, *Deutsche Flotte,* 110–14.

23. "Kurzbiographie," BAMA, N 255/1. Henni was born on 27 June 1853 and baptized on 4 August 1853, Auszug aus dem Geburts- und Taufregister der evangelischen Kirchengemeinde Leer, 1853, BAMA, N 255/1. The Klopp family later became one of the leading families in the river port in part because of their ownership of the international trading firm Bünting & Co; see Heinrich Böckmann to author, 12 May 1990.
24. Jachmann to Falckenstein, 18 February 1871, BAMA, RM 1/2318; Personalbogen, BAMA, N 255/1.
25. Quoted in Steltzer, *Deutsche Flotte*, 117. See also Mantey, *Marinegeschichte*, 104–7.
26. Witthöfft, *Lexikon*, 1:148.
27. Stosch to Gustav Freytag, 24 October 1871; quoted in Hubatsch, *Admiralstab*, 36. Stosch had considerable political ambitions. His progressive politics and friendship with the crown prince made him a major political rival of and liberal alternative to the conservative Chancellor Bismarck. His political conflicts with Bismarck did not always serve the navy well. See, particularly, Frederic B. M. Hollyday, *Bismarck's Rival: A Political Biography of General and Admiral Albrecht von Stosch* (1960).
28. Mantey, *Marinegeschichte*, 110.
29. Denkschrift betreffend eine Darlegung wie weit der in den Motiven zum Anleiche-Gesetz von 9 November 1867 enthaltene Plan für die Entwickelung der Kaiserlichen Marine; Der Flottengründungsplan von 1873; Denkschrift betreffend die weitere Entwicklung der Kaiserlichen Marine, BAMA, RM 1/1849. See also Lambi, *Power Politics*, 4–5.
30. Promemoria betreffend die übergabe des Hafens von Geestemünde und die Königliche Marine, 2 July 1866; Naval Ministry to Hardenberg, 9 July 1866; Olberg to Naval Ministry, BAMA, RM 1/492.
31. Personalbogen, BAMA, N 255/1; RM 1/1617, Vorschläge zur Bildung einer Torpedo-Abteilung, 25 April, 1871, BAMA, RM 1/1617; Olberg to Roon, 28 November 1871, Marine-Intendantur to Marineministerium, 28 January 1872, BAMA, RM 1/493.
32. Stosch to Marinestationen, 10 March 1873, and 20 June 1876, BAMA, RM 1/784.
33. Tirpitz, *Memoirs*, 1:26.
34. Heinrich Böckmann to author, 12 May 1990; "Kurzbiographie," BAMA, N 255/1.
35. Quoted in Tirpitz, *Memoirs*, 1:28.
36. Personalbogen, BAMA, N 255/1; Hildebrand, *Kriegsschiffe*, 2:97.
37. Stosch, Promemoria zum Immediatvortrag, 1 March 1872, BAMA, RM 1/215.
38. Aufgaben zur Bearbeitung, 7 February 1873, BAMA, RM 31/41.

39. Stationsbefehl von 7 September 1872, BAMA, RM 31/41. Later directors included Diederichs's mentor, Rear Admiral Rudolf Schering (1886–90), and friend Vice Adm. Iwan Oldekop (1895–99).
40. Studien-Plan der Vorlesungen, 1872–73, 20 September 1872, BAMA, RM 31/42.
41. Personalbogen, BAMA, N 255/1; AKO, 20 May 1873, BAMA, RM 1/2833.
42. Abgangs-Zeugnis für Marineakademie, 6 July 1874, BAMA, N 255/1.
43. Tages-Rapport, 4 June 1873, BAMA, RM 1/308.
44. Stosch to Henk, 20 May 1873. Ibid. Henk's original proposals are in Henk to Stosch, 11 April 1872, BAMA, RM 1/144.
45. Henk to Stosch, 17 and 24 June, 1 July 1873, BAMA, RM 1/144.
46. Henk to Admiralty, 29 July 1873, BAMA, RM 1/144.
47. Henk to Stosch, 3 and 14 August, 11 September 1873, BAMA, RM 1/144.
48. "Kurzbiographie," BAMA, N 255/1. Fritz also noted that his father suffered later in life from fever, erysipelas, rheumatism, and sciatica. He nonetheless slept long, deep, and well, and never suffered from insomnia.
49. Abgangs-Zeugnis für Marineakademie, 6 July 1874, BAMA, N 255/1.
50. Hildebrand, *Kriegsschiffe,* 5:78–79; see also, Disposition für das Schiessen an Bord SM Artillerieschiff *Renown,* 1874, undated, and Monts to CO/MSNS, 5 September 1874, BAMA, RM 1/2459.
51. See Edwin Gray, *The Devil's Device: Robert Whitehead and the History of the Torpedo* (Annapolis, Md.: Naval Institute Press, 1991).
52. Bestimmungen über die Bildung der Torpedo-Abteilung und die Einrichtung des Torpedowesens, 20 September 1871, BAMA, RM 1/2459. The navy eventually canceled plans to develop a site at Geestemünde.
53. Albert Röhr, "Vorgeschichte und Chronik des Torpedowesens," *Schiff und Zeit* 7 (1978): 47–51.
54. Witthöfft, *Marinelexikon,* 2:102. The *Rangliste für 1875* lists staff members.
55. Diederichs holographically recorded details of his mission in an earlier version, dated 1883, of his service file, which contains information slightly different from the later, official version. Both are in BAMA, N 255/1. See also, Gray, *Devil's Device,* 96–97.
56. Promemoria betreffend die Bildung des Admiralstabes, 19 April 1875, and AKO, 25 May 1875, BAMA, RM 1/120.
57. Kaiser Wilhelm formally designated the serving officers in AKO, 14 December 1875, BAMA, RM 1/2835.
58. Bernhard Sage to author, 13 February 2001. *Elbe* sank during a torpedo test on 17 September 1881.
59. Personalbogen, BAMA, N 255/1; Hildebrand, *Kriegsschiffe,* 6:70–71. For Zieten's fitting out, see Admiralty to Mensing, 29 June 1876; Tages-Rapport, 12 August, 13, 16, 17 September 1876, BAMA, RM 1/2654.

60. Stosch to Werner, 10 and 19 May 1877, BAMA, RM 31/38.
61. Diederichs to Werner, 25 May 1877, BAMA, RM 31/38.
62. Stosch to Werner, 6 June 1877; Diederichs to Werner, 11 June 1877, BAMA, RM 31/38.
63. Knorr to Werner, 20 June 1877, BAMA, RM 31/453.
64. Heusner to MSNS, 27 September 1877; Tages-Rapport, 28 September 1877, BAMA, RM 31/453.
65. Tages-Rapport, 2 October 1877, BAMA, RM 31/453.
66. Werner to Diederichs, 31 December 1877, BAMA, RM 31/453.
67. Personalbogen, BAMA, N 255/1.
68. Stosch to Werner, 29 November 1877 and 20 December 1877; Geschäftsordnung für die Kommission zur Bearbeitung eines Armierungs Plan für SMS Zieten, 5 January 1878, BAMA, RM 3/453.
69. Tages-Rapport, 16 April 1878, BAMA, RM 3/453. See also Goltz to Marinestation, 6 March 1878; Stosch to Marinestation, 8 April 1878; Tages-Rapport, 6 May 1878.
70. *Rangliste für 1877–1878*, 12.
71. Oldekop to Diederichs, 18 January 1878, BAMA, N 255/8.
72. Jeschke to Diederichs, 12 February 1878, BAMA, N 255/8.
73. AKO, 29 January 1878, and Stosch to Werner, 26 December 1877, BAMA, RM 1/319.
74. Schering to Diederichs, 2 May 1878, BAMA, RM 1/319.
75. Oldekop to Diederichs, 7 May 1878, BAMA, RM 1/319.
76. Barandon to Diederichs, 15 July 1878, BAMA, RM 1/319.
77. Personalbogen, BAMA, N 255/1.
78. Barandon to Diederichs, 15 July 1878, BAMA, N 255/1.
79. "Kurzbiographie," BAMA, N 255/1.
80. AKO, 13 August 1897, BAMA, RM 1/2838.

Chapter 3. To East Asia, 1878–1880

1. Mantey, *Marinegeschichte*, 46–47, 60–63.
2. Boelcke, *So Kam das Meer zu Uns*, 13–24, 235–39.
3. Holographic notes, folio 59–60, BAMA, N 255/1; Michael Salewski, "Die Preussische Expedition nach Japan, 1859–1861," *Revue Internationale d'Histoire Militaire* 70 (1988): 39–57.
4. Admiralität, *Die Preussische Expedition nach Ost-Asien* (Berlin: Decker, 1873), 4:353–68.
5. Jachmann to OKM, 18 January 1868, BAMA, RM 1/819.
6. Brandt to Bülow, 24 July 1877, BAMA, RM 1/2381.
7. Stosch to Schering, 10 September 1878, BAMA, RM 1/2639.

8. Personalbogen, BAMA, N 255/1.
9. Gröner, *German Warships,* 1:86–87; Hildebrand, *Kriegsschiffe,* 4:97–98.
10. Entry for 20 November 1878, BAMA, N 255/43.
11. Entries for 21–27 November 1878, BAMA, N 255/43.
12. Stosch to Schering, 11 November 1878, and Admiralty order, 7 August 1878, BAMA, RM 1/2639.
13. Entries for 30 November and 1–3 December 1878, BAMA, N 255/43.
14. Entries for 4–7 December 1878, BAMA, N 255/43; Schering to Admiralty, 7 December 1878, BAMA, RM 1/2639.
15. Promemoria, 12 October 1878; Schering to Admiralty, 16 December 1878, BAMA, RM 1/2639.
16. Entries for 9–17 December 1878, BAMA, N 255/43.
17. Schering to Admiralty, 23 December 1878, RM 1/2639; entries for 23–29 December 1878, BAMA, N 255/43.
18. Entries for 31 December 1878, 1 and 2 January 1879, BAMA, N 255/43.
19. Schering to Admiralty, 25 January 1879, BAMA, RM 1/2639; entries for 8–18 January 1879, BAMA, N 255/43.
20. Schering to Admiralty, 19 and 25 January 1879, BAMA, RM 1/2639; entries for 20–27 January 1879, BAMA, N 255/43.
21. Schering to Admiralty, 14 February 1879, BAMA, RM 1/2639; entries for 2–8 February 1879, BAMA, N 255/43.
22. Entries for 29 January–9 February 1879, BAMA, N 255/43.
23. Schering to Admiralty, 22 February 1879; Schering to Admiralty, 10 March 1879, BAMA, RM 1/2639.
24. Schering to Admiralty, 10 March 1879, BAMA, RM 1/2639.
25. Entries for 24 February to 2 March 1879, BAMA, N 255/43; Schering to Admiralty, 10 March 1879, BAMA, RM 1/2639.
26. Schering to Admiralty, 5 April 1879, BAMA, RM 1/2639; entries for 17–26 March 1879, BAMA, N 255/43.
27. Entries for 29 March–10 April 1879, BAMA, N 255/43.
28. Entries for 15 and 16 April 1879, BAMA, N 255/43.
29. Entries for 30 April and 1 May 1879, BAMA, N 255/43.
30. Entries for 5, 8, 9, 13–16, 19–21, and 24 May 1879, BAMA, N 255/43; Schering to Admiralty, 17 June 1879, BAMA, RM 1/2639.
31. Schering to Brandt, 12 April 1879, BAMA, RM 1/2381.
32. Brandt to Schering, 28 April 1879, BAMA, RM 1/2381.
33. Schering to Brandt, 14 May 1879, BAMA, RM 1/2381.
34. See chapter six.
35. Entry for 29–31 May 1879, BAMA, N 255/43.
36. Schering to Admiralty, 17 June 1879, BAMA, RM 1/2639.

37. Entry for 27 June 1879, BAMA, RM 1/2639.
38. Schering to Admiralty, 26 July 1879, BAMA, RM 1/2639.
39. Entries for 11, 18, and 31 July 1879, BAMA, N 255/43; Schering to Admiralty, 26 July 1879 and 2 September 1879, BAMA, RM 1/2639.
40. Schering to Admiralty, 26 July 1879, BAMA, RM 1/2639.
41. Entries for 3, 4, 7, 8, 11, 23, and 24 July 1879, BAMA, N 255/43.
42. Entries for 6, 7, 8, 12 August 1879, BAMA, N 255/43.
43. Schering to Admiralty, 2 September 1879, BAMA, RM 1/2639; entries for 6, 14, 30, 31 August 1879, BAMA, N 255/43.
44. Brandt to Schering, 18 August 1879, BAMA, RM 1/2639.
45. Schering to Admiralty, 29 September, 24 October, and 1 November 1879; Brandt to Schering, 18 August 1879; Schering to Second Matrosendivision (Wilhemshaven), BAMA, RM 1/2639; entries for 12, 13, 14, 16, 26 September 1879, BAMA, N 255/43.
46. Entries, 12–14, 16, and 26 September 1879, BAMA, N 255/43.
47. Entry for 21 October 1879, BAMA, N 255/43.
48. *North China Daily News,* 23 and 24 March 1880.
49. Schering to Admiralty, 1 November and 1 December 1879, 1 January 1880, BAMA, RM 1/2639.
50. Quoted in *North China Daily News,* 23 February 1880.
51. Schering to Admiralty, 31 January 1880, BAMA, RM 1/2639; entries for 14, 18, 20 February and 21, 23, 25, 27, and 28 March 1880, BAMA, N 255/43.
52. Entry for 8 March 1879, BAMA, N 255/43.
53. Hsü, *Ili Crisis,* 57–74.
54. Schering to Admiralty, 1 and 23 March 1880, BAMA, RM 1/2639.
55. *North China Daily News,* 25 March 1880.
56. Brandt to Schering, 17 March 1880, BAMA, RM 1/2639.
57. Brandt to Schering, 12 April 1880, BAMA, RM 1/2639.
58. Schering to Admiralty, 1 June 1880, BAMA, RM 1/2639.
59. Schering to Admiralty, 1 July 1880, BAMA, RM 1/2639.
60. Schering to Admiralty, 3 July 1880; Hohenlohe to Stosch, 29 June 1880, BAMA, RM 1/2639.
61. Schering to Admiralty, 17 July 1880, BAMA, RM 1/2639. Diederichs arranged to purchase nearly 150 tons of coal for a total cost of 48 marks. Schering's report also cited the presence of three German firms and twenty-five nationals in Saigon.
62. Stosch to Hohenlohe, 25 June 1880, BAMA, RM 1/2639.
63. Schering to Admiralty, 9 August 1880, BAMA, RM 1/2639.
64. Schering to Admiralty, 19 August 1880, BAMA, RM 1/2639.
65. Schering to Admiralty, 10 September 1880, BAMA, RM 1/2639.

66. Schering to Admiralty, 4 November 1880, BAMA, RM 1/2639.
67. Promemoria, 10 May 1880; Wilhelm to Monts, 10 May 1880, BAMA, RM 1/2385; Berger to Admiralty, 20 November 1880, BAMA, RM 1/2639.
68. Berger to Admiralty, 20 November 1880, BAMA, RM 1/2639.
69. The model is currently on display at the Laboe Naval Museum near Kiel.

Chapter 4. Defending the Coasts, 1880–1890

1. *Rangliste für 1881*, 20–22.
2. Organisation der Marineakademie und Schule, 16 October 1875, BAMA, RM 1/184.
3. James Soley, *Report on Foreign Systems of Naval Education* (1880), 173–89.
4. Entwurf zu einem Lehrplan der Marineakademie, 1875, BAMA, RM 31/41.
5. Stunden-Plan, 1880–1881, 22 September 1880, BAMA, RM 31/42.
6. Rolf Hobson, "The German School of Naval Thought and the Origins of the Tirpitz Plan, 1875–1890," *Institut für Forsvarsstudier* 2 (1996): 22.
7. See Stenzel, *Kriegsführung zur See*.
8. Personalbogen, BAMA, N 255/1.
9. Diederichs reviewed early German operational planning in Immediatvortrag, 17 February 1900, BAMA, RM 5/879.
10. Knorr, Verfügung, 12 March 1882, BAMA, RM 5/1631.
11. Die Verwendung der Flotte im Krieg gegen Russland, 3 June 1882; Allgemeiner Kriegsplan, 4 August 1882, BAMA, RM 5/1631.
12. Mobilization plan, 28 July 1882, BAMA, RM 5/1631. For details on *Blücher* see Hildebrand, *Kriegsschiffe*, 1:150–51; for details on the division's ships see Gröner, *German Warships*, 1:42–44, 84–85.
13. Stosch report, 22 September 1882, BAMA, RM 1/2862.
14. Betrachtungen über die Verteidigung der Deutschen Küsten gegen Seemächte, welche gleichzeitig von Ostsee und Nordsee auftreten, 9 November 1882, BAMA, RM 1/2862.
15. Lambi, *Power Politics*, 12–14. Fritz von Diederichs makes several references to his father's admiration for Moltke; see, particularly, "Kurzbiographie," BAMA, N 255/1.
16. The navy began construction of the canal in 1887. Kaiser Wilhelm II officially opened the Kaiser Wilhelm Canal in 1895.
17. Betrachtungen über die Verteidigung der Deutschen Küsten gegen Seemächte, welche gleichzeitig von Ostsee und Nordsee auftreten, 9 November 1882, BAMA, RM 1/2862.
18. Tages-Rapport, 1 May 1883, BAMA, RM 1/2544.
19. Wickede to Admiralty, 8 February 1883; Übungs-Programm der Panzer-Geschwader, March 1883, BAMA, RM 1/335.

20. Wickede to Admiralty, 28 May and 21 June 1883, BAMA, RM 1/335.
21. Wickede to Admiralty, 19 and 29 July 1883, 1 September 1883, BAMA, RM 1/335.
22. Personalbogen, BAMA, N 255/1.
23. Tirpitz, *Memoirs*, 1:37. See also Sondhaus, *Weltpolitik*, 150–153.
24. Personalbogen, BAMA, N 255/1.
25. Denkschrift betreffend die weitere Entwickelung der Kaiserliche Marine, 5 December 1883, BAMA, RM 1/1848. Caprivi submitted the memorandum to the Reichstag in March 1884 for approval; see Germany, Reichstag, *Stenographische Berichte,* V Legislativ-Periode, IV Session, 1884, vol. 3, Anlage, Nr. 26.
26. See particularly Theodore Ropp, *The Development of a Modern Navy: French Naval Policy, 1871–1904* (1987), 155–80.
27. Denkschrift betreffend die weitere Entwickelung der Kaiserliche Marine, 5 December 1883, BAMA, RM 1/1848.
28. Mantey, *Marinegeschichte*, 136–45. See also, A. Harding Ganz, "The Role of the Imperial German Navy in Colonial Affairs," Ph.D. diss., Ohio State University, 1972.
29. Personalbogen, BAMA, N 255/1.
30. Hildebrand, *Kriegsschiffe,* 5:134–35. *Stosch* returned to service in 1888 as a training ship.
31. Personalbogen, BAMA, N 255/1. Family photo albums provide interior and exterior views of the new home; see BAMA, N 255/44.
32. Personalbogen, BAMA, N 255/1; AKO, 25 March 1885, BAMA, RM 1/2845.
33. Exercier-Reglement für die Flotte, BAMA, RM 1/253.
34. See, for example, Carl L. Boyd, "The Ten Wasted Years, 1888–1898: The Kaiser Finds an Admiral," *Journal of the Royal United Service Institution* 111 (1966): 291–97.
35. AKO, 16 April 1887, BAMA, RM 1/2848; Personalbogen, BAMA, N 255/1.
36. Tages-Rapport, 16 August 1887, BAMA, RM 1/2729; Indienststellung von Schiffen und Fahrzeugen für 1887, BAMA, RM 1/2615.
37. Caprivi to stations, 2 February 1887, BAMA, RM 1/345.
38. Gröner, *Warships,* 137–38.
39. Personalbogen, BAMA, N 255/1.
40. Tirpitz, *Memoirs,* 1:39; Arden Bucholz, *Moltke, Schlieffen, and Prussian War Planning* (1993), 29–35.
41. Diederichs to Caprivi, 23 March 1888, BAMA, RM 1/563; Tages-Rapports for 26 April, 3 May, and 16 May 1888, BAMA, RM 1/2615. The operational plan is in Denkschrift über Küstenkrieg in der Nordsee, 20 October 1887, BAMA, RM 5/1656.
42. Tages-Rapport, 16 August 1887; MSNS to Admiralty, 24 August 1888; Admiralty to MSNS [Marinestation der Nord See], 25 August 1888, BAMA, RM 1/2729.

43. AKO, 24 January 1888; Zeit-Einteilung für die Sommer-Übungen, 24 January 1888, BAMA, RM 1/339; Knorr to Admiralty, 14 September, 1888, BAMA, RM 1/2729.
44. Personalbogen; AKO, 20 January 1889, BAMA, N 255/1.
45. BAMA, RM 1/2530, Goltz to MSNS, 1 March 1889; N 255/1, Personalbogen.
46. Ordre de bataille für die Manöverflotte 1889, 6 February 1889, BAMA, RM 1/340; Goltz reported *Bayern*'s boiler problems in Goltz to stations, 19 March 1889, BAMA, RM 1/2685. See also, Hildebrand, *Kriegsschiffe,* 5:89–91.
47. Personalbogen, BAMA, N 255/1.

Chapter 5. The Kaiser's Navy, 1890–1897

1. Biographical works include Lamar Cecil, *Wilhelm II: Prince and Emperor, 1859–1900* (1989–1996); Michael Balfour, *The Kaiser and His Times* (1964); John C. G. Röhl, *Germany without Bismarck: The Crisis of Government in the Second Reich, 1890–1900* (1967) and *The Kaiser and His Court: Wilhelm II and the Government of Germany* (1987); and Thomas Kohut, *Wilhelm II and the Germans: A Study in Leadership* (1991).
2. "Kurzbiographie," BAMA, N 255/1; Diederichs to Fritz von Diederichs, 20 and 25 December 1902, N 255/6.
3. Carl L. Boyd, "The Wasted Ten Years," 291.
4. Quoted in Michael Balfour, *The Kaiser and His Times,* 124.
5. Notizen und Aufzeichnungen, 1888–1901, BAMA, N 260/11.
6. Wilhelm implemented these changes with two AKOs, dated 28 and 30 March 1889, RM 2/2823. See also Hubatsch, *Admiralstab,* 49–53.
7. Personalbogen, BAMA, N 255/1.
8. Gary E. Weir, *Building the Kaiser's Navy: The Imperial Navy Office and German Industry in the von Tirpitz Era, 1890–1919* (1992), 16–17; Tjard Schwarz and Ernst von Halle, *Die Schiffbauindustrie in Deutschland und im Auslande,* vol. 2, *Der deutsche Schiffbau* (1902), 155–67.
9. Folio 14, BAMA, N 255/1.
10. Qualifikationsbericht für 1 January 1891, BAMA, RM 2/827. Superior officers submitted fitness reports on their subordinates in writing to the emperor, by way of Senden, every new year.
11. Gröner, *Warships,* 1:8–13.
12. Alfred Thayer Mahan, *The Influence of Sea Power on History, 1660–1783* (1890).
13. Quoted in William E. Livezey, *Mahan on Sea Power* (1947), 124.
14. Tirpitz, *Memoirs,* 1:62.
15. Unsere Maritim-Militärische Fortentwickelung, April 1891, BAMA, N 253/42. See also Lambi, *Power Politics,* 63–65.

16. Denkschrift über die Neuorganisation unserer Panzerflotte, n.d., BAMA, N 253/56.
17. Tirpitz, *Memoirs,* 1:75.
18. Lambi, *Power Politics,* 91–112.
19. See, particularly, "Kurzbiographie," BAMA, N 255/1; Diederichs to Fritz von Diederichs, 20 and 25 December 1898, BAMA, N 255/6.
20. Senden to Tirpitz, 2 September 1891, BAMA, N 253/308.
21. Qualifikationsbericht für 1 Januar 1892, BAMA, RM 2/827.
22. *Rangliste für 1893,* 27.
23. See particularly Walter R. Herrick, *The American Naval Revolution* (1966); and William Braisted, *The United States Navy in the Pacific, 1897–1909* (1969).
24. Hollmann to Diederichs, 27 April 1893, BAMA, N 255/21.
25. Paunceforte to Diederichs, 24 May 1893, BAMA, N 255/21; see also Doris D. Maguire, ed., *French Ensor Chadwick: Selected Letters and Papers* (1981).
26. See Taylor Peck, *Round-Shot to Rockets: A History of the Washington Navy Yard and U.S. Naval Gun Factory* (1949).
27. Harris to Diederichs, 11 May 1898; Chadwick to Diederichs, 17 August 1893, BAMA, N 255/21.
28. Windsor Hotel receipt, 8 June 1893, BAMA, N 255/21.
29. Mary Anne Cowell and Edward C. Whitman, "Newport and Navy Torpedoes: An Enduring Legacy," *Undersea Warfare* 2 (2000), Internet www.chinfolnavy.mil /navpalib/cno/n87/usw/issue7/newport.htm [accessed 24 July 2001].
30. See Dienstschrift X: Das für den diesjährigen Sommerkursus beabsichtige Programm des Naval War College, 9 August 1894, BAMA, N 253/34.
31. Witthöft, *Marinelexikon,* 1:188.
32. Relation über die Herbstmanöver der Marine im Jahre 1893, BAMA, RM 4/62; Erfahrung aus dem Sommer 1893 über Verwendung der Schiffsartillerie und Aufgaben für 1894, 14 March 1894, BAMA, N 253/34.
33. Valois to Diederichs, 8 November 1893, BAMA, N 255/21.
34. "Fackelzug auf der Kaiserlichen Werft in Gaarden bei Kiel," 28 October 1893, BAMA, N 25/45.
35. *Rangliste für 1894,* 17–18.
36. AKO, 2 January 1894, BAMA, RM 1/2857; Personalbogen, BAMA, N 255/1.
37. The photograph is in BAMA, N 255/21. Wilhelm added a holographic note, "Zur Errinerung an den 20/II 1894, Wilhelmshaven."
38. Hildebrand, *Kriegsschife,* 4:36.
39. Dienstschrift IX, Allgemeine Erfahrungen aud den Manövern der Herbstübungsflotte, 16 June 1894, BAMA, N 253/51.
40. Generalidee für das Kaisermanöver; Generalidee für das II. Manöver; Specialbestimmungen für das Deutsche Geschwader, n.d., BAMA, RM 4/64.

41. Kurzbiographie and Personalbogen, BAMA, N 255/1.
42. Tirpitz to Diederichs, 27 June 1895, BAMA, N 255/8.
43. Witthöfft, *Marinelexikon,* 2:14. A second stage of construction, begun in 1907 to reflect the construction of *Dreadnought*-class battleships, widened the canal to one hundred meters and deepened it to eleven meters.
44. Hildebrand, *Kriegsschiffe,* 4:108.
45. Senden to Diederichs, 6 January 1895, BAMA, N 255/8.
46. Knorr toWilhelm, 10 December 1895, BAMA, RM 2/827.
47. Qualifikationsbericht für 1 Januar 1896, BAMA, RM 2/827.
48. AKO, 13 August 1895, BAMA, N 255/1.
49. Witthöfft, *Marinelexikon,* 1:157. Witthöft describes Knorr as a "bold daredevil with a vehement temperament."
50. Bendemann to Diederichs, 27 October, 1 November, and 1 December 1895, BAMA, N 255/8; Diederichs to Tirpitz, 30 November 1896, BAMA, N 253/261.
51. Knorr, Immediatbericht betreffend der Etatenwurf der Marine, 28 November 1895; AKO, 16 December 1895; Tirpitz, Immediatbericht betreffend der Vorschläge des Kommandierenden Admirals zum Schiffbauprogramm, December 1895, BAMA, N 253/3.
52. Wilhelm Langer, *The Diplomacy of Imperialism, 1890–1902* (1972), 222–48. Paul Kennedy, *The Rise of the Anglo-German Antagonism, 1860–1914* (1980), 220–22.
53. Wilhelm II, *Die Reden Kaiser Wilhelms II* (1904), 2:9.
54. Tirpitz, Annahme des Staatssekretäramtes, 28 January 1898, BAMA, N 253/3.
55. The events of Tirpitz's campaign for office are well told elsewhere; see particularly Hallmann, *Der Weg,* 183–87; Steinberg, *Yesterday's Deterrent,* 61–97; and Lambi, *Power Politics,* 113–17.
56. Senden to Tirpitz, 21 March 1896, BAMA, N 160/5.
57. Hopman, *Logbuch,* 217.
58. Geschichtspunkte für einen Operationsplan der heimischen Streitkräfte bei einem Kriege Deutschland allein gegen England allein, 5 March 1896, BAMA, RM 5/1609. See also Paul Kennedy, "The Development of German Naval Operations against England, 1896–1914," *The English Historical Review* 89 (1974): 48–76; and Lambi, *Power Politics,* 120–21.
59. Spending money on coastal defense also violated the Tirpitz plan, which wanted to focus all funding on the development of the battle fleet. Diederichs nonetheless persisted in this idea while chief of the *Admiralstab* after 1899.
60. Seiner Exzellenz Vorzulegen, 23 April 1896, BAMA, RM 5/1609.
61. Diederichs to Koester, 25 April 1896, BAMA, RM 4/83.
62. Diederichs to Tirpitz, 30 November 1896, BAMA, N 253/361.
63. Seiner Exzellenz mit Folgenden gehorsamst vorgelegt, 12 July 1896, BAMA, RM 4/83.

64. Programm für die Übungsflotte, 1896, BAMA, RM 4/83.
65. Diederichs to Tirpitz, 30 November 1896, BAMA, N 253/361.
66. AKO, 10 and 12 October 1896, BAMA, N 255/1.
67. Diederichs to Tirpitz, 30 November 1896, BAMA, N 253/361.
68. Diederichs to Tirpitz, 30 November 1896, BAMA, N 253/361.

CHAPTER 6. A MAILED FIST, 1897–1898

1. "Die Besetzung von Tsingtau, 14 November 1897," 1, BAMA, N 255/24. Diederichs wrote a detailed account of his involvement in the seizure of Kiaochou Bay between 1906 and 1908, basing it on his own memory, official documents, and contemporary correspondence with wife Henni, son Fritz, and various naval colleagues. Fritz von Diederichs transcribed the document in 1939. Diederichs's handwritten manuscript is in N 255/23 with the original transcription in RM 3/11938.
2. Qualifikationsbericht für January 1897, BAMA, RM 2/827.
3. Besetzung, 2, BAMA, N 255/24.
4. Prussia, *Die Preussiche Expedition nach Ost-Asien* (Berlin: Decker, 1873), 4:353–68.
5. Promemoria, 10 May 1880, BAMA, RM 1/2385.
6. Joseph Conrad, *Heart of Darkness*, 78.
7. Annual *Rangliste* note the presence only of gunboats *Wolf* and *Iltis* from 1880 to 1893.
8. See, for example, John Rawlinson, *China's Struggle for Naval Development, 1839–1895* (1967), and Lillian Dotson, *The Sino-Japanese War of 1894–1895: A Study in Asian Power Politics* (1967).
9. AKO, 25 September 1894; Goltz to Hollmann, 6 October 1894, BAMA, RM 4/83.
10. AKO, 16 January 1895, BAMA, RM 4/83.
11. Hoffmann to Knorr, 12 November 1895, BAMA, RM 3/6692.
12. Jachmann to OKM, 18 January 1868, BAMA, RM 1/819. Diederichs reviewed these issues, adding pertinent documents, in Besetzung, 4–7, BAMA, N 255/24.
13. Wilhelm to Hohenlohe, 17 November 1894, Politisches Archivs des Auswärtiges Amtes, Bonn, Federal Republic of Germany, R 18156.
14. Hollmann to Marschall, 17 April 1895, BAMA, RM 5/5928.
15. Hohenlohe to Wilhelm, 19 March 1895, BAMA, RM 5/5928.
16. Marschall to Hatzfeldt, 1 February 1895, BAMA, RM 5/5928.
17. No. 595: Heyking to Holstein, 17 January 1897, in Norman Rich and M. H. Fishers, eds., *The Holstein Papers*, vol. 4, *Correspondence, 1897–1909* (Cambridge: Cambridge University Press, n.d.), 4–5.
18. Schenck to Hohenlohe, 23 November 1894; Marschall to Hatzfeldt, 1 February 1895; and Hohenlohe to Wilhelm, 19 March 1895, PAAA, R 18156; Marschall to

Hollmann, 11 March 1895; and Hollmann to Marschall, 17 April 1895, BAMA, RM 5/5928.

19. See, particularly, Minge C. Bee, "Origins of German Far Eastern Policy," *Chinese Social and Political Science Review* 21 (1937): 65–97.

20. Wilhelm to Knorr, 23 September 1895, PAAA, R 18159. See also Ralph Norem, "German Catholic Missions in Shantung," *The Chinese Social and Political Science Review* 19 (1935–36): 45–64.

21. Hoffmann to Knorr, 8 October 1895, and Knorr to Wilhelm, 10 October 1895, BAMA, RM 5/5915.

22. Marschall to Hohenlohe, 2 September 1895, PAAA, R 18158.

23. Knorr, Immediatvortrag, 8 November 1895, BAMA, RM 38/28.

24. Hoffmann to Knorr, 8 October 1895 and 12 November 1895, BAMA, RM 5/5915; Knorr to Wilhelm, 10 October, 1895; Senden to Knorr, 3 November 1895, and Hoffmann to Knorr, 26 August 1895, BAMA, RM 3/6692; Hollmann to Marschall, 17 April 1895, BAMA, RM 5/5928; Knorr to Wilhelm, 8 November 1895, BAMA, RM 38/28; Diederichs to Henni von Diederichs, 15 November 1897; and N 255/6, Diederichs to Fritz von Diederichs, 4 April 1898, BAMA, N 255/4.

25. Diederichs to Marschall, 21 April 1896, PAAA, R 2231.

26. Tirpitz, *Memoirs*, 1:91.

27. Tirpitz to Knorr, 21 November 1896, BAMA, RM 38/29.

28. Tirpitz to Knorr, 5 September 1896, BAMA, N 253/45.

29. Senden to Tirpitz, 22 November 1896, BAMA, N 253/45. Senden termed Diederichs's dismissal as "extremely unfortunate" and praised his tenure as chief of staff. He attributed the problem to irreconcilable policy differences with Knorr. He bemoaned Diederichs's future, "No one knows what will happen to him since he has already declined appointment to the Inspectorate. Nor do I know who will succeed him."

30. Tirpitz to Senden, 21 January 1897, quoted in Steinberg, *Yesterday's Deterrent*, 103.

31. Knorr, Immediatvortrag, 28 November 1896, BAMA, RM 3/6693.

32. Knorr, Immediatvortrag, 15 December 1896, BAMA, RM 2/1855.

33. Hoffmann to Franzius, 17 December 1896, BAMA, RM 3/6693. Franzius described his experiences in *Kiautschou: Deutschlands Erwerbung in Ostasien* (1902).

34. Tirpitz deleted the phrase "such as Germany" in the final draft transmitted to the OKM. The original draft is in Tirpitz to Knorr, 6 December 1896, BAMA, RM 38/28; the final draft is in Tirpitz to Knorr, 6 December 1896, BAMA, N 253/45.

35. Besetzung, 8, BAMA, N 255/24.

36. Diederichs to Henni von Diederichs, 4, 6, and 13 May 1897, BAMA, N255/4; Besetzung, 2–3, BAMA, N 255/24.
37. Besetzung, 3–4, BAMA, N 255/24; Diederichs also described the incident in Diederichs to Henni von Diederichs, 31 May 1897, BAMA, N 255/4.
38. Diederichs to Henni von Diederichs, 3 and 6 June 1897, BAMA, N 255/4.
39. Diederichs to Henni von Diederichs, 6 June 1897, BAMA, N 255/4; Zeye to OKM, 6 June 1897, BAMA, RM 3/3156.
40. Franzius, Untersuchung den Häfen an der ostasiatischen Küste, 27 August 1897, BAMA, RM 3/6693.
41. Diederichs described his discussions with Franzius, "who sends heartfelt greetings," in BAMA, N 255/4, Diederichs to Henni von Diederichs, 13 June 1897, BAMA, N 255/4. He also based his account on a conversation with his new flag lieutenant, Lt. Cdr. Gustav von Ammon; see Besetzung, 8, BAMA, N 255/24. For Zeye's report, see Zeye to OKM, 10 June 1897, BAMA, RM 3/6697. Zeye returned from East Asia in early 1898 to a post in Tirpitz's RMA. His ploy, however, failed to secure him the acclaim he sought.
42. Tätigskeitbericht [action report] für Juni 1897, BAMA 3/3156.
43. Diederichs to Knorr, 30 August 1897, BAMA, RM 38/28.
44. Diederichs to Knorr, 21 August 1897, BAMA, RM 3/6694.
45. Besetzung, 8, BAMA, N 255/24.
46. Tätigskeitbericht für Juni 1897, BAMA 3/3156; Diederichs to Henni von Diederichs, 27 June 1897, BAMA, N 255/4.
47. Besetzung, 10, BAMA, N 255/24; Diederichs to Henni von Diederichs, 6 and 10 July, BAMA, N 255/4.
48. Diederichs to Knorr, 21 August 1897, BAMA, RM 3/6694.
49. Besetzung, 9, BAMA, N 255/24; Diederichs to Henni von Diederichs, 6 July 1897, BAMA, N 255/4.
50. Diederichs to Knorr, 21 August 1897, BAMA, RM 3/6694.
51. Tätigskeitbericht für Juli 1897, BAMA, RM 3/3156; Besetzung, 11, BAMA, N 255/24; Diederichs to Henni von Diederichs, 22 July 1897, BAMA, N 255/4.
52. Diederichs to Henni von Diederichs, 30 July 1897, BAMA, N 255/4.
53. Diederichs to Henni von Diederichs, 24 and 26 August 1897, BAMA, N 255/4.
54. Diederichs, Militär-Politische Bericht über die Lage in China, 21 August 1897, BAMA, RM 5/5930.
55. Diederichs to Henni von Diederichs, 3, 13, and 19 September 1897, BAMA, N 255/4.
56. Diederichs to Henni von Diederichs, 6 and 8 October 1897, BAMA, N 255/4.
57. Diederichs to Henni, 14 October 1897, BAMA, N 255/4; Tätigskeitbericht für October 1897, BAMA, RM 3/3156. The Diederichs-Buller correspondence is in BAMA, N 255/9.

58. Tätigskeitbericht für October 1897, BAMA, RM 3/3156; Diederichs to Henni von Diederichs, 19 October 1897, BAMA, N 255/4.
59. Diederichs to Knorr, 30 August 1897, BAMA, RM 38/28.
60. Tirpitz to Bülow, 12 October 1897, PAAA, R 18167.
61. Senden to Diederichs, 7 October 1897, BAMA, N 255/8.
62. Koester to Diederichs, 14 October 1897; and Koester to Tirpitz, 14 October 1897, BAMA, RM 3/6693.
63. Koester to Tirpitz, 2 November 1897, BAMA, RM 3/6694. Tirpitz later claimed credit for the decision to select Kiao-chou; see, Tirpitz, *Memoirs*, 1:91–98. Admiral Koester, however, properly credited Diederichs for the final decision; see Koester to Diederichs, 30 December 1897, BAMA, N 255/8.
64. Besetzung, 13–14, BAMA, N 255/24.
65. Brussatis to Diederichs, 31 October 1897, BAMA, RM 3/5930. Brussatis submitted a more formal and lengthier report in Brussatis to Diederichs, 31 October 1897, BAMA, RM 3/5931.
66. Diederichs to OKM, 1 November 1897, BAMA, RM 5/5930.
67. Koester to Tirpitz, 1 November 1897; Koester to Foreign Ministry, 1 November 1897; Koester to Diederichs, 3 November 1897, BAMA, RM 5/5930.
68. Diederichs to Henni von Diederichs, 4 November 1897, BAMA, N 255/4.
69. Besetzung, 14, BAMA, N 255/24.
70. Heyking to Diederichs, 6 November 1897, BAMA, RM 5/5930.
71. Norem, "German Missions," 45–50. The *Ta Tao Hui* were part of the Boxer movement.
72. Diederichs to Knorr, 6 and 7 November 1897, BAMA, RM 2/1835.
73. Hohenlohe to Wilhelm, 6 November 1897, BAMA, RM 2/1835.
74. Wilhelm to Hohenlohe, 6 November 1897, BAMA, RM 2/1835.
75. Quoted in Gerd Fesser, "'Hunderte deutscher Kaufleute werden Jauchzen,'" *Die Zeit*, 21 November 1997, 16.
76. Wilhelm to Diederichs, 7 November 1897, BAMA, RM 2/1835.
77. Diederichs to Knorr, 8 November 1897, BAMA, RM 2/1835.
78. Besetzung, 16, BAMA, N 255/24.
79. Tätigskeitbericht für November 1897, BAMA, RM 3/3156.
80. Diederichs to Knorr, 15 November 1897, BAMA, RM 3/6697.
81. Besetzung, 17, BAMA, N 255/24.
82. Diederichs to Henni von Diederichs, 10 November 1897, BAMA, N 255/4.
83. Besetzung, 17, BAMA, N 255/24.
84. *Prinzess Wilhelm* Kriegstagebuch, 11 and 12 November 1897, BAMA, RM 38/31.
85. Besetzung, 18, BAMA, N 255/24.
86. Diederichs to Fritz von Diederichs, 4 April 1898, BAMA, N 255/6.

87. Besetzung, 20–22, BAMA, N 255/24.
88. Anhang, BAMA, N 255/24. Diederichs's formal report, which also included a copy of the proclamation is in Diederichs to Knorr, 15 November 1897, BAMA, RM 3/6697. War diaries for *Prinzess Wilhelm* (RM 38/31) and *Kaiser* (RM 38/33) contain more succinct information. Frau Gisela von Diederichs graciously showed me the original Chinese-language proclamation in 1994.
89. Diederichs to Knorr, 14 November 1897, BAMA, RM 2/1835.
90. Koester to Diederichs, 13 November 1897, BAMA, RM 2/1835.
91. Diederichs to Koester, 14 November 1897, BAMA, RM 2/1835.
92. Besetzung, 23, BAMA, N 255/24.
93. Knorr to Diederichs, 15 November 1897, BAMA, RM 2/1835.
94. Diederichs to Henni, 15 November 1897, BAMA, N 255/4.
95. Senden to Diederichs, 9 November 1897, BAMA, N 255/8.
96. Hoffmann to Diederichs, 29 November 1897, BAMA, N 255/8.
97. Koester to Diederichs, 30 December 1897, BAMA, N 255/8.
98. #630: Holstein to Hatzfeldt, 13 November 1897, *Holstein Papers,* 4:48–53.
99. Besetzung, 23–28, BAMA, N 255/24.
100. Eiswert to Diederichs, 20 November 1897, BAMA, N 255/8.
101. Knorr to Wilhelm, 17 November 1897, BAMA, RM 3/3156.
102. Knorr to Wilhelm, 19 November 1897, BAMA, RM 3/3156.
103. Wilhelm, *Reden,* 2:80.
104. *Prinzess Wilhelm* Kriegstagebuch, 15 and 16 November 1897, RM 38/31.
105. Diederichs to OKM, 30 November 1897, BAMA, RM 3/6697; Besetzung, 31–35, BAMA, N 255/24.
106. Besetzung, 34, BAMA, N 255/24.
107. BAMA, N 255/24, 34–36; Diederichs to OKM, 30 November 1897, BAMA, RM 3/6697.
108. Besetzung, 36, BAMA, N 255/24.
109. *Prinzess Wilhelm* Kriegstagebuch, 28 November 1897, BAMA, RM 38/31; Diederichs to OKM, 30 November 1897, BAMA, RM 3/6697.
110. Besetzung, 36–37, BAMA, N 255/24; *Prinzess Wilhelm* Kriegstagebuch, 30 and 31 November 1897, BAMA, RM 38/31.
111. Zeye to Diederichs, 15 December 1897, BAMA, RM 3/6697.
112. Diederichs to Knorr, 7 January 1898, BAMA, RM 3/6697.
113. Besetzung, 37–40, BAMA, N 255/24.
114. Diederichs to Knorr, 9 December 1897, BAMA, RM 3/6697; Besetzung, 39–40, BAMA, N 255/24. For the negotiations, see Chiang Siang-tseh, "The Impact of the Kiaochow Affair on Chinese Foreign and Domestic Policy, 1897–1898," master's thesis, University of Washington, 1948.

115. Besetzung, 40, BAMA, N 255/24; Diederichs to Henni von Diederichs, 27 December 1897 and 2 January 1898, BAMA, N 255/4.
116. Diederichs to Henni von Diederichs, 12, 18, and 23 December 1897, BAMA, N 255/4; Diederichs to OKM, 12 January 1898, BAMA, RM 3/6697.
117. *Kaiser* Kriegstagebuch, 29 December 1897 and 2 January 1898, BAMA, RM 31/33.
118. Besetzung, 41, BAMA, N 255/24.
119. Diederichs to OKM, 12 January 1898, BAMA, RM 3/6697; Besetzung, 42, BAMA, N 255/24.
120. Diederichs to OKM, 12 January 1898, BAMA, RM 3/6697.
121. Besetzung, 41–43, BAMA, N 255/24.
122. Diederichs to Henni von Diederichs, 24 January 1898, BAMA, N 255/4; Diederichs to Knorr, 15 February 1898, BAMA, RM 3/6697.
123. Besetzung, 44–47, BAMA, N 255/24; Diederichs to Knorr, 3 February 1898, BAMA, RM 3/6697.
124. Besetzung, 47, BAMA, N 255/24; *Prinzess Wilhelm* Kriegstagebuch, 14 February 1898, BAMA, RM 38/31; *Kaiser* Kriegstagebuch, 18 February 1898, BAMA, RM 38/33.
125. "Convention respecting the lease of Kiaochow," 6 March 1898, in *Treaties and Agreements concerning China, 1894–1919* (1921), 4:112–16.
126. Diederichs to Fritz von Diederichs, 4 April 1898, BAMA, N 255/6. See also Diederichs to Henni von Diederichs, 26 February 1898, BAMA, N 255/4; and Senden to Diederichs, 30 March 1898, BAMA, N 255/9.
127. Diederichs to Henni von Diederichs, 28 May 1898, BAMA, N 255/5.
128. Diederichs to Henni, 31 January 1898, BAMA, N 255/4.
129. Henni von Diederichs to Diederichs, 3 March 1898, BAMA, N 255/3; Diederichs to Henni von Diederichs, 21 and 28 March 1898, BAMA, N 255/4.
130. Henni von Diederichs to Diederichs, 27 April 1898, BAMA, N 255/3.
131. Diederichs to Knorr, 3 June 1898, BAMA, RM 3/3157; Diederichs to Henni von Diederichs, 4 and 11 March, 15, 23 and 30 April, and 8 May 1898, BAMA, N 255/4.
132. Diederichs to Henni von Diederichs, 8 May 1898, BAMA, N 255/4.

Chapter 7. The Philippines, Summer 1898

1. Diederichs to Henni von Diederichs, 14 May 1898, BAMA, N 255/4. See also, David F. Trask, *The War with Spain in 1898* (1981), and Julius W. Pratt, *Expansionists of 1898: The Acquisition of Hawaii and the Spanish Islands* (1936).
2. Bülow quoted Wilhelm's marginal gloss on a diplomatic document, dated 3 April 1898, and then added his own remarks; see Bernhard von Bülow, *Memoirs of Prince von Bülow*, vol 1, *From Secretary of State to Imperial Chancellor, 1897–1903*, trans.

F. A.Vogt (1931), 255. See also Leon Guerrero, "The Kaiser and the Philippines," *Philippine Studies* 9 (1961): 584–600; and Lester Shippee, "Germany and the Spanish-American War," *American Historical Review* 30 (1925): 754–77.

3. Diederichs to Henni von Diederichs, 14 and 19 May 1898, BAMA, N 255/4. Dewey's initial account of the battle is in Dewey to Long, 4 May 1898, NARA, Record Group 45, Area File no. 10. See also Nathan Sargent, *Admiral Dewey and the Manila Campaign* (1947), and Ronald Spector, *Admiral of the New Empire: The Life and Career of George Dewey* (1974).

4. Klehmet to Bülow, 16 March 1898, Bundesarchiv, Koblenz, NL 16/22. Tirpitz also told Klehmet that Germany should first expand its position in China, citing the Yangtze basin, before making imperialistic moves elsewhere.

5. Finley Peter Dunne, *Mr. Dooley in Peace and in War* (Boston: Small, Maynard, 1899), 43.

6. Knorr to Wilhelm, 20 April 1898, BAMA, RM 2/1834.

7. Knorr to Wilhelm, 13 July 1898, BAMA, RM 2/1834.

8. Anlage betreffend Flottenstützpunkt in den Philippinen und Sulu Inseln, 13 July 1898, BAMA, RM 2/1834.

9. Marginal gloss, Knappe to Hohenlohe, 1 February 1897, BAMA, RM 2/2991.

10. Hay to Henry Cabot Lodge, 27 July 1898, in Alfred. L. P. Dennis, *Adventures in American Diplomacy, 1896–1906* (1928), 28.

11. Heinrich to Foreign Ministry, 11 April 1898, PAAA, R 19474.

12. Krüger to Foreign Ministry, 12 May 1898, PAAA, R 19474.

13. Williams to Caldwell, 10 March 1898, LC, Dewey Papers, General Correspondence.

14. Krüger to Diederichs, 20 April 1898, BAMA, RM 38/29.

15. Diederichs to Knorr, 3 June and 10 July 1898, BAMA, RM 3/3157.

16. Obenheimer to Diederichs, 8 May 1898, BAMA, RM 3/4263.

17. Obenheimer to Diederichs, 27 May 1898, BAMA, RM 3/4263. Obenheimer also assumed responsibility for Swiss nationals. The French captain arranged to take his nationals aboard *Bruix*, while the British consul also leased steamers for evacuees. See Chichester to Holland, 3 June 1898, Public Record Office, London, ADM 125/142, The Spanish-American War and the Rebellion in the Philippines.

18. Obenheimer to Diederichs, 17 May 1898, BAMA, RM 3/4263. The Spanish garrison in Iloilo sent a telegram to Obenheimer on 10 May: "All the Iloilo volunteers greet the squadron thankfully and send their hearty greetings. Long live Germany! Long live Spain!"

19. Quoted in Alfred Vagts, "Hopes and Fears of an American-German War, 1870–1915," *Political Science Quarterly* 54 (1939): 522.

20. Sargent, *Manila Campaign,* 11–12. See also, *Olympia* logbook, 8 March 1898, NARA, Record Group 24; Dewey to Diederichs, 9 March 1898, LC, Dewey

Papers, Squadron Letters.
21. Dewey, *Life and Letters,* 200; George Dewey Diary, entries for 12 and 30 March 1898, LC, Dewey Papers; Adalbert M. Dewey, *The Life and Letters of Admiral Dewey from Montpelier to Manila, 1837–1898* (1899), 200; Clara E. Schieber, *The Transformation of American Sentiment toward Germany, 1870–1914* (1923), 110–11.
22. Sargent, *Manila Campaign,* 11.
23. Obenheimer to Diederichs, 12 May 1898, BAMA, RM 3/4263.
24. Frederick Pohl, "Die Tätigkeit SMS *Irene* in den Gewässern der Philippinen, 1896–1899," *Marine Rundschau* 7 (1902): 761–62. An English translation of this article is in *Germany, the Philippines, and the Spanish-American War: Four Accounts by Officers of the Imperial German Navy,* ed. Karl-Heinz Wionzek (2000), 39–46.
25. See "Spanish Vessels in the Philippines," February 1898, LC, Dewey Papers.
26. Long to Dewey, 27, 29 and 30 May 1898, LC, Dewey Papers.
27. *Concord* logbook, 9 May 1898 and 17 June 1898, NARA, RG 24.
28. Diederichs to Dewey, 10 July 1898, in BAMA, RM 38/44; Sargent, *Manila Campaign,* 56; Dudley N. Carpenter Journal, Naval Historical Foundation Collection, LC.
29. See, for example, *Concord* log, 24 June 1898; *Petrel* log, 6, 13, and 14 June 1898, NARA, RG 24.
30. George Dewey, *Autobiography of George Dewey, Admiral of the Navy* (1913), 252. Augustin initially maintained communications with Madrid via another cable between Manila and Iloilo, thence by steamer to Labuan, Borneo, and by cable again to Madrid; see Obenheimer to Diederichs, 20 May 1898, BAMA, RM 3/4264.
31. Ernest Heilmann, "Activities of the German Squadron at Manila Bay," NARA, Record Group 45, Subject Files. Heilmann was a member of *Irene*'s draft aboard *Darmstadt.* Because he spoke English, he later served as Obenheimer's orderly. He eventually immigrated to the United States and enlisted in the U.S. Navy. The Reichsmarineamt had earlier leased *Darmstadt* for seven hundred thousand marks to carry forty-seven officers and 1,120 seamen to Kiao-chou in early 1898; see Transport Verlag, 11 December 1897, BAMA, RM 3/9408.
32. Diederichs to Knorr, 27 June 1898, BAMA, RM 3/3157; Dewey, *Autobiography,* 256–57; No. 224: Pratt to Day, 2 June 1898, in United States, Department of State, Despatches from United States Consuls in Singapore, 1833–1906 (National Archives microfilm publication T128).
33. Bülow to Tirpitz, 18 May 1898; Tirpitz to Knorr, 28 May 1898, BAMA, RM 3/2992.
34. Knorr to Diederichs, 2 June 1898, BAMA, RM 38/43.
35. Diederichs to Knorr, 10 July 1898, BAMA, RM 3/3157.
36. Otto von Diederichs, "Darstellung der Vorgänge vor Manila von Mai bis August

1898," *Marine Rundschau* 25 (1914): 253–54. An English translation of this article appears as "A Statement of Events in Manila, May–August 1898," *Journal of the Royal United Services Institute* 59 (1914): 421–46; another translation appears as "An Account of Events off Manila from May to August 1898," in Wionzek, *Germany, the Philippines, and the Spanish-American War*, 1–36.

37. Diederichs to Henni von Diederichs, 19 and 20 May 1898, BAMA, N 255/5.
38. Diederichs to Knorr, 25 June 1898, BAMA, RM 3/4263.
39. Diederichs to Henni von Diederichs, 12 June 1898, BAMA, N 255/5. Diederichs provided an additional description of the battle and battle site in Diederichs to Henni von Diederichs, 17 June 1898, BAMA, N 255/5.
40. Diederichs disputed Dewey's contention that only one German firm existed in Manila. He listed eleven such firms in his article. There were additional German merchants in Iloilo and Cebu, as well as other firms under the protection of the German flag. The German consul also handled consular duties for Austria, Holland, Italy, Portugal, and Switzerland. See Diederichs, "Darstellung," 259–60.
41. Dewey, *Autobiography*, 257; Diederichs, "Darstellung," 260.
42. Diederichs to Knorr, 25 June 1898, BAMA, RM 3/4263.
43. Diederichs, "Darstellung," 254–56.
44. Diederichs to Knorr, 25 June 1898, BAMA, RM 3/4263.
45. Dewey, *Autobiography*, 262; Diederichs, "Darstellung," 263–64. Captain Chichester noted his and Rawson-Walker's visit to the Spanish officials in Chichester to Holland, 12 May 1898, PRO, ADM 125/143.
46. Diederichs to Fritz von Diederichs, 17 June 1898, BAMA, N 255/6.
47. Diederichs to Knorr, 23 June 1898, BAMA, RM 2/1855.
48. Diederichs to Knorr, 24 July 1898, BAMA, RM 3/4264.
49. Diederichs to Knorr, 23 June 1898, BAMA, RM 2/1855.
50. *Olympia* logbook, 18 and 19 June 1898, NA, RG 24; *Kaiser* logbook, 18 and 19 June, BAMA, RM 92/67.
51. Diederichs to Knorr, 23 June 1898, BAMA, RM 2/1855.
52. John T. McCutcheon, *Drawn from Memory* (1950), 119.
53. "Register of Salutes and Official Visits," Military Papers, Dewey Papers, LC.
54. Diederichs to Knorr, 4 July 1898, BAMA, RM 3/3157.
55. Diederichs to Knorr, 23 June 1898, BAMA, RM 2/1855.
56. Dewey, *Autobiography*, 262–65.
57. Diederichs, "Darstellung," 266–67. Captain Chichester confirmed Diederichs's explanations; see Chichester to Holland, 9 July 1898, PRO, ADM 125/143.
58. Diederichs to Knorr, 25 June 1898, BAMA, RM 38/43.
59. Diederichs to Henni von Diederichs, 29 June and 4 July 1898, BAMA, N 255/5.
60. Quoted in "The Philippines and Their Future," *Literary Digest* 17 (1898): 85–86.
61. Quoted in "Anti-German Agitation in the United States," *Literary Digest* 17

(1898): 354.

62. White to Day, 18 and 23 June 1898, United States, Department of State, Despatches from United States Ministers to Germany, 1799–1906, NARA microfilm M 44.

63. Williams to Wildman, 22 June 1898; Wildman to Williams, 29 June 1898, quoted in Edwin Wildman, "What Dewey Feared in Manila Bay," *Forum* 59 (1918): 523.

64. When the ships finally reached the mouth of Manila Bay on 30 June, lookouts spotted the masts of three unidentified warships above the Mariveles hills. The two cruisers immediately cleared for action, fearing that the warships belonged to Camara's relief squadron. The ships, however, were *Kaiser, Cormoran,* and *Kaiserin Augusta,* which were anchored in the bay for coaling and crew transfer. See, Charles Julian Diary, 25 and 30 June 1898, Naval Historical Foundation Collection, Washington, D.C.

65. Obenheimer to Diederichs, 4 July 1898, BAMA, RM 38/43. See also United States, Department of the Treasury, *The United States Revenue Cutter Service in the War with Spain, 1898* (Washington, D.C.: U.S. Government Printing Office, 1899), 16.

66. United States, Bureau of Insular Affairs, *A Pronouncing Gazetteer and Geographical Dictionary of the Philippine Islands* (1902), 840.

67. Diederichs to Obenheimer, 2 July 1898, BAMA, RM 38/43.

68. Diederichs to Obenheimer, 3 July 1898, BAMA, RM 38/43.

69. Heilman, "Activities," NARA, RG 45.

70. Chichester to Holland, 9 July 1898, PRO, ADM 125/143. Captain Chichester and Admiral de la Bedolliéré also protested the insurgents' improper use of the flag; see Chichester to Holland, 13, 14, and 17 July 1898, PRO, ADM 125/143.

71. Obenheimer to Diederichs, 7 July 1898, BAMA, RM 38/43.

72. Dewey to Long, 13 July 1898, LC, Dewey Papers, Special Correspondence.

73. Heilmann, "Activities," NARA, RG 45.

74. *Raleigh* logbook, 7 July 1898; *Concord* logbook, 7 July 1898, NARA, RG 45.

75. Obenheimer to Diederichs, 7 July 1898, BAMA, RM 38/43.

76. Diederichs to Obenheimer, 8 July 1898, BAMA, RM 38/43; Diederichs to Knorr, 9 July 1898, BAMA, RM 3/3180; Diederichs to Knorr, 18 October 1898, BAMA, RM 3/3157.

77. Diederichs to Knorr, 27 July 1898, BAMA, RM 3/3180.

78. "The Status of the Philippines," *New York Times,* 15 July 1898, 6.

79. Quoted in "Topics in Brief," *Literary Digest* 17 (1898): 38.

80. All references quoted in "Germany and the Philippines Situation," *Literary Digest* 17 (1898): 91–93.

81. Quoted in "The Situation in the Philippines," *Literary Digest* 17 (1898): 202.

82. Obenheimer to Diederichs, 7 July 1898, BAMA, RM 38/43.

83. *Raleigh* logbook, 7 July 1898, NARA, RG 24.
84. Coghlan to Dewey, 10 July 1898, NARA, RG 45, Area File 10.
85. Dewey to George Goodwin Dewey, 9 July 1898, in Department of the Navy, Operational Archives, George Goodwin Dewey Papers, Washington, D.C.
86. Diederichs to Henni von Diederichs, 18 July 1898, BAMA, N 255/5.
87. Diederichs to Fritz von Diederichs, 5 July 1898, BAMA, N 255/6.
88. Henni von Diederichs to Diederichs, 24 July 1898, BAMA, N 255/3.
89. Henni von Diederichs to Diederichs, 12 July 1898, BAMA, N 255/3. See also Henni von Diederichs to Diederichs, 21 July 1898, BAMA, N 255/3.
90. *McCulloch* logbook, 5 July 1898, NARA, RG 45.
91. Synopsis of Interview with Vice Admiral von Diedrichs [sic] on board the *Kaiser* at Manila, 7 July 1898, NARA, RG 45, Area File 10, RG 45, NA. Emphasis in the original. Diederichs's account, which differs only slightly from Brumby's, is in Diederichs to Knorr, 14 July 1898, BAMA, RM 38/43.
92. Diederichs to Dewey, 10 July 1898, BAMA, RM 38/44.
93. Diederichs forwarded Hintze's report in Diederichs to Knorr, 14 July 1898, BAMA, RM 2/1855. Hintze recorded his exchange with Dewey in English. Henry V. Butler (see Addendum, 15 November 1930, NARA, RG 45, Area File 10, RG 45, NA), who had served aboard *Olympia* as an ensign, remembered the Dewey-Hintze exchange in 1930:

> Dewey said: "Does Admiral von Diedrichs [sic] think he commands here or do I? Tell your Admiral if he wants war I am ready." German officer said to Lt. Brumby: "Mein Gott! What is the matter with your Admiral?" Brumby said: "Nothing, he means every word he says and you better tell your Admiral exactly what it was."

> Dewey seems to have violated his own navy's blockade regulations: "The men-of-war of neutral powers should, as a matter of courtesy, be allowed free passage to and from a blockaded port." See United States, Department of the Navy, Instructions to Blockading Vessels and Cruisers, General Order No. 492, 20 June 1898, 2. Although Dewey might not have had a recent copy of these instructions, they were presumably on file with the Navy Department.

94. Diederichs to Knorr, 14 July 1898, BAMA, RM 2/1855.
95. Dewey to Diederichs, 11 July 1898, BAMA, RM 38/43. Brumby also delivered copies of the letter to the senior French, English, Japanese, and Austrian officers in port.
96. Diederichs to Dewey, 11 July 1898, LC, Dewey Papers, Letters.
97. Dewey to Diederichs, 12 July 1898, BAMA, RM 38/43.

98. Diederichs to Knorr, 14 July 1898, BAMA, RM 38/43.
99. Chichester to Holland, 14 July 1898, PRO, ADM 125/143; Diederichs to Knorr, 14 July 1898, BAMA, RM 38/43. Chichester generally sided with Dewey in condemning alleged German violations. At one point, he noted, "This sort of petty annoyance on the part of the Germans towards the Americans is very noticeable and, to say the least of it, wanting in manners." See Chichester to Holland, 25 July 1898, PRO, ADM 125/143. Vice Adm. Sir Arthur Seymour, who had replaced Buller as commander of the British naval forces in East Asian waters, concurred: "The proceedings of the German Ships in the Philippines, regardless of the wishes and interests of the United States Admiral, are certainly a breach of courtesy towards him, if not more serious." See Seymour minute, 30 July 1898, PRO, ADM 125/143.
100. Diederichs to Dewey, 13 July 1898, LC, Dewey Papers, Letters.
101. Diederichs to Stubenrauch, 11 July 1898, BAMA, RM 38/44.
102. Memorandum for Commanding Officer, USS *Baltimore,* LC, Dewey Papers, Flag Secretary Letters.
103. Oscar King Davis, *Released for Publication* (1925), 12–13. Dewey later had Frederick Palmer, the ghost writer of his autobiography, omit this incident; see Bailey, "Dewey and the Germans at Manila Bay," *American Historical Review* 45 (1939): 69.
104. Dewey to Diederichs, 23 July 1898, BAMA, N 256/8.
105. Diederichs, "Darstellung," 267.
106. Knorr to Wilhelm II, 30 July 1898, BAMA, RM 2/1855. Wilhelm commended Diederichs for his actions throughout the July crisis: "The commander of the cruiser squadron acted correctly in the identification question." See Wihelm to Knorr, 21 July 1898, BAMA, RM 3/4263. He later added, "Diederichs handled the matter with gravity, tact, and vigor." See marginal note, Knorr to Wilhelm, 22 August 1898, BAMA, RM 2/1855.
107. Dewey to Wildman, 18 July 1898, in Wildman, "What Dewey Feared," 528.
108. Diederichs to Knorr, 9 August 1898, BAMA, RM 38/44.
109. Diederichs to Knorr, 2 August 1898, BAMA, RM 3/4264.
110. Diederichs to Knorr, 18 August 1898, BAMA, RM 3/4264.
111. Diederichs to Knorr, 28 August 1898, BAMA, RM 3/4264.
112. Diederichs to Henni von Diederichs, 18 August 1898, BAMA, N 255/5. Diederichs's lengthy report on the fall of Manila is in RM 3/4264. Diederichs to Knorr, 28 August 1898, BAMA, RM 3/4264. See also, Bailey, "Dewey and the Germans," 78–79; Sargent, *Manila Campaign,* 79–81.
113. Sargent noted, for example, that Chichester's maneuver "was quietly executed,

114. Diederichs to Knorr, 28 August 1898, BAMA, RM 3/4264.
115. Chichester to Holland, 14 August 1898, PRO, ADM 125/143.
116. The reports of Dewey and his captains are in U.S. Department of the Navy, NARA, M 625, Area File of the Naval Records Collection, 1775–1910; Area File 10, NARA microfilm M 625. American consul O. F. Williams, who observed the battle from the bridge of USS *Baltimore,* made no mention of German interference in his report to the State Department; see Williams to Day, 13 August 1898, United States, Department of State, Despatches from United States Consuls in Manila, 1817–1899, NARA microfilm, T 43.
117. Augustin had formally given his parole to the Americans in the presence of Diederichs and Krüger; see Krüger to Merritt, 16 August 1898, LC, Dewey Papers. See also, Diederichs to Knorr, 28 August 1898, BAMA, RM 3/4264; Köllner to Diederichs, 16 August 1898, BAMA, RM 3/3208.
118. Holland to Seymour, 18 August 1898, PRO, ADM 125/143.
119. "The German Navy," *New York Times,* 18 August 1898, 6.
120. Dunne, *Mr. Dooley,* 40–41.
121. Knorr to Wilhelm, 18 August 1898, BAMA, RM 2/1855.
122. Senden to Diederichs, 23 August 1898, BAMA, N 255/9.
123. Diederichs to Knorr, 28 August 1898, BAMA, RM 3/4264.
124. Diederichs to Köllner, 20 August 1898, BAMA, RM 38/46.
125. Diederichs to Knorr, 28 August 1898, BAMA, RM 3/4264.
126. Pohl, "Tätigkeit," 764–66.
127. See United States, Department of State, *Foreign Relations of the United States, 1898* (1899), 905–66.
128. Dunne, *Mr. Dooley,* 61.
129. An English translation of the treaty is in Jackson to Hay, 6 June 1899, United States, Department of State, Despatches from United States Ministers to Germany, 1799–1905, NARA microfilm, M 44.
130. Diederichs to Fritz von Diederichs, 8 October 1898, BAMA, N 255/6.
131. Diederichs to Henni von Diederichs, 2 March 1899, BAMA, N 255/5.
132. Quoted in Spector, *Admiral,* 82.
133. Rieloff to Hohenlohe, 30 May 1899, BAMA, RM 3/4266.
134. Spector, *Admiral,* 103.
135. Hildebrand, *Kriegsschiffe,* 3:121–23.
136. Diederichs to Henni von Diederichs, 1 and 2 September 1898, BAMA, N 255/5.

but it meant much, and no doubt was as thoroughly understood by the foreign men-of-war as it was appreciated by our own." See *Manila Campaign,* 84.

137. [Indecipherable] to Diederichs, 18 November 1898, BAMA, N 255/9; see also Diederichs to Henni von Diederichs, 11 and 17 September 1898, BAMA, N 255/5.
138. Diederichs to Knorr, 19 October 1898, BAMA, RM 38/28. Knorr forwarded the report to Kaiser Wilhelm with the reminder that "with Kiao-chou, an island in the Philippines, and [an island in the East Indies] as bases, our East Asian squadron will possess a secure basis for independent operations." See Aus den Berichten des Chef des Kreuzergeschwaders über Niederländischen Indien, 10 December 1898, BAMA, RM 4/917.
139. Diederichs to Fritz von Diederichs, 8 October 1898, BAMA, N 255/6. But it was Diederichs's flag lieutenant, Paul von Hintze, who would parlay his naval experience into a diplomatic career. Hintze left the navy in 1906, eventually rising through the diplomatic service to become Imperial Germany's last foreign minister at the end of World War I in 1918. See also Johannes Hürter, ed., *Paul von Hintze: Marineoffizier, Diplomat, Staatssekretär: Dokumenteeiner Karriere zwischen Militär und Politik, 1903–1918* (Munich: Herald Boldt Verlag, 1998).
140. Diederichs to Henni von Diederichs, 29 October and 5 November 1898, BAMA, N 255/5.
141. Diederichs to Henni von Diederichs, 24 November 1898, BAMA, N 255/5.
142. Hildebrand, *Kriegsschiffe,* 3:123, n20.
143. Henni von Diederichs to Diederichs, 13 November and 11 December 1898, BAMA, N 255/3.
144. Henni von Diederichs to Diederichs, 2, 4, and 11 January 1899, BAMA, N 255/3.
145. Henni von Diederichs to Diederichs, 17 and 31 January 1899, BAMA, N 255/3.
146. Diederichs to Henni von Diederichs, 2 and 27 March 1899, BAMA, N 255/5. He received formal notification of his new appointment in AKO, 2 April 1899, N 255/1.

Chapter 8. Constant Strife, 1899–1902

1. Diederichs to Henni, 24 February and 2 March 1899, BAMA, N 255/5; Personalbogen, BAMA, N 255/1.
2. I am indebted to Professor Patrick Kelly, Department of History, Adelphi University, for introducing me to this concept.
3. Quoted in Walther Hubatsch, *Kaiserliche Marine: Aufgaben und Leistungen* (1975), 275.
4. Patrick Kelly, "Tirpitz and the Origins of the Torpedo Arm, 1877–1889," 244, n. 24.
5. Allgemeine Geschichtspunkte bei der Feststellung unserer Flottenstärken nach Schiffsklassen und Schiffstypen, 15 June 1897, BAMA, N 253/4.
6. Motive für die Organizationsänderung der Marine, n.d., BAMA, N 253/39.

7. Steinberg, *Yesterday's Deterrent*, 138–39. See also, AKOs, 7 February and 7 March 1898, BAMA, RM 1/2860.
8. Koester to Diederichs, 20 December 1897, BAMA, N 255/8.
9. Oldekop to Diederichs, 18 December 1897, 5 February and 6 March 1898, BAMA, N 255/13.
10. Diederichs to Henni von Diederichs, 12 February 1898, BAMA, N 255/4.
11. Tirpitz to Bülow, 12 October 1897, PAAA, R 18167.
12. Bülow also noted, "The dispatch of our Cruiser Division to Kiao-chou Bay and the occupation of that bay is, on the one hand, proper compensation for the murder of German Catholic missionaries and, on the other hand, the best security that such an occurrence will not happen again." See Germany, Reichstag, *Stenographische Berichte über die Verhandlungen des Reichstags, 1897–1898*, 5th session, 4th meeting, 6 December 1897, 60.
13. See, particularly, Steinberg, *Yesterday's Deterrent*, 149–200.
14. Zur Organisationsfrage, 27 July 1897, BAMA, N 160/11. See also, Hubatsch, *Admiralstab*, 73–84.
15. Tirpitz to Wilhelm, 24 April 1898, BAMA, N 160/7.
16. Diederichs to Henni von Diederichs, 11 March and 5 April 1898, BAMA, N 255/4.
17. Thiele to Diederichs, 12 April 1898, BAMA, N 255/7.
18. Karcher to Diederichs, 5 May 1898, BAMA, N 255/9.
19. Tirpitz to Wilhelm, 14 June 1898, BAMA, N 253/39.
20. Henni von Diederichs to Diederichs, 20 July 1898, BAMA, N 255/3; see also, Henni von Diederichs to Diederichs, 27 April 1898, BAMA, N 255/3.
21. Diederichs to Henni von Diederichs, 15 April 1898, BAMA, N 255/4.
22. Oldekop to Diederichs, 23 August 1898, BAMA, N 255/13.
23. AKO, 19 December 1898, BAMA, RM 3/2.
24. Knorr himself did not discuss these issues. His unpublished memoirs, in BAMA, N 578, end in 1889.
25. AKO, 14 March 1899, BAMA, RM 3/2640. The Admiralty Staff's responsibility for ships on foreign station is in Groeben to Bendemann, 17 March 1899, BAMA, RM 5/268.
26. Hubatsch, *Admiralstab*, 84.
27. Tirpitz, Immediatvortrag, 15 June 1897, BAMA, N 253/4.
28. Victor Valois, *Seegeltung, Seemacht, Seeherrschaft: kurze Betrachtungen über Seekriegsführung* (1899). Valois commanded the *Kreuzergeschwader* between 1890 and 1892.
29. Auszüge aus der Schrift von Freiherr Kurt von Maltzahn mit Bemerkungen von Tirpitz, 1899, BAMA, N 253/345.
30. AKO, 28 Septmber 1899, BAMA, RM 3/2.

31. Oldekop to Diederichs, 29 October, 12 and 16 November, and 11 December 1899, BAMA, N 255/13.
32. Groeben to Bendemann, 17 March 1899, BAMA, RM 5/268.
33. Bendemann, Verfügung #2, 15 March 1899, BAMA, RM 5/270.
34. Groeben to Bendemann, 17 March 1899, BAMA, RM 5/268.
35. Wilhelm to Bendemann, 27 March 1899, BAMA, RM 5/268.
36. AKOs, 16 August and 18 September 1899, BAMA, RM 1/2862.
37. "Kurzbiographie," BAMA, N 255/1.
38. Bronsart von Schellendorff, *The Duties of the General Staff*, 4th ed. (1905), 30–48.
39. Diederichs to Tirpitz, 21 November 1899, BAMA, N 253/361.
40. AKO, 20 December 1899, BAMA, RM 1/2862; Tirpitz to Bendemann, 3 December 1899, BAMA, RM 5/1945.
41. Denkschrift zum Immediatvortrag betreffend Ausarbeitungen zur Flottenvorlage der Operationen gegen England und Amerika, 20 January 1900, BAMA, RM 5/1945.
42. Denkschrift zum Immediatvortrag betreffend Immediatbericht des Admiral von Koesters über seine Kenntnisnahme in Admiralstabsarbeiten und Vorschläge über Entwicklung des Admiralstabes, [February 1900], BAMA, RM 5/879. Lambi, in *The Navy and Power Politics*, 192, argues that Diederichs produced the memorandum in January 1901, but internal evidence points to February 1900 as the correct date.
43. Diederichs, Immediatvortrag, 26 February 1900, BAMA, RM 5/879. See also, Holger H. Herwig and David Trask, "Naval Operations between Germany and the United States of America, 1891–1913: A Study of Strategic Planning in the Age of Imperialism," *Militärgeschichtliche Mitteilungen* 2 (1971): 1–32. Planning continued under Diederichs's successor, Büchsel, until 1906, when it became apparent that Germany's likely foes would come from Europe, not North America.
44. Operationsbefehle für das Kreuzergeschwader und S. M. Schiffe im Auslande, 1 February 1900, BAMA, RM 38/125.
45. Dreibund Pacht, 5 December 1900, BAMA, RM 5/1669.
46. Koester to Wilhelm, 29 January 1900; Senden to Diederichs, 7 February 1900, BAMA, RM 4/273.
47. Denkschrift zum Immediatvortrag betreffend Immediatbericht des Admiral von Koesters über seine Kenntnisnahme in Admiralstabsarbeiten und Vorschläge über Entwicklung des Admiralstabes, [February 1900], BAMA, RM 5/879.
48. Diederichs, Immediatvortrag, 17 Feburary 1899, BAMA, RM 5/879.
49. Diederichs to Tirpitz, 29 March 1900, BAMA, RM 2/1553.
50. Tirpitz, *Memoirs*, 1:151.
51. Tirpitz, Immediatvortrag, 28 September 1899, BAMA, N 253/5.

52. The relevant documents for the second *Flottengesetz* are in BAMA, N 253/19.
53. See, particularly, Paul Kennedy, "Tirpitz, England, and the Second Navy Law of 1900: A Strategical Critique," *Militärgeschichtliche Mitteilungen* (1970): 740–52; Lambi, *Power Politics,* 143–51.
54. "Kurzbiographie," BAMA, N 255/1.
55. Senden to Bendemann, 6 May 1900; Koester to Bendemann, 1 October 1900, BAMA, RM 38/179.
56. Tirpitz to Koester, 4 May 1900, BAMA, RM 31/7.
57. Thomsen to Tirpitz, 10 May 1900, BAMA, RM 31/7.
58. Koester to Tirpitz, 31 May 1900, BAMA, RM 31/7.
59. Diederichs to Hintze, 4 May 1900, BAMA, N 536/7.
60. Diederichs to Bendemann, 22 July 1900, BAMA, RM 38/179.
61. Diederichs to Bendemann, 11 August 1900, BAMA, RM 38/179.
62. Diederichs to Hintze, 5 August 1900, BAMA, N 536/7.
63. Diederichs to Bendemann, 16 November 1900, BAMA, RM 38/179.
64. Tirpitz to Diederichs, 5 November 1900, BAMA, RM 5/1669.
65. Diederichs to Bendemann, 26 December 1900, BAMA, RM 38/179.
66. Diederichs, Immediatvortrag, 12 January 1901, BAMA, RM 2/1553.
67. Diederichs, Immediatvortrag, 22 January 1901, BAMA, RM 2/1553.
68. Geschäftsverteilungsplan des Admiralstabs der Marine, 9 March 1901, BAMA, RM 2/1553.
69. Senden to Diederichs, 4 and 16 February 1901, BAMA, RM 5/270.
70. Tirpitz, Immediatvortrag, 13 February 1901, BAMA, RM 2/1553.
71. Senden to Tirpitz, 20 February 1901, BAMA, RM 5/573.
72. Tirpitz, Immediatvortrag, 1 March 1901, BAMA, RM 5/573.
73. AKO, 16 March 1901, BAMA, RM 3/2647.
74. Senden to Bendemann, 15 February 1901, BAMA, RM 38/179. Koester continued to complain that Tirpitz's plans undermined the fleet's readiness.
75. Senden to Bendemann, 8 June 1901, BAMA, RM 38/179.
76. Tirpitz, Immediatvortrag, 28 November 1898, BAMA, N 253/4.
77. Alfred Thayer Mahan, *The Influence of Sea Power upon the French Revolution and Empire, 1793–1812* (1892), 1:321.
78. AKO, 12 June 1899, BAMA, RM 5/1894.
79. Diederichs to Schlieffen, 9 February 1900; Diederichs to commanding general, Seventeenth Army Corps, 6 March and 8 April 1901, BAMA, RM 5/1894.
80. Diederichs to Tirpitz, 20 May and 4 October 1901, BAMA, RM 5/1894.
81. Diederichs, Immediatvortrag, 11 January 1901, BAMA, RM 5/881.
82. Goltz to Tirpitz, 28 March 1901, BAMA, RM 5/1894.
83. Diederichs to Tirpitz, 10 February 1901, BAMA, N 253/20.
84. AKO, 23 March 1901, BAMA, N 253/20.

85. Diederichs to Bendemann, 7 April 1901, BAMA, RM 38/179.
86. Senden to Bendemann, 8 June 1901, BAMA, RM 38/179.
87. AKO, 24 June 1901, BAMA, N 253/20.
88. Senden to Bendemann, 10 July 1901, BAMA, RM 38/179.
89. Diederichs to Senden, 16 July 1901, BAMA, N 160/11.
90. Diederichs to Bendemann, 2 August 1901, BAMA, RM 38/179.
91. Diederichs to Wilhelm, 1 April 1901, BAMA, RM 2/2005.
92. Diederichs to Tirpitz, 24 February 1901, BAMA, RM 2/2005.
93. Tirpitz to Diederichs, 13 March 1901, BAMA, RM 2/2005.
94. Diederichs to Tirpitz, 21 March 1901, BAMA, RM 2/2005.
95. Diederichs to Wilhelm, 1 April 1901, BAMA, RM 2/2005.
96. Büchsel to Diederichs, 16 March 1901; Diederichs to Senden, 16 April 1901, BAMA, RM 2/2005.
97. Diederichs to Tirpitz, 7 October 1901, and Tirpitz to Diederichs, 7 October 1901, BAMA, RM 2/2005. *Panther* was currently undergoing a refit. The two torpedo boats would have to be activated from the fleet reserve. See also Holger H. Herwig, *Germany's Vision of Empire in Venezuela, 1871–1914* (1986).
98. "Kurzbiographie," BAMA, N 255/1.
99. AKO, 27 January 1902, BAMA, RM 1/2865.
100. Diederichs to Senden, 25 March 1902, BAMA, RM 5/270.
101. Wilhelm to Tirpitz, 28 June 1902, BAMA, RM 3/108.
102. Diederichs, Immediatvortrag, 16 April 1902, BAMA, RM 5/918.
103. "Kurzbiographie," BAMA, N 255/1.
104. AKO, 18 May 1902, BAMA, N 255/1.
105. *Rangliste für 1901*, 13.
106. Tirpitz to Senden, 21 April 1902, BAMA, RM 3/39.
107. AKO, 19 August 1902, BAMA, N 255/1.
108. Dienstlaufbahnzeugniss über der Admiral und Chef des Admiralstabes Otto von Diederichs, 24 August 1902; Tirpitz to Admiralstab, 25 September 1902, BAMA, RM 5/566.
109. Quoted in Hubatsch, *Admiralstab*, 109.
110. "Kurzbiographie," BAMA, N 255/1.
111. These included Vice Adm. Wilhelm Büchsel, Adm. Max von Fischel, Vice Adm. August von Heeringen, Adm. Hugo von Pohl, and Vice Adm. Gustav Bachmann; see Kelly, "Tirpitz and the Origins of the Torpedo Arm," 244 n. 24.

CHAPTER 9. WATCHING FROM AFAR, 1902–1918

1. Henni von Diederichs to Diederichs, 23 June 1898, BAMA, N 255/3.
2. Diederichs to Hintze, 5 January and 23 September 1903, BAMA, N 536/7.

BAMA, N 255/47, contains exterior and interior photographs of the villa.
3. Admiral Archibald Buller, the commander of British forces in East Asia, used the term in a letter to Diederichs; see Buller to Diederichs, 14 January 1898, BAMA, N 255/8.
4. Great Britain, Foreign Office, *Kiaochow and Weihaiwei* (1920), 1–41.
5. "Kurzbiographie," BAMA, N 255/1.
6. Diederichs to Hintze, 19 January 1903, BAMA, N 536/7.
7. Diederichs to Hintze, 23 September 1903, BAMA, N 536/7.
8. Diederichs to Fritz von Diederichs, 12 February 1904, BAMA, N 255/6.
9. Aufnahme-Urkunde, 26 November 1904, BAMA, N 255/1.
10. Erskine Childers, *The Riddle of the Sands* (1903). See also, David Stafford, "Spies and Gentlemen: The Birth of the British Spy Novel, 1893–1914," *Victorian Studies* 24 (1981): 489–509.
11. See particularly, A. J. Marder, *The Anatomy of British Sea Power: A History of British Naval Policy in the Pre-Dreadnought Era, 1880–1905* (1940); A. J. Marder, *From the Dreadnought to Scapa Flow: The Royal Navy in the Fisher Era, 1904–1919*, vol. 1, *The Road to War, 1904–1914* (1961); Peter Padfield, *The Great Naval Race: The Anglo-German Naval Rivalry, 1900–1914* (1974); Paul M. Kennedy, *The Rise of the Anglo-German Antagonism, 1860–1914* (1980).
12. Diederichs to Hintze, 20 November 1907, BAMA, N 536/7.
13. See, for example, Fritz Fischer, *Germany's Aims in the First World War* (1967); Volker Berghahn, *Germany and the Approach of War in 1914* (1993), and Gregor Schöllgen, ed., *Escape into War: The Foreign Policy of Imperial Germany* (1990).
14. Diederichs to Fritz von Diederichs, 20 December 1908, BAMA, N 255/6. Fritz describes his father's reticence about discussing service issues while on active duty in "Kurzbiographie," BAMA, N 255/1.
15. Diederichs to Fritz von Diederichs, 25 December 1908, BAMA, N 255/6.
16. Diederichs to Fritz von Diederichs, 11 September 1909, BAMA, N 255/6.
17. Germany, Reichstag, *Stenographische Berichte über die Verhandlungen des Reichstags*, XIII. Legislaturperiode, dreizigsten Sitzung, Band 293, 19 February 1914, 7505.
18. See, for example, *Berliner Tageblatt*, "Diederichs gegen Dewey," 28 February 1914, 1.
19. Hoffmann to Diederichs, 14 May 1914, BAMA, N 255/12.
20. N1 to Fritz von Diederichs, 9 March 1914, BAMA, RM 5/3712.
21. The pertinent documents are in Great Britain, Public Record Office, DPP 1/26, Records of the Director of Public Prosecutions.
22. Gisela von Diederichs, interview by author, 24 June 1994, Baden-Baden, Federal Republic of Germany.

23. Sidney Felstead, *German Spies at Bay: An Actual Record of the German Espionage in Great Britain, 1914–1918* (1920), 5.
24. Hoffmann to Diederichs, 15 August 1914, BAMA, N 255/12.
25. Tim Hughes to author, 21 August 2001. The pertinent records are digested in Great Britain, Public Record Office, Foreign Office, Correspondence Indexes.
26. See Charles Burdick, *The Japanese Siege of Tsingtau: World War I in Asia* (1976), and John Schrecker, *Imperialism and Chinese Nationalism: Germany in Shantung* (1971). For the fate of the Cruiser Squadron, see R. K. Lochner, *The Last Gentleman of War: The Raider Exploits of the Cruiser* Emden (1988), and Keith Yates, *Graf Spee's Raiders: Challenge to the Royal Navy, 1914–1915* (1995).
27. See particularly, Herwig, *"Luxury Fleet,"* 5, 144–45. For the history of the German Navy during World War I, see also Paul Halpern, *A Naval History of World War I* (1994), and Richard Hough, *The Great War at Sea: 1914–1918* (1983).
28. See particularly, V. E. Tarrant, *Jutland: The German Perspective* (1995). Adm. Gustav Bachmann, Diederichs's former adjutant at the *Admiralstab,* described the battle in a birthday letter in September 1916. Bachmann's son won an Iron Cross while serving aboard SMS *Moltke* during the battle. See Bachmann to Diederichs, 13 September 1916, BAMA, N 255/14.
29. The pertinent documents, including Diederichs's Will and Testament, are in BAMA, N 255/1.
30. Daniel Horn, *The German Naval Mutinies of World War I* (1969).
31. Dan Van der Vat, *The Grand Scuttle: The Sinking of the German Fleet at Scapa Flow in 1919* (1982).
32. Oldekop to Herman von Diederichs, 10 March 1918, BAMA, N 255/13. Oldekop, who had retired to Hanover in 1899, died in 1936 at age ninety-two.

Bibliography

Archival Sources

Bundesarchiv, Koblenz

NL 16   Nachlass Bülow

Bundesarchiv-Militärarchiv, Freiburg im Breisgau

N 160	Nachlass Senden
N 253	Nachlass Tirpitz
N 255	Nachlass Diederichs
N 536	Nachlass Hintze
N 560	Nachlass Knorr
RM 1	Admiralität
RM 2	Marine-Kabinett
RM 3	Reichsmarineamt
RM 4	Oberkommando der Marine
RM 5	Admiralstab der Marine
RM 8	Bildungswesen der Marine
RM 31	Marinestation der Ostsee
RM 38	Kreuzergeschwader
RM 92	Schwere und Mittlere Kampfschiffe

Library of Congress, Washington, D.C.

Charles Julian Diary, Naval Historical Foundation Collection
Dudley N. Carpenter Journal, Naval Historical Foundation Collection
George Dewey Papers, Manuscript Division

National Archives and Records Administration, Washington, D.C.

RG 24, RECORDS OF THE BUREAU OF NAVAL PERSONNEL, LOGS OF SHIPS AND STATIONS, 1801–1946

Boston logbook
Concord logbook
Hugh McCulloch logbook
Raleigh logbook
Olympia logbook

RG 45, OFFICE OF NAVAL RECORDS AND LIBRARY

Subject File VI-8, Relations between the United States and Germany, 1848–1910
Ernst Heilmann, Activities of the German Squadron at Manila Bay
Notes regarding assistance desired by Germany from the United States in forming a Navy, 1848–1849

Politisches Archiv des Auswärtigen Amtes, Bonn

R 18156–59	Erwerbungen der Grossmächte in China (geheim)
R 19462	Spanische Besitzungen in Asien 1
R 19474	Spanische Besitzungen in Asien 1 (geheim)
R 2231	Die Kaiserliche Deutsche Marine

Public Record Office, London

ADM 125/143	The Spanish-American War and the Rebellion in the Philippines
DPP 1/26	Records of the Director of Public Prosecution: F. Diedericks [*sic*]

U.S. Department of the Navy, Washington, D.C.

Area File of the Naval Records Collection, 1775–1910. Area File No. 10. National Archives microfilm publication M 625.

George Goodwin Dewey Papers. Operational Archives.
Hutch I. Cone Diary. Naval Historical Foundation.
Squadron Letters. National Archives microfilm publication M 89.

U.S. Department of State, Washington, D.C.

Despatches from United States Consuls in Amoy, 1844–1906. National Archives microfilm publication M 100.
Despatches from United States Consuls in Manila, 1817–1899. National Archives microfilm publication T 43.
Despatches from United States Consuls in Singapore, 1833–1906. National Archives microfilm publication T 128.
Despatches from United States Ministers to China, 1843–1906. National Archives microfilm publication M 92.
Despatches from United States Ministers to Germany, 1799–1906. National Archives microfilm publication M 44.

Published Documents and Memoirs

Bülow, Bernhard von. *Memoirs of Prince von Bülow.* Vol. 1, *From Secretary of State to Imperial Chancellor, 1897–1903.* Translated by F. A. Vogt. Boston: Little, Brown, 1931.
Davis, Oscar King. *Released for Publication.* Boston: Houghton Mifflin, 1925.
Dewey, Adalbert, ed. *The Life and Letters of Admiral Dewey from Montpelier to Manila, 1837–1898.* New York: Woodfall, 1899.
Dewey, George. *Autobiography of George Dewey, Admiral of the Navy.* New York: Charles Scribner's Sons, 1916.
Germany. Auswärtiges Amt. *Die Grosse Politik der Europäischen Kabinette, 1871–1914.* Vol. 15, *Rings um die Erste Haager Friedenskonferenz.* Edited by Johannes Lepsius, A. M. Bartholdy, and Friedrich Thimme. Berlin: Deutsche Verlagsgesellschaft für Politik und Geschichte, 1924.
———. Reichstag. *Stenographische Berichte über die Verhandlungen des Reichstags, 1897/1898.* I. Legislaturperiode. 5ten Session. 4ten Sitzung. 6 December 1897
———. Reichstag. *Stenographische Berichte über die Verhandlungen des Reichstags, 1912–1914.* XIII. Legislaturperiode. 13en Sitzung. 19 February 1914.
Great Britain. Foreign Office. *Kiaochow and Weihaiwei.* London: HMSO, 1920.
Hopman, Albert. *Das Logbuch eines deutschen Seeoffiziers.* Berlin: 1924.
Hürter, Johannes, ed. *Paul von Hintze: Marineoffizier, Diplomat, Staatssekretär: Dokumente einer Karriere zwischen Militär und Politik, 1903–1918.* Munich: Herald Boldt Verlag, 1998.
MacMurray, John, ed. *Treaties and Agreements concerning China, 1894–1919.* New York: Oxford University Press, 1921.

Maguire, Doris, ed. *French Ensor Chadwick: Selected Letters and Papers.* Washington, D.C.: University Press of America, 1981.

Palmer, Frederick. *With My Own Eyes: A Personal Story of Battle Years.* Indianapolis, Ind.: Bobbs-Merrill, 1932.

Rich, Norman, and M. H. Fishers, eds. *The Holstein Papers.* Vol. 4. *Correspondence, 1897–1909.* Cambridge: Cambridge University Press, n.d.

Tirpitz, Alfred von. *My Memoirs.* 2 vols. New York: Dodd, Mead, 1919.

United States. Bureau of Insular Affairs. *A Pronouncing Gazetteer and Geographical Dictionary of the Philippine Islands.* Washington, D.C.: U.S. Government Printing Office, 1902.

———. Department of the Navy. *Instructions to Blockading Vessels and Cruisers.* General Order no. 492. 20 June 1898.

———. Department of State. *Foreign Relations of the United States, 1880.* Washington, D.C.: U.S. Government Printing Office, 1881.

———. Department of State. *Foreign Relations of the United States, 1898.* Washington, D.C.: U.S. Government Printing Office, 1899.

———. Department of the Treasury. *The United States Revenue Cutter Service in the War with Spain, 1898.* Washington, D.C.: U.S. Government Printing Office, 1899.

———. Department of War. *Correspondence Relating to the War with Spain.* 2 vols. Washington, D.C.: U.S. Government Printing Office, 1902.

Wilhelm II. *Die Reden Kaiser Wilhelms II.* Leipzig: Philip Reclam, 1904.

Wionzek, Karl-Heinz, ed. *Germany, the Philippines, and the Spanish-American War: Four Accounts by Officers of the Imperial German Navy.* Manila: National Historical Institute, 2000.

Secondary Sources

"Anti-German Agitation in the United States." *Literary Digest* 17 (1898): 354.

Artelt, Jork. *Tsingtau: Deutsche Stadt und Festung in China, 1897–1914.* Düsseldorf: Droste Verlag, 1984.

Bailey, Thomas. "Dewey and the Germans at Manila Bay." *American Historical Review* 45 (1939): 59–81.

Balfour, Michael. *The Kaiser and His Times.* Boston: Houghton Mifflin, 1964.

Barnard, Henry. *Military Schools and Courses of Instruction in the Science and Art of War.* New York: E. Steiger, 1872.

Bee, Minge C. "Origins of German Far Eastern Policy." *Chinese Social and Political Science Review* 21 (1937): 65–97.

Berghahn, Volker. *Germany and the Approach of War in 1914.* London: Macmillan, 1993.

———. *Der Tirpitz-Plan: Genesis und Verfall einer innen-politischen Krisenstrategie unter Wilhelm II*. Düsseldorf: Droste Verlag, 1971.

Boelcke, Willi A. *So Kam das Meer zu Uns: die Preussisch-deutsche Kriegsmarine in Ubersee, 1822 bis 1914*. Frankfurt am Main: Ullstein, 1981.

Boyd, Carl. "The Wasted Ten Years, 1888–1898: The Kaiser Finds an Admiral." *Journal of the Royal United Service Institution* 111 (1966): 291–97.

Braisted, William. *The United States Navy in the Pacific, 1897–1909*. New York: Greenwood Press, 1969.

Brysch, Thomas. *Marinepolitik im preussischen Abgeordnetenhaus und Deutschen Reichstag, 1850–1888*. Hamburg: Verlag E. S. Mittler, 1996.

Bucholz, Arden. *Moltke, Schlieffen, and Prussian War Planning*. Providence, R.I.: Berg, 1993.

Bueb, Volkmar. *Die "Junge Schule" der französischen Marine Strategie und Politik, 1875–1900*. Boppard am Rhein: Herald Boldt Verlag, 1971.

Burdick, Charles. *The Japanese Siege of Tsingtau: World War I in Asia*. Hamden, Conn.: Shoestring Press, 1976.

Carroll, E. Malcolm. *Germany and the Great Powers, 1866–1914: A Study in Public Opinion and Foreign Policy*. New York: Prentice-Hall, 1938.

Cecil, Lamar. *The German Diplomatic Service, 1871–1914*. Princeton, N.J.: Princeton University Press, 1976.

———. *Wilhelm II: Prince and Emperor, 1859–1900*. 2 vols. Chapel Hill: University of North Carolina Press, 1989–1996.

Chiang Siang-tseh, "The Impact of the Kiaochow Affair on Chinese Foreign and Domestic Policy, 1897–1898." M.A. thesis, University of Washington, 1948.

Childers, Erskine. *The Riddle of the Sands*. London: Smith Elder, 1903.

Clemente, Steven. *For King and Kaiser! The Making of the Prussian Army Officer, 1860–1914*. Westport, Conn.: Greenwood Press, 1992.

Clifford, John. "Admiral Dewey and the Germans, 1903: A New Perspective." *Mid-America* 49 (1967): 214–20.

Conrad, Joseph. *Heart of Darkness*. New York: Signet Classics, 1978.

Cowell, Mary Anne, and Edward C. Whitman. "Newport and Navy Torpedoes: An Enduring Legacy." *Undersea Warfare* 2 (2000). Internet www.chinfolnavy.mil/navpalib/cno/n87/usw/issue7/newport.htm. Accessed 24 July 2001.

Cronsaz, Alfred von. *Die Organization des Brandenburgischen und Preussischen Heeres seit 1640*. Berlin: Reimschneider Verlag, 1873.

Dennis, Alfred L. P. *Adventures in American Diplomacy, 1896–1906*. New York: E. P. Dutton, 1928.

Deutschen Adelsarchiv. *Genealogisches Handbuch des Adels: Adelslexikon*. Edited by Walter von Hueck. Limburg am Lahn: C. A. Starke, 1974.

Diederichs, Frederick von. *Die Systeme der Staatswissenschaften von Say, Jacob und Politz nach ihren Hauptmomenten und mit besonderer Rücksicht auf die sogenannte Nationalökonomie: Nebst Ideen zur neuen, sachgemässen Begründung und Behandlung der berührten Materien.* Cologne: Bachem Verlag, 1833.

Diederichs, Otto von. "Darstellung der Vorgänge vor Manila von Mai bis August 1898." *Marine Rundschau* 25 (1914): 253–54.

———. "A Statement of Events in Manila, May–August 1898." *Journal of the Royal United Services Institute* 59 (1914): 421–46.

Dotson, Lilian. *The Sino-Japanese War of 1894–1895: A Study in Asian Power Politics.* Ann Arbor, Mich.: University Microfilms, 1967.

Dunne, Finley Peter. *Mr. Dooley: In Peace and in War.* Boston: Small, 1899.

Duppler, Jörg. *Der Juniorpartner: England und die Entwicklung der Deutschen Marine, 1848–1890.* Herford: E. S. Mittler, 1985.

———. *Prinz Adalbert von Preussen: Gründer der Deutschen Marine.* Herford: E. S. Mittler, 1986.

Ellicott, J. M. "The Cold War between von Diederichs and Dewey in Manila Bay." *U.S. Naval Institute Proceedings* 81 (1955): 1236–39.

Eschenburg, Harald. *Prinz Heinrich von Preussen: der Grossadmiral im Schatten des Kaisers.* Heide: Westholsteinische Verlagsanstalt, 1989.

Fairbanks, John. *Trade and Diplomacy on the China Coast: The Opening of the Treaty Ports, 1842–1854.* Cambridge: Harvard University Press, 1953.

Fay, Peter W. *The Opium War, 1840–1842.* Chapel Hill: University of North Carolina Press, 1975.

Felstead, Sidney. *German Spies at Bay: An Actual Record of the German Espionage in Great Britain, 1914–1918.* London: Hutchinson, 1920.

Ferber, Konstantin. *Organisation und Dienstbetrieb der Kaiserlich deutschen Marine.* Berlin: Mittler und Sohn, 1901.

Fesser, Gerd. "'Hunderte deutscher Kaufleute werden Jauchzen.'" *Die Zeit*, vol. 21, November 1997, 16.

Fischer, Fritz. *Germany's Aims in the First World War.* New York: W. W. Norton, 1967.

The Franco-German War, 1870–1871. Part 1, *History of the War to the Downfall of the Empire.* Vol. 1, *From the Outbreak of Hostilities to the Battle of Gravelotte.* Vol. 2, *From the Battle of Gravelotte to the Downfall of the Empire.* Translated by F. C. H. Clarke. London: Her Majesty's Stationery Office, 1874, 1876.

———. Part 2, *History of the War against the Republic.* Vol. 1, *From the Investment of Paris to the Re-Occupation of Orleans.* Translated by F. C. H. Clarke. London: His Majesty's Stationery Office, 1880.

Franzius, Georg. *Kiautschou: Deutschlands Erwerbung in Ostasien*. Berlin: Schall und Grund, 1902.
Ganz, Albert H. "The Role of the Imperial German Navy in Colonial Affairs." Ph.D. dissertation, Ohio State University, 1972.
Gemzell, Carl-Axel. *Organization, Conflict, and Innovation: A Study of German Naval Strategic Planning, 1888–1940*. Stockholm: Esselte Studium, 1973.
"The German Navy." *New York Times*, 18 August 1898, 6.
Giese, Fritz. *Die Alte und die Neue Marine*. Bonn: Athenäum Verlag, 1957.
Graubohm, Herbert. *Die Ausbildung in der deutschen Marine: von ihrer Grüung bis zum Jahre 1914*. Düsseldorf: Droste, 1977.
Gröner, Erich. *Die deutschen Kriegsschiffe, 1815–1945*. 2 vols. Munich: J. F. Lehmanns Verlag, 1966.
———. *German Warships, 1815–1945*. Vol. 1, *Major Surface Vessels*. Revised and expanded by Dieter Jung and Martin Maass. Annapolis, Md.: Naval Institute Press, 1982.
Guerrero, Leon. "The Kaiser and the Philippines." *Philippine Studies* 9 (1961): 584–600.
Güth, Rolf. *Von Revolution zu Revolution: Entwicklungen und Führungsprobleme der Deutschen Marine, 1848–1918*. Herford: Verlag Mittler und Sohn, 1978.
Hallmann, Hans. *Krügerdepesche und Flottenfrage*. Stuttgart: Kohlhammer, 1927.
———. *Der Weg zum deutschen Schlachtflottenbau*. Stuttgart: Kohlhammer, 1933.
Halpern, Paul. *A Naval History of World War I*. Annapolis, Md.: Naval Institute Press, 1994.
Hansen, Claus. *Deutschland wird Seemacht: der Aufbau der Kaiserlichen Marine, 1867–1880*. Munich: Urbes, 1991.
Hansen, Hans Jürgen. *The Ships of the German Fleets, 1848–1945*. London: Hamlyn, 1973.
Hassell, Ulrich von. *Alfred von Tirpitz: Sein Leben und Wirken*. Stuttgart: Belser, 1920.
Heinsius, Paul. "Anfänge der Deutschen Marine." In *Die Erste Deutsche Flotte, 1848–1857*, edited by Walther Hubatsch, 13–27. Herford: E. S. Mittler und Sohn, 1981.
Herrick, Walter R. *The American Naval Revolution*. Baton Rouge: Louisiana State University, 1966.
Herwig, Holger H. *The German Naval Officer Corps: A Social and Political History, 1890–1918*. Oxford: Clarendon Press, 1973.
———. *Germany's Vision of Empire in Venezuela, 1871–1914*. Princeton, N.J.: Princeton University Press, 1986.

———. *The Influence of A. T. Mahan upon German Sea Power.* Newport, R.I.: Naval War College, 1990.

———. *"Luxury Fleet": The Imperial German Navy, 1888–1918.* London: Allen and Unwin, 1980.

———. *Politics of Frustration: The United States in German Naval Planning, 1889–1941.* Boston: Little, Brown, 1976.

Herwig, Holger H., and David F. Trask. "Naval Operations between Germany and the United States of America, 1898–1913: A Study of Strategic Planning in the Age of Imperialism." *Militärgeschichte Mitteilungen* 2 (1970): 1–32.

Hildebrand, Hans, Albert Röhr, and Hans-Otto Steinmetz. *Die Deutschen Kriegsschiffe.* 6 vols. Herford: Koehlers Verlagsgesellschaft, 1982.

Hildebrand, Hans, Albert Röhr, Hans-Otto Steinmetz, and Ernest Henriot. *Deutschlands Admirale, 1849–1945.* 4 vols. Osnabrück: Biblio, 1988–96.

Hobson, Rolf. "The German School of Naval Thought and the Origins of the Tirpitz Plan, 1875–1890." *Institut für Forsvarsstudier* 2 (1996): 1–93.

Hollyday, Frederic B. M. *Bismarck's Rival: A Political Biography of General and Admiral Albrecht von Stosch.* Durham, N.C.: Duke University Press, 1960.

Horn, Daniel. *The German Naval Mutinies of World War I.* New Brunswick, N.J.: Rutgers University Press, 1969.

Hough, Richard. *The Great War at Sea: 1914–1918.* Oxford: Oxford University Press, 1983.

Howard, Michael. *The Franco-Prussian War: The German Invasion of France, 1870–1871.* New York: Macmillan, 1962.

Hsü, Immanuel. *The Ili Crisis: A Study of Sino-Russian Diplomacy, 1871–1881.* Oxford: Clarendon Press, 1965.

Hubatsch, Walther. *Der Admiralstab und die Obersten Marinebehörden in Deutschland, 1848–1945.* Frankfurt am Main: Bernard & Graefe, 1958.

———. *Die Ara Tirpitz: Studien zur deutschen Marinepolitik, 1890–1918.* Göttingen: Munsterschmidt, 1955.

———. *Kaiserliche Marine: Aufgaben und Leistungen.* Munich: Lehmanns Verlag, 1975.

———, ed. *Die Erste Deutsche Flotte, 1848–1857.* Herford: E. S. Mittler und Sohn, 1981.

Hurd, Archibald, and Henry Castle. *German Sea-Power: Its Rise, Progress, and Economic Basis.* New York: Charles Scribner's Sons, 1913.

Irmer, Julius. *Kiautschou: Die diplomatische Vorbereitung der Erwerbung, 1894–1898.* Cologne: Gilde Verlag, 1932.

Johnson, Robert E. *Far China Station: The U.S. Navy in Asian Waters, 1800–1898.* Annapolis, Md.: Naval Institute Press, 1979.

Jung, Sang Su. *Deutschland und das Gelbe Meer: die deutsche Weltpolitik in Ostasien, 1897–1902.* Berlin: Lang, 1996.

Kehr, Eckart. *Battleship Building and Party Politics in Germany, 1894–1901.* Edited, translated, and introduced by Pauline and Eugene Anderson. Chicago: University of Chicago Press, 1973.

Kelly, Patrick. "Tirpitz and the Origins of the Torpedo Arm, 1877–1889." In *New Interpretations in Naval History: Selected Papers from the Eleventh Naval History Symposium,* edited by Robert Love, 219–49. Annapolis, Md.: Naval Institute Press, 2001.

Kennedy, Paul. "The Development of German Naval Operations against England, 1896–1914." *The English Historical Review* 89 (1974): 48–76.

———. *The Rise of the Anglo-German Antagonism, 1860–1914.* London: The Ashford Press, 1980.

———. "Tirpitz, England, and the Second Navy Law of 1900: A Strategical Critique," *Militärgeschichtliche Mitteilungen* 2 (1970): 740–52.

Kennedy, Paul, and John Moses, eds. *Germany in the Pacific and Far East, 1870–1914.* St. Lucia, Queensland: University of Queensland Press, 1977.

Koch, Paul. "General von Roon als Marineminister." *Marine-Rundschau* 14 (1903): 397–401.

Kohut, Thomas. *Wilhelm II and the Germans: A Study in Leadership.* Oxford: Oxford University Press, 1991.

Koop, Gerhard, and Erich Mulitze. *Die Marine in Wilhelmshaven.* Bonn: Bernard & Gräfe Verlag, 1997.

Laing, E. A. M. "Admiral Dewey and the Foreign Warships at Manila, 1898." *Mariner's Mirror* 52 (1966): 167–71.

Lambi, Ivo N. *The Navy and German Power Politics, 1862–1914.* Boston: Allen and Unwin, 1984.

Langer, William. *The Diplomacy of Imperialism, 1890–1902.* New York: Alfred A. Knopf, 1972.

Leutner, Mechthild, ed. *"Musterkolonie Kiautschou": Die Expansion des Deutschen Reiches in China.* Berlin: Akademie Verlag, 1997.

Livezey, William. *Mahan on Sea Power.* Norman: University of Oklahoma Press, 1947.

Lochner, R. K. *The Last Gentleman of War: The Raider Exploits of the Cruiser Emden.* Annapolis, Md.: Naval Institute Press, 1988.

Mahan, Alfred Thayer. *The Influence of Sea Power on History, 1660–1783.* Boston: Little, Brown, 1890.

———. *The Influence of Sea Power upon the French Revolution and Empire, 1793–1812.* 2 Vols. Boston: Little, Brown, 1892.

Mantey, Eberhard von. *Deutsche Marinegeschichte.* Charlottenburg: Offene Worte, 1926.

Marder, A. J. *The Anatomy of British Sea Power: A History of British Naval Policy in the Pre-Dreadnought Era, 1880–1905.* New York: Knopf, 1940.

———. *From the Dreadnought to Scapa Flow: The Royal Navy in the Fisher Era, 1904–1919.* Vol. 1, *The Road to War, 1904–1914.* London: Oxford University Press, 1961.

McCutcheon, John T. *Drawn from Memory.* Indianapolis, Ind.: Bobbs-Merrill, 1950.

Melville, Herman. *Moby-Dick.* New York: Bantam, 1967.

Norem, Ralph. "German Catholic Missions in Shantung." *The Chinese Social and Political Science Review* 19 (1935–36): 45–64.

Padfield, Peter. *The Great Naval Race: The Anglo-German Naval Rivalry, 1900–1914.* London: Hart-Davis, 1974.

Paulsen, George. *German Education: Past and Present.* New York: C. Scribner's Sons, 1908.

Peck, Taylor. *Round-Shot to Rockets: A History of the Washington Navy Yard and U.S. Naval Gun Factory.* Annapolis, Md.: Naval Institute Press, 1949.

Peter, Karl. *Seeoffizieranwärter-Ausbildurg in Preussen-Deutschland von 1848–1945.* Freiburg: Militärgeschichtforsamt, n.d.

Petter, Wolfgang. *Die überseeische Stützpunktpolitik der preussisch-deutschen Kriegsmarine, 1859–1883.* Freiburg: Petter, 1975.

Pflanze, Otto. *Bismarck and the Development of Germany.* Princeton, N.J.: Princeton University Press, 1963.

"The Philippines and Their Future." *Literary Digest* 17 (1898): 85–86.

Pohl, Frederick. "Die Tätigkeit SMS *Irene* in den Gewässern der Philippinen, 1896–1899." *Marine Rundschau* 7 (1902): 759–66.

Pratt, Julius W. *Expansionists of 1898: The Acquisition of Hawaii and the Spanish Islands.* Chicago: Quadrangle Books, 1936.

Prussia. *Liste der Königlich Preussische Marine pro 1866.* Berlin: Hermann Theinhardt, 1866.

———. *Organisation und Dienstbetrieb der Kaiserlich Deutschen Marine.* Berlin: Mittler und Sohn, 1901.

———. *Die Preussische Expedition nach Ost-Asien.* 4 vols. Berlin: Decker, 1873.

———. *Ranglisten der Königlich Preussischen Marine aus den Jahren 1848 bis 1864.* Berlin: Mittler und Sohn, 1894.

Rawlinson, John. *China's Struggle for Naval Development, 1839–1895.* Cambridge: Harvard University Press, 1967.

Richthofen, Ferdinand Freiherr von. *Schantung und Seine Eingangspforte Kiautschou.* Berlin: Dietrich Reimer, 1898.

Röhl, John C. G. *Germany without Bismarck: The Crisis of Government in the Second Reich, 1890–1900.* Berkeley: University of California Press, 1967.

———. *The Kaiser and His Court: Wilhelm II and the Government of Germany.* Cambridge: Cambridge University Press, 1987.

Röhr, Albert. *Deutsche Marinechronik.* Oldenburg: Gerhard Stalling, 1974.

———. "Vorgeschichte und Chronik des Torpedowesens." *Schiff und Zeit* 7 (1978): 47–51.

Ropp, Theodore. *The Development of a Modern Navy: French Naval Policy, 1871–1904.* Annapolis, Md.: Naval Institute Press, 1987.

Russell, James Earle. *German Higher Schools: The History, Organization and Methods of Secondary Education in Germany.* New York: Longmans, 1905.

Salewski, Michael. "Kiel und die Marine." In *Geschichte der Stadt Kiel*, edited by Jürgen Jensen and Peter Wulf, 272–86. Neumünster: Karl Wachholtz Verlag, 1991, 272–86.

———. "Die Preussische Expedition nach Japan, 1859–1861." *Revue Internationale d'Histoire Militaire* 70 (1988): 39–57.

———. *Tirpitz: Aufstieg, Macht, Scheitern.* Göttingen: Musterschmidt, 1979.

Sargent, Nathan. *Admiral Dewey and the Manila Campaign.* Washington, D.C.: Naval Historical Foundation, 1947.

Schellendorf, Bronsart von. *The Duties of the General Staff.* 4th ed. London: His Majesty's Stationery Office, 1905.

Schieber, Clara. *The Transformation of American Sentiment toward Germany, 1870–1914.* New York: Russell and Russell, 1923.

Schiller, Friedrich von. *Die Jungfrau von Orleans: Eine romantische Tragödie.* Edited by B. W. Wells. Boston: D. C. Heath, 1901.

———. *Schillers Gedichte.* Berlin: Weichert, n.d.

Schöllgen, Gregor, ed. *Escape into War: The Foreign Policy of Imperial Germany.* London: Berg, 1990.

Schottelius, Herbert, and Wilhelm Deist. *Marine und Marinepolitik im Kaiserlichen Deutschland, 1871–1914.* Düsseldorf: Droste Verlag, 1972.

Schrecker, Paul. *Imperialism and Chinese Nationalism: Germany in Shantung.* Cambridge: Harvard University Press, 1971.

Schüddekopf, Otto-Ernst. *Die Stützpunktpolitik des Deutschen Reiches, 1890–1914.* Berlin: Junker und Dünnhaupt, 1941.

Schultz-Naumann, Joachim. *Unter Kaisers Flagge: Deutschlands Schutzgebiete im Pazifik und in China.* Munich: Universitas Verlag, 1985.

Schüssler, Wilhelm, ed. *Weltmachtstreben und Flottenbau.* Witten/Ruhr: Luther Verlag, 1956.

Schwarz, Tjard, and Ernst von Halle. *Die Schiffbauindustrie in Deutschland und im Auslande.* Vol. 2, *Der deutsche Schiffbau.* Berlin: Mittler und Sohn, 1902.

Shippee, Lester. "Germany and the Spanish-American War." *American Historical Review* 30 (1925): 754–77.

Simsa, Paul. *Marine Intern: Entwicklung und Fehlentwicklung der deutschen Marine, 1888–1939.* Stuttgart: Motorbuch Verlag, 1972.

Smith, Woodruff D. *The German Colonial Empire.* Chapel Hill: University of North Carolina Press, 1978.

Soley, James. *Report on Foreign Systems of Naval Education.* Washington, D.C.: U.S. Government Printing Office, 1880.

Sondhaus, Lawrence. *Naval Warfare, 1815–1914.* New York: Routledge, 2001.

———. *Preparing for Weltpolitik: German Sea Power before the Tirpitz Era.* Annapolis, Md.: Naval Institute Press, 1997.

———. "'The Spirit of the Army' at Sea: The Prussian-German Naval Officer Corps, 1847–1897." *International History Review* 17 (1995): 459–84.

Spector, Ronald. *Admiral of the New Empire: The Life and Career of George Dewey.* Baton Rouge: Louisiana State University Press, 1974.

Spence, Jonathan. *God's Chinese Son: The Taiping Heavenly Kingdom of Hong Xiuquan.* New York: Norton, 1996.

Stafford, David. "Spies and Gentlemen: The Birth of the British Spy Novel, 1893–1914." *Victorian Studies* 24 (1981): 489–509.

"The Status of the Philippines." *New York Times,* 15 July 1898, 6.

Steinberg, Jonathan. *Yesterday's Deterrent: Tirpitz and the Birth of the German Battle Fleet.* New York: Macmillan, 1965.

Steltzer, Hans Georg. *Die Deutsche Flotte: ein historischer überblick von 1640 bis 1918.* Frankfurt am Main: Societäts-Verlag, 1989.

Stenzel, Alfred. *Kriegsführung zur See: Lehre vom Seekriege.* Hannover: Hahnsche Buchhandlung, 1913.

Stolberg-Wernigerode, Count Otto zu. *Germany and the United States of America during the Era of Bismarck.* Translated by Otto E. Lessing. Reading, Pa.: The Henry Janssen Foundation, 1937.

Tantum, W. H. *German Army, Navy Uniforms and Insignia, 1871–1918.* Greenwich, Conn.: Old Greenwich, 1968.

Tarrant, V. E. *Jutland: The German Perspective.* Annapolis, Md.: Naval Institute Press, 1995.

Townsend, Mary Evelyn. *The Rise and Fall of Germany's Colonial Empire, 1884–1918.* New York: Macmillan, 1930.

Trask, David. *The War with Spain in 1898.* New York: Free Press, 1981.

Trotha, Adolf von. *Grossadmiral Alfred von Tirpitz: Flottenbau and Reichsgedanke.* Breslau: Korn, 1932.

Vagts, Alfred. *Deutschland und die Vereinigten Staaten in der Weltpolitik.* New York: Macmillan, 1935.

———. "Hopes and Fears of an American-German War, 1870–1915." *Political Science Quarterly* 54 (1939): 514–35.

Valois, Victor. *Seegeltung, Seemacht, Seeherrschaft: kurze Betrachtungen über Seekriegsführung.* Berlin: Reimer, 1899.

Van der Vat, Dan. *The Grand Scuttle: The Sinking of the German Fleet at Scapa Flow in 1919.* London: Hodder and Stoughton, 1982.

Walle, Heinrich. "Das deutsche Kreuzergeschwader in Ostasien, 1897 bis 1914: politische Absichten und militärische Wirkung." In *Der Einsatz von Seestreitkräften im Dienst der Auswärtigen Politik,* edited by Heinrich Walle, 32–60. Herford: Mittler, 1983.

Weir, Gary E. *Building the Kaiser's Navy: The Imperial Naval Office and German Industry in the Tirpitz Era, 1890–1919.* Annapolis, Md.: Naval Institute Press, 1992.

Wetzel, David. *A Duel of Giants: Bismarck, Napoleon III, and the Origins of the Franco-Prussian War.* Madison: University of Wisconsin Press, 2001.

Wildman, Edwin. "What Dewey Feared in Manila Bay." *Forum* 59 (1919): 513–35.

Wilson, H. W. *The Downfall of Spain: Naval History of the Spanish-American War.* New York: Burt Franklin, 1971.

Wionzek, Karl-Heinz, ed. *Germany, the Philippines, and the Spanish-American War: Four Accounts by Officers of the Imperial German Navy.* Manila: National Historical Institute, 2000.

Witthöfft, Hans Jürgen. *Lexikon zur deutschen Marinegeschichte.* 2 vols. Herford: Koehlers Verlagsgesellschaft, 1977.

Yates, Keith. *Graf Spee's Raiders: Challenge to the Royal Navy, 1914–1915.* Annapolis, Md.: Naval Institute Press, 1995.

Index

Adalbert of Prussia, Prince (1811–73), 10–12, 14–16, 20, 26–27, 30, 34, 40, 57–58
Aden, 66–67
Admiral Duperre, 92
Admiralstab der Marine (Admiral Staff of the Navy): on coastal defense, 246–50; development of, 231–33; enlargement of, 242–46; functions of, 229, 233–36; independence and authority of, 250–56; reorganization of, 236–42
Admiralstabsabteilung (Admiral Staff Detachment), 125, 128
Admiralstabsoffizier, 49, 121
Admiralstabsreise, 106–8
Admiralty, abolition of, 111
Admiralty's Military Department (*Militärische Abteilung* or Department A), 89
Africa, 102–4, 124, 135
Aguinaldo, Emilio, 203
Ahlefeld, Hunold von, 89

Akitsushima (cruiser), 196, 209
Alabama (CSS), 23
Alberts, Hermann, 231
Albrecht, Eduard, 16, 27
Alexandrine (cruiser), 135, 136
Algeciras Conference, 260
Alsace, 38, 39
Alsace-Lorrain, 262
Alsen, 13
Altona, 32–33
Amaranth, 6–7, 58
Amazone (SMS), 6, 15, 57
Ammon, Gustav von, 147, 148, 153, 159, 161–62
Amoy, China, 7, 60, 72, 78–79, 136, 137, 139–43, 151, 220
Anglo-Chinese Treaty (1846), 139
Anton, Karl, 34
Arabian Sea, 67
Arcadia (SS), 132
Arcona (SMS): in Cruiser Division in East Asia, 147–48, 150, 153, 157, 165; in Cruiser Squadron in East Asia,

Arcona (SMS) (*continued*)
  167–69, 185, 195, 205, 218, 220;
  Diederichs's assignment to, 31–32;
  Hoffmann's command of, 135–36;
  investigative expedition to East Asia,
  59; in Light Division, 90; in Training
  Squadron, 45
Ariadne (corvette), 45, 56
Arminius (armored monitor), 35
Arnim, Volkmar von, 256
Atlanta *Constitution,* 205
Aube, Théophile, 101
August, 8
Augusta (SM sloop), 38–39
Augustin, Frau, 194
Augustin y Davilo, Basilio, 187, 192–94, 196–97, 201, 211–12, 214–15
Ausfallflotte, 93–95, 127
Ausfallkorvetten, 107
Auslandskreuzer, 31, 54, 113, 134
Aussereuropäische Abteilung, 244
Austria, 9, 23–25
Austria-Hungary, 196, 236
Aviso (dispatch boat), 89

Bachmann, Gustav, 231, 256
Baden-Baden, 133, 223, 242, 257, 259
Baltic Sea, 13–14, 32, 37, 38, 92–96, 107, 129
Baltimore (USS), 195, 196, 200
Banan (steamer), 212
Bangkok, 8
Barandon, Carl, 56, 121, 130
Basilisk (SM gunboat), 48
Bastille Day (1870), 34
Batavia (Jakarta), Dutch East Indies, 179, 180, 215, 218–19
Batsch, Carl: appointment of cadets, 1; 17; command of *Niobe,* 16; aboard *Luise,* 62; training cruise of, 18–24
"Battle of Fehmarn Sound," 96
Battle of Königgrätz, 20
Battle of the Falklands, 263
battleships (*Schlachtschiffe*): anticipated missions of, 100; approval of Tirpitz's plan for, 249, 251; in British war plan, 127, 225–26; conversions to, 113, 115; emphasis on, 230; increased construction of, in 1908, 260; in mobile strike force, 95; proposal of fleet, 123–25; in war games, 107. *See also* Navy Law (*Flottengesetz*)
Bayard (barbette ship), 196, 212
Bay of Biscay, 64
Becker, Adolf, 89
Becker, Gottlieb, 148, 159, 167, 169
Becks, Willibert, 73
Bedolliére, Philippe de la, 196, 209, 218
Bendemann, Felix von: and Boxer Rebellion, 243; on coastal defense, 247; complaints to, 123, 241–42, 249, 251; at *Marineakademie,* 44; request for financial and logistical support from RMA, 252; role in development of Admiralstab, 231, 246; support of Diederichs, 246, 256; visit with Henni, 220–21; and war with United States, 236
Berger, Adolf, 28–30
Berlin, 10, 47–50, 56, 93, 130, 223–24
Berlin *Lokal Anzeiger,* 205
Bibra, Ernst von, 166
Bismarck, Elizabeth von, 2
Bismarck, Otto von, 2, 12, 30, 34, 39–40, 59, 102–3, 110
Bismarck-class corvettes, 127

Black Sea, 57
Blanc, Louis von, 16, 83, 106
Blitz (SMS), 107
Blücher (SMS), 89–90, 129
B-N-D incident, 200–204, 207–10
Bombay, 67–68
"Bombay Marine," 67
Bonaventure (light cruiser), 196
Borkum Island, 32–33, 37, 38, 95, 98–99, 129–30, 247–49
Bormann, Geheime-Oberrechnungsrat, 2
Boston (cruiser), 195
Bouet-Willaumez, Louis, 37, 38
Bouvet (French packet), 39
Boxer Rebellion, 241, 243
Brandenburg (battleship), 119, 223
Brandenburg-class battleships, 113
Brandt, Maximilian von, 59–60, 71–72, 76, 79
Bremen, 10. *See also* Weser (Bremen) Estuary
Breusing, Alfred, 231
Bruix (cruiser), 185, 196
Brumby, Thomas M., 200, 207, 208, 216
Brussatis, Reinhold, 147, 155, 167, 174–75, 176, 187
Büchsel, Wilhelm, 16, 252–53, 255, 256, 258
Buller, Sir Archibald, 153, 156, 173
Bülow, Bernhard von, 154, 155, 157, 164, 182, 190, 226
Bundesmarine (Federal Navy), 30
Burski, Otto von, 156
Bussard-class light cruisers, 113
Buss- und Bettag, 23–24
Buthmann, Seaman, 172

Butterlin, Adolf, 25, 27
Butterwegge, Hugo, 62

Cadiz, 22–23
Calcutta, 68–69
Callao (gunboat), 195
Camäleon (gunboat), 105, 107
Cameroon, 103
canals, 96
Canton, 7, 58
Capelle, Eduard von, 225
Cape Town, South Africa, 82, 254
Cape Tres Forcas, 57–58
Cape Verde Islands, 20, 83
Caprivi, Leo von, 99–102, 105, 106, 110, 111, 121–22
Carlos V (cruiser), 188
Carlowitz and Company, 154–55
Caroline Islands, 104, 204
Cavite, 183, 184, 215–16
Cebu, 184, 215
Centurion (HMS), 153, 173
Ceylon, 68
Chadwick, French E., 117
Chang Chih-tung, 155
Chang Kao-yüan, 160–62, 168, 169–71
Charleston (cruiser), 211
Chefoo, 76, 148–49
Chicago, 117
Chichester, Edward, 148, 193, 196, 202, 209, 213–14, 217, 219
Childers, Erskine, 259
Chi-mo, 173–77
China: base sites in, 137–43, 145–57; Boxer Rebellion in, 243; Diederichs's arrival in, 7–8; German relations with, 58–59; and Japan, 135–36; *Luise* in, 76–78; resistance to occupation of

China (*continued*)
  Kiao-chou, 169–77; revival of German interest in, 134–35
Chinese New Year, 173–74
cholera, 73
Christiansand (Oslo), 46
Christian VIII (ship-of-the-line), 11
Ch'ung-kou, 7
Churchill, Winston, 264
Chusan Island, 137, 139–43, 147, 151, 154
Clausewitz, Karl von, 87
coaling depots, 219, 236
coastal defense, 99–102, 127, 235, 246–50
"Coastal War on the North Sea," 107
Coghlan, J. B., 203, 210
Colomb, Adalbert von, 89
Colombo, 68
Columbian Exposition, 117
commerce raiding, 101–2, 105, 114, 115, 120, 230, 264
Companie de Filipinas, 201–4, 207
Concepts of Political Economy (Diederichs), 2
Concord (USS), 188, 195, 203, 205–6
Conrad, Joseph, 134
Constantinople, 57
Cormoran (SMS): in Cruiser Division in East Asia, 136, 147–48, 150, 153, 155, 157–59, 161; in Cruiser Squadron in the Philippines, 185, 186, 190, 195, 196, 199–200, 212, 215, 218; in Cruiser Squadron at Tsingtao, 166–69, 171, 174, 175, 179; dispatched to rescue *Kaiser*, 220
Corregidor Island, 184
Courbet, 92
Cowes regatta, 106, 108, 111

Crefeld (SS), 176
Crimean War (1854–56), 12, 13, 57
Cruiser Division (*Kreuzerdivision*), 134–65
cruisers (*Kreuzers*), 100, 102, 115, 134, 230, 264
Cruiser Squadron (*Kreuzergeschwader*): in Africa, 135; conversion from Cruiser Division, 165; demise of, 263; in East Asia, 167–220; home port at Tsingtao, 258; and Tirpitz, 242, 243, 253; and war with United States, 236
"cruiser war." *See* commerce raiding
Cuba, 182, 217
Cuxhaven, 37
Cyclops (gunboat), 70–72, 76, 79

Dagupan, 200
Daily Telegraph (London), 261
Dalwigk zu Lichtenfels, Gottfried Freiherr von, 231
Dampfkanonenboot II–Klasse gunboats, 35–36
Danish War of 1864, 12
Danzig, 9, 14, 16, 61
Danzig (SMS), 57–58, 58
Darmstadt (SS), 175–76, 189–90, 196
Davis, Oscar King, 210
Denmark, 10–14, 127
Detroit News, 205
Detroit Tribune, 205
Deutsches Bund (the German Confederation), 9
Deutschland (SMS), 98, 119, 165, 178, 180, 195, 218, 222
Dewey, George: on arrival of *Irene* in Manila, 186; autobiography, 262; at battle of Manila, 182–83, 212–14;

Diederichs's relationship with, 191–92, 198, 207–10, 217–18; on German-Spanish conspiracy, 193–94; operational plans against Germany, 235; problems with Germans at Subic Bay, 200–205, 207–10; problems with Germans in Manila, 186–200, 217; on rescue of Augustin's family, 194; on U.S. performance at battle of Cavite, 216

Dick, Karl, 231

Diederichs, Christoph, 2

Diederichs, Ernst Otto von: at Admiralstab, 233; on Americans, 206, 208, 216; appointment to cadet, 1, 17; appointment to chief of the First Inspectorate, 121; appointment to commander of Cruiser Squadron, 169; appointment to Manöverflotte, Second Division, 118–23; in army, 4–5; assignment to *Luise,* 55–56; in Baden-Baden, 257, 259; as chief of Cruiser Division, 134–36; as chief of staff, 123–30; commissioning as lieutenant jg, 28; correspondence with Dewey, 207–10; death, 264; desire to return to sea, 54–55; in Dewey's autobiography, 262; early life, 1–3; education, 2–3; illness, 3, 5, 46–47, 73, 75, 88, 99, 105, 150–51, 153, 206; marriage, 42; in merchant marines, 5–6; in officer training, 26–27; promotion to commander, 80; promotion to full admiral, 253; promotion to Kapitän zur See, 104; promotion to lieutenant, 33; promotion to lieutenant commander, 44; promotion to midshipman, 24–25; promotion to rear admiral, 116; receipt of *Dienstauszeichnungs-Kreuz* (Distinguished Service Cross), 105; receipt of *Festungs-Inspection* medal, 107; receipt of Order of the Red Eagle, Fourth Class, 100; receipt of Order of the Royal Crown, Third Class, 106; receipt of Royal Crown Order, Second Class, 108; retirement of, 115–16, 130–33, 254–56

Diederichs, Friedrich von, 1–2, 10

Diederichs, Friedrich von (Fritz) (son): arrest for espionage, 262–63; in Berlin, 48; birth, 44; in Chefoo, 148–49; on clash between father and Tirpitz, 240; compliments paid, 150; correspondence with, 261–62; on father's character, 28; on father's relationship with Wilhelm, 256; on father's retirement, 255; on *Irene,* 130, 134; at Kiao-chou, 172; at Kiel, 104; on leave from *Oldenburg,* 223; naval career of, 206, 219, 221; on naval policy against Britain, 258; at opening of Kaiser Wilhelm Canal, 122

Diederichs, Henni (Klopp): in Berlin, 48, 130, 223; and birth of Fritz, 44; and birth of Herman, 52; correspondence with, 178–79, 181, 206, 220–22, 227; courtship of, 39; on dangers of gunnery training, 47; death, 264; to Egypt, 132–33; forty-fourth birthday, 148; illness, 105, 144, 151, 178, 206; to Italy, 88; at Kiel, 104; marriage, 42; moves to Gaarden, 113; moves to Leer, 56; at opening of Kaiser Wilhelm Canal, 122; on retirement, 255; on Tirpitz's ambition, 228

Diederichs, Henriette Molinari, 2

Diederichs, Herman von: birth, 52; on deaths of parents, 264, 265; on father's retirement, 255; on *Gneisenau*, 130, 132–33; at Kiel, 104; on leave from *Brandenburg*, 223; at opening of Kaiser Wilhelm Canal, 122
Diederichs, Leopold, 2
Diederichsstein monument, 263
Dienstschrift IX (Tirpitz), 120, 230
Dimitri Danskov (Russian steam frigate), 21
Direktion des Bildungswesens der Marine, 104
Drache (gunboat), 36
Drachenfels (collier), 197
Dreadnought (HMS), 260
Dreibund conference, 242
Dreikaiserbund (Three Emperors' League), 46, 88
Du Bois, Georg, 148, 150
Düppel, 13
Dürstenbrook: campus, 87; hotel, 26
Dutch East Indies, 218–19

East Asia. *See specific countries*
Eastern Extension Telegraph Company, 189
East Indies, 219
East Prussian Fusiliers, 5
Eckernförde, 11, 98
Edward, Prince of Wales, 111
Egypt, 132–33
Eider Canal, 18, 96, 121–22
Eider River, 18
Elbe (SMS), 50, 59
Elbe Estuary, 13, 32, 35, 94–95, 107, 129, 249
Elcano (steamer), 212

Elisabeth (sail frigate), 83
Ellerbek, 18
Emden, 32, 36–39
Emden (SMS), 264
Ems (Emden) Estuary, 13, 32, 35, 36–39, 95, 98, 108, 247, 248
Ems Telegram, 34
Entente Cordiale, 260
Erzherzog Friedrich (steam sloop), 23–24
Eulenburg, Friedrich Graf von, 59
Europäische Abteilung, 244

Falke (SMS), 106–7
Fehmarn Belt, 17
Fei Ying, 164
First Danish War (1848–50), 13
Fischel, Max, 225
Fischer, Fritz, 260
Fischtorpedos ("fish" torpedo), 47, 96
Fisher, Sir John, 259–60
"fish" torpedoes (*Fischtorpedos*), 47, 96
Fiume, Austria, 48–49, 50
Fiume Mark I torpedo, 49
Fontane, Thomas, 62, 63, 64, 66, 77
Fort Wilhelm, 41
Fourichon, Martin, 37, 38
France: and Britain, 260; in China, 58, 137; and commerce raiding, 101–2; demand for revenge, 262; on German base at Kiao-chou, 152; in Philippines, 196; plan for war against, 89, 92–95, 97, 102, 106, 120, 123, 232, 235–37. *See also* Franco-German War (1870)
Franco-German War (1870), 23, 33–39, 136, 262
Frankfurt, 10–11
Franzius, Georg, 112, 143, 146–47, 154

Frauenlob (schooner), 59
Freiburg im Breisgau, 223
Freya (SMS), 70
Friedrich, Crown Prince (son of Wilhelm I), 32, 46
Friedrich Carl (SMS), 35, 42–43, 88, 91, 97–99, 106
Friedrich der Grosse (armored frigate), 56, 119
Friedrich III, Kaiser, 110
Friedrichsort, 18, 24, 48, 52, 87, 90–91, 98
Friedrich Wilhelm, Crown Prince, 109
Friedrich Wilhelm III, King, 2
Friendship, 8
Frisian Islands, 32–33, 99, 108, 248
Frundsberg (sloop), 196, 209
Fu Ch'ing, 164
Funchal, Madeira, 19, 22

Gaarden, 87, 113
Geestemünde, 32, 41–42
Gefion (Danish frigate), 11
Gefion (SMS): assignment to, 31; in Cruiser Squadron, 165, 218; cruise to Black Sea, 57; field trip on, 87; officer training on, 86; in Philippines, 184, 195; restoration of, 25; at Tsingtao, 178, 180
Geissler, Richard, 103
German Bight, 247, 249
German East Africa, 103
Gibraltar, 64
Gneisenau (corvette), 89, 104, 122, 130, 132–33
Goltz, Helmut von der, 248–49
Goltz, Max von der, 111, 116
Grant, U. S., 67, 74

Grapow, Max (von), 231, 232
Great Bitter Lakes, 65
Great Britain: on base at Wei-hai-wei, 173; in China, 58, 137, 138; and commerce raiding, 101–2; declaration of war on Germany, 263; in East Asia, 142; on German base at Kiao-chou, 152; German threat to, 109; in Philippines, 196, 206, 211; threat of, 115, 120, 124, 225, 234, 259–61, 264; war plan against, 125–30, 235, 237, 258; Wilhelm II on, 110
Greater German General Staff, 232–33, 245
Gridley, C. V., 187
Grille (SMS), 32–33, 45, 74, 89, 108, 111
Guam, 217
gunboats, 106, 128
Gutschow, Dr., 75, 105

Habicht (SMS), 254
Hacke, Friedrich Graf von, 98
Hakodate, 75–76, 150
Hamburg-Altona, 32–33
Hansa (SMS), 54
Hay, John, 184
Heart of Darkness (Conrad), 134
Heeringen, August von, 125–26, 128, 225
Heilmann, Ernest, 202, 203–4
Heinrich, Prince of Prussia (1862–1929): as acting chief of Cruiser Squadron, 221, 222; breach of naval protocol, 186–87; as a child, 33; command of Cruiser Squadron, First Division, 165; on conditions in Philippines, 184; delayed arrival in Tsingtao, 178–80; and *Kaiser*'s accident in Samsah Bay, 220; in navy, 111; on *Prinz Adalbert*, 63; support of Tirpitz, 256

Heldt, Edward, 34, 38
Helgoland, 37, 95, 129
Helsinki, 46
Henk, Wilhelm von, 45–46, 119
Henry, Prince of Prussia, 74
Henry the Navigator, Prince, 23
Heringa, A. D., 219
Herminia (steamer), 212
Hertha (corvette), 45, 83
Hertz, Theodor, 48
Herz, Alfred, 62
Heusner, Eduard von, 48, 50, 52, 53, 54, 89, 112
Heyking, Eduard von: on assault at Wuchang, 155–56; on bases in China, 137, 138, 148–49, 171–72, 177; on Chang's repatriation, 170; meeting with Franzius, 146; on seizure of Kiao-chou, 158–59; at Wuhan, 153
Heyking, Elisabeth von, 28, 148
High Seas Fleet (*Hochseeflotte*), 264–65
Hildebrandt, Richard, 62
Hintze, Paul von, 190, 207–8, 217, 218, 258, 260
Hobson, Rolf, 87
Hoffmann, Paul: acquaintance with, 21; on base in East Asia, 141, 142, 144; command of Cruiser Division, 135–36; comments about, 145; on Dewey's autobiography, 262; in East Asia, 138; on Fritz's arrest, 263; at Marineschule, 26; rank of, 33; on second Navy Law, 240; on seizure of Kiao-chou, 163–64
Hohenlohe, Chlodwig von, 124, 137, 156
Hohenzollern (yacht), 122
Hohenzollern regime, 32, 259

Hohenzollern-Sigmaringen, Leopold von, 34
Hokkaido Island, 75–76, 150
Holland, Swinton, 214
Hollmann, Friedrich von: on base sites, 137, 141, 142; on cruisers and commerce raiding, 115; dismissal as state secretary, 133; evaluation of Diederichs, 116; and operational planning, 124–25; at *Reichsmarineamt*, 112, 144; and Tirpitz, 224
Holstein, 10, 23
Holtenau, 18
Hong Kong: British in, 58, 137, 138; Diederichs in, 8, 145; German ships in, 7; *Kaiser* in, 219–20; *Luise* in, 60, 70–71, 80–81; transport of Augustin to, 214
Honorable East India Company, 67, 69
Honshu, 73
Hooghly River, 68–69
Hugh McCulloch (revenue cutter), 195, 200–204, 206–10
Hydrographic Bureau, 61, 67

Ili, 79
Iloilo, port of, 184, 215
Iltis (gunboat), 83, 147
Iltis Denkmal, 147
Iltis monument, 220
Immediatstellung, 229
Immortalité (HMS), 148, 185, 196, 212–14
Imperial German Empire (*Kaiserlich Deutsche Reich*), 39–40
imperialism, 103
India, 63, 67–69
Indochina, 137

Infanterieismus, 42, 66, 71, 134–35
The Influence of Sea Power upon History (Mahan), 114
Ingenohl, Friedrich, 225
intelligence section, 238, 243, 244, 246
Invincible (HMS), 260
Iphigenia (light cruiser), 196, 212–14
Irene (SMS): and BND incident, 200–204, 207–10; in Cruiser Division in East Asia, 147–48, 150, 153, 157, 165; in Cruiser Squadron in East Asia, 179, 204–5, 218; Fritz on, 130, 134; and German-American tensions, 200–206; Hoffmann's command of, 135; at Kiao-chou, 172; in Philippines, 185–86, 195, 196, 218; return to Manila in 1898, 216; transferring of crews to, 190
Isabella, Queen, 23, 34
Isendahl, Walter, 263
Isla Grande, 184, 200–205, 207
Isle of Man, 263
Ismaili, 65
Italy, 236
Itsushima (cruiser), 196

Jachmann, Eduard von: and *Arcona*, 32; in Danish War of 1864, 12; in Franco-German War, 34–36, 38, 39; at Marineschule, 27; on *Niobe*, 18; as operational commander, 30; operational plan of, 95; retirement of, 40; role of, 14
Jade Bight, 107
Jadebusen, 13, 32, 94–95, 99, 105, 249
Jade squadron, 36
Jägerbuschen M/71 rifles, 160
Jäger (gunboat), 36

Jameson, L. S., 124
Japan: attacks against Russia at Port Arthur, 94; and China, 135–38; at Kiao-chou, 263; *Luise* in, 71–76; in Philippines, 196; relations with West, 58; visit to, 152–53
Jardenes, Fermin, 212, 213
Jäschke, Paul, 90, 91
Jasmund, 12–13
Jeschke, Heinrich, 55
Jeune école ("Young School"), 101, 102, 105, 114, 230

Kagoshima, 153
Kaiserin Augusta (triple-screw), 113, 165, 173, 185, 190–91, 195–96, 212, 214–15, 218
Kaiserlich Deutsche Reich (Imperial German Empire), 39–40
Kaiserliche Admiralität (Imperial German Admiralty), 40–41
Kaiserliche Marine (Imperial Navy): creation of, 40–41; and diplomatic crisis with Russia, 88; leadership of, 99; operational planning for, 92, 95; reorganization of, 224–31; and torpedo exercises, 106; Wilhelm on, 111
Kaiserliche Werft (Imperial Shipyard at Kiel), 87, 108, 112–20
Kaiser (SMS): accident at Amoy, 141; accident in Samsah Bay, 220; in Cruiser Division in East Asia, 136, 145–50, 153–54, 156–61, 163, 166; in Cruiser Squadron in East Asia, 169, 170–72, 174, 179, 190, 194–97, 207, 209–10, 212–14, 216, 218–20, 222; on maneuver squadron, 98, 99
Kaiser Wilhelm Canal, 18, 122, 128, 129, 249

Kaplen, Johan, 231
Karcher, Guido, 227–28
Kaufmann, Diver, 75, 78
Kaufmann, Machinist's Mate, 70, 73
Kearsarge (USS), 23
Keyserling, Walter Freiherr von, 231
Kiao-chou: administration of, 255; Chinese resistance to occupation of, 169–77; development of, 113, 166–67, 258; plan to purchase land at, 155; as potential base site, 139–44, 147, 149–52, 154; protection of, 173–76, 236; seizure of, 155–63, 164–69; surrender of in World War I, 263; Tirpitz on, 154–55, 177–78, 226; winter in, 172–73
Kiao-chou Bay, China, 131, 138, 146–47, 258
Kiel: assignment to Marineakademie at, 43–47, 84–88, 91, 97, 104–8; canal at, 96, 106, 121–22; development of base at, 13, 14; and Franco-German War, 35; *Friedrich Carl* at, 98; *Gefion* at, 25; Marineschule at, 26–27; Matrosendivision at, 31; *Niobe*'s cruise to, 17–18; and operational planning, 90–93; regatta at, 122; torpedo testing at, 49–51, 53; training at, 15; *Übungsgeschwader* at, 45; *Vineta* at, 46–47
Kiel Canal, 106, 121–22
Kirkwall, Orkney Island, 119–20
"Kleiner Leisberg," 257
Klön, Feodor von, 23
Klopp, Amalie, 39
Klopp, Clara Elisabeth Henriette (Henni). *See* Diederichs, Henni (Klopp)
Klopp, Herman, 39

Knockaloe, 263
Knorr, Anna, 178, 221, 228
Knorr, Eduard von: acquaintance with, 21; on acquisition of bases, 183–84; in Africa, 103, 104; approval of *Kaiserin Augusta* for Cruiser Division, 165; on Augustin incident, 215; on base in East Asia, 139–44, 147; on Cruiser Division, 136; on 1896 maneuvers, 129–30; evaluation of Diederichs, 113, 116, 123; in Franco-German War, 39; at Kiel naval station, 121; and operational planning, 89; on Philippines, 185, 190; reports to, 118, 219; retirement of, 221, 229; and Tirpitz, 225–28; on war with Britain, 125; working relationship with Diederichs, 123, 128
Kobe, 73, 153
Koester, Gustav von, 256
Koester, Hans: on Admiralstab, 241, 246; evaluation of Diederichs, 123; on fleet expansion, 225–26; on Kiao-chou, 154–56, 164; with Manöverflotte, 118, 119; on operational plans, 237; rank, 253; on second Navy Law, 240; support of Diederichs, 254; "Tactical Exercises for the Fleet," 105
Köllner, Leopold, 173, 214, 215
Königgrätz, Bohemia, 25
Königliche Preussische Admiralität, 11
Königliche Werft (Royal Shipyard), 18
König Wilhelm (frigate), 35, 93, 106, 119, 121
Korea, 138, 150
Kreigsakademie, 232
Kreuzers (cruisers). *See* cruisers (*Kreuzers*)

Kreuzerdivision. See Cruiser Division (*Kreuzerdivision*)
Kreuzergeschwader. See Cruiser Squadron (*Kreuzergeschwader*)
Kreuzerkrieg. See commerce raiding
Kriegsgeschichtliches Dezernat, 244
Kronprinz, 35, 98
Krüger, Friedrich von, 184–86, 198, 200–201, 213, 214
Kruger, Paul, 124
Kruger Telegram, 124
Küstenflotille, 9, 10
Kyoto, 153

Lake Remmelsburger, 48
Landtag, Prussian (the provincial diet), 12
Lans, Wilhelm, 129
Leer, 36, 39, 44, 56
Leisberg, 257
Lemke, Marine, 21
Leonowens, Anna, 8
Leyte (gunboat), 195
Liaotung peninsula, 138
Lichtenthal, 257
Liebe, C. A., 26, 44
Light Division, 89–90
Li Hung-chang, 149, 170, 177
Lilie, Hermann, 89
Linnet (gunboat), 196
Li Ping-heng, 169
Lisbon, 23, 30
"little war" (*klein Krieg*), 95
Livonius, Otto, 89–90
Lizard Point, England, 83
London *Daily Telegraph*, 261
Long, John D., 188
Longe, Diedrich, 9, 14

Longmoon (SS), 166
Lorraine, 38, 39, 262
Lössow, Kopka von, 176
Luchs (SM gunboat), 251–52
Luise (SMS), 60–84; activities of, 61–62; assignment to, 55–56; deactivation of, 83–85; Diederichs's duties on, 60–62; in operational planning against Russia, 90, 91
Luzon, 184–86
Luzon Straits, 182

MacLean, Archibald, 30, 33, 73
Madagascar, 81–83
Madeira Island, 19, 22
Mahan, Alfred Thayer, 88, 114, 118
Maltzahn, Curt, 230–31
Manchuria, 137, 152
Manila, 182–200, 211–18. *See also* Philippines
Manöverflotte, 108, 118–23, 129
Manövergeschwader (maneuver squadron), 105–6
Manteuffel, Otto Freiherr von, 11
Mantey, Eberhard von, 41, 235
Maracaibo, Venezuela, 253
Mariana Islands, 204
Marie (cruiser), 135, 136
Marie Wilhelmina, 8
Marineakademie (Naval War College): assignment to, 43–47; reorganization of, 239, 241, 245; teaching duties at, 84–88, 91, 97, 104–8
Marinegenerale (navy generals), 99
Marinekabinett (Naval Cabinet, or MK), 111–12
Marineministerium (Ministry of the Navy), 12

Marinerundschau, 261
Marineschule, 15, 26–27, 85–87
Marinestation der Nordsee, 32
Marineverordnungsblatt, 43
Mariveles Bay, 184, 197, 212
Marschall, Hermann von, 137, 138, 142
Marschall-Viebrok, Alfred, 89
Mars (SMS), 122
Matrosendivision, 18, 27–28, 31, 32, 42–43, 46, 56–57, 121
Matsushima (IJNS), 196, 201, 212
Mauritius, 81
Mauser Jägerbüsche M/71, 42
McCutcheon, John T., 195
McKinley, William, 183, 189, 190, 198
McNair, Frederick, 191–92
Mediterranean Sea, 12
Meller, Johannes, 36, 38
memoranda: "Consideration of the Defense of German Coasts against Sea Powers which Attack Simultaneously from the Baltic Sea and North Sea," 91–92, 97, 98; "General Experiences from the Maneuvers of the Fall Training Fleet," 120; "Memorandum Concerning the Further Development of the Imperial Navy," 100; "Memorandum Concerning the Reorganization of the Armored Fleet," 115; "A Military and Political Report on the Situation in China," 151; "Our Further Maritime and Military Development," 114–15
Mensing, Franz, 50
Merritt, Wesley, 211–13, 216
Meteor (SM gunboat), 39
Metz, 38

Militärische Abteilung (Admiralty's Military Department, or Department A), 89
Militärische Verwendung der Schiffe, 89, 100
Militär-wissenschaftliche Angelegenheiten, 89
"A Military and Political Report on the Situation in China," 151
Mindanao Island, 184
Minelayer No. 6, 51, 52
Mirs Bay, 138
Mitsubishi Dockyard and Engine Works, 185
Moltke, Helmut von, 25, 38, 92, 93, 114, 232
Moltke (SMS), 122, 133
Monadnock (U.S. monitor), 215–16
Monongahela (USS), 75
Montebello Island, 138
Monterrey (U.S. monitor), 211
Montojo y Passaron, Patricio, 187–88, 193
Monts, Alexander Graf von, 48, 106, 111
Morocco, 260
Mücke (SM armored gunboat), 105–7
Murck, Heinrich, 9
Musquito (SMS), 16, 19, 28–33
Mutsuhito, Meiji emperor, 152

Nachrichtenbüro, 244
Nachrichtwesen, 246
Nagasaki, 72, 153, 179, 181, 185
Naniwa (cruiser), 196, 212
Napoleon, Emperor Louis, III, 34, 38
Napoleonic Wars (1792–1815), 8–9, 127
Nassau (SMS), 260
Natter (SM gunboat), 35–39

Naval Gun Factory, 117
Naval Torpedo Station on Goat Island, 117
Naval War College, Newport, R.I., 117–18
Navigation School, 14
Navy Law (*Flottengesetz*), 224, 226–28, 230, 233–34, 239–41, 244, 247–48, 259
New Course (*Neue Kurs*), 109–12
Newport, R.I., 117
New York Evening Post, 205
New York *Herald,* 218
New York Times, 205, 214–15
Nicholas II, Czar, 129
Niobe (SMS), 1, 16–25, 29
Norddeutschen Bund (North German Confederation), 30
Norman, Admiral, 196
Normannia (SS), 117
North China Daily News, 77, 79, 143, 158
North Sea: Admiralstabsreise in, 106–8; coastal defense concerns in, 247–48; and Franco-German War, 35, 37, 38; *Friedrich Carl* in, 98–99; *Luise* in, 63; maneuvers in, 129; and operational planning, 92–96, 107; Prussian fleet in, 13–14; strategic importance of, 120, 127; training exercises in, 119; and Wilhelmshaven naval base, 32
Norway, 119
Nostitz, Georg von, 103
Novelle, 260
Nymphe (sloop), 38, 90

Obenheimer, August, 185–87, 189, 200–205, 216
Oberkommando der Marine (OKM) (the Naval High Command), 10, 111, 112, 115, 123–30, 221, 225, 227–30
Oldekop, Iwan: conflict with Tirpitz, 230–31; on death of Diederichs, 265; desire to return to sea, 54–56; on Diederichs's transfer to Wilhelmshaven, 116; on *Niobe,* 16–18; in officer training, 26–27; promotion to midshipman, 25; retirement of, 231; support for Diederichs's plan for enlargement of Admiralstab, 246; on Tirpitz's fleet plan, 226, 228
Oldenburg (SMS), 219, 223
Olga (light corvette), 89
Olongapo, 184, 200–203
Olympia (USS), 117, 185, 186, 188, 194, 195, 207–8, 217
operational planning: of Admiralstab, 234–38; against Britain, 124–30, 235, 237; and Caprivi, 99–102; of Jachmann, 95; at *Militärische Verwendung der Schiffe,* 100; in North Sea, 92–96, 107; origins of, 88–93; of Tirpitz, 114–15, 120. *See also* strategic thinking
Orkney Island, 119–20
Oscar I, king of Sweden, 45–46

Palmer, Frederick, 262
Panther (SMS), 253, 260
Panzerfahrzeugsflottille, 107
Paris, 38
Pascal (cruiser), 196, 212
Paschen, Karl, 104, 106
Pasig lighthouse, 197
Peace of Prague, 25
Peking, 79–80, 148–49, 258
Pelayo (cruiser), 188

Perry, Matthew, 58
Personalien, 89
Pescadore Islands, 138
Petrel (gunboat), 195, 212
Petr Velicki, 93
Philadelphia Navy Yard, 117
Philippines: Diederichs dispatched to, 190–91; potential base sites in, 199–201, 206; protection of German interests in, 185–86, 236; strategic potential of, 182–84; United States in, 185, 191–93, 198, 211–17; visit to, 180. *See also* Kiao-chou; Manila; Subic Bay
Pique (gunboat), 196
Plover (gunboat), 196
Plüddemann, Max, 26, 27
Plymouth, England, 19, 24, 29, 63, 83
Pohl, Hugo, 74, 225
Pomerania, 9
Port Arthur, 94
Port Louis, Mauritius, 81
Porto Grande, St. Vincente Island, 22
Port Said, 65
Portsmouth, England, 108
Portugal, 23, 30
Preussen (SS), 144, 146
Prinz Adalbert (SMS), 35, 53, 63, 73–75, 104
Prinzessin Louise (trading ship), 58
Prinzess Wilhelm (cruiser): in Cruiser Division in East Asia, 136, 147–50, 153–54, 156–62, 166; in Cruiser Squadron in East Asia, 169, 170, 173, 179, 181, 185, 190, 195–96, 212, 218, 220
Prinz Heinrich (steamer), 214, 222

Prussia, 9, 10–11, 25. *See also* Franco-German War (1870)
Prussian-German General Staff, 232
Prussian Ministry of War, 11
Prussian Navy, 5–6, 8–10, 14–16
Puerto Rico, 217
Pygmy (HMS), 196, 200

Raleigh (cruiser), 195, 203, 205–6
Rama IV, King, 8
Ranavalona, Queen, 82
Ranger (U.S. sloop), 72
Rattler (gunboat), 196
Ratzeburg, Julius, 32
Rauch, Gustav von, 8–9
Rawson-Walker, E. H., 186, 193
Rebeur-Paschwitz, Lt. (sg) von, 235
Red Sea, 65–66
Reibnitz, Paul von, 16
Reichsmarineamt (RMA), 111–12, 177, 225, 227–28, 246, 248–52, 254
Renown (SMS), 47, 86
Ressorteifer, 224, 249, 256
Reyner, Karl, 154–55
Rhodes, Cecil, 124
The Riddle of the Sands (Childers), 259
Riedel, Louis, 85
Rieloff, Wilhelm, 214, 218
"risk fleet," 239–40, 264. *See also* Navy Law (*Flottengesetz*)
RMA. *See Reichsmarineamt* (RMA)
Roon, Albrecht von, 12–14, 30, 31, 40, 59, 88
Rota, 22
Rover (training sloop), 16, 19, 21, 29
Royal Prussian Admiralty, 12
Russia: and Britain, 260; in China, 58, 137, 138, 152; plan for war against,

89–94, 97, 102, 106, 120, 123, 232, 235–37; seizure of Ili, 79

Sachsen (SMS), 108
sail, 13
Sakhalin Island, 150
Salamander (gunboat), 36, 105, 107
Samoa, 139–40
Samsah, 139–43
Samsah Bay, 220
San Nicolas (steamer), 212
Sargent, Nathan, 186, 187
Schelle, Erwin, 30
Schering, Rudolf, 55, 60, 71–72, 100, 104
Schiller, Friedrich, 3, 28
Schlachtschiffe (battleships). *See* battleships (*Schlachtschiffe*)
Schleswig, 10, 23
Schlieffen, Alfred von, 93, 232, 235
Schröder, Jan, 10, 11, 57
Schulze, Johann Heinrich, 176
Scorpion (*Jäger*-class gunboat), 52
Scotland, 119
sea control (*Seeherrschaft*), 120
sea power, 114, 183, 234
Second Danish War (1864), 14
Seebatallion, 18
Seeferkel (sea piglet), 35–36
Seeherrschaft. *See* sea control (*Seeherrschaft*)
Seekadetten-Institut (Midshipmen Institute), 14, 15
Seekadetten-Prüfung, 24
Seekriegslehre (Lessons of Naval Warfare) (Maltzahn), 230–31
Seemacht, Seegeltung, Seeherrschaft (Valois), 230

Senden-Bibran, Gustav Freiherr von: acquaintance with, 21; on Augustin incident, 215; on cruisers, 115; on Diederichs's prospects for assignments, 131, 133; on Diederichs's transfer to Wilhelmshaven, 116; on enlargement of Admiralstab, 243, 244, 246; as first chief of Marinekabinett, 111; gift for, 152; Henni on ambition of, 221; at Marineakademie, 44; at Marineschule, 26, 27; on occupation of Kiao-chou, 177; on potential base sites, 141, 142, 154; on Prince Heinrich's disobedience, 220; rank of, 33; on regatta competition, 122; selfishness of, 256; and Tirpitz, 125, 227, 228, 249–50, 253, 254
Seoul, 150
Seville, 22
Shanghai, 7, 58, 77–79, 137, 138, 146, 153, 179, 220
Shantung Peninsula, 76, 138, 140, 151–52, 156
Siegfried-class battleships, 113
Simonstown, Cape Colony, 83
Singapore, 8, 69–70, 81, 219
Sino-French War (1884–1885), 137
Sino-Japanese War (1894–1895), 135, 138, 152, 157–58, 209, 262
Sino-Prussian Treaty (1861), 156, 159, 176
Society of the Divine Word, 156
sorties, 95
Souchon, Wilhelm, 231
South Africa, 254
South America, 251–52
South China Sea, 145, 182

Spain, 22–23, 181
Spanish-American War, 180–83
Spee, Maximilian Graf von, 263
squadron warfare (*Geschwaderkrieg*), 115, 120
steam, 13
Stein (corvette), 122
Stenzel, Alfred, 29, 56, 85, 87–88, 92, 231
Stiege, Oskar, 133
Stockholm, 46
St. Olaf (screw frigate), 46
Stosch, Albrecht von: on canal construction, 96; chief of *Kaiserliche Admiralität*, 40–41; creation of *Admiralstabsoffizier*, 49; *Infanterieismus* policy of, 66, 134–35; and operational planning, 88–91; Tirpitz's relationship with, 228; and torpedos, 48, 50–53; on training, 42, 43, 86
Stosch (SMS), 83, 103–4, 122, 135, 148
St. Paul *Dispatch*, 205
Stralsund, 9, 14, 35
Stralsund (SM schooner), 9
strategic thinking, 87–88, 123–25. *See also* operational planning
Struggle for Schleswig (Klön), 23
Stubenrauch, Felix, 173, 194, 213, 218, 219
Stubenrauch, Wilhelm, 89
Subic Bay, 184, 200–205, 207–10
Suchow, 8
Suez Canal, 65
Sumatra, 219
Sumbawa, 219
Sundewall, Henrik, 59
Swatow, 138

Sweden, 9, 45–46
Swift (gunboat), 196

"Tactical Exercises for the Fleet" (Koester), 105
Der Tag, 265
Taiping Rebellion (1856–64), 7
Taiwan, 137
Taku forts, 149
Tamatave, Madagascar, 81–83
Ta Tao Hui (Society of the Great Knife), 156
Thetis (sail frigate), 59
Thiele, Adolf, 148, 156, 159, 167, 170, 172, 254
Thiele, August, 112, 122, 227, 254
Thomson, August, 26, 27, 241, 256
Tientsin, 60
Tirpitz, Alfred von: ambition of, 221, 227–29; on assignment of *Luchs*, 251–52; attitude toward navy, 13; authority of, 224, 249, 251–54; on bases in East Asia, 141–44, 148, 151, 190; on battleships, 225–26; on Caprivi's conservatism, 99; on coastal defense plan, 247–49; comments about, 145; departure from East Asia, 146; on Diederichs's retirement, 255–56; on Diederichs's transfer to Wilhelmshaven, 116; on enlargement of Admiralstab, 243–46; as head of Reichsmarineamt, 112; on implications of Spanish-American War, 182–83; intraservice rivalry with Diederichs, 233, 238, 241, 242, 250; and Kiao-chou, 154–55, 177–78, 226; on *Niobe*, 16; plan against Britain, 258–60, 264; plan against Russia, 90;

promotion to midshipman, 25; relationship with Knorr, 123, 130; and reorganization of Naval High Command, 229–31; resignation of, 264; second Navy Law of, 233–34, 239–41; on Stosch's army methods, 42; strategic thinking of, 88, 105, 109, 114–15, 120, 123–25, 133; and torpedos, 50, 52, 53, 87, 106, 146, 177, 225, 255; Wilhelm's failure to promote, 125

Togo, 103

Tokyo, 73–75, 152

torpedo boats, 101

Torpedo Depot, Friedrichsort, 48, 52, 98

Torpedo Depot, Kiel, 49–51

torpedoes: development of, 47–56, 118; and operational planning, 92–99; testing of, 70, 72, 74, 77, 78; training with, 87, 106, 107. *See also* Whitehead torpedoes

Torpedo Research and Development Commission (*Torpedo-Versuchs-und-Prüfung Kommission,* or TVK), 47–53

Torpedo Research Station, Newport, R.I., 117–18

Torpedo Service (*Torpedowesen*), 48–50, 52–54, 56, 66, 87

Training Squadron (*Übungsgeschwader*), 45

Trans-Siberian Railroad, 152

Transvaal Republic, 124

Treaty of Frankfurt (1871), 39, 40

Treaty of Paris (1898), 217

Treaty of Peking (1861), 134

Treaty of Shimonoseki (1895), 138

Treaty of Versailles, 265

Treutler, Herman von, 152

Trinidad (collier), 212

Triple Alliance (*Dreibund*), 236

Triple Entente, 260

Tsingtao: development of, after retirement, 258; German defense of, 169–76; *Kaiser*'s final visit to, 222; permission to develop and fortify naval base at, 177; as potential base site, 140, 152, 159–63, 165–68; Prince Heinrich visit to, 178–80; *Prinzess Wilhelm* at, 220

Tsungli-Yamen, 149, 170

typhus, 30

Übungsgeschwader (Training Squadron), 45

Ulan, 90

United States: attack on Manila, 211–18; imperialism of, 181–82; intentions in Philippines, 185, 191–93, 198; operational plan against, 234–37; tensions with Germany at Subic Bay, 200–205, 207–10; tensions with Germany in Manila, 186–200, 213–14, 217. *See also* Spanish-American War

United States Navy, 116–17, 140

University of Kiel, 26, 85

Valletta, Malta, 64

Valois, Viktor, 16, 44, 45, 112, 118, 230, 246

Van der Tann (SMS), 260

Venezuela, 253

Vernichtungsschlacht, 87–88

Victoria, Crown Princess, 32, 109

Victoria, Empress, 122

Victoria, Queen of Great Britain, 109, 111, 117

Vineta (SMS), 44–46
Viper (gunboat), 105, 107

war games, 106–8
War of National Liberation (1813–14), 9
Washington, D.C., 117
Washington Navy Yard, 117
Weichkhmann, Johannes, 38
Wei-hai-wei, 138, 141, 147–48, 173
Weltmacht und Seemacht, 114
Werftdivision, 121
Werner, Reinhold, 51, 52
Weser (Bremen) Estuary, 13, 32, 35, 94–95, 107, 249
Wespe (gunboat), 36–39
White, James, 199
Whitehead, Robert, 47–48
Whitehead torpedoes, 48–50, 53, 60–62, 66, 68, 72, 74, 118
Wickede, Wilhelm von, 45, 47, 98–99
Wildman, Rounseville, 187, 199, 214
Wilhelm I, Kaiser (1861–88), 12, 22–23, 32, 34, 40, 49, 106, 110
Wilhelm II, Kaiser, 33; abolition of OKM, 221, 229–30; appointments to Admiralstab, 231, 233; on base sites in East Asia, 138, 141, 143, 144, 154; on British threat, 260–61; on coastal defense, 247; on Cruiser Division, 135; on Cruiser Squadron, First Division, 165; and Diederichs's retirement, 255; on enlargement of Admiralstab, 242–46; escort to England for regatta, 108; on exchange between Dewey and Diederichs, 208; and Kiao-chou, 156–57, 163, 177; on *König Wilhelm,* 119; "New Course," 109–12; on possession of Philippines, 184, 190; promotion of Diederichs to rear admiral, 116; refusal of Tirpitz's resignation, 228; relationship with Diederichs, 256, 259, 261; relationship with Tirpitz, 253–54; on reorganization of Admiralstab, 238, 241–42; on seizure of Taiwan, 137; on Society of the Divine Word, 156; on Spanish-American War, 182; on strategic planning, 124–25; on Tirpitz's fleet plan, 123–25, 133, 224, 226, 228–29, 230; on *Weltmacht und Seemacht,* 114
Wilhelmina, Queen of the Netherlands, 218
Wilhelmshaven: assignment to Matrosendivision in, 46, 56–57; development of base at, 13; *Friedrich Carl* at, 98; inauguration of *Marinestation der Nordsee* at, 32; Kaiser Wilhelm II at, 119; mobile strike force at, 95; and operational planning, 92, 93; and proposed canal, 96; replacement of Geestemünde, 41–42; torpedo testing at, 49–50; transfer to, 116; *Übungsgeschwader* at, 45; war games at, 107
Williams, O. F., 184, 199
Winkler, Raimund, 231
Wismar, 37
Wolf (gunboat), 70, 71, 73, 76, 79, 83
World's Fair (Chicago), 117
World War I, 262–63
Wuchang, 153, 155–56
Wuhan (Wuchang-Hankow), 153
Wusung, 146

Yangtze Basin, 137, 138, 151, 258
Yokohama, Japan, 60, 73–75, 150–51

Zanzibar, 103

Zeye, Hugo: as assistant to Büchsel, 255; departure from Kiao-chou, 172; as military governor of Kiao-chou, 165–68, 169–71; planned meetings with, 145–47; and seizure of Kiao-chou, 158–59, 161, 177; in "torpedo gang," 225; to Wuhan, 153

Ziegler, Captain, 209

Zieten (SMS), 48, 50–53

About the Author

Terrell D. Gottschall earned a doctorate in nineteenth-century European history and diplomacy from Washington State University in 1981. He has taught at Andrews University in Berrien Spring, Michigan, and Union College in Lincoln, Nebraska. Professor Gottschall currently teaches at Walla Walla College in College Place, Washington. He has written about German naval history for the *International Journal of Naval History*, the *International Journal of Maritime History*, and *Columbia* and presented several papers at the Naval History Symposium held at the United States Naval Academy, Annapolis, Maryland. He also wrote the introduction to Hellmuth von Mücke's book, *The Emden-Ayesha Adventure: German Raiders in the South Seas and Beyond, 1914* (Annapolis, Md.: Naval Institute Press, 2000). Terry Gottschall lives in Walla Walla, Washington, with his wife, Merry, and three children.

The Naval Institute Press is the book-publishing arm of the U.S. Naval Institute, a private, nonprofit, membership society for sea service professionals and others who share an interest in naval and maritime affairs. Established in 1873 at the U.S. Naval Academy in Annapolis, Maryland, where its offices remain today, the Naval Institute has members worldwide.

Members of the Naval Institute support the education programs of the society and receive the influential monthly magazine *Proceedings* and discounts on fine nautical prints and on ship and aircraft photos. They also have access to the transcripts of the Institute's Oral History Program and get discounted admission to any of the Institute-sponsored seminars offered around the country.

The Naval Institute also publishes *Naval History* magazine. This colorful bimonthly is filled with entertaining and thought-provoking articles, first-person reminiscences, and dramatic art and photography. Members receive a discount on *Naval History* subscriptions.

The Naval Institute's book-publishing program, begun in 1898 with basic guides to naval practices, has broadened its scope to include books of more general interest. Now the Naval Institute Press publishes about one hundred titles each year, ranging from how-to books on boating and navigation to battle histories, biographies, ship and aircraft guides, and novels. Institute members receive significant discounts on the Press's more than eight hundred books in print.

Full-time students are eligible for special half-price membership rates. Life memberships are also available.

For a free catalog describing Naval Institute Press books currently available, and for further information about subscribing to *Naval History* magazine or about joining the U.S. Naval Institute, please write to:

Membership Department
U.S. Naval Institute
291 Wood Road
Annapolis, MD 21402-5034
Telephone: (800) 233-8764
Fax: (410) 269-7940
Web address: www.navalinstitute.org